PENGUIN CLASSICS

CULTURE AND ANARCHY
AND OTHER SELECTED PROSE

MATTHEW ARNOLD (1822–88) was the son of the famous Dr Thomas Arnold, headmaster of Rugby. After a fairly carefree time as a student at Oxford, where he graduated in 1844 with second class honours, he spent several years travelling and writing experimental verse. His first volume of poetry was published in 1849 and surprised his friends and family with its concern for moral issues. It was his third volume, *Poems*, published in 1853, that established his reputation. Although there were still some fine poems to come, his growing absorption in social and political matters turned him increasingly towards prose. In 1851 he became an inspector of schools, a position which he held throughout his life except for a ten-year period from 1857 until 1867 when he was Professor of Poetry at Oxford. His influence as a social and literary critic and as a controversial thinker on religious and educational issues is still felt.

P. J. KEATING was Reader in English Literature at the University of Edinburgh until 1991, when he took early retirement in order to concentrate on writing. His publications include *The Working Classes in Victorian Fiction* (1971); *Into Unknown England: Selections from the Social Explorers* (1976); *The Haunted Study: A Social History of the English Novel 1875–1914* (1989); and *Kipling the Poet* (1994). In addition to *Matthew Arnold: Culture and Anarchy and Other Selected Prose*, he has also edited for Penguin *Cranford* and *Cousin Phillis* by Elizabeth Gaskell, and Rudyard Kipling's *Selected Poems*. His latest book is *Autobiographical Tales* (2013), published by Priskus Books.

MATHEW ARNOLD

Culture and Anarchy
and Other Selected Prose

Edited and Introduced by
P. J. KEATING

PENGUIN BOOKS

PENGUIN CLASSICS

UK | USA | Canada | Ireland | Australia
India | New Zealand | South Africa

Penguin Classics is part of the Penguin Random House group of companies
whose addresses can be found at global.penguinrandomhouse.com.

This edition first published in the Penguin English Library as *Arnold: Selected Prose* 1970
Published in Penguin Classics 1987
This edition first published by Penguin Classics 2015

013

Introduction and Notes copyright © P. J. Keating, 1970
All rights reserved

Set in 10.25/12.25 pt PostScript Adobe Sabon
Typeset by Jouve (UK), Milton Keynes
Printed in Great Britain by Clays Ltd, Elcograf S.p.A.

ISBN: 978-0-141-39624-8

Contents

CULTURE AND ANARCHY
AND OTHER SELECTED PROSE

ESSAYS IN CRITICISM

MY COUNTRYMEN

CULTURE AND ANARCHY

FRIENDSHIP'S GARLAND

ESSAYS IN CRITICISM: SECOND SERIES

Preface

No anthologist of a writer so prolific and of such varied interest as Matthew Arnold is likely to be fully satisfied with his final choice. My guiding principle has been not to attempt an inclusive portrait of an important nineteenth-century writer, but to select those prose writings which make Arnold a living force for the modern reader: the same principle adopted by Arnold himself in his editions of Wordsworth and Byron. There is much else I would have liked to include, but with more space at my disposal I would almost certainly have chosen further examples of those aspects of Arnold's work already represented here; more from the Homer lectures and *Friendship's Garland*, 'A French Critic on Milton', 'The Bishop and the Philosopher' and the essay on Dr Johnson. As it stands the final choice is hardly unconventional save for the central place given to *Friendship's Garland*, which has, I feel, been unfairly neglected. Major omissions were dictated by the same principle. The writings on religion, to which Arnold gave pride of place when he anthologized himself in 1880, I have omitted completely, because, of all Arnold's work, these seem to me to carry least well to the modern reader. I have also omitted some favourite anthology pieces, often with regret, to make way for *Friendship's Garland*.

The greater part of Arnold's work was published originally in periodicals and newspapers, and extensively revised (with personal and topical allusions removed or modified) for publication in book form. This means that works such as the Preface to *Essays in Criticism* (1865) and *Culture and Anarchy*, for instance, with which the modern reader is familiar, are not the same works known to the original readers in the 1860s. In substance they are unchanged but in spirit they are often very different. This creates special textual problems. One type of Arnold edition would be for the historian: a text reprinting the first edition to show the work known to the original reader. Such an edition would be of great value but this is not the place for it. The other approach is to print, as I have done, the version which represents Arnold's final intention and which incorporates his latest revisions. I have based the text on the last English edition published during Arnold's lifetime: the edition used for each individual work is mentioned in the Notes. All footnotes in the present text, even when signed Ed., are Arnold's, though I have silently removed several footnotes (usually referring to editions of works from which Arnold is quoting) which I considered liable to obstruct rather than help the reader. Editorial sub-titles are mine.

Arnold is so allusive a writer that complete annotation could not reasonably be expected of any editor. In order to avoid swamping the text with notes, while, at the same time, providing the much-needed additional information, it has sometimes been necessary for me to pursue an inconsistent, though not I hope arbitrary, policy on when and when not to provide annotation. It is a great pleasure to acknowledge the invaluable help given in this respect, as in many others, by R. H. Super's edition of *The Complete Prose Works of Matthew Arnold* (University of Michigan Press, 1960, in progress), of which six volumes have so far been published. I am also indebted to the following: Kenneth Allott (ed.), *The Poems of Matthew Arnold* ('Longmans Annotated English Poets', 1965); Fraser Neiman (ed.), *Essays, Letters and Reviews by Matthew Arnold* (Harvard University Press, 1960); John Dover Wilson (ed.), *Culture and Anarchy* (Cambridge University Press, 1932, rev. edn. 1935); and Howard Foster Lowry (ed.), *The Letters of Matthew Arnold to Arthur Hugh Clough* (Oxford University Press, 1932).

I would like to express my gratitude to Mr Patrick Scott for his advice and help on a wide range of problems: and to Mr J. D. Cloud, Mr Gerd Wagner and Dr J. R. Watson, who helped me in various ways.

P. J. K., 1970

Introduction

> And so for a time he seems to have grown rather cold towards
> the Muses, his earliest and always his truest loves. Social,
> political, and religious matters tempted him away from
> literature.*

George Saintsbury's early judgement that Arnold's social and
religious writings were the aberrations of a major poet and literary critic is well known, and at this late date, as full-scale
studies on every conceivable aspect of Arnold's thought and
work proliferate, needs perhaps no rebuttal. But the mono-
graphic nature of most of these studies tends to reinforce
Saintsbury's fundamental belief that there were at least five
Matthew Arnolds, of which two were true and three were false;
the permutation may vary but the attitude implicit in the approach
recurs. It is easy enough to understand why so many critics prefer to regard Arnold as poet, the son of his father, ethnologist,
Francophile, ethical idealist, educationist, political theorist, literary critic or middle-class scourge, rather than to 'see him
steadily and see him whole.' He wrote on a wide variety of
subjects and his life seems to divide naturally into periods during which one of his interests dominated, or even temporarily
eclipsed, the others. One principal division is between the poet
and the writer of prose. Most of his poetry was written before
1858, when he was thirty-six years old, almost all of his prose
afterwards. The further classification of his prose, by subject
matter, obscures the strong underlying sense of purpose that
informs his work as a whole.

Arnold's first published essay, the Preface to *Poems* (1853),
is disturbingly ambiguous. It is best seen as a manifesto from a

---

* G. Saintsbury, *Matthew Arnold* (1899), 126.

practising poet on the verge of admitting defeat. The apparently total concern with problems of literary criticism cannot conceal the fact that Arnold is really at odds with society, and viewed retrospectively it is clear that the life-long battle with the critics, which was later to inspire his greatest work, begins here. He is not yet ready to admit that it is impossible to talk about literature without talking about society, but the step is a short one and four years later, in his inaugural lecture as Professor of Poetry at Oxford, he committed himself firmly to this belief. In doing so he surrendered poetry to prose. There were still some fine poems to come and to the day of his death Arnold was to dream of completing his tragedy on Lucretius, but when, in 1861, he told his mother that he intended finishing off his literary criticism by his fortieth year so that he could 'give the next ten years earnestly to poetry',* he was fooling himself.

The relative neglect of Arnold the humorist, the unwillingness on the part of even many of his most perceptive critics to recognize him as one of the funniest of Victorian writers, is less easy to understand. The reason appears to lie partly in the continuing belief (explicitly formulated by Saintsbury but stretching back to the reaction of Arnold's contemporaries) that much of his humour is in bad taste:† and partly in the tendency of literary critics to discuss his literary criticism in isolation from his social criticism. Behind both attitudes is the fear that laughter will somehow dilute the tone of high moral seriousness that literary critics in particular so admire in him. Yet it is harmful to Arnold's reputation as a living classic of our literature (as opposed to our social thought) to exaggerate the profundity of his ideas or the solemnity of their expression. Arnold decided what he wanted to say very early and in charting his development as a prose writer one finds oneself exploring not so much a mind disinterestedly exercised by the moral and social problems

* Letter, 15 August 1861.
† 'Perhaps it is simply bad for people to be invited to lecture at Oxford. At all events, this combination of academic hauteur and lazy man-about-town insolence enlivens, and disfigures, much of his criticism and all of his controversial writings forever after.' George Watson, on the Preface to *Essays in Criticism* (1865), *The Literary Critics* (Penguin, 1962), 152.

of mid-Victorian England, as a mind constantly struggling to find new ways of expressing certain basic ideas unshakeably held to be true. And in this struggle laughter plays a crucial role. From the beginning Arnold's work was grounded in controversy, but while his views on the style of writing and polemical techniques appropriate to controversial debate changed several times, his essential position remained the same.

In a celebrated passage of 'The Function of Criticism at the Present Time' Arnold instanced the 'return of Burke upon himself' as 'one of the finest things in English literature'. He goes on to explain why:

> That is what I call living by ideas: when one side of a question has long had your earnest support, when all your feelings are engaged, when you hear all round you no language but one, when your party talks this language like a steam-engine and can imagine no other, – still to be able to think, still to be irresistibly carried, if so it be, by the current of thought to the opposite side of the question, and, like Balaam, to be unable to speak anything *but what the Lord has put in your mouth*. I know nothing more striking, and I must add that I know nothing more un-English.

This idea (and the phrase) Arnold found extremely attractive. It recurs in a variety of contexts throughout his work. Yet there are few figures, of comparable intellectual force, that one can less imagine returning upon themselves than Arnold, so sure is he (so cocksure, his critics claimed) of the rightness of his views. When his sister accused him of becoming as dogmatic as Ruskin, he pointed out that 'the difference was that Ruskin was dogmatic and *wrong*',* and there is no reason to believe he had his tongue too firmly in his cheek. In a very real sense the apostle of disinterestedness was the most inflexible of Victorian intellectuals. The moment in 'My Countrymen' when he bows before the critical onslaught, confesses that he is overwhelmed and must make a return upon himself, is one of great irony.

There were, however, two occasions in Arnold's life when he

* Letter to his mother, 13 October 1863.

felt compelled to change direction. They occur too early to be regarded as returns upon himself, and are best seen as formative stages in the development of the position he holds in the very greatest of his prose works – 'The Function of Criticism at the Present Time', 'My Countrymen', *Culture and Anarchy* and *Friendship's Garland*. The first turning point came with his realization of the importance of education in a democratic society, the second with his loss of faith in the middle classes.

In April 1851 Arnold was appointed, on the recommendation of Lord Lansdowne whose private secretary he had been for three years, to an Inspectorship of Schools, a post he held until 1886. It is sometimes suggested that this strange choice of career was a stoical act by which the young poet determined to submerge his melancholy view of life in regular, routine work, and certainly evidence for such an interpretation is to be found in the letters he wrote to Clough at this time. A more pressing, if more mundane, reason was that he wanted to get married and needed to earn his living. By neither poetry nor politics (the two obvious careers open to him) could he immediately achieve these ends and, ironically, teaching he found uncongenial. One point is certain. He did not become a School Inspector through any sense of commitment to the cause of education. On 15 October 1851 he wrote to his wife:

> I think I shall get interested in the schools after a little time; their effects on the children are so immense, and their future effects in civilizing the next generation of the lower classes, who, as things are going, will have most of the political power of the country in their hands, may be so important.

This half-hearted attempt to justify his own position is as near as he gets to enthusiasm about education in the early letters, and even this is soon lost in a flood of complaints about his day-to-day routine, the vastness of the area for which he was responsible, the constant travelling, poor food, lodgings, and the appalling ignorance of the children he examined.

Eight years later he was appointed Foreign Assistant

Commissioner to the Newcastle Commission on elementary education; his task being to examine the educational systems of France, the French cantons of Switzerland, and Holland, and to write a report upon them. He was delighted with the job and a letter to his sister, written on 16 February 1859, captures precisely his frame of mind just a few weeks before he left for the Continent:

> You know that I have no special interest in the subject of public education, but a mission like this appeals even to the general interest which every educated man cannot help feeling in such a subject. I shall for five months get free from the routine work of it, of which I sometimes get very sick, and be dealing with its history and principles. Then foreign life is still to me perfectly delightful, and *liberating* in the highest degree, although I get more and more satisfied to live generally in England, and convinced that I shall work best in the long-run by living in the country which is my own. But when I think of the borders of the Lake of Geneva in May, and the narcissuses, and the lilies, I can hardly sit still.

By the time he returned to England five months later Arnold's position, as outlined in this letter, had been completely reversed. It was now public education rather than the narcissuses and lilies that agitated him. So much importance did he attach to his findings that he took the unusual step of obtaining permission to publish the report in book form, and it appeared in 1861 as *The Popular Education of France* with an introductory essay 'Democracy'. This essay marks Arnold's emergence as a critic of Victorian England. In it can be seen the extension of ideas advanced earlier in his inaugural lecture 'On the Modern Element in Literature' (at this time still unpublished) as well as the first public expression of ideas later to inform his more famous works. Where 'Democracy' differs most markedly from his later social criticism is in its deliberately muted tone.

Even at this early date Arnold was no stranger to controversy. His two most important previous publications, the Preface to *Poems* (1853) and the lectures *On Translating Homer*

(published only four months before 'Democracy') had both
aroused fierce antagonism. In the 1853 Preface Arnold had
adopted a staid, dignified, slightly priggish academic style of
writing; in the Homer lectures he had given full rein to his talent for massacring scapegoats. Neither style was suitable for
the present task. The Preface and Homer lectures had been
directed at specialist audiences, and in their entirely different
ways had depended for their success on Arnold's skill at
in-fighting, grounded as they were in one of his most constant
beliefs – that anyone with the temerity to place his personal
views before the public must be fully prepared to take care of
himself. But with 'Democracy' he was setting out to woo the
middle classes, to convince by reasoned argument, to persuade
a large audience that many of its most cherished opinions were
false. It was, therefore, crucial that he should not alienate his
prospective audience, and the intense desire to avoid frighten-
ing or offending the reader is apparent throughout the essay:

> No sensible man will lightly go counter to an opinion firmly held
> by a great body of his countrymen. He will take for granted, that
> for any opinion which has taken deep root among a people so
> powerful, so successful, and so well worthy of respect as the
> people of this country, there certainly either are, or have been,
> good and sound reasons. He will venture to impugn such an
> opinion with real hesitation, and only when he thinks he per-
> ceives that the reasons which once supported it exist no longer, or
> at any rate seem about to disappear very soon. For undoubtedly
> there arrive periods, when, the circumstances and conditions of
> government having changed, the guiding maxims of government
> ought to change also.

The position adopted here seems far removed from the humble
hack-writer of *Friendship's Garland* who skulks in his garret
while the Philistines prowl outside seeking revenge, but the
change that takes place is more one of tone than of basic attitude. Arnold's hesitancy especially should not fool us, for
whenever he begins to heavily qualify his observations or adopt
a mask of humility he is invariably preparing to pounce, and

the blow when it comes is all the more effective for the reader having been lulled into a mood of false comfort. In 'Democracy' Arnold is too busy trying to establish a close relationship with his readers to use this technique in any other than its most simple form, but even so we can already see how, in the above quotation, the absolute certainty of the final statement makes nonsense of the heavily qualified preceding sentences. The understanding that 'there arrive periods, when, the circumstances and conditions of government having changed, the guiding maxims of government ought to change also' is what Arnold wants to get across to the reader. This belief in historical relativism together with its corollary – the development of a frame of mind able to recognize and work with the dominant forces making for change – is the key-note of Arnold's view of society. Indeed, it would be scarcely an exaggeration to say that Arnold's evaluation of people (whether individually or in groups) is always made according to how they react to the spirit of the age, the *Zeitgeist*.

There are four main categories. First, those who recognize the *Zeitgeist* and work with it, even if this entails making a return upon themselves. Secondly, those who appear to recognize the *Zeitgeist* but in reality deny it by speaking or acting on behalf of a section of society rather than the whole. Thirdly, those who are capable of recognizing the *Zeitgeist* but stand blindly against it. And fourthly, those people, constituting the greater part of society, who are totally incapable of reaching any answer to this problem for themselves. This last group (subdivided into three classes) is, of course, the important one. Arnold is fully aware that in an emergent democracy it is here that true power lies, and in the final instance it is possible to say that almost every intellectual stand taken by Arnold results from his awareness of the pressures of a mass society. Arnold himself is only making an indirect bid for influence over this mass society, his principal targets being those men who have already set themselves up as leaders in whatever field, political, critical, religious, journalistic. It is Harrison, Roebuck, Bright, Gladstone, Colenso, Bradlaugh, Miall, Lowe, Sala or Bottles that he wants to convert. If the more intelligent members of the aristocracy, middle or working classes are converted in the process then all the better, but it is the leaders not the led that he concentrates on; the men who, in offering guidance during a period of crisis, have proclaimed themselves fit to shape and define English democracy. Some are beyond salvation and these must accordingly be exploded or bludgeoned, others may be reached by reason, yet others by being made to look ridiculous in the eyes of the people they are trying to impress. For Arnold education is the central issue because society does not need to be told *what* to think but *how* to think. Thought must lead to action but thought must come first. He is, in T. S. Eliot's famous phrase, less a critic than a propagandist for criticism.*

'Democracy' is an early exercise in this technique:

> This movement of democracy, like other operations of nature, merits properly neither blame nor praise. Its partisans are apt to give it credit which it does not deserve, while its enemies are apt to upbraid it unjustly.

As the coming of democracy is inevitable it is equally foolish to stand stubbornly against it or to welcome it unthinkingly. The only sensible questions to ask are: how can democracy be made to work in the most efficient manner? and, is English society ready to adapt itself to this new force, this 'operation of nature'? Arnold answers that England is entirely unfitted to come to terms with an epoch when 'new ideas are powerfully fermenting in a society, and profoundly changing its spirit'. The working classes are as yet undeveloped, the aristocracy is defunct, and the middle classes, in whom hope for the future rests, are crippled by an outmoded educational system and an irrational, though historically understandable, fear of the State. Yet, the development of the State (a strong central authority acting on behalf of the whole nation) is the only way to avoid the threatening chaos of class conflict. Arnold's courage in making this stand against *laissez-faire* doctrine says much for his faith at this time in the reasoning powers of the middle

---

* 'The Perfect Critic', *The Sacred Wood* (1920).

classes, for, as Lionel Trilling has said: 'he might as well have told the English middle class that only Popery or Mohammedanism could save the national life from meanness as that in the State lay spiritual salvation'.* Anticipating objections that State control means loss of liberty, Arnold argues that the State, through an enlightened educational system, can provide the lead once given by the aristocracy, thus solving the central problem of democracy, 'how to find and keep high ideals'. Above all else people must be taught how to think:

> In modern epochs the part of a high reason, of ideas, acquires constantly increasing importance in the conduct of the world's affairs. A fine culture is the complement of a high reason, and it is in the conjunction of both with character, with energy, that the ideal for men and nations is to be placed ... Culture without character is, no doubt, something frivolous, vain, and weak; but character without culture is, on the other hand, something raw, blind, and dangerous.

Here already is the central thesis of *Culture and Anarchy* as well as the answer to its detractors. It remained only for Arnold to restate, in as reasonable a tone as possible, the need for objectivity:

> Undoubtedly we are drawing on towards great changes; and for every nation the thing most needful is to discern clearly its own condition, in order to know in what particular way it may best meet them. Openness and flexibility of mind are at such a time the first of virtues.

Arnold's growing anger throughout the 1860s (his constant search for new ways of making the same points) is the result of this essay, this approach, failing to make the impact he felt it deserved. The change of tone was not sudden. During 1861 and 1862 he was directly involved in the battle to force Lowe (his superior in the department of education) to modify his plan to

* *Matthew Arnold* (1939, rev. ed. 1949), 179.

introduce a system of 'payment by results' into English education, a form of state intervention contrary in every respect to
that advocated in 'Democracy'; and in *A French Eton* (1864)
Arnold once again tried to persuade the middle classes that
they had everything to gain and nothing to lose by backing the
State. But already we can see that he is losing patience, and the
publication of 'The Function of Criticism at the Present Time'
in the same year shows him as having accepted that reasonableness will not persuade the English to believe in reason. By the
close of the decade the whole argument of 'Democracy' was to
be contained in Arminius's defiant scream 'Get Geist.'

Arnold's campaign to bring *Geist*, intellect, reason, or light,
to the British public was conducted first and foremost through
the periodicals, and it was his ambiguous relationship with the
periodical journalism of the 1860s that largely determined the
shape and tone of the books that eventually emerged. Arnold
did not originally plan to publish *Culture and Anarchy* and
Friendship's Garland in book form. They were composed over
a number of years, each chapter or letter appearing separately,
with each subsequent chapter or letter taking up and answering
criticisms aimed at the originals. They are best regarded as
parts of a running debate from which, for the modern reader at
least, the opposition has been silently removed. Neither book
presents a polished argument which moves in logical stages,
but rather leaps and turns as the author mocks, attacks, or
refutes his often invisible critics. It is this that gives Arnold's
prose its peculiar characteristic; that of a monologue masquer-
ading as a dialogue. The notorious allusiveness also plays a
part in this. Few of his opponents are living names to any but
the student with a specialist knowledge of Victorian literature
and society, and beyond this he is often taking issue with people
who are living names only to a specialist in Matthew Arnold.
What is so surprising is how rarely this allusiveness obstructs
the modern reader. The reason for this lies partly in the total
relevance to any mass-democratic society of Arnold's central
issues; partly in the fact that he seldom allows himself to wal-
low in his ability to savage opponents without relating his

attack to those central issues; and most of all in his constant concern with the problems of communication.

No view of Arnold is more misguided than that which sees him as a disinterested aesthete isolated from the pressures of everyday events. It was a charge frequently levelled against him by his contemporaries and one which particularly riled him:

> 'Death, sin, cruelty stalk among us, filling their maws with inno-
> cence and youth,' and me, in the midst of the general tribulation,
> handing out my pouncet-box.
>
> (*Culture and Anarchy,* Chapter 2)

To make this mistake is to confuse the disinterestedness he advocated as the prime need of modern society with the totally interested way he conducted his campaign. He was, for instance, fully aware of the kind of audience his work attracted: 'I never expect anything of mine to have exactly the popular quality necessary for making a sensation, and perhaps I hardly wish it. But I daresay it will be read by some influential people . . .'*
His target, as has already been mentioned, was that handful of influential people, and this necessarily entailed attacking his competitors. But they are attacked not so much for what they are as for what they represent. The no-holds-barred policy is justified by the need at all costs to counteract irresponsibility. His furious assault on Francis Newman has ultimately little to do with Homer and everything to do with Newman, a man of position and influence, misleading English opinion at a crucial moment:

> in England . . . there exists too little of what I may call a public
> force of correct literary opinion, possessing within certain limits
> a clear sense of what is right and wrong, sound and unsound, and
> sharply recalling men of ability and learning from any flagrant
> misdirection of these their advantages. I think, even, that in our
> country a powerful misdirection of this kind is often more likely to
> subjugate and pervert opinion, than to be checked and corrected

* Letter to his mother, 19 February 1862 (p. 421 below).

by it. Hence a chaos of false tendencies, wasted efforts, impotent conclusions, works which ought never to have been undertaken.

Newman has to be ridiculed because he is contributing to the chaos. A scholarly refutation of Newman's method would appeal only to those readers capable of making such a refutation for themselves, while leaving untouched the greater number of people likely to accept his opinions as correct simply because of the position he holds. The intellectual insularity of the English makes them particularly susceptible to arbitrary judgments. If they could once be persuaded of their foolishness (or their inability to understand that there is a 'final judgment' on such matters) then a Newman would present no danger and there would be no need for Arnold to establish himself as their mentor:

> Any one who can introduce a little order into this chaos by establishing in any quarter a single sound rule of criticism, a single rule which clearly marks what is right as right, and what is wrong as wrong, does a good deed; and his deed is so much the better the greater force he counteracts of learning and ability applied to thicken the chaos. Of course no one can be sure that he has fixed any such rules; he can only do his best to fix them; but somewhere or other, in the literary opinion of Europe, if not in the literary opinion of one nation, in fifty years, if not in five, there is a final judgment on these matters, and the critic's work will at last stand or fall by its true merits.

What clearly emerges from the Homer lectures is that Arnold is not talking solely of literary criticism but of 'the endeavour, in all branches of knowledge – theology, philosophy, history, art, science – to see the object as in itself it really is.' This 'critical effort', which has distinguished European thought throughout the nineteenth century, has passed England by and now threatens to turn her into an intellectual backwater.

In 'Democracy' he had urged the middle classes to recognize the truth of this and by means of state education develop qualities of intelligence to complement the practical virtues they already so abundantly possessed; in the Homer lectures he had displayed Newman as the kind of false guide nurtured by a society lacking intelligence. In his article 'The Bishop and the Philosopher', a review of Bishop Colenso's study of the Pentateuch, published in *Macmillan's Magazine* of January 1863, Arnold once again set himself the task of destroying false guides, but the satire is darker and the hope that the English might yet be stirred to a great critical effort has disappeared. Reason is still appealed to but now the reader is caricatured as well as the author under review:

> Heedless of what may be said about him, the Englishman is generally content to pursue his own way, producing, indeed, little in the sphere of criticism, but producing from time to time in the sphere of pure creation masterpieces which attest his intellectual power and extort admiration from his detractors. Occasionally, however, he quits this safe course. Occasionally, the uncritical spirit of our race, determines to perform a great public act of self-humiliation. Such an act it has recently accomplished. It has just sent forth as its scapegoat into the wilderness, amidst a titter from educated Europe, the Bishop of Natal.

Colenso's book, like Newman's, is one of those 'works which ought never to have been undertaken' because it neither edifies the little-instructed nor further informs the much-instructed. What it does do is confirm the Englishman in his insularity (the force of the above passage comes from Colenso being made the passive agent of the reader) and lowers even further England's esteem in the eyes of 'educated Europe'. More than ever Arnold is firmly convinced that in the State lies the possibility of salvation for English democracy, but no longer does he see education solely in middle-class terms. He had earlier proclaimed the aristocracy and the working classes unfit to rule: he now begins to jettison the middle classes as well.

'The Function of Criticism at the Present Time' has long been regarded as one of Arnold's finest achievements. It is without doubt an immensely polished performance, exuding a poise and confidence unequalled in his earlier work. There is little in it that is really new: its strength lies in the way Arnold pulls together the various strands of thought he had been pursuing for the previous decade to make a definite statement. From this moment his position is absolutely clear and 'The Function of Criticism' becomes, both for Arnold and for his critics, a *point de repère*. Continually looking over his shoulder, especially to 'On the Modern Element', the Homer lectures and the Colenso review, he establishes his historical position in the concept of the epochs of concentration and expansion, and employs this to explain the superiority of European over English literature of the nineteenth century. For Arnold the eighteenth century had been the very type of an epoch of concentration; a society directed by an aristocracy capable of acting for and defining that society, and which, in its ability to respond rationally rather than mechanically, had provided England with the necessary qualities to reign supreme in Europe during the chaotic aftermath of the French Revolution. But the French Revolution was the most important event in recent history. It penetrated a whole nation 'with an enthusiasm for pure reason, and with an ardent zeal for making its prescriptions triumph'; it made France 'the country in Europe where *the people* is most alive.' Alone among the nations of Europe, England had remained oblivious to this 'enthusiasm for pure reason' and had not understood, to use Arnold's earlier phrase from 'Democracy', that 'the circumstances and conditions of government having changed, the guiding maxims of government ought to change also.' England's insularity is reflected in its social structure (still aristocratically governed though the aristocracy has long since lost the will to rule; and still praising practical at the expense of intellectual virtues), and in the literature of the Romantic period, which had its source in 'a great movement of feeling, not in a great movement of mind'. Even Wordsworth, whom Arnold greatly admired, must be judged inferior to Goethe because he 'did not know enough'.

It is the Englishman's error that he is unable to perceive that the epoch of concentration has made way for an epoch of expansion; or rather his error that he can only half perceive this. Material expansion he understands better than anyone else, but the need to control and direct an expanding society by an open-minded examination of the forces making for change is beyond his comprehension. Criticism alone can save him. Only by 'a disinterested endeavour to learn and propagate the best that is known and thought in the world' will the Englishman be brought to understand that the evaluation of any issue (literary, political, social or theological) according to nationalistic, partisan, practical or material principles means all too often an acceptance of the second-rate and leads ultimately to a mere 'apparition of intellectual life'. It is the function of criticism *at the present time* to prevent this happening; to help create the frame of mind appropriate to an epoch of expansion.

Great English critics, Arnold acknowledges, had spoken in a similar manner before him, and the men he mentions are significantly social not literary critics – Cobbett, Carlyle and Ruskin. They must be regarded as failures because they surrendered their original objectivity to partisan involvement. In announcing his willingness to learn from these predecessors Arnold places himself in one of the most important lines of tradition in nineteenth-century English literature – that of the prophet or sage:

> I say, the critic must keep out of the region of immediate practice
> in the political, social, humanitarian sphere, if he wants to make
> a beginning for that more freely speculative treatment of things,
> which may perhaps one day make its benefits felt even in this
> sphere, but in a natural and thence irresistible manner.

No other single passage in 'The Function of Criticism' caused Arnold more trouble than this. Mockingly interpreted by Frederic Harrison as the point of view of 'a critic of new books' or a 'professor of *belles-lettres*', it became the starting-point of *Culture and Anarchy*.

The response provoked by 'The Function of Criticism' both delighted and disturbed Arnold. It delighted him because, as he had explained to his mother during an earlier controversy:

> When first I read a thing of this kind I am annoyed; then I think
> how certainly in two or three days the effect of it upon me will
> have wholly passed off; then I begin to think of the openings it

gives for observations in answer, and from that moment, when a
free activity of the spirit is restored, my gaiety and good spirits
return, and the article is simply an object of interest to me.*

It would be difficult to better this, Arnold's own analysis of the
way his mind worked. In the cut and thrust of controversy conducted through the periodicals and newspapers (he was
notoriously unhappy with public speaking) Arnold was fully at
ease, so much so that he determined to restrict his contributions to the press 'partly because the habit of newspaper writing
would soon become too fascinating and exciting'.† Yet it was
this atmosphere which brought out his best qualities – the ability, and the courage, to ring the changes endlessly (with satire,
wit, seriousness and mocking irony) on those opinions he was
convinced were right; the deep love of England‡ (his Franco-
philia properly read indicates just this), and the profound
understanding that what he was witnessing in England was the
emergence of a mass-democratic society.
   If he was delighted with the replies to 'The Function of Criticism' because they provided him with the inspiration and
ammunition to return to the attack, he was disturbed because
it meant that he had once again been seriously misunderstood.
By stating so unequivocally his belief that the critic should 'keep
out of the region of immediate practice' he had opened the way
to the description of himself as the bored aesthete reaching for
his pouncet-box as protection against the odour of involvement. And this in spite of one of the main purposes of the essay
being to illustrate the relevance of criticism to social problems,
with the justly celebrated assault on Roebuck and Adderley
and the 'Wragg is in custody' passage, synthesized by

---

* Letter to his mother, 30 July 1861 (p. 420).
† Letter to his mother, 3 February 1866 (pp. 422–3).
‡ 'I have a conviction that there is a real, an almost imminent danger of England losing immeasurably in all ways, declining into a sort of greater Holland,
for want of what I must still call ideas, for want of perceiving how the world
is going and must go, and preparing herself accordingly. This conviction
haunts me, and at times even overwhelms me with depression'. Letter to Miss
Arnold, November 1865 (pp. 421–2).

disinterestedness, acting as the culminating exemplum. It now became one of his major concerns to correct this misunderstanding, to explain how criticism (or 'culture'), defined as 'a disinterested endeavour to learn and propagate the best that is known and thought in the world', led neither to non-involvement nor to an automatic solution of every problem, but rather created the frame of mind by which the most sensible solution could be discovered. Time and time again he returned to this, with Chapter 6 of *Culture and Anarchy*, 'Our Liberal Practitioners', his most sustained attempt to argue the point.

The greater part of Arnold's energy between now and the close of the 1860s was devoted to the running debate with his critics. The publication of *Essays in Criticism,* in February 1865, provided him with the first opportunity to reply, and in his Preface, in the very act of denying any intention of replying to criticisms originally made against the reprinted articles, he proceeded to do just that and to create a savage parody of middle-class life. The sharpness of tone, and especially the calculated viciousness of his attack on Ichabod Wright (much of which was omitted from subsequent editions), stand in marked contrast to the sweet reasonableness exhibited in the essays making up the collection. The contrast is important and deliberate. 'I often wished,' Sir Leslie Stephen wrote, 'that I too had a little sweetness and light that I might be able to say such nasty things of my enemies.'* Arnold encouraged his enemies to pursue him and replied with 'My Countrymen', the Arminius letters and *Culture and Anarchy.*

As Arnold's main purpose was now to restate and reaffirm, in however different a manner, his own position, interest changes from what is being said to how it is being said. Given the piecemeal nature of composition it was inevitable that new ideas should be thrown up, but there are really only two which modify the view of society advanced earlier – the 'alien' and 'Hebraism and Hellenism'. The former concept developed naturally out of Arnold's disillusionment with all three classes, and places hope for the future on those individuals (regardless

---

* *Studies of a Biographer,* II (1898).

of class or background) whose view of life is not determined by stock notions and ideas. The contrast between Hebraism and Hellenism holds a more central place in these works and Arnold himself attached great importance to it. It is perhaps best seen as a supplement to the epochs of concentration and expansion in that it attempts to explain, in historical terms, the isolation of England from the mainstream of European thought. Between them Hebraism and Hellenism have moulded the Western world, the aim of both being 'man's perfection or salvation'. But whereas Hellenism was founded on 'spontaneity of consciousness', the desire to 'get rid of one's ignorance, to see things as they are, and by seeing them as they are to see them in their beauty', Hebraism, the dominant defining force in English society, had stressed 'strictness of conscience', morality as an end in itself. The Renaissance inspired a resurgence of Hellenism throughout Europe, but in England this mainstream was transformed into a tributary by Puritanism. To this theory can be traced Arnold's obsession with the Nonconformist as an English middle-class archetype, and the interest in racial characteristics which he explored in *On the Study of Celtic Literature* (1867).

The most striking aspect of these works is the way they are dominated by Arnold's personality. The confidence which enabled him to make a definitive statement of 'The Function of Criticism' is more apparent than ever, and the increased circulation of his ideas brought about by criticisms of that essay made it possible for him to enter his own work as a character; a character whose position is so well known that it can be toyed with, held up to ridicule or even inverted, without, paradoxically, suffering any diminution. Indeed, carried out with Arnold's skill, this dangerous method leads to his opponents' arguments always appearing to be foolish, and his own, made stark in outline by a whittling away to fundamentals, unavoidably sane. Accused of being unpractical he *becomes* unpractical, accused of being dogmatic he *becomes* humble, making a series of ironic returns upon himself until he is back where he started:

I do not quite know what to say about the transcendental system of philosophy, for I am a mere dabbler in these great matters, and to grasp and hold a system of philosophy is a feat much beyond my strength; but I certainly did talk about British Philistines, and to call people Philistines when they are doing just what the wisest men in the country have settled to be quite right, does seem unreasonable, not to say indecent. Being really the most teachable man alive, I could not help making, after I had read the article in the *Saturday Review,* a serious return, as the French say, upon myself; and I resolved never to call my countrymen Philistines again till I had thought more about it, and could be quite sure I was not committing an indecency.

(My Countrymen)

This is still Arnold taking on all comers ('I love to range all the evidence in black and white before me, though it tends to my own discomfiture'), but later in the same essay he places his own views in the mouths of foreigners and, as the recipient of those views, adopts the persona of an English Philistine. From this it is only a further short step for him to become himself once again; himself as seen by Leo of the *Daily Telegraph*:

'A fig for your fine distinctions,' cried I. 'Secretly or openly, will any one dare call Bottles, if he contracts a marriage of this kind, a profligate man?'

Poor Mr Matthew Arnold, upon this, emerged suddenly from his corner, and asked hesitatingly: 'But will any one dare call him a man of delicacy?' The question was so utterly unpractical that I took no notice of it whatever ...

(Friendship's Garland, Letter 8)

But the usual technique is simply to reverse roles, so that it is Arnold who takes 'the *Star* for wisdom and charity, and the *Telegraph* for taste and style'; Arminius who describes the Atlantic cable as 'that great rope, with a Philistine at each end of it talking inutilities'; it is Arnold who is horrified when Arminius tells him: 'Your middle-class man thinks it the highest pitch of development and civilization when his letters are carried twelve times a day from Islington to Camberwell'; and Arnold who 'catches at Mr Lowe's powerful help' and proclaims 'the heart of the English nation is its middle class'. Critics of Arnold's views materialize as though their very existence depended on a single phrase. Harrison, for his praise of the working classes, becomes a Jacobin, while the 'young lions of the *Daily Telegraph*' sign their letters and are addressed as 'Leo'. A single foolish phrase from an opponent is gleefully seized and used as a kind of embalming fluid, to eternally mummify John Hepworth Dixon, Colenso, Sala, Bright, and a host of others. Throughout it all Arnold's pet subjects recur – the public schools, Nonconformist life, the Deceased Wife's Sister Bill, Liberalism, Culture – discussed rationally at one moment only to be dramatized and reduced to farce at another.

As a counterbalance to this process of *reductio ad absurdum* Arnold is constantly reducing his own argument to fundamentals so that he can eventually communicate by means of complex concepts simplified into mere catch-phrases. The three classes are analysed, found wanting, and labelled 'Barbarians', 'Philistines' and 'Populace' (personified in *Friendship's Garland* they become Lord Lumpington, Bottles and Zephaniah Diggs). England's industrial might is symbolized by Coles's Truss Manufactory on the 'finest site in Europe'; and the Englishman is urged to complement his energy and valuable common sense with 'light', 'sweetness', 'Geist', or 'culture'. As E. K. Brown has pointed out, Arnold is not so much 'submitting a reasoned case to the reader's intelligence' as 'laying siege to his emotions'.*
This approach enabled him to answer his critics, reach new readers and, most important of all, turn his ideas into common currency. The effects of his slogans he watched as eagerly as any modern advertising agent. 'I think *Barbarian* will stick,' he wrote to his mother in February 1868, and four months later: 'I should think I heard the word *Philistines* used at least a hundred times during dinner, and *Barbarians* very often.' He was particularly pleased when Disraeli praised him for his 'great achievement in launching phrases'. By 1869 Arnold, though still, in his own phrase, 'an unpopular author', was moving in influential circles and feeling some satisfaction with the impact

* *Matthew Arnold: A Study in Conflict* (Chicago, 1948), 11.

he had made. 'However much I may be attacked,' he wrote to his mother, 'my manner of writing is certainly one that takes hold of people and proves effective.'*

But only part of the effectiveness of Arnold's work at this time can be explained by his dedication to the clarification and communication of his ideas. Many people were willing to listen to him because his single-mindedness and certainty appeared more attractive during the tumultuous years of the late 1860s than they would have done ten years earlier. The death of Palmerston in 1865, the emergence of Disraeli and Gladstone as the leading political figures of the day, and the agitation for the extension of the franchise to the working classes, seemed to augur a resurgence of the social conflict of the 1840s. Arnold himself was fearful that this might happen. His use of the word 'anarchy', with its popular connotations of disorder and arbitrary violence, is indicative of this fear, as is his notorious endorsement, in the first edition of *Culture and Anarchy*, of his father's advice to deal with rioters by flogging the rank and file and flinging the ring-leaders from the Tarpeian Rock. That he deleted this sentence from later editions hardly excuses the tone of this, one of his rare approvals of a practical measure. It does, however, further emphasize the authoritarian nature of Arnold's views. 'Force till right is ready' he had advocated in the 'Function of Criticism', and he makes it clear in *Culture and Anarchy* that others besides rioters are to be severely dealt with; Mr Beales and Mr Bradlaugh and 'the young lions of the *Daily Telegraph*' are also to be 'sacrificed'. Anyone, indeed, whose actions are likely to prevent others from attaining '*real* thought and *real* beauty; *real* sweetness and *real* light'. In Lionel Trilling's words: 'Arnold . . . believed so firmly in reason that he was certain it justified the use of its antithesis, force, without which it was powerless.'†

Yet even his own fear Arnold turned to good advantage. Indirectly, the monster marches and Hyde Park riots are invoked in order to give his portraits of the middle classes (as

* Letter, 27 February 1869.
† *Matthew Arnold*, 260.

tea-sipping Nonconformists) and the aristocracy (as sportsmen isolated on their country estates) the qualities of inflated cartoons; to make these ways of life seem totally ridiculous and irrelevant to the modern world. More directly, he is able to employ the fear of working-class agitation to berate the middle classes for ignoring his warning that democracy 'like other operations of nature' was inevitable and not to be feared so long as preparation was made for its arrival. Preparation was not made and the revolution (that Arnold always insisted must eventually come about) now looked like taking a violent rather than a peaceful course:

> This is the old story of our system of checks and every Englishman doing as he likes, which we have already seen to have been convenient enough so long as there were only the Barbarians and the Philistines to do what they liked, but to be getting inconvenient, and productive of anarchy, now that the Populace wants to do what it likes too.

In spite of this, *Culture and Anarchy* is by no means a pessimistic book. There are moments when Arnold ignores his own advice and allows his ordinary self to triumph over his best self, but these are merely temporary lapses, recognized as such and easily corrected. There is none of the hysterical fear that permeates *Shooting Niagara* (1867), Carlyle's response to the same events. From cover to cover Carlyle breathes forth a prophecy of damnation and fire, while *Culture and Anarchy* closes with a joke against some of Arnold's favourite butts. In his lecture on Emerson (published in *Discourses in America*) Arnold regretfully drew a comparison between the voice of the Carlyle he remembered from his youth ('fresh, comparatively sound and reaching our hearts with true pathetic eloquence') and that of the later Carlyle ('so sorely strained, over-used, and mis-used') and decided that Carlyle could not 'well support a return upon him'. Arnold must have been fully aware that he himself had taken over Carlyle's role as official Victorian prophet. The qualities that had made Carlyle so influential in the 1830s and 40s (the prophetic tone and the courage to stand alone in order to berate, guide, advise and insult the emerging democratic society) were outmoded and ineffectual by the 1860s. For Arnold, Carlyle had committed the unforgivable sin – he had lost touch with the spirit of the age.

By the time *Friendship's Garland* was published in book form, Arnold had already begun to turn away from social criticism and was writing the first of the religious books which were to make him a best-selling author for the first time in his life. For the modern reader these works (together, perhaps, with the political essays he wrote during the last years of his life) have far less interest than the literary or social criticism. Arnold's concern with religious issues does not, of course, suddenly develop in the late 1860s, nor is the form his concern takes unrelated to his work on other subjects. On the contrary, in *St Paul and Protestantism* (1870), *Literature and Dogma* (1873), *God and the Bible* (1875), and *Last Essays on Church and Religion* (1877), he applied to religion the same critical method he had already demonstrated in his studies of literature and society – the stripping away of accretions in order 'to see the object as in itself it really is'. As in his social criticism this entailed destroying both stock notions and blind misdirected energy, the establishing of a middle way (the natural truth of Christianity) between those who 'cling to the traditionary religion with their eyes shut' and those who busy themselves with 'fantastic projects, which can never come to anything, but which prevent their seeing the real character of the situation'.* But these works, widely read and discussed as they were in the 1870s, important as they are to the Arnold specialist, do not carry well to the modern reader. Unlike his other essays they do not transcend the particular age and problems which inspired them.

In the Preface to *Last Essays on Church and Religion* Arnold announced his intention of devoting the remainder of his life to the study of literature. He was careful to point out that this was not a departure from his earlier studies, but an extension of them: 'I am returning, after all, to a field where work of the most important kind has to be done, though indirectly, for

* Preface to *Last Essays on Church and Religion* (1877).

religion.' This return to literary criticism, the point where he had begun, gives an unusual neatness to Arnold's career. It should not, however, be interpreted as a retreat from social issues, nor as a kind of penance paid to the Muses he had so long neglected. He dedicated his last ten years primarily to literary criticism because, of all fields of study, this, he was convinced, was of the greatest importance to society. It is Arnold's view of literature that must finally be looked at.

It would be as wrong to expect from Arnold a neat, coherent theory of literature as it would to expect a neat, coherent theory of society, so firm was his commitment to historical relativism, so contemptuous was he of systems and system-makers. Literature and criticism hold central places in his total view of life but he never conceives of literature as other than a part of society, nor of the critic as being concerned solely with literature. His most unequivocal statement on these two points is in the Preface to *Mixed Essays* (1879): 'Whoever seriously occupies himself with literature will soon perceive its vital connection with other agencies . . . literature is a part of civilization; it is not the whole.'

First and foremost is Arnold's faith in literature as an educative force. Simple didacticism he rejects scornfully. Literature does not try to direct man's thoughts on specified issues, but fosters the ability to understand and judge by awakening a sense of calm objectivity in the face of life. In the Preface to *Poems* (1853) this power is given pre-eminently to classical literature. Arnold's argument, in this his first published essay, contains in embryo almost every important feature of his later literary criticism. Modern life is characterized by its fragmentation:

The confusion of the present times is great, the multitude of voices counselling different things bewildering, the number of existing works capable of attracting a young writer's attention and of becoming his models, immense. What he wants is a hand to guide him through the confusion, a voice to prescribe to him the aim which he should keep in view, and to explain to him that the value of the literary works which offer themselves to his attention is relative to their power of helping him forward on his road towards this aim.

Literature as 'part of civilization' reflects this chaos and is conditioned by it. The modern poet has no sense of form, of 'total impression', and can produce only 'occasional bursts of fine writing' and showers 'of isolated thoughts and images'. Guidance is required and for guidance one must turn to the best:

> I know not how it is, but their commerce with the ancients appears to me to produce, in those who constantly practise it, a steadying and composing effect upon their judgment, not of literary works only, but of men and events in general.

The great writer is someone intensely concerned with his age, but capable of conceiving of it in its totality and of conveying this conception to others. This involves a rising above the simple level of interpretation, the writing *about* one's own society:

> they are more truly than others under the empire of facts, and more independent of the language current among those with whom they live. They wish neither to applaud nor revile their age; they wish to know what it is, what it can give them, and whether this is what they want. What they want, they know very well; they want to educe and cultivate what is best and noblest in themselves.

This, however, typifies only the golden age of Greek literature. By the time of Empedocles 'the calm, the cheerfulness, the disinterested objectivity have disappeared; the dialogue of the mind with itself has commenced; modern problems have presented themselves'.

At this early stage Arnold is writing as a poet, largely addressing other poets about poetry. But in spite of this, most of his important assumptions about literature are to be found either in the 1853 Preface or in 'On the Modern Element in

Literature'. They are later to be supported by a greater range of evidence and by more stringent reasoning; they are to be reworked and encapsulated in striking phrases ('imaginative reason', 'natural magic', 'literature a criticism of life') but in essence they have already been formulated, at the very beginning of his career as a prose writer. As a poet Arnold was unable to solve this central problem of the fragmentation of modern life, though the critic in him was able to see what was wrong. In turning from poetry to criticism he was acknowledging defeat on one level, and on another triumphing over defeat by responding to the true demands of the age. The creative faculty he recognizes as superior to the critical faculty but there is a time for criticism and a time for creativity. What the mid-nineteenth century most requires is a breathing space during which may be developed a mood of calm objectivity to withstand the threatened chaos:

> There is so much inviting us! – what are we to take? what will nourish us in growth towards perfection? That is the question which, with the immense field of life and of literature lying before him, the critic has to answer; for himself first, and afterwards for others. In this idea of the critic's business the essays brought together in the following pages have had their origin; in this idea, widely different as are their subjects, they have, perhaps, their unity.
>
> ('The Function of Criticism')

In this sense the critic is preparing the ground for a creative epoch, a time when society is 'in the fullest measure, permeated by fresh thought, intelligent and alive'. This has been the distinguishing mark of the great creative periods of the past and they will occur again but only 'when criticism has done its work'.

To this, the role of the critic, must be added the special function of the critic's chosen medium, prose. Arnold's statement in 'The Study of Poetry' that 'Dryden and Pope are not classics of our poetry, they are classics of our prose', has been much debated, and (the inevitable result of Arnold's love of catch-phrases) much misunderstood. For Arnold, the special task of post-Restoration literature was to establish a 'clear, plain and 'short' prose style appropriate to an age of reason.* His own prose work he considered to be in the same tradition, and, as we have seen, clarity, brevity and plainness were the very qualities he had so carefully developed. In doing so he was recognizing the spirit of his age, just as Johnson and Dryden, as prose writers, were recognizing and responding to the spirit of their age. The eighteenth-century poets (excepting Gray) were bound by the spirit of the age but did not respond to it and merely carried the qualities of prose into their poetry. The same reasoning lies behind Arnold's denigration or even neglect of his contemporary poets who continued striving to produce poetry which requires 'synthesis and exposition', in an age which most demanded 'analysis and discovery':

> This is why great creative epochs in literature are so rare, this is why there is so much that is unsatisfactory in the productions of many men of real genius; – because, for the creation of a master-work of literature two powers must concur, the power of the man and the power of the moment, and the man is not enough without the moment . . .
>
> ('The Function of Criticism')

Poetry is always considered by Arnold to be superior to prose. Prose is functional; the medium of criticism and reason. Poetry is the true medium of imaginative literature:

> it is to the poetical literature of an age that we must, in general, look for the most perfect, the most adequate interpretation of that age, – for the performance of a work which demands the most energetic and harmonious activity of all the powers of the human mind.

* This argument, best known from 'The Study of Poetry', Arnold had earlier advanced in his preface to *The Six Chief Lives from Johnson's Lives of the Poets* (1878).

By virtue of the unique status of poetry, its qualities are less easy to determine than those of prose. Arnold's clearest attempt at definition is in 'Maurice de Guérin':

> The grand power of poetry is its interpretative power; by which I mean, not a power of drawing out in black and white an explanation of the mystery of the universe, but the power of so dealing with things as to awaken in us a wonderfully full, new and intimate sense of them, and of our relations with them.

Here is anticipated Arnold's more famous, or infamous, pronouncement in 'The Study of Poetry', that poetry will ultimately assume the role hitherto taken by religion: 'More and more mankind will discover that we have to turn to poetry to interpret life for us, to console us, to sustain us.' It will serve this educative, therapeutic, religious function because it is the highest expression of which man is capable; through it contact can be made with the very mystery of the universe; and in it can be found a stable scale of values, a positive to cling to, which remains firm while all other creeds and beliefs are crumbling.

If poetry is to fulfil this purpose then the role of the critic is crucial; he becomes a priest whose task is to determine a scale of values: 'For in poetry the distinction between excellent and inferior, sound and unsound or only half-sound, true and untrue or only half-true, is of paramount importance.' The critic must recognize and welcome the best but he must also be capable of extracting what is distinctive from those writers not quite of the first order; as he must also be capable of deciding what, in a major writer's work, is of permanent value and what inferior; inferior, that is, as measured against the same writer's best and the best in an absolute sense. Arnold's literary essays should be considered as exercises in both of these tasks; on the one hand, his attempts to 'extract the honey' from Joubert, Maurice de Guérin and Heine, and, on the other, his qualified praise of writers such as Chaucer and Burns.

For the modern reader Arnold survives not merely as a classic of our criticism but as a classic of our prose. He would not have been surprised to hear it. In turning away from poetry and towards prose he was proclaiming himself the right man for the right moment. It has already been sufficiently stressed how seriously he was concerned with developing a personal prose style, and his interest in the prose styles of his contemporaries – men who were using the right medium at the right time but in the wrong way – is everywhere apparent. He firmly believed that in the literature of an age can be found epitomized the qualities it most values, and, for Arnold, there was no surer test of the health of a society (past or present) than the style it countenanced. Believing this and trying to make it prevail in his own work, he was particularly committed to destroying those of his contemporaries whose prose styles manifested the very qualities most likely to contribute to the chaos of the age. In the attacks on Newman, Macaulay, Sala and John Hepworth Dixon, for their floridity, obscurity and longwindedness (as opposed to Arnold's own simplicity, clarity and brevity), or in his exploration of the ways in which a fragmented society is served by a multitude of newspapers or voices, each carefully nurturing a style of writing or speaking calculated to appeal to one small piece of man rather than the whole, is to be found perhaps the essential Arnold. Here is the literary, social and religious critic in one; his analysis and criticism of a particular aspect of life informed by the strongest possible faith in and concern for the whole; his destructive power made positive by his own example; his criticism surviving as great literature.

P. J. Keating, 1970

Select Bibliography

Edward Alexander, *Matthew Arnold and John Stuart Mill* (1965)

E. K. Brown, *Matthew Arnold: A Study in Conflict* (Chicago, 1948)

Sidney M. B. Coulling, 'The Evolution of *Culture and Anarchy*', *Studies in Philology* LX (1963)

  'Matthew Arnold and the *Daily Telegraph*', *Review of English Studies* XII (1961)

  'Matthew Arnold's 1853 Preface: Its Origin and Aftermath', *Victorian Studies* VII (1964)

T. S. Eliot, 'Arnold and Pater', *Selected Essays* (1951)

  The Use of Poetry and the Use of Criticism (1963)

John Holloway, 'Matthew Arnold and the Modern Dilemma', *The Charted Mirror* (1960)

  The Victorian Sage (1953)

F. R. Leavis, 'Arnold as Critic', *Scrutiny* VII (1938)

Patrick J. McCarthy, *Matthew Arnold and the Three Classes* (New York, 1964)

George Saintsbury, *Matthew Arnold* (1899)

Geoffrey Tillotson, *Criticism and the Nineteenth Century* (1951)

Kathleen Tillotson, 'Matthew Arnold and Carlyle', *Proceedings of the British Academy* (1956)

Lionel Trilling, *Matthew Arnold* (1939)

Culture and Anarchy
and Other Selected Prose

Preface to First Edition of
Poems (1853)

In two small volumes of Poems, published anonymously, one in 1849, the other in 1852, many of the poems which compose the present volume have already appeared. The rest are now published for the first time.

I have, in the present collection, omitted the poem from which the volume published in 1852 took its title.[1] I have done so, not because the subject of it was a Sicilian Greek born between two and three thousand years ago, although many persons would think this a sufficient reason. Neither have I done so because I had, in my own opinion, failed in the deline-ation which I intended to effect. I intended to delineate the feelings of one of the last of the Greek religious philosophers, one of the family of Orpheus and Musæus, having survived his fellows, living on into a time when the habits of Greek thought and feeling had begun fast to change, character to dwindle, the influence of the Sophists to prevail. Into the feelings of a man so situated there entered much that we are accustomed to consider as exclusively modern; how much, the fragments of Empedocles himself which remain to us are sufficient at least to indicate. What those who are familiar only with the great monuments of early Greek genius suppose to be its exclusive characteristics, have disappeared; the calm, the cheerfulness, the disinterested objectivity have disappeared; the dialogue of the mind with itself has commenced; modern problems have presented themselves; we hear already the doubts, we witness the discouragement, of Hamlet and of Faust.

The representation of such a man's feelings must be interesting, if consistently drawn. We all naturally take pleasure, says Aristotle, in any imitation or representation whatever; this is the basis of our love of poetry; and we take pleasure in them, he adds, because all knowledge is naturally agreeable to us; not to the philosopher only, but to mankind at large.[2] Every representation, therefore, which is consistently drawn may be supposed to be interesting, inasmuch as it gratifies this natural interest in knowledge of all kinds. What is *not* interesting, is that which does not add to our knowledge of any kind; that which is vaguely conceived and loosely drawn; a representation which is general, indeterminate, and faint, instead of being particular, precise, and firm.

Any accurate representation may therefore be expected to be interesting; but, if the representation be a poetical one, more than this is demanded. It is demanded, not only that it shall interest, but also that it shall inspirit and rejoice the reader; that it should convey a charm, and infuse delight. For the Muses, as Hesiod says, were born that they might be 'a forgetfulness of evils, and a truce from cares:' and it is not enough that the poet should add to the knowledge of men, it is required of him also that he should add to their happiness. 'All art,' says Schiller, 'is dedicated to Joy, and there is no higher and no more serious problem, than how to make men happy. The right art is that alone, which creates the highest enjoyment.'

A poetical work, therefore, is not yet justified when it has been shown to be an accurate, and therefore interesting representation; it has to be shown also that it is a representation from which men can derive enjoyment. In presence of the most tragic circumstances, represented in a work of art, the feeling of enjoyment, as is well known, may still subsist; the representation of the most utter calamity, of the liveliest anguish, is not sufficient to destroy it; the more tragic the situation, the deeper becomes the enjoyment; and the situation is more tragic in proportion as it becomes more terrible.

What then are the situations, from the representation of which, though accurate, no poetical enjoyment can be derived? They are those in which the suffering finds no vent in action; in which a continuous state of mental distress is prolonged, unrelieved by incident, hope, or resistance; in which there is everything to be endured, nothing to be done. In such situations there is inevitably something morbid, in the description of them something monotonous. When they occur in actual life, they are painful, not tragic; the representation of them in poetry is painful also.

To this class of situations, poetically faulty as it appears to me, that of Empedocles, as I have endeavoured to represent him, belongs; and I have, therefore, excluded the poem from the present collection.

And why, it may be asked, have I entered into this explanation respecting a matter so unimportant as the admission or exclusion of the poem in question? I have done so, because I was anxious to avow that the sole reason for its exclusion was that which has been stated above; and that it has not been excluded in deference to the opinion which many critics of the present day appear to entertain against subjects chosen from distant times and countries: against the choice, in short, of any subjects but modern ones.[3]

'The poet,' it is said,* and by an intelligent critic, 'the poet who would really fix the public attention must leave the exhausted past, and draw his subjects from matters of present import, and *therefore* both of interest and novelty.'

Now this view I believe to be completely false. It is worth examining, inasmuch as it is a fair sample of a class of critical dicta everywhere current at the present day, having a philosophical form and air, but no real basis in fact; and which are calculated to vitiate the judgment of readers of poetry, while they exert, so far as they are adopted, a misleading influence on the practice of those who make it.

What are the eternal objects of poetry, among all nations, and at all times? They are actions; human actions; possessing an inherent interest in themselves, and which are to be communicated in an interesting manner by the art of the poet. Vainly will the latter imagine that he has everything in his own

---

* In the *Spectator* of April 2, 1853. The words quoted were not used with reference to poems of mine.

power; that he can make an intrinsically inferior action equally delightful with a more excellent one by his treatment of it. He may indeed compel us to admire his skill, but his work will possess, within itself, an incurable defect.

The poet, then, has in the first place to select an excellent action; and what actions are the most excellent? Those, certainly, which most powerfully appeal to the great primary human affections: to those elementary feelings which subsist permanently in the race, and which are independent of time. These feelings are permanent and the same; that which interests them is permanent and the same also. The modernness or antiquity of an action, therefore, has nothing to do with its fitness for poetical representation; this depends upon its inherent qualities. To the elementary part of our nature, to our passions, that which is great and passionate is eternally interesting; and interesting solely in proportion to its greatness and to its passion. A great human action of a thousand years ago is more interesting to it than a smaller human action of today, even though upon the representation of this last the most consummate skill may have been expended, and though it has the advantage of appealing by its modern language, familiar manners, and contemporary allusions, to all our transient feelings and interests. These, however, have no right to demand of a poetical work that it shall satisfy them; their claims are to be directed elsewhere. Poetical works belong to the domain of our permanent passions; let them interest these, and the voice of all subordinate claims upon them is at once silenced.

Achilles, Prometheus, Clytemnestra, Dido,[4] – what modern poem presents personages as interesting, even to us moderns, as these personages of an 'exhausted past'? We have the domestic epic dealing with the details of modern life which pass daily under our eyes; we have poems representing modern personages in contact with the problems of modern life, moral, intellectual, and social; these works have been produced by poets the most distinguished of their nation and time; yet I fearlessly assert that Hermann and Dorothea, Childe Harold, Jocelyn, the Excursion,[5] leave the reader cold in comparison with the effect produced upon him by the latter books of the Iliad, by the

Oresteia, or by the episode of Dido. And why is this? Simply because in the three last-named cases the action is greater, the personages nobler, the situations more intense: and this is the true basis of the interest in a poetical work, and this alone.

It may be urged, however, that past actions may be interesting in themselves, but that they are not to be adopted by the modern poet, because it is impossible for him to have them clearly present to his own mind, and he cannot, therefore, feel them deeply, nor represent them forcibly. But this is not necessarily the case. The externals of a past action, indeed, he cannot know with the precision of a contemporary; but his business is with its essentials. The outward man of Œdipus or of Macbeth, the houses in which they lived, the ceremonies of their courts, he cannot accurately figure to himself; but neither do they essentially concern him. His business is with their inward man; with their feelings and behaviour in certain tragic situations, which engage their passions as men; these have in them nothing local and casual; they are as accessible to the modern poet as to a contemporary.

The date of an action, then, signifies nothing; the action itself, its selection and construction, this is what is all-important. This the Greeks understood far more clearly than we do. The radical difference between their poetical theory and ours consists, as it appears to me, in this: that, with them, the poetical character of the action in itself, and the conduct of it, was the first consideration; with us, attention is fixed mainly on the value of the separate thoughts and images which occur in the treatment of an action. They regarded the whole; we regard the parts. With them, the action predominated over the expression of it; with us, the expression predominates over the action. Not that they failed in expression, or were inattentive to it; on the contrary, they are the highest models of expression, the unapproached masters of the *grand style*.[6] But their expression is so excellent because it is so admirably kept in its right degree of prominence; because it is so simple and so well subordinated; because it draws its force directly from the pregnancy of the matter which it conveys. For what reason was the Greek tragic poet confined to so limited a range of subjects? Because there are so few actions which unite in themselves, in the highest degree, the conditions of excellence: and it was not thought that on any but an excellent subject could an excellent poem be constructed. A few actions, therefore, eminently adapted for tragedy, maintained almost exclusive possession of the Greek tragic stage. Their significance appeared inexhaustible; they were as permanent problems, perpetually offered to the genius of every fresh poet. This, too, is the reason of what appears to us moderns a certain baldness of expression in Greek tragedy; of the triviality with which we often reproach the remarks of the chorus, where it takes part in the dialogue: that the action itself, the situation of Orestes, or Merope, or Alcmæon, was to stand the central point of interest, unforgotten, absorbing, principal; that no accessories were for a moment to distract the spectator's attention from this; that the tone of the parts was to be perpetually kept down, in order not to impair the grandiose effect of the whole. The terrible old mythic story on which the drama was founded stood, before he entered the theatre, traced in its bare outlines upon the spectator's mind; it stood in his memory, as a group of statuary, faintly seen, at the end of a long and dark vista: then came the poet, embodying outlines, developing situations, not a word wasted, not a sentiment capriciously thrown in: stroke upon stroke, the drama proceeded: the light deepened upon the group; more and more it revealed itself to the riveted gaze of the spectator: until at last, when the final words were spoken, it stood before him in broad sunlight, a model of immortal beauty.

This was what a Greek critic demanded; this was what a Greek poet endeavoured to effect. It signified nothing to what time an action belonged. We do not find that the Persæ occupied a particularly high rank among the dramas of Æschylus, because it represented a matter of contemporary interest; this was not what a cultivated Athenian required. He required that the permanent elements of his nature should be moved; and dramas of which the action, though taken from a long-distant mythic time, yet was calculated to accomplish this in a higher degree than that of the Persæ, stood higher in his estimation accordingly. The Greeks felt, no doubt, with their exquisite sagacity of taste, that an action of present times was too near them, too much mixed up with what was accidental and passing, to form a sufficiently grand, detached, and self-subsistent object for a tragic poem. Such objects belonged to the domain of the comic poet, and of the lighter kinds of poetry. For the more serious kinds, for *pragmatic* poetry, to use an excellent expression of Polybius, they were more difficult and severe in the range of subjects which they permitted. Their theory and practice alike, the admirable treatise of Aristotle, and the unrivalled works of their poets, exclaim with a thousand tongues – 'All depends upon the subject; choose a fitting action, penetrate yourself with the feeling of its situations; this done, everything else will follow.'

But for all kinds of poetry alike there was one point on which they were rigidly exacting; the adaptability of the subject to the kind of poetry selected, and the careful construction of the poem.

How different a way of thinking from this is ours! We can hardly at the present day understand what Menander meant, when he told a man who inquired as to the progress of his comedy that he had finished it, not having yet written a single line, because he had constructed the action of it in his mind. A modern critic would have assured him that the merit of his piece depended on the brilliant things which arose under his pen as he went along. We have poems which seem to exist merely for the sake of single lines and passages; not for the sake of producing any total impression. We have critics who seem to direct their attention merely to detached expressions, to the language about the action, not to the action itself. I verily think that the majority of them do not in their hearts believe that there is such a thing as a total impression to be derived from a poem at all, or to be demanded from a poet; they think the term a commonplace of metaphysical criticism. They will permit the poet to select any action he pleases, and to suffer that action to go as it will, provided he gratifies them with occasional bursts of fine writing, and with a shower of isolated thoughts and images. That is, they permit him to leave their poetical sense ungratified, provided that he gratifies their rhetorical sense and their curiosity. Of his neglecting to gratify these, there is little danger. He needs rather to be warned against the danger of attempting to gratify these alone; he needs rather to be perpetually reminded to prefer his action to everything else; so to treat this, as to permit its inherent excellences to develop themselves, without interruption from the intrusion of his personal peculiarities; most fortunate, when he most entirely succeeds in effacing himself, and in enabling a noble action to subsist as it did in nature.

But the modern critic not only permits a false practice; he absolutely prescribes false aims. – 'A true allegory of the state of one's own mind in a representative history,' the poet is told, 'is perhaps the highest thing that one can attempt in the way of poetry.' And accordingly he attempts it. An allegory of the state of one's own mind, the highest problem of an art which imitates actions! No assuredly, it is not, it never can be so: no great poetical work has ever been produced with such an aim. Faust itself, in which something of the kind is attempted, wonderful passages as it contains, and in spite of the unsurpassed beauty of the scenes which relate to Margaret, Faust itself, judged as a whole, and judged strictly as a poetical work, is defective: its illustrious author, the greatest poet of modern times, the greatest critic of all times, would have been the first to acknowledge it; he only defended his work, indeed, by asserting it to be 'something incommensurable.'

The confusion of the present times is great, the multitude of voices counselling different things bewildering, the number of existing works capable of attracting a young writer's attention and of becoming his models, immense. What he wants is a hand to guide him through the confusion, a voice to prescribe to him the aim which he should keep in view, and to explain to him that the value of the literary works which offer themselves to his attention is relative to their power of helping him forward on his road towards this aim. Such a guide the English writer at the present day will nowhere find. Failing this, all that can be looked for, all, indeed, that can be desired, is, that his attention should be fixed on excellent models; that he may reproduce, at any rate, something of their excellence, by penetrating himself with their works and by catching their spirit, if he cannot be taught to produce what is excellent independently.

Foremost among these models for the English writer stands Shakespeare: a name the greatest perhaps of all poetical names; a name never to be mentioned without reverence. I will venture, however, to express a doubt, whether the influence of his works, excellent and fruitful for the readers of poetry, for the great majority, has been of unmixed advantage to the writers of it. Shakespeare, indeed, chose excellent subjects; the world could afford no better than Macbeth, or Romeo and Juliet, or Othello; he had no theory respecting the necessity of choosing subjects of present import, or the paramount interest attaching to allegories of the state of one's own mind; like all great poets, he knew well what constituted a poetical action; like them, wherever he found such an action, he took it; like them, too, he found his best in past times. But to these general characteristics of all great poets he added a special one of his own; a gift, namely, of happy, abundant, and ingenious expression, eminent and unrivalled: so eminent as irresistibly to strike the attention first in him, and even to throw into comparative shade his other excellences as a poet. Here has been the mischief. These other excellences were his fundamental excellences *as a poet*; what distinguishes the artist from the mere amateur, says Goethe, is *Architectonicè* in the highest sense; that power of execution, which creates, forms, and constitutes: not the profoundness of single thoughts, not the richness of imagery, not the abundance of illustration. But these attractive accessories of a poetical work being more easily seized than the spirit of the whole, and these accessories being possessed by Shakespeare in an unequalled degree, a young writer having recourse to Shakespeare as his model runs great risk of being vanquished and absorbed by them, and, in consequence, of reproducing, according to the measure of his power, these, and these alone. Of this preponderating quality of Shakespeare's genius, accordingly, almost the whole of modern English poetry has, it appears to me, felt the influence. To the exclusive attention on the part of his imitators to this it is in a great degree owing, that of the majority of modern poetical works the details alone are valuable, the composition worthless. In reading them one is perpetually reminded of that terrible sentence on a modern French poet: – *Il dit tout ce qu'il veut, mais malheureusement il n'a rien à dire.*

Let me give an instance of what I mean. I will take it from the works of the very chief among those who seem to have been formed in the school of Shakespeare: of one whose exquisite genius and pathetic death render him for ever interesting. I will take the poem of Isabella, or the Pot of Basil, by Keats. I choose this rather than the Endymion, because the latter work (which a modern critic has classed with the Fairy Queen!), although undoubtedly there blows through it the breath of genius, is yet as a whole so utterly incoherent, as not strictly to merit the name of a poem at all. The poem of Isabella, then, is a perfect treasure-house of graceful and felicitous words and images: almost in every stanza there occurs one of those vivid and picturesque turns of expression, by which the object is made to flash upon the eye of the mind, and which thrill the reader with a sudden delight. This one short poem contains, perhaps, a greater number of happy single expressions which one could quote than all the extant tragedies of Sophocles. But the action, the story? The action in itself is an excellent one; but so feebly is it conceived by the poet, so loosely constructed, that the effect produced by it, in and for itself, is absolutely null. Let the reader, after he has finished the poem of Keats, turn to the same story in the Decameron: he will then feel how pregnant and interesting the same action has become in the hands of a great artist, who above all things delineates his object; who subordinates expression to that which it is designed to express.

I have said that the imitators of Shakespeare, fixing their attention on his wonderful gift of expression, have directed their imitation to this, neglecting his other excellences. These excellences, the fundamental excellences of poetical art, Shakespeare no doubt possessed them, – possessed many of them in a splendid degree; but it may perhaps be doubted whether even he himself did not sometimes give scope to his faculty of expression to the prejudice of a higher poetical duty. For we must never forget that Shakespeare is the great poet he is from his skill in discerning and firmly conceiving an excellent action, from his power of intensely feeling a situation, of intimately associating himself with a character; not from his gift of expression, which rather even leads him astray, degenerating sometimes into a fondness for curiosity of expression, into an irritability of fancy, which seems to make it impossible for him to say a thing plainly, even when the press of the action demands the very directest language, or its level character the very simplest. Mr Hallam, than whom it is impossible to find a saner and more judicious critic, has had the courage (for at the present day it needs courage) to remark, how extremely and faultily difficult Shakespeare's language often is. It is so: you many find main scenes in some of his greatest tragedies, King Lear for instance, where the language is so artificial, so curiously tortured, and so difficult, that every speech has to be read two or three times before its meaning can be comprehended. This over-curiousness of expression is, indeed, but the excessive employment of a wonderful gift, – of the power of saying a thing in a happier way than any other man; nevertheless, it is carried so far that one understands what M. Guizot meant, when he said that Shakespeare appears in his language to have tried all styles except that of simplicity. He had not the severe and scrupulous self-restraint of the ancients, partly no doubt, because he had a far less cultivated and exacting audience. He has, indeed, a far wider range than they had, a far richer fertility of thought; in this respect he rises above them. In his strong conception of his subject, in the genuine way in which he is penetrated with it, he resembles them, and is unlike the moderns. But in the accurate limitation of it, the conscientious rejection of superfluities, the simple and rigorous development of it from the first line of his work to the last, he falls below them, and comes nearer to the moderns. In his chief works, besides what he has of his own, he has the elementary soundness of the ancients; he has their important action and their large and broad manner; but he has not their purity of method. He is, therefore, a less safe model; for what he has of his own is personal, and inseparable from his own rich nature; it may be imitated and exaggerated, it cannot be learned or applied as an art. He is above all suggestive; more valuable, therefore, to young writers as men than as artists. But clearness of arrangement, rigour of development, simplicity of style, – these may to a certain extent be learned; and these may, I am convinced, be learned best from the ancients, who, although infinitely less suggestive than Shakespeare, are thus, to the artist, more instructive.

What then, it will be asked, are the ancients to be our sole models? the ancients with their comparatively narrow range of experience, and their widely different circumstances? Not, certainly, that which is narrow in the ancients, nor that in which we can no longer sympathize. An action like the action of the Antigone of Sophocles, which turns upon the conflict between the heroine's duty to her brother's corpse and that to the laws of her country, is no longer one in which it is possible that we should feel a deep interest. I am speaking, too, it will be remembered, not of the best sources of intellectual stimulus for the general reader, but of the best models of instruction for the individual writer. This last may certainly learn of the ancients, better than anywhere else, three things which it is vitally important for him to know: – the all-importance of the choice of a subject; the necessity of accurate construction; and the subordinate character of expression. He will learn from them how unspeakably superior is the effect of the one moral impression left by a great action treated as a whole, to the effect produced by the most striking single thought or by the happiest image. As he penetrates into the spirit of the great classical works, as he becomes gradually aware of their intense significance, their noble simplicity, and their calm pathos, he will be convinced that it is this effect, unity and profoundness of moral impression, at which the ancient poets aimed; that it is this which constitutes the grandeur of their works, and which makes them immortal. He will direct his own efforts towards producing the same effect. Above all, he will deliver himself from the jargon of modern criticism, and escape the danger of producing poetical works conceived in the spirit of the passing time, and which partake of its transitoriness.

The present age makes great claims upon us; we owe it service, it will not be satisfied without our admiration. I know not how it is, but their commerce with the ancients appears to me to produce, in those who constantly practise it, a steadying and composing effect upon their judgment, not of literary works only, but of men and events in general. They are like persons who have had a very weighty and impressive experience; they are more truly than others under the empire of facts, and more independent of the language current among those with whom they live. They wish neither to applaud nor to revile their age; they wish to know what it is, what it can give them, and whether this is what they want. What they want, they know very well; they want to educe and cultivate what is best and noblest in themselves; they know, too, that this is no easy task – χαλεπὸν, Pittacus said, χαλεπὸν ἐσθλὸν ἔμμεναι[7] – and they ask themselves sincerely whether their age and its literature can assist them in the attempt. If they are endeavouring to practise any art, they remember the plain and simple proceedings of the old artists, who attained their grand results by penetrating themselves with some noble and significant action, not by inflating themselves with a belief in the pre-eminent importance and greatness of their own times. They do not talk of their mission, nor of interpreting their age, nor of the coming poet; all this, they know, is the mere delirium of vanity; their business is not to praise their age, but to afford to the men who live in it the highest pleasure which they are capable of feeling. If asked to afford this by means of subjects drawn from the age itself, they ask what special fitness the present age has for supplying them. They are told that it is an era of progress, an age commissioned to carry out the great ideas of industrial development and social amelioration. They reply that with all this they can do nothing; that the elements they need for the exercise of their art are great actions, calculated powerfully and delightfully to affect what is permanent in the human soul; that so far as the present age can supply such actions, they will gladly make use of them; but that an age wanting in moral grandeur can with difficulty supply such, and an age of spiritual discomfort with difficulty be powerfully and delightfully affected by them.

A host of voices will indignantly rejoin that the present age is inferior to the past neither in moral grandeur nor in spiritual health. He who possesses the discipline I speak of will content himself with remembering the judgments passed upon the present age, in this respect, by the men of strongest head and widest culture whom it has produced; by Goethe and by Niebuhr.[8] It will be sufficient for him that he knows the opinions held by these two great men respecting the present age and its literature; and that he feels assured in his own mind that their aims and demands upon life were such as he would wish, at any rate, his own to be; and their judgment as to what is impeding and disabling such as he may safely follow. He will not, however, maintain a hostile attitude towards the false pretensions of his age; he will content himself with not being overwhelmed by them. He will esteem himself fortunate if he can succeed in banishing from his mind all feelings of contradiction, and irritation, and impatience; in order to delight himself with the contemplation of some noble action of a heroic time, and to enable others, through his representation of it, to delight in it also.

I am far indeed from making any claim, for myself, that I possess this discipline; or for the following poems, that they breathe its spirit. But I say, that in the sincere endeavour to learn and practise, amid the bewildering confusion of our times, what is sound and true in poetical art, I seemed to myself to find the only sure guidance, the only solid footing, among the ancients. They, at any rate, knew what they wanted in art, and we do not. It is this uncertainty which is disheartening, and not hostile criticism. How often have I felt this when reading words of disparagement or of cavil: that it is the uncertainty as to what is really to be aimed at which makes our difficulty, not the dissatisfaction of the critic, who himself suffers from the same uncertainty! *Non me tua fervida terrent Dicta; . . . Dii me terrent, et Jupiter hostis.*[9]

Two kinds of *dilettanti*, says Goethe, there are in poetry: he who neglects the indispensable mechanical part, and thinks he has done enough if he shows spirituality and feeling; and he who seeks to arrive at poetry merely by mechanism, in which he can acquire an artisan's readiness, and is without soul and matter. And he adds, that the first does most harm to art, and the last to himself. If we must be *dilettanti*: if it is impossible for us, under the circumstances amidst which we live, to think clearly, to feel nobly, and to delineate firmly: if we cannot attain to the mastery of the great artists; – let us, at least, have so much respect for our art as to prefer it to ourselves. Let us not bewilder our successors; let us transmit to them the practice of poetry, with its boundaries and wholesome regulative laws, under which excellent works may again, perhaps, at some future time, be produced, not yet fallen into oblivion through our neglect, not yet condemned and cancelled by the influence of their eternal enemy, caprice.

Preface to Second Edition of
Poems (1854)

I have allowed the Preface to the former edition of these Poems to stand almost without change, because I still believe it to be, in the main, true. I must not, however, be supposed insensible to the force of much that has been alleged against portions of it, or unaware that it contains many things incompletely stated, many things which need limitation. It leaves, too, untouched the question, how far and in what manner the opinions there expressed respecting the choice of subjects apply to lyric poetry, – that region of the poetical field which is chiefly cultivated at present. But neither do I propose at the present time to supply these deficiencies, nor, indeed, would this be the proper place for attempting it. On one or two points alone I wish to offer, in the briefest possible way, some explanation.

An objection has been warmly urged to the classing together, as subjects equally belonging to a past time, Œdipus and Macbeth. And it is no doubt true that to Shakespeare, standing on the verge of the Middle Ages, the epoch of Macbeth was more familiar than that of Œdipus. But I was speaking of actions as they presented themselves to us moderns: and it will hardly be said that the European mind, in our day, has much more affinity with the times of Macbeth than with those of Œdipus. As moderns, it seems to me, we have no longer any direct affinity with the circumstances and feelings of either. As individuals, we are attracted towards this or that personage, we have a capacity for imagining him, irrespective of his times, solely according to a law or personal sympathy; and those subjects for which we feel this personal attraction most strongly, we may hope to treat successfully. Prometheus or Joan of Arc, Charlemagne or

Agamemnon, – one of these is not really nearer to us now than another. Each can be made present only by an act of poetic imagination; but this man's imagination has an affinity for one of them, and that man's for another.

It has been said that I wish to limit the poet, in his choice of subjects, to the period of Greek and Roman antiquity; but it is not so. I only counsel him to choose for his subjects great actions, without regarding to what time they belong. Nor do I deny that the poetic faculty can and does manifest itself in treating the most trifling action, the most hopeless subject. But it is a pity that power should be wasted; and that the poet should be compelled to impart interest and force to his subject, instead of receiving them from it, and thereby doubling his impressiveness. There is, it has been excellently said, an immortal strength in the stories of great actions; the most gifted poet, then, may well be glad to supplement with it that mortal weakness, which, in presence of the vast spectacle of life and the world, he must for ever feel to be his individual portion.

Again, with respect to the study of the classical writers of antiquity; it has been said that we should emulate rather than imitate them. I make no objection; all I say is, let us study them. They can help to cure us of what is, it seems to me, the great vice of our intellect, manifesting itself in our incredible vagaries in literature, in art, in religion, in morals: namely, that it is *fantastic*, and wants *sanity*. Sanity, – that is the great virtue of the ancient literature; the want of that is the great defect of the modern, in spite of all its variety and power. It is impossible to read carefully the great ancients, without losing something of our caprice and eccentricity; and to emulate them we must at least read them.

On the Modern Element in Literature

(What follows was delivered as an inaugural lecture in the Poetry Chair at Oxford. It was never printed, but there appeared at the time several comments on it from critics who had either heard it, or heard reports about it. It was meant to be followed and completed by a course of lectures developing the subject entirely, and some of these were given. But the course was broken off because I found my knowledge insufficient for treating in a solid way many portions of the subject chosen. The inaugural lecture, however, treating a portion of the subject where my knowledge was perhaps less insufficient, and where besides my hearers were better able to help themselves out from their own knowledge, is here printed. No one feels the imperfection of this sketchy and generalizing mode of treatment more than I do; and not only is this mode of treatment less to my taste now than it was eleven years ago, but the style too, which is that of the doctor rather than the explorer, is a style which I have long since learnt to abandon. Nevertheless, having written much of late about Hellenism and Hebraism,[1] and Hellenism being to many people almost an empty name compared with Hebraism, I print this lecture with the hope that it may serve, in the absence of other and fuller illustrations, to give some notion of the Hellenic spirit and its works, and of their significance in the history of the evolution of the human spirit in general. M. A.)

It is related in one of those legends which illustrate the history of Buddhism, that a certain disciple once presented himself before his master, Buddha, with the desire to be permitted to undertake a mission of peculiar difficulty. The compassionate teacher represented to him the obstacles to be surmounted and the risks to be run. Pourna – so the disciple was called – insisted, and replied, with equal humility and adroitness, to the successive objections of his adviser. Satisfied at last by his answers of the fitness of his disciple, Buddha accorded to him the desired permission; and dismissed him to his task with these remarkable words, nearly identical with those in which he himself is said to have been admonished by a divinity at the outset of his own career: – 'Go then, O Pourna,' are his words; 'having been delivered, deliver; having been consoled, console; being arrived thyself at the farther bank, enable others to arrive there also.'[2]

It was a moral deliverance, eminently, of which the great Oriental reformer spoke; it was a deliverance from the pride, the sloth, the anger, the selfishness, which impair the moral activity of man – a deliverance which is demanded of all individuals and in all ages. But there is another deliverance for the human race, hardly less important, indeed, than the first – for in the enjoyment of both united consists man's true freedom – but demanded far less universally, and even more rarely and imperfectly obtained; a deliverance neglected, apparently hardly conceived, in some ages, while it has been pursued with earnestness in others, which derive from that very pursuit their peculiar character. This deliverance is an intellectual deliverance.

An intellectual deliverance is the peculiar demand of those ages which are called modern; and those nations are said to be imbued with the modern spirit most eminently in which the demand for such a deliverance has been made with most zeal, and satisfied with most completeness. Such a deliverance is emphatically, whether we will or no, the demand of the age in which we ourselves live. All intellectual pursuits our age judges according to their power of helping to satisfy this demand; of all studies it asks, above all, the question, how far they can contribute to this deliverance.

I propose, on this my first occasion of speaking here, to attempt such a general survey of ancient classical literature and history as may afford us the conviction – in presence of the doubts so often expressed of the profitableness, in the present day, of our study of this literature – that, even admitting to their fullest extent the legitimate demands of our age, the literature of ancient Greece is, even for modern times, a mighty agent of intellectual deliverance; even for modern times, therefore, an object of indestructible interest.

But first let us ask ourselves why the demand for an intellectual deliverance arises in such an age as the present, and in what the deliverance itself consists? The demand arises, because our present age has around it a copious and complex present, and behind it a copious and complex past; it arises, because the present age exhibits to the individual man who contemplates it the spectacle of a vast multitude of facts awaiting and inviting his comprehension. The deliverance consists in man's comprehension of this present and past. It begins when our mind begins to enter into possession of the general ideas which are the law of this vast multitude of facts. It is perfect when we have acquired that harmonious acquiescence of mind which we feel in contemplating a grand spectacle that is intelligible to us; when we have lost that impatient irritation of mind which we feel in presence of an immense, moving, confused spectacle which, while it perpetually excites our curiosity, perpetually baffles our comprehension.

This, then, is what distinguishes certain epochs in the history of the human race, and our own among the number; – on the one hand, the presence of a significant spectacle to contemplate; on the other hand, the desire to find the true point of view from which to contemplate this spectacle. He who has found that point of view, he who adequately comprehends this spectacle, has risen to the comprehension of his age: he who communicates that point of view to his age, he who interprets to it that spectacle, is one of his age's intellectual deliverers.

The spectacle, the facts, presented for the comprehension of the present age, are indeed immense. The facts consist of the events, the institutions, the sciences, the arts, the literatures, in which human life has manifested itself up to the present time: the spectacle is the collective life of humanity. And everywhere there is connection, everywhere there is illustration: no single event, no single literature, is adequately comprehended except in its relation to other events, to other literatures. The literature of ancient Greece, the literature of the Christian Middle Age, so long as they are regarded as two isolated literatures, two isolated growths of the human spirit, are not adequately comprehended; and it is adequate comprehension which is the demand of the present age. 'We must compare,' – the illustrious Chancellor of Cambridge said the other day to his hearers at Manchester, – 'we must compare the works of other ages with those of our own age and country; that, while we feel proud of the immense development of knowledge and power of production which we possess, we may learn humility in contemplating the refinement of feeling and intensity of thought manifested in the works of the older schools.' To know how others stand, that we may know how we ourselves stand; and to know how we ourselves stand, that we may correct our mistakes and achieve our deliverance – that is our problem.

But all facts, all the elements of the spectacle before us, have not an equal value – do not merit a like attention: and it is well that they do not, for no man would be adequate to the task of thoroughly mastering them all. Some have more significance for us, others have less; some merit our utmost attention in all their details, others it is sufficient to comprehend in their general character, and then they may be dismissed.

What facts, then, let us ask ourselves, what elements of the spectacle before us, will naturally be most interesting to a highly developed age like our own, to an age making the demand which we have described for an intellectual deliverance by means of the complete intelligence of its own situation? Evidently, the other ages similarly developed, and making the same demand. And what past literature will naturally be most interesting to such an age as our own? Evidently, the literatures which have most successfully solved for *their* ages the problem which occupies ours: the literatures which in their day and for their own nation have adequately comprehended, have adequately represented, the spectacle before them. A significant, a highly-developed, a culminating epoch, on the one hand, – a comprehensive, a commensurate, an adequate literature, on the other, – these will naturally be the objects of deepest interest to our modern age. Such an epoch and such a literature are, in fact, *modern*, in the same sense in which our own age and literature are modern; they are founded upon a rich past and upon an instructive fulness of experience.

It may, however, happen that a great epoch is without a perfectly adequate literature; it may happen that a great age, a great nation, has attained a remarkable fulness of political and social development, without intellectually taking the complete measure of itself, without adequately representing that development in its literature. In this case, the *epoch*, the *nation* itself, will still be an object of the greatest interest to us; but the *literature* will be an object of less interest to us: the facts, the material spectacle, are there; but the contemporary view of the facts, the intellectual interpretation, are inferior and inadequate.

It may happen, on the other hand, that great authors, that a powerful literature, are found in an age and nation less great and powerful than themselves; it may happen that a literature, that a man of genius, may arise adequate to the representation of a greater, a more highly developed age than that in which they appear; it may happen that a literature completely interprets its epoch, and yet has something over; that it has a force, a richness, a geniality, a power of view which the materials at its disposition are insufficient adequately to employ. In such a case, the literature will be more interesting to us than the epoch. The interpreting power, the illuminating and revealing intellect, are there; but the spectacle on which they throw their light is not fully worthy of them.

And I shall not, I hope, be thought to magnify too much my office if I add, that it is to the poetical literature of an age that we must, in general, look for the most perfect, the most adequate interpretation of that age, – for the performance of a work which demands the most energetic and harmonious activity of all the powers of the human mind. Because that activity of the whole mind, that genius, as Johnson nobly describes it, 'without which judgment is cold and knowledge is inert; that energy which collects, combines, amplifies, and animates,' is in poetry at its highest stretch and in its most energetic exertion.[3]

What we seek, therefore, what will most enlighten us, most

contribute to our intellectual deliverance, is the union of two things; it is the coexistence, the simultaneous appearance, of a great epoch and a great literature.

Now the culminating age in the life of ancient Greece I call, beyond question, a great epoch; the life of Athens in the fifth century before our era I call one of the highly developed, one of the marking, one of the modern periods in the life of the whole human race. It has been said that 'Pericles of Athens was a vigorous man, at the summit of his bodily strength and mental energy.' There was the utmost energy of life there, public and private; the most entire freedom, the most unprejudiced and intelligent observation of human affairs. Let us rapidly examine some of the characteristics which distinguish modern epochs; let us see how far the culminating century of ancient Greece exhibits them; let us compare it, in respect of them, with a much later, a celebrated century; let us compare it with the age of Elizabeth in our own country.

To begin with what is exterior. One of the most characteristic outward features of a *modern* age, of an age of advanced civilization, is the banishment of the ensigns of war and bloodshed from the intercourse of civil life. Crime still exists, and wars are still carried on; but within the limits of civil life a circle has been formed within which man can move securely, and develop the arts of peace uninterruptedly. The private man does not go forth to his daily occupation prepared to assail the life of his neighbour or to have to defend his own. With the disappearance of the constant means of offence the occasions of offence diminish; society at last acquires repose, confidence, and free activity. An important inward characteristic, again, is the growth of a tolerant spirit; that spirit which is the offspring of an enlarged knowledge; a spirit patient of the diversities of habits and opinions. Other characteristics are the multiplication of the conveniences of life, the formation of taste, the capacity for refined pursuits. And this leads us to the supreme characteristic of all: the intellectual maturity of man himself; the tendency to observe facts with a critical spirit; to search for their law, not to wander among them at random; to judge by the rule of reason, not by the impulse of prejudice or caprice.

Well, now, with respect to the presence of all these character-istics in the age of Pericles, we possess the explicit testimony of an immortal work, – of the history of Thucydides. 'The Atheni-ans first,' he says – speaking of the gradual development of Grecian society up to the period when the Peloponnesian War commenced – 'the Athenians first left off the habit of wearing arms:' that is, this mark of superior civilization had, in the age of Pericles, become general in Greece, had long been visible at Athens. In the time of Elizabeth, on the other hand, the wearing of arms was universal in England and throughout Europe. Again, the conveniences, the ornaments, the luxuries of life, had become common at Athens at the time of which we are speak-ing. But there had been an advance even beyond this; there had been an advance to that perfection, that propriety of taste which proscribes the excess of ornament, the extravagance of luxury. The Athenians had given up, Thucydides says, had given up, although not very long before, an extravagance of dress and an excess of personal ornament which, in the first flush of newly-discovered luxury, had been adopted by some of the richer classes. The height of civilization in this respect seems to have been attained; there was general elegance and refinement of life, and there was simplicity. What was the case in this respect in the Elizabethan age? The scholar Casaubon, who set-tled in England in the reign of James I., bears evidence to the want here, even at that time, of conveniences of life which were already to be met with on the continent of Europe. On the other hand, the taste for fantastic, for excessive personal adornment, to which the portraits of the time bear testimony, is admirably set forth in the work of a great novelist, who was also a very truthful antiquarian – in the *Kenilworth* of Sir Walter Scott. We all remember the description, in the thirteenth and fourteenth chapters of the second volume of *Kenilworth*, of the barbarous magnificence, the 'fierce vanities,' of the dress of the period.

Pericles praises the Athenians that they had discovered sources of recreation for the spirit to counterbalance the labours of the body: compare these, compare the pleasures which charmed the whole body of the Athenian people through the yearly round of their festivals with the popular shows and pastimes in

Kenilworth. 'We have freedom,' says Pericles, 'for individual diversities of opinion and character; we do not take offence at the tastes and habits of our neighbour if they differ from our own.' Yes, in Greece, in the Athens of Pericles, there is toleration; but in England, in the England of the sixteenth century? – the Puritans are then in full growth. So that with regard to these characteristics of civilization of a modern spirit which we have hitherto enumerated, the superiority, it will be admitted, rests with the age of Pericles.

Let us pass to what we said was the supreme characteristic of a highly developed, a modern age – the manifestation of a critical spirit, the endeavour after a rational arrangement and appreciation of facts. Let us consider one or two of the passages in the masterly introduction which Thucydides, the contemporary of Pericles, has prefixed to his history. What was his motive in choosing the Peloponnesian War for his subject? Because it was, in his opinion, the most important, the most instructive event which had, up to that time, happened in the history of mankind. What is his effort in the first twenty-three chapters of his history? To place in their correct point of view all the facts which had brought Grecian society to the point at which that dominant event found it; to strip these facts of their exaggeration, to examine them critically. The enterprises undertaken in the early times of Greece were on a much smaller scale than had been commonly supposed. The Greek chiefs were induced to combine in the expedition against Troy, not by their respect for an oath taken by them all when suitors to Helen, but by their respect for the preponderating influence of Agamemnon; the siege of Troy had been protracted not so much by the valour of the besieged as by the inadequate mode of warfare necessitated by the want of funds of the besiegers. No doubt Thucydides' criticism of the Trojan War is not perfect; but observe how in these and many other points he labours to correct popular errors, to assign their true character to facts, complaining, as he does so, of men's habit of *uncritical* reception of current stories. 'So little a matter of care to most men,' he says, 'is the search after truth, and so inclined are they to take up any story which is ready to their hand.' 'He himself,' he continues, 'has endeavoured to give a true picture, and believes that in the main he has done so. For some readers his history may want the charm of the uncritical, half-fabulous narratives of earlier writers; but for such as desire to gain a clear knowledge of the past, and thereby of the future also, which will surely, after the course of human things, represent again hereafter, if not the very image, yet the near resemblance of the past – if such shall judge my work to be profitable, I shall be well content.'

What language shall we properly call this? It is *modern* language; it is the language of a thoughtful philosophic man of our own days; it is the language of Burke or Niebuhr assigning the true aim of history. And yet Thucydides is no mere literary man; no isolated thinker, speaking far over the heads of his hearers to a future age – no: he was a man of action, a man of the world, a man of his time. He represents, at its best indeed, but he represents, the general intelligence of his age and nation; of a nation the meanest citizens of which could follow with comprehension the profoundly thoughtful speeches of Pericles.

Let us now turn for a contrast to a historian of the Elizabethan age, also a man of great mark and ability, also a man of action, also a man of the world, Sir Walter Ralegh. Sir Walter Ralegh writes the *History of the World*, as Thucydides has written the *History of the Peloponnesian War*; let us hear his language; let us mark his point of view: let us see what problems occur to him for solution. 'Seeing,' he says, 'that we digress in all the ways of our lives – yea, seeing the life of man is nothing else but digression – I may be the better excused in writing their lives and actions.' What are the preliminary facts which he discusses, as Thucydides discusses the Trojan War and the early naval power of Crete, and which are to lead up to his main inquiry? Open the table of contents of his first volume. You will find: – 'Of the firmament, and of the waters above the firmament, and whether there be any crystalline Heaven, or any primum mobile.' You will then find: – 'Of Fate, and that the stars have great influence, and that their operations may diversely be prevented or furthered.' Then you come to two entire chapters on the place of Paradise, and on the two chief trees in the garden of Paradise. And in what style, with what power of criticism, does Ralegh treat the subjects so selected? I turn to the 7th section of the third chapter of his first book, which treats 'Of their opinion which make Paradise as high as the moon, and of others which make it higher than the middle region of the air.' Thus he begins the discussion of this opinion: – 'Whereas Beda saith, and as the schoolmen affirm Paradise to be a place altogether removed from the knowledge of men ("locus a cognitione hominum remotissimus"), and Barcephas conceived that Paradise was far in the east, but mounted above the ocean and all the earth, and near the orb of the moon (which opinion, though the schoolmen charge Beda withal, yet Pererius lays it off from Beda and his master Rabanus); and whereas Rupertus in his geography of Paradise doth not much differ from the rest, but finds it seated next or nearest Heaven –' So he states the error, and now for his own criticism of it. 'First, such a place cannot be commodious to live in, for being so near the moon it had been too near the sun and other heavenly bodies. Secondly, it must have been too joint a neighbour to the element of fire. Thirdly, the air in that region is so violently moved and carried about with such swiftness as nothing in that place can consist or have abiding. Fourthly,' – but what has been quoted is surely enough, and there is no use in continuing.

Which is the ancient here, and which is the modern? Which uses the language of an intelligent man of our own days? which a language wholly obsolete and unfamiliar to us? Which has the rational appreciation and control of his facts? which wanders among them helplessly and without a clue? Is it our own countryman, or is it the Greek? And the language of Ralegh affords a fair sample of the critical power, of the point of view, possessed by the majority of intelligent men of his day; as the language of Thucydides affords us a fair sample of the critical power of the majority of intelligent men in the age of Pericles.

Well, then, in the age of Pericles we have, in spite of its antiquity, a highly-developed, a modern, a deeply interesting epoch. Next comes the question: Is this epoch adequately interpreted by its highest literature? Now, the peculiar characteristic of the highest literature – the poetry – of the fifth century in Greece before the Christian era, is its *adequacy*; the peculiar characteristic of the poetry of Sophocles is its consummate, its unrivalled *adequacy*; that it represents the highly developed human nature of that age – human nature developed in a number of directions, politically, socially, religiously, morally developed – in its completest and most harmonious development in all these directions; while there is shed over this poetry the charm of that noble serenity which always accompanies true insight. If in the body of Athenians of that time there was, as we have said, the utmost energy of mature manhood, public and private; the most entire freedom, the most unprejudiced and intelligent observation of human affairs – in Sophocles there is the same energy, the same maturity, the same freedom, the same intelligent observation; but all these idealized and glorified by the grace and light shed over them from the noblest poetical feeling. And, therefore, I have ventured to say of Sophocles, that he 'saw life steadily, and saw it whole.' Well may we understand how Pericles – how the great statesman whose aim was, it has been said, 'to realize in Athens the idea which he had conceived of human greatness,' and who partly succeeded in his aim – should have been drawn to the great poet whose works are the noblest reflection of his success.

I assert, therefore, though the detailed proof of the assertion must be reserved for other opportunities, that, if the fifth century in Greece before our era is a significant and modern epoch, the poetry of that epoch – the poetry of Pindar, Aeschylus, and Sophocles – is an adequate representation and interpretation of it.

The poetry of Aristophanes is an adequate representation of it also. True, this poetry regards humanity from the comic side; but there is a comic side from which to regard humanity as well as a tragic one; and the distinction of Aristophanes is to have regarded it from the true point of view on the comic side. He, too, like Sophocles, regards the human nature of his time in its fullest development; the boldest creations of a riotous imagination are in Aristophanes, as has been justly said, based always upon the foundation of a serious thought: politics, education, social life, literature – all the great modes in which the human life of his day manifested itself – are the subjects of his thoughts, and of his penetrating comment. There is shed, therefore, over his poetry the charm, the vital freshness, which is felt when man and his relations are from any side adequately, and therefore genially, regarded. Here is the true difference between Aristophanes and Menander. There has been preserved an epitome of a comparison by Plutarch between Aristophanes and Menander, in which the grossness of the former, the exquisite truth to life and felicity of observation of the latter, are strongly insisted upon; and the preference of the refined, the learned, the intelligent men of a later period for Menander loudly proclaimed. 'What should take a man of refinement to the theatre,' asks Plutarch, 'except to see one of Menander's plays? When do you see the theatre filled with cultivated persons, except when Menander is acted? and he is the favourite refreshment,' he continues, 'to the overstrained mind of the laborious philosopher.' And everyone knows the famous line of tribute to this poet by an enthusiastic admirer in antiquity: – 'O Life and Menander, which of you painted the other?' We remember, too, how a great English statesman is said to have declared that there was no lost work of antiquity which he so ardently desired to recover as a play of Menander. Yet Menander has perished, and Aristophanes has survived. And to what is this to be attributed? To the instinct of self-preservation in humanity. The human race has the strongest, the most invincible tendency to *live*, to *develop* itself. It retains, it clings to what fosters its life, what favours its development, to the literature which exhibits it in its vigour; it rejects, it abandons what does not foster its development, the literature which exhibits it arrested and decayed. Now, between the times of Sophocles and Menander a great check had befallen the development of Greece; – the failure of the Athenian expedition to Syracuse, and the consequent termination of the Peloponnesian War in a result unfavourable to Athens. The free expansion of her growth was checked; one of the noblest channels of Athenian life, that of political activity, had begun to narrow and to dry up. That was the true catastrophe of the ancient world; it was then that the oracles of the ancient world should have become silent, and that its gods should have forsaken their temples; for from that date the intellectual and spiritual life of Greece was left without an adequate material basis of political and practical life; and both began inevitably to decay. The opportunity of the ancient world was then lost, never to return; for neither the Macedonian or the Roman world, which possessed an adequate material basis, possessed, like the Athens of earlier times, an adequate intellect and soul to inform and inspire them; and there was left of the ancient world, when Christianity arrived, of Greece only a head without a body, and of Rome only a body without a soul.

It is Athens after this check, after this diminution of vitality, – it is man with part of his life shorn away, refined and intelligent indeed, but sceptical, frivolous, and dissolute, – which the poetry of Menander represented. The cultivated, the accomplished might applaud the dexterity, the perfection of the representation – might prefer it to the free genial delineation of a more living time with which they were no longer in sympathy. But the instinct of humanity taught it, that in the one poetry there was the seed of life, in the other poetry the seed of death; and it has rescued Aristophanes, while it has left Menander to his fate.

In the flowering period of the life of Greece, therefore, we have a culminating age, one of the flowering periods of the life of the human race: in the poetry of that age we have a literature commensurate with its epoch. It is most perfectly commensurate in the poetry of Pindar, Aeschylus, Sophocles, Aristophanes; these, therefore, will be the supremely interesting objects in this literature; but the stages in literature which led up to this point of perfection, the stages in literature which led downward from it, will be deeply interesting also. A distinguished person,[4] who has lately been occupying himself with Homer, has remarked that an undue preference is given, in the studies of Oxford, to these poets over Homer. The justification of such a preference, even if we put aside all philological considerations, lies, perhaps, in what I have said. Homer himself is eternally interesting; he is a greater poetical power than even Sophocles or Aeschylus; but his age is less interesting than himself. Aeschylus and Sophocles represent an age as interesting as themselves; the names, indeed, in their dramas are the names of the old heroic world, from which they were far separated; but these names are taken, because the use of them permits to the poet that free and ideal treatment of his characters which the highest tragedy demands; and into these figures of the old world is poured all the fulness of life and of thought which the new world had accumulated. This new world in its maturity of reason resembles our own; and the advantage over Homer in their great significance for *us*, which Aeschylus and Sophocles gain by belonging to this new world, more than compensates for their poetical inferiority to him.

Let us now pass to the Roman world. There is no necessity to accumulate proofs that the culminating period of Roman history is to be classed among the leading, the significant, the modern periods of the world. There is universally current, I think, a pretty correct appreciation of the high development of the Rome of Cicero and Augustus; no one doubts that material civilization and the refinements of life were largely diffused in it; no one doubts that cultivation of mind and intelligence were widely diffused in it. Therefore, I will not occupy time by showing that Cicero corresponded with his friends in the style of the most accomplished, the most easy letter-writers of modern times; that Caesar did not write history like Sir Walter Ralegh. The great period of Rome is, perhaps, on the whole, the greatest, the fullest, the most significant period on record; it is certainly a greater, a fuller period than the age of Pericles. It is an infinitely larger school for the men reared in it; the relations of life are immeasurably multiplied, the events which happen are on an immeasurably grander scale. The facts, the spectacle of this Roman world, then, are immense: let us see how far the literature, the interpretation of the facts, has been adequate.

Let us begin with a great poet, a great philosopher, Lucretius.[5] In the case of Thucydides I called attention to the fact that his habit of mind, his mode of dealing with questions, were modern; that they were those of an enlightened, reflecting man among ourselves. Let me call attention to the exhibition in Lucretius of a modern *feeling* not less remarkable than the modern *thought* in Thucydides. The predominance of thought, of reflection, in modern epochs is not without its penalties; in the unsound, in the over-tasked, in the over-sensitive, it has produced the most painful, the most lamentable results; it has produced a state of feeling unknown to less enlightened but perhaps healthier epochs – the feeling of depression, the feeling of *ennui*. Depression and *ennui*; these are the characteristics stamped on how many of the representative works of modern times! they are also the characteristics stamped on the poem of Lucretius. One of the most powerful, the most solemn passages of the work of Lucretius, one of the most powerful, the most solemn passages in the literature of the whole world, is the well-known conclusion of the third book. With masterly touches he exhibits the lassitude, the incurable tedium which pursue men in their amusements; with indignant irony he upbraids them for the cowardice with which they cling to a life which for most is miserable; to a life which contains, for the most fortunate, nothing but the old dull round of the same unsatisfying objects for ever presented. 'A man rushes abroad,' he says, 'because he is sick of being at home; and suddenly comes home again because he finds himself no whit easier abroad. He posts as fast as his horses can take him to his country-seat: when he has got there he hesitates what to do; or he throws himself down moodily to sleep, and seeks forgetfulness in that; or he makes the best of his way back to town again with the same speed as he fled from it. Thus everyone flies from himself.' What a picture of *ennui*! of the disease of the most modern societies, the most advanced civilizations! 'O man,' he exclaims again, 'the lights of the world, Scipio, Homer, Epicurus, are dead; wilt thou hesitate and fret at dying, whose life is well-nigh dead whilst thou art yet alive; who consumest in sleep the greater part of thy span, and when awake dronest and ceasest not to dream; and carriest about a mind troubled with baseless fear, and canst not find what it is that aileth thee when thou staggerest like a drunken wretch in the press of thy cares, and welterest hither and thither in the unsteady wandering of thy spirit!' And again: 'I have nothing more than you have already seen', he makes Nature say to man, 'to invent for your amusement; *eadem sunt omnia semper* – all things continue the same for ever.'

Yes, Lucretius is modern; but is he adequate? And how can a

man adequately interpret the activity of his age when he is not in sympathy with it? Think of the varied, the abundant, the wide spectacle of the Roman life of his day; think of its fulness of occupation, its energy of effort. From these Lucretius withdraws himself, and bids his disciples to withdraw themselves; he bids them to leave the business of the world, and to apply themselves *'naturam cognoscere rerum* – to learn the nature of things'; but there is no peace, no cheerfulness for him either in the world from which he comes, or in the solitude to which he goes. With stern effort, with gloomy despair, he seems to rivet his eyes on the elementary reality, the naked framework of the world, because the world in its fulness and movement is too exciting a spectacle for his discomposed brain. He seems to feel the spectacle of it at once terrifying and alluring; and to deliver himself from it he has to keep perpetually repeating his formula of disenchantment and annihilation. In reading him, you understand the tradition which represents him as having been driven mad by a poison administered as a love-charm by his mistress, and as having composed his great work in the intervals of his madness. Lucretius is, therefore, over-strained, gloom-weighted, morbid; and he who is morbid is no adequate interpreter of his age.

I pass to Virgil; to the poetical name which of all poetical names has perhaps had the most prodigious fortune; the name which for Dante, for the Middle Age, represented the perfection of classical antiquity. The perfection of classical antiquity Virgil does not represent; but far be it from me to add my voice to those which have decried his genius;[6] nothing that I shall say is, or can ever be, inconsistent with a profound, an almost affectionate veneration for him. But with respect to him, as with respect to Lucretius, I shall freely ask the question, *Is he adequate?* Does he represent the epoch in which he lived, the mighty Roman world of his time, as the great poets of the great epoch of Greek life represented theirs, in all its fulness, in all its significance?

From the very form itself of his great poem, the Aeneid, one would be led to augur that this was impossible. The epic form, as a form for representing contemporary or nearly contemporary events, has attained, in the poems of Homer, an unmatched, an immortal success; the epic form as employed by learned poets for the reproduction of the events of a past age has attained a very considerable success. But for *this* purpose, for the poetic treatment of the events of a *past* age, the epic form is a less vital form than the dramatic form. The great poets of the modern period of Greece are accordingly, as we have seen, the *dramatic* poets. The chief of these – Aeschylus, Sophocles, Euripides, Aristophanes – have survived: the distinguished epic poets of the same period – Panyasis, Chœrilus, Antimachus – though praised by the Alexandrian critics, have perished in a common destruction with the undistinguished. And what is the reason of this? It is, that the dramatic form exhibits, above all, *the actions of man as strictly determined by his thoughts and feelings*; it exhibits, therefore, what may be always accessible, always intelligible, always interesting. But the epic form takes a wider range; it represents not only the thought and passion of man, that which is universal and eternal, but also the forms of outward life, the fashion of manners, the aspects of nature, that which is local or transient. To exhibit adequately what is local and transient, only a witness, a contemporary, can suffice. In the *reconstruction*, by learning and antiquarian ingenuity, of the local and transient features of a past age, in their representation by one who is not a witness or contemporary, it is impossible to feel the liveliest kind of interest. What, for instance, is the most interesting portion of the Aeneid, – the portion where Virgil seems to be moving most freely, and, therefore, to be most animated, most forcible? Precisely that portion which has most a *dramatic* character; the episode of Dido; that portion where locality and manners are nothing – where persons and characters are everything. We might presume beforehand, therefore, that if Virgil, at a time when contemporary epic poetry was no longer possible, had been inspired to represent human life in its fullest significance, he would not have selected the epic form. Accordingly, what is, in fact, the character of the poem, the frame of mind of the poet? Has the poem the depth, the completeness of the poems of Aeschylus or Sophocles, of those adequate and consummate representations of human life? Has the poet the serious cheerfulness of Sophocles, of a man who has mastered

the problem of human life, who knows its gravity, and is, therefore, serious, but who knows that he comprehends it, and is
therefore cheerful? Over the whole of the great poem of Virgil,
over the whole Aeneid, there rests an ineffable melancholy: not
a rigid, a moody gloom, like the melancholy of Lucretius; no, a
sweet, a touching sadness, but still a sadness; a melancholy
which is at once a source of charm in the poem, and a testimony
to its incompleteness. Virgil, as Niebuhr has well said, expressed
no affected self-disparagement, but the haunting, the irresistible
self-dissatisfaction of his heart, when he desired on his death-
bed that his poem might be destroyed. A man of the most delicate genius, the most rich learning, but of weak health, of the
most sensitive nature, in a great and overwhelming world; conscious, at heart, of his inadequacy for the thorough spiritual
mastery of that world and its interpretation in a work of art;
conscious of this inadequacy – the one inadequacy, the one
weak place in the mighty Roman nature! This suffering, this
graceful-minded, this finely-gifted man is the most beautiful, the
most attractive figure in literary history; but he is not the
adequate interpreter of the great period of Rome.

We come to Horace: and if Lucretius, if Virgil want cheerfulness, Horace wants seriousness. I go back to what I said of
Menander: as with Menander so it is with Horace: the men of
taste, the men of cultivation, the men of the world are enchanted
with him; he has not a prejudice, not an illusion, not a blunder.
True! yet the best men in the best ages have never been thoroughly satisfied with Horace. If human life were complete
without faith, without enthusiasm, without energy, Horace,
like Menander, would be the perfect interpreter of human life:
but it is not; to the best, to the most living sense of humanity, it
is not; and because it is not, Horace is inadequate. Pedants are
tiresome, men of reflection and enthusiasm are unhappy and
morbid; therefore, Horace is a sceptical man of the world. Men
of action are without ideas, men of the world are frivolous and
sceptical; therefore, Lucretius is plunged in gloom and in stern
sorrow. So hard, nay, so impossible for most men is it to develop
themselves in their entirety; to rejoice in the variety, the
movement of human life with the children of the world; to be

serious over the depth, the significance of human life with the wise! Horace warms himself before the transient fire of human animation and human pleasure while he can, and is only serious when he reflects that the fire must soon go out: –

> Damna tamen celeres reparant coelestia lunae:
> Nos, ubi decidimus –

'For nature there is renovation, but for man there is none!' – it is exquisite, but it is not interpretative and fortifying.

In the Roman world, then, we have found a highly modern, a deeply significant, an interesting period – a period more significant and more interesting, because fuller, than the great period of Greece; but we have not a commensurate literature. In Greece we have seen a highly modern, a most significant and interesting period, although on a scale of less magnitude and importance than the great period of Rome; but then, co-existing with the great epoch of Greece there is what is wanting to that of Rome, a commensurate, an interesting literature.

The intellectual history of our race cannot be clearly understood without applying to other ages, nations, and literatures the same method of inquiry which we have been here imperfectly applying to what is called classical antiquity. But enough has at least been said, perhaps, to establish the absolute, the enduring interest of Greek literature, and, above all, of Greek poetry.

ON TRANSLATING
HOMER 1861

From Lecture 2

'The Two Tribunals'

I must repeat what I said in beginning, that the translator of Homer ought steadily to keep in mind where lies the real test of the success of his translation, what judges he is to try to satisfy. He is to try to satisfy *scholars*, because scholars alone have the means of really judging him. A scholar may be a pedant, it is true, and then his judgment will be worthless; but a scholar may also have poetical feeling, and then he can judge him truly; whereas all the poetical feeling in the world will not enable a man who is not a scholar to judge him truly. For the translator is to reproduce Homer, and the scholar alone has the means of knowing that Homer who is to be reproduced. He knows him but imperfectly, for he is separated from him by time, race, and language; but he alone knows him at all. Yet people speak as if there were two real tribunals in this matter – the scholar's tribunal, and that of the general public. They speak as if the scholar's judgment was one thing, and the general public's judgment another; both with their shortcomings, both with their liability to error; but both to be regarded by the translator. The translator who makes verbal literalness his chief care 'will,' says a writer in the National Review whom I have already quoted, 'be appreciated by the scholar accustomed to test a translation rigidly by comparison with the original, to look perhaps with excessive care to finish in detail rather than boldness and general effect, and find pardon even for a version that seems bare and bald, so it be scholastic and faithful.' But, if the scholar in judging a translation looks to detail rather than to general effect, he judges it pedantically and ill. The appeal, however, lies not from the pedantic scholar to the general public, which can only like or dislike Chapman's version, or Pope's, or Mr Newman's, but cannot *judge* them; it lies from the pedantic scholar to the scholar who is not pedantic, who knows that Homer is Homer by his general effect, and not by his single words, and who demands but one thing in a translation – that it shall, as nearly as possible, reproduce for him the *general effect* of Homer. This, then, remains the one proper aim of the translator: to reproduce on the intelligent scholar, as nearly as possible, the general effect of Homer. Except so far as he reproduces this, he loses his labour, even though he may make a spirited Iliad of his own, like Pope, or translate Homer's Iliad word for word, like Mr Newman.[1] If his proper aim were to stimulate in any manner possible the general public, he might be right in following Pope's example; if his proper aim were to help schoolboys to construe Homer, he might be right in following Mr Newman's. But it is not: his proper aim is, I repeat it yet once more, to reproduce on the intelligent scholar, as nearly as he can, the general effect of Homer.

When, therefore, Cowper says, 'My chief boast is that I have adhered closely to my original;' when Mr Newman says, 'My aim is to retain every peculiarity of the original, to be *faithful*, exactly as is the case with the draughtsman of the Elgin marbles;' their real judge only replies: 'It may be so; reproduce then upon us, reproduce the effect of Homer, as a good copy reproduces the effect of the Elgin marbles.'

When, again, Mr Newman tells us that 'by an exhaustive process of argument and experiment' he has found a metre which is at once the metre of 'the modern Greek epic,' and a metre 'like in moral genius' to Homer's metre, his judge has still but the same answer for him: 'It may be so; reproduce then on our ear something of the effect produced by the movement of Homer.'

But what is the general effect which Homer produces on Mr Newman himself? because, when we know this, we shall know whether he and his judges are agreed at the outset, whether we may expect him, if he can reproduce the effect he feels, if his hand does not betray him in the execution, to satisfy his judges and to succeed. If, however, Mr Newman's impression from Homer is something quite different from that of his judges, then it can hardly be expected that any amount of labour or talent will enable him to reproduce for them *their* Homer.

Mr Newman does not leave us in doubt as to the general effect which Homer makes upon him. As I have told you what is the general effect which Homer makes upon me – that of a most rapidly moving poet, that of a poet most plain and direct in his style, that of a poet most plain and direct in his ideas, that of a poet eminently noble – so Mr Newman tells us his general impression of Homer. 'Homer's style,' he says, 'is direct, popular, forcible, quaint, flowing, garrulous.' Again; 'Homer rises and sinks with his subject, is prosaic when it is tame, is low when it is mean.'

I lay my finger on four words in these two sentences of Mr Newman, and I say that the man who could apply those words to Homer can never render Homer truly. The four words are these; *quaint, garrulous, prosaic, low.* Search the English language for a word which does not apply to Homer, and you could not fix on a better than *quaint*, unless perhaps you fixed on one of the other three.

Again; 'to translate Homer suitably,' says Mr Newman, 'we need a diction sufficiently antiquated to obtain pardon of the reader for its frequent homeliness.' 'I am concerned,' he says again, 'with the artistic problem of attaining a plausible aspect of moderate antiquity, while remaining easily intelligible.' And, again, he speaks of 'the more antiquated style suited to this subject.' Quaint! antiquated! – but to whom? Sir Thomas Browne is quaint, and the diction of Chaucer is antiquated: does Mr Newman suppose that Homer seemed quaint to Sophocles, when he read him, as Sir Thomas Browne seems quaint to us, when we read him? or that Homer's diction seemed antiquated to Sophocles, as Chaucer's diction seems antiquated to us? But we cannot really know, I confess, how Homer seemed to Sophocles: well then, to those who can tell us how he seems to them, to the living scholar, to our only present witness on this matter – does Homer make on the Provost of Eton,[2] when he reads him, the impression of a poet quaint and antiquated?

does he make this impression on Professor Thompson, or Professor Jowett?[3] When Shakespeare says, 'The princes *orgulous*',[4] meaning 'the proud princes,' we say, 'This is antiquated'; when he says of the Trojan gates, that they,

> With massy staples
> And corresponsive and fulfilling bolts
> *Sperr* up the sons of Troy[5] –

we say, 'This is both quaint and antiquated.' But does Homer ever compose in a language which produces on the scholar at all the same impression as this language which I have quoted from Shakespeare? Never once. Shakespeare is quaint and antiquated in the lines which I have just quoted; but Shakespeare, need I say it? can compose, when he likes, when he is at his best, in a language perfectly simple, perfectly intelligible; in a language which, in spite of the two centuries and a half which part its author from us, stops us or surprises us as little as the language of a contemporary. And Homer has not Shakespeare's variations: Homer always composes as Shakespeare composes at his best; Homer is always simple and intelligible, as Shakespeare is often; Homer is never quaint and antiquated, as Shakespeare is sometimes.

When Mr Newman says that Homer is garrulous, he seems, perhaps, to depart less widely from the common opinion than when he calls him quaint; for is there not Horace's authority for asserting that 'the good Homer sometimes nods,' *bonus dormitat Homerus?* and a great many people have come, from the currency of this well-known criticism, to represent Homer to themselves as a diffuse old man, with the full-stocked mind, but also with the occasional slips and weaknesses, of old age. Horace has said better things than his 'bonus dormitat Homerus;' but he never meant by this, as I need not remind anyone who knows the passage, that Homer was garrulous, or anything of the kind. Instead, however, of either discussing what Horace meant, or discussing Homer's garrulity as a general question, I prefer to bring to my mind some style which *is* garrulous, and to ask myself, to ask you, whether anything at all of the impression made by that style, is ever made by the style of Homer. The mediæval romancers, for instance, are garrulous; the following, to take out of a thousand instances the first which comes to hand, is in a garrulous manner. It is from the romance of Richard Cœur de Lion:

> Of my tale be not a-wondered!
> The French says he slew an hundred
> (Whereof is made this English saw)
> Or he rested him any thraw.
> Him followed many an English knight
> That eagerly holp him for to fight –

and so on. Now the manner of that composition I call garrulous; everyone will feel it to be garrulous; everyone will understand what is meant when it is called garrulous. Then I ask the scholar – does Homer's manner ever make upon you, I do not say, the same impression of its garrulity as that passage, but does it make, ever for one moment, an impression in the slightest way resembling, in the remotest degree akin to, the impression made by that passage of the mediæval poet? I have no fear of the answer.

I follow the same method with Mr Newman's two other epithets, *prosaic*, and *low*. 'Homer rises and sinks with his subject,' says Mr Newman; 'is prosaic when it is tame, is low when it is mean.' First I say, Homer is never, in any sense, to be with truth called prosaic; he is never to be called low. He does not rise and sink with his subject; on the contrary, his manner invests his subject, whatever his subject be, with nobleness. Then I look for an author of whom it may with truth be said, that he 'rises and sinks with its subject, is prosaic when it is tame, is low when it is mean.' Defoe is eminently such an author; of Defoe's manner it may with perfect precision be said, that it follows his matter; his lifelike composition takes its character from the facts which it conveys, not from the nobleness of the composer. In Moll Flanders and Colonel Jack, Defoe is undoubtedly prosaic when his subject is tame, low when his subject is mean. Does Homer's manner in the Iliad, I ask the scholar, ever make upon him an impression at all like the impression made by Defoe's manner in Moll Flanders and Colonel Jack? Does it not, on the contrary, leave him with an impression of nobleness, even when it deals with Thersites or with Irus?[6]

Well then, Homer is neither quaint, nor garrulous, nor prosaic, nor mean; and Mr Newman, in seeing him so, sees him differently from those who are to judge Mr Newman's rendering of him. By pointing out how a wrong conception of Homer affects Mr Newman's translation, I hope to place in still clearer light those four cardinal truths which I pronounce essential for him who would have a right conception of Homer; that Homer is rapid, that he is plain and direct in word and style, that he is plain and direct in his ideas, and that he is noble.

Mr Newman says that in fixing on a style for suitably rendering Homer, as he conceives him, he 'alights on the delicate line which separates the *quaint* from the *grotesque*.' 'I ought to be quaint,' he says, 'I ought not to be grotesque.' This is a most unfortunate sentence. Mr Newman is grotesque, which he himself says he ought not to be; and he ought not to be quaint, which he himself says he ought to be.

'No two persons will agree,' says Mr Newman, 'as to where the quaint ends and the grotesque begins;' and perhaps this is true. But, in order to avoid all ambiguity in the use of the two words, it is enough to say, that most persons would call an expression which produced on them a very strong sense of its incongruity, and which violently surprised them, *grotesque*; and an expression, which produced on them a slighter sense of its incongruity, and which more gently surprised them, *quaint*. Using the two words in this manner, I say, that when Mr Newman translates Helen's words to Hector in the sixth book,

Δᾶερ ἐμεῖο, κυνὸς κάκομηχάνου, ὀκρυοέσσης –

O, brother thou of me, who am a mischief-working vixen,
A numbing horror –

he is grotesque; that is, he expresses himself in a manner which produces on us a very strong sense of its incongruity, and which violently surprises us. I say, again, that when Mr Newman translates the common line,

Τὴν δ' ἠμείβετ' ἔπειτα μέγας κορυθαίολος Ἕκτωρ –

Great Hector of the motley helm then spake to her responsive –

or the common expression ἐϋκνήμιδες Ἀχαιοί, 'dapper-greav'd Achaians' – he is quaint; that is, he expresses himself in a manner which produces on us a slighter sense of incongruity, and which more gently surprises us. But violent and gentle surprise are alike far from the scholar's spirit when he reads in Homer κυνὸς κακομηχάνου, or, κορυθαίολος Ἕκτωρ, or, ἐϋκνήμιδες Ἀχαιοί. These expressions no more seem odd to him than the simplest expressions in English. He is not more checked by any feeling of strangeness, strong or weak, when he reads them, than when he reads in an English book 'the painted savage,' or, 'the phlegmatic Dutchman.' Mr Newman's renderings of them must, therefore, be wrong expressions in a translation of Homer; because they excite in the scholar, their only competent judge, a feeling quite alien to that excited in him by what they profess to render.

Mr Newman, by expressions of this kind, is false to his original in two ways. He is false to him inasmuch as he is ignoble; for a noble air, and a grotesque air, the air of the address,

Δᾶερ ἐμεῖο, κυνὸς κακομηχάνου, ὀκρυοέσσης –

and the air of the address,

O, brother thou of me, who am a mischief-working vixen,
A numbing horror –

are just contrary the one to the other: and he is false to him inasmuch as he is odd; for an odd diction like Mr Newman's, and a perfectly plain natural diction like Homer's – 'dapper-greav'd Achaians' and ἐϋκνήμιδες Ἀχαιοί – are also just contrary the one to the other. Where, indeed, Mr Newman got his diction, with whom he can have lived, what can be his test of antiquity and rarity for words, are questions which I ask myself with bewilderment. He has prefixed to his translation a list of what he calls 'the more antiquated or rarer words' which he has used. In this list appear, on the one hand, such words as *doughty*, *grisly*, *lusty*, *noisome*, *ravin*, which are familiar, one would think, to all the world; on the other hand, such words as *bragly*, meaning, Mr Newman tells us, 'proudly fine;' *bulkin*, 'a calf;' *plump*, 'a mass;' and so on. 'I am concerned,' says Mr Newman, 'with the artistic problem of attaining a plausible aspect of moderate antiquity, while remaining easily intelligible.' But it seems to me that *lusty* is not antiquated; and that *bragly* is not a word readily understood. That this word, indeed, and *bulkin*, may have 'a plausible aspect of moderate antiquity,' I admit; but that they are 'easily intelligible,' I deny.

Mr Newman's syntax has, I say it with pleasure, a much more Homeric cast than his vocabulary; his syntax, the mode in which his thought is evolved, although not the actual words in which it is expressed, seems to me right in its general character, and the best feature of his version. It is not artificial or rhetorical like Cowper's syntax or Pope's: it is simple, direct, and natural, and so far it is like Homer's. It fails, however, just where, from the inherent fault of Mr Newman's conception of Homer, one might expect it to fail – it fails in nobleness. It presents the thought in a way which is something more than unconstrained – over-familiar; something more than easy – free and easy. In this respect it is like the movement of Mr Newman's version, like his rhythm; for this, too, fails, in spite of some good qualities, by not being noble enough; this, while it avoids the faults of being slow and elaborate, falls into a fault in the opposite direction, and is slip-shod . . .

'To See the Object as in Itself It Really Is'

Mr Newman, indeed, says in his preface, that if any one dislikes his translation, 'he has his easy remedy; to keep aloof from it.' But Mr Newman is a writer of considerable and deserved reputation; he is also a Professor of the University of London, an institution which by its position and by its merits acquires every year greater importance. It would be a very grave thing if the authority of so eminent a Professor led his students to misconceive entirely the chief work of the Greek world; that work which, whatever the other works of classical antiquity have to give us, gives it more abundantly than they all. The eccentricity, too, the arbitrariness, of which Mr Newman's conception of Homer offers so signal an example, are not a peculiar failing of Mr Newman's own; in varying degrees, they are the great defect of English intellect, the great blemish of English literature. Our literature of the eighteenth century, the literature of the school of Dryden, Addison, Pope, Johnson, is a long reaction against this eccentricity, this arbitrariness: that reaction perished by its own faults, and its enemies are left once more masters of the field. It is much more likely that any new English version of Homer will have Mr Newman's faults than Pope's. Our present literature, which is very far, certainly, from having the spirit and power of Elizabethan genius, yet has in its own way these faults, eccentricity and arbitrariness, quite as much as the Elizabethan literature ever had. They are the cause that, while upon none, perhaps, of the modern literatures has so great a sum of force been expended as upon the English literature, at the present hour this literature, regarded not as an object of mere literary interest but as a living intellectual instrument, ranks only third in European effect and importance among the literatures of Europe; it ranks after the literatures of France and Germany. Of these two literatures, as of the intellect of Europe in general, the main effort, for now many years, has been a *critical* effort; the endeavour, in all branches of knowledge – theology, philosophy, history, art, science – to see the object as in itself it really is. But, owing to the presence in English literature of this eccentric and arbitrary spirit, owing to the strong tendency of English writers to bring to the consideration of their object some individual fancy, almost the last thing for which one would come to English literature is just that very thing which now Europe most desires – *criticism*. It is useful to

notice any signal manifestation of those faults, which thus limit
and impair the action of our literature. And, therefore, I have
pointed out, how widely, in translating Homer, a man even of
real ability and learning may go astray, unless he brings to the
study of this clearest of poets one quality in which our English
authors, with all their great gifts, are apt to be somewhat
wanting – simple lucidity of mind.

ON TRANSLATING HOMER:
LAST WORDS 1862

'Reply to Mr Newman'

. . . I never have replied, I never will reply, to any literary assail-
ant; in such encounters tempers are lost, the world laughs, and
truth is not served. Least of all should I think of using this
Chair as a place from which to carry on such a conflict. But
when a learned and estimable man thinks he has reason to
complain of language used by me in this Chair, – when he
attributes to me intentions and feelings towards him which are
far from my heart, I owe him some explanation, – and I am
bound, too, to make the explanation as public as the words
which gave offence. This is the reason why I revert once more
to the subject of translating Homer. But being thus brought
back to that subject, and not wishing to occupy you solely with
an explanation which, after all, is Mr Newman's affair and
mine, not the public's, I shall take the opportunity, – not certainly to enter into any conflict with any one, – but to try to
establish our old friend, the coming translator of Homer, yet a
little firmer in the positions which I hope we have now secured
for him; to protect him against the danger of relaxing, in the
confusion of dispute, his attention to those matters which alone
I consider important for him; to save him from losing sight, in
the dust of the attacks delivered over it, of the real body of
Patroclus.[1] He will probably, when he arrives, requite my solicitude very ill, and be in haste to disown his benefactor; but my
interest in him is so sincere that I can disregard his probable
ingratitude.

First, however, for the explanation. Mr Newman has

published a reply to the remarks which I made on his translation of the Iliad. He seems to think that the respect which at the outset of those remarks I professed for him must have been professed ironically; he says that I use 'forms of attack against him which he does not know how to characterise;' that I 'speak scornfully' of him, treat him with 'gratuitous insult, gratuitous rancour;' that I 'propagate slanders' against him, that I wish to 'damage him with my readers,' to 'stimulate my readers to despise' him. He is entirely mistaken. I respect Mr Newman sincerely; I respect him as one of the few learned men we have, one of the few who love learning for its own sake; this respect for him I had before I read his translation of the Iliad, I retained it while I was commenting on that translation, I have not lost it after reading his reply. Any vivacities of expression which may have given him pain I sincerely regret, and can only assure him that I used them without a thought of insult or rancour. When I took the liberty of creating the verb to *Newmanize,* my intentions were no more rancorous than if I had said to *Miltonise;*[2] when I exclaimed, in my astonishment at his vocabulary, – 'With whom can Mr Newman have lived?' – I meant merely to convey, in a familiar form of speech, the sense of bewilderment one has at finding a person to whom words one thought all the world knew seem strange, and words one thought entirely strange, intelligible. Yet this simple expression of my bewilderment Mr Newman construes into an accusation that he is 'often guilty of keeping low company,' and says that I shall 'never want a stone to throw at him.' And what is stranger still, one of his friends gravely tells me that Mr Newman 'lived with the fellows of Balliol.'[3] As if that made Mr Newman's glossary less inexplicable to me! As if he could have got his glossary from the fellows of Balliol! As if I could believe, that the members of that distinguished society, – of whose discourse, not so many years afterwards, I myself was an unworthy hearer, – were in Mr Newman's time so far removed from the Attic purity of speech which we all of us admired, that when one of them called a calf a *bulkin,* the rest 'easily understood' him; or, when he wanted to say that a newspaper-article was 'proudly fine,' it mattered little whether he said it was that or *bragly!* No; his having lived with the fellows of Balliol does not explain Mr Newman's glossary to me. I will no longer ask 'with whom he can have lived,' since that gives him offence; but I must still declare that where he got his test of rarity or intelligibility for words is a mystery to me.

That, however, does not prevent me from entertaining a very sincere respect for Mr Newman and since he doubts it, I am glad to reiterate my expression of it. But the truth of the matter is this: I unfeignedly admire Mr Newman's ability and learning; but I think in his translation of Homer he has employed that ability and learning quite amiss. I think he has chosen quite the wrong field for turning his ability and learning to account. I think that in England, partly from the want of an Academy, partly from a national habit of intellect to which that want of an Academy is itself due, there exists too little of what I may call a public force of correct literary opinion, possessing within certain limits a clear sense of what is right and wrong, sound and unsound, and sharply recalling men of ability and learning from any flagrant misdirection of these their advantages. I think, even, that in our country a powerful misdirection of this kind is often more likely to subjugate and pervert opinion, than to be checked and corrected by it.* Hence a chaos of false tendencies, wasted efforts, impotent conclusions, works which ought never to have been undertaken. Any one who can introduce a little order into this chaos by establishing in any quarter a single sound rule of criticism, a single rule which clearly marks what is right as right, and what is wrong as wrong, does a good deed; and his deed is so much the better the greater force he counteracts of learning and ability applied to thicken the chaos. Of course no one can be sure that he has fixed any

* 'It is the fact, that scholars of fastidious refinement, but of a judgment which I think far more masculine than Mr Arnold's, have passed a most encouraging sentence on large specimens of my translation. I at present count eight such names.' – 'Before venturing to print, I sought to ascertain how unlearned women and children would accept my verses. I could boast how children and half-educated women have extolled them, how greedily a working man has inquired for them, without knowing who was the translator.' – Mr Newman's *Reply*, pp. 2, 12, 13.

such rules; he can only do his best to fix them; but somewhere or other, in the literary opinion of Europe, if not in the literary opinion of one nation, in fifty years, if not in five, there is a final judgment on these matters, and the critic's work will at last stand or fall by its true merits.

Meanwhile, the charge of having in one instance misapplied his powers, of having once followed a false tendency, is no such grievous charge to bring against a man; it does not exclude a great respect for himself personally, or for his powers in the happier manifestation of them. False tendency is, I have said, an evil to which the artist or the man of letters in England is peculiarly prone; but everywhere in our time he is liable to it, – the greatest as well as the humblest. 'The first beginnings of my Wilhelm Meister,' says Goethe, 'arose out of an obscure sense of the great truth that man will often attempt something for which nature has denied him the proper powers, will undertake and practise something in which he cannot become skilled. An inward feeling warns him to desist' (yes, but there are, unhappily, cases of absolute judicial blindness!), 'nevertheless he cannot get clear in himself about it, and is driven along a false road to a false goal, without knowing how it is with him. To this we may refer everything which goes by the name of false tendency, dilettantism, and so on. A great many men waste in this way the fairest portion of their lives, and fall at last into wonderful delusion.' Yet after all, – Goethe adds, – it sometimes happens that even on this false road a man finds, not indeed that which he sought, but something which is good and useful for him; 'like Saul, the son of Kish, who went forth to look for his father's asses, and found a kingdom.' And thus false tendency as well as true, vain effort as well as fruitful, go together to produce that great movement of life, to present that immense and magic spectacle of human affairs, which from boyhood to old age fascinates the gaze of every man of imagination, and which would be his terror, if it were not at the same time his delight.

So Mr Newman may see how wide-spread a danger it is, to which he has, as I think, in setting himself to translate Homer, fallen a prey. He may be well satisfied if he can escape from it by paying it the tribute of a single work only. He may judge how unlikely it is that I should 'despise' him for once falling a prey to it. I know far too well how exposed to it we all are; how exposed to it I myself am. At this very moment, for example, I am fresh from reading Mr Newman's reply to my lectures; a reply full of that erudition in which (as I am so often and so good-naturedly reminded, but indeed I know it without being reminded), Mr Newman is immeasurably my superior. Well, the demon that pushes us all to our ruin is even now prompting me to follow Mr Newman into a discussion about the digamma,[4] and I know not what providence holds me back. And some day, I have no doubt, I shall lecture on the language of the Berbers, and give him his entire revenge.[5]

But Mr Newman does not confine himself to complaints on his own behalf, he complains on Homer's behalf, too. He says that my 'statements about Greek literature are against the most notorious and elementary fact'; that I 'do a public wrong to literature by publishing them;' and that the Professors to whom I appealed in my three Lectures, 'would only lose credit if they sanctioned the use I make of their names.' He does these eminent men the kindness of adding, however, that 'whether they are pleased with this parading of their names in behalf of paradoxical error, he may well doubt,' and that 'until they endorse it themselves, he shall treat my process as a piece of forgery.' He proceeds to discuss my statements at great length, and with an erudition and ingenuity which nobody can admire more than I do. And he ends by saying that my ignorance is great.

Alas! that is very true. Much as Mr Newman was mistaken when he talked of my rancour, he is entirely right when he talks of my ignorance. And yet, perverse as it seems to say so, I sometimes find myself wishing, when dealing with these matters of poetical criticism, that my ignorance were even greater than it is. To handle these matters properly there is needed a poise so perfect, that the least overweight in any direction tends to destroy the balance. Temper destroys it, a crotchet destroys it, even erudition may destroy it. To press to the sense of the thing itself with which one is dealing, not to go off on some collateral issue about the thing, is the hardest matter in the world. The 'thing itself' with which one is here dealing, – the critical perception of poetic truth, – is of all things the most volatile, elusive, and evanescent; by even pressing too impetuously after it, one runs the risk of losing it. The critic of poetry should have the finest tact, the nicest moderation, the most free, flexible, and elastic spirit imaginable; he should be indeed the 'ondoyant et divers,' the *undulating and diverse* being of Montaigne.[6] The less he can deal with his object simply and freely, the more things he has to take into acount in dealing with it, – the more, in short, he has to encumber himself, – so much the greater force of spirit he needs to retain his elasticity. But one cannot exactly have this greater force by wishing for it; so, for the force of spirit one has, the load put upon it is often heavier than it will well bear. The late Duke of Wellington said of a certain poet that 'it was a pity his education had been so far too much for his abilities.' In like manner, one often sees erudition out of all proportion to its owner's critical faculty. Little as I know, therefore, I am always apprehensive, in dealing with poetry, lest even that little should prove 'too much for my abilities.'

With this consciousness of my own lack of learning, – nay, with this sort of acquiescence in it, with this belief that for the labourer in the field of poetical criticism learning has its disadvantages, – I am not likely to dispute with Mr Newman about matters of erudition. All that he says on these matters in his Reply I read with great interest: in general I agree with him; but only, I am sorry to say, up to a certain point. Like all learned men, accustomed to desire definite rules, he draws his conclusions too absolutely; he wants to include too much under his rules; he does not quite perceive that in poetical criticism the shade, the fine distinction, is everything; and that, when he has once missed this, in all he says he is in truth but beating the air . . .

'The Grand Style'

. . . Nothing has raised more questioning among my critics than these words, – *noble, the grand style*. People complain that I do not define these words sufficiently, that I do not tell them enough about them. 'The grand style, – but what *is* the grand style?' – they cry; some with an inclination to believe in it, but puzzled; others mockingly and with incredulity. Alas! the grand style is the last matter in the world for verbal definition to deal with adequately. One may say of it as is said of faith: 'One must feel it in order to know what it is.' But, as of faith, so, too, one may say of nobleness, of the grand style: 'Woe to those who know it not!' Yet this expression, though indefinable, has a charm; one is the better for considering it; *bonum est, nos hic esse*; nay, one loves to try to explain it, though one knows that one must speak imperfectly. For these, then, who ask the question, – What is the grand style? – with sincerity, I will try to make some answer, inadequate as it must be. For those who ask it mockingly I have no answer, except to repeat to them, with compassionate sorrow, the Gospel words: *Moriemini in peccatis vestris*, – Ye shall die in your sins.

But let me, at any rate, have the pleasure of again giving, before I begin to try and define the grand style, a specimen of what it *is*:

> Standing on earth, not rapt above the pole,
> More safe I sing with mortal voice, unchanged
> To hoarse or mute, though fall'n on evil days,
> On evil days though fall'n, and evil tongues . . .[7]

There is the grand style in perfection; and anyone who has a sense for it, will feel it a thousand times better from repeating those lines than from hearing anything I can say about it.

Let us try, however, what *can* be said, controlling what we say by examples. I think it will be found that the grand style arises in poetry, *when a noble nature, poetically gifted, treats with simplicity or with severity a serious subject*. I think this definition will be found to cover all instances of the grand style in poetry which present themselves. I think it will be found to exclude all poetry which is not in the grand style. And I think it contains no terms which are obscure, which themselves need defining. Even those who do not understand what is meant by calling poetry noble, will understand, I imagine, what is meant by speaking of a noble nature in a man. But the noble or powerful nature, – the *bedeutendes individuum* of Goethe, – is not enough. For instance, Mr Newman has zeal for learning, zeal for thinking, zeal for liberty, and all these things are noble, they ennoble a man; but he has not the poetical gift: there must be the poetical gift, the 'divine faculty,' also. And, besides all this, the subject must be a serious one (for it is only by a kind of licence that we can speak of the grand style in comedy); and it must be treated *with simplicity or severity*. Here is the great difficulty: the poets of the world have been many; there has been wanting neither abundance of poetical gift nor abundance of noble natures; but a poetical gift so happy, in a noble nature so circumstanced and trained, that the result is a continuous style, perfect in simplicity or perfect in severity, has been extremely rare. One poet has had the gifts of nature and faculty in unequalled fulness, without the circumstances and training which make this sustained perfection of style possible. Of other poets, some have caught this perfect strain now and then, in short pieces or single lines, but have not been able to maintain it through considerable works; others have composed all their productions in a style which, by comparison with the best, one must call secondary.

The best model of the grand style simple is Homer; perhaps the best model of the grand style severe is Milton. But Dante is remarkable for affording admirable examples of both styles; he has the grand style which arises from simplicity, and he has the grand style which arises from severity; and from him I will illustrate them both. In a former lecture I pointed out what that severity of poetical style is, which comes from saying a thing with a kind of intense compression, or in an allusive, brief, almost haughty way, as if the poet's mind were charged with so many and such grave matters, that he would not deign to treat any one of them explicitly. Of this severity the last line of the following stanza of the Purgatory is a good example. Dante has been telling Forese that Virgil had guided him through Hell, and he goes on:

> Indi m' han tratto su gli suoi conforti,
> Salendo e rigirando la Montagna
> *Che drizza voi che il mondo fece torti.*

'Thence hath his comforting aid led me up, climbing and circling the Mountain *which straightens you whom the world made crooked.*' These last words, 'la Montagna *che drizza voi che il mondo fece torti,*' – 'the Mountain *which straightens you whom the world made crooked,*' – for the Mountain of Purgatory, I call an excellent specimen of the grand style in severity, where the poet's mind is too full charged to suffer him to speak more explicitly. But the very next stanza is a beautiful specimen of the grand style in simplicity, where a noble nature and a poetical gift unite to utter a thing with the most limpid plainness and clearness:

> Tanto dice di farmi sua compagna
> Ch' io sarò là dove fia Beatrice;
> Quivi convien che senza lui rimagna.

'So long,' Dante continues, 'so long he (Virgil) saith he will bear me company, until I shall be there where Beatrice is; there it behoves that without him I remain.' But the noble simplicity of that in the Italian no words of mine can render.

Both these styles, the simple and the severe, are truly grand; the severe seems, perhaps, the grandest, so long as we attend most to the great personality, to the noble nature, in the poet its author; the simple seems the grandest when we attend most to the exquisite faculty, to the poetical gift. But the simple is no doubt to be preferred. It is the more *magical*: in the other there is something intellectual, something which gives scope for a play of thought which may exist where the poetical gift is either wanting or present in only inferior degree: the severe is much more imitable, and this a little spoils its charm. A kind of semblance of this style keeps Young going, one may say, through all the nine parts of that most indifferent production, the Night Thoughts. But the grand style in simplicity is inimitable:

αἰὼν ἀσφαλής
οὐκ ἔγεντ᾽ οὔτ᾽ Αἰακίδᾳ παρὰ Πηλεῖ,
οὔτε παρ᾽ ἀντιθέῳ Κάδμῳ λέγονται μὰν βροτῶν
ὄλβον ὑπέρτατον οἱ σχεῖν, οἵ τε καὶ χρυσαμπύκων
μελπομενᾶν ἐν ὄρει Μοισᾶν, καὶ ἐν ἑπταπύλοις
ἄϊον Θήξαις...*

There is a limpidness in that, a want of salient points to seize
and transfer, which makes imitation impossible, except by a
genius akin to the genius which produced it ...

'Tennyson and Wordsworth'

One sees how needful it is to direct incessantly the English translator's attention to the essential characteristics of Homer's poetry,
when so accomplished a person as Mr Spedding,[8] recognizing
these characteristics as indeed Homer's, admitting them to be
essential, is led by the ingrained habits and tendencies of English
blank verse thus repeatedly to lose sight of them in translating
even a few lines. One sees this yet more clearly, when Mr Spedding, taking me to task for saying that the blank verse used for
rendering Homer 'must not be Mr Tennyson's blank verse,'
declares that in most of Mr Tennyson's blank verse all Homer's
essential characteristics, – 'rapidity of movement, *plainness of
words and style, simplicity and directness of ideas*, and, above
all, nobleness of manner, are as conspicuous as in Homer himself.' This shows, it seems to me, how hard it is for English
readers of poetry, even the most accomplished, to feel deeply and
permanently what Greek plainness of thought and Greek simplicity of expression really are: they admit the importance of these
qualities in a general way, but they have no ever-present sense of
them; and they easily attribute them to any poetry which has

* 'A secure time fell to the lot neither of Peleus the son of Æacus, nor of the
god-like Cadmus; howbeit these are said to have had, of all mortals, the
supreme of happiness, who heard the golden-snooded Muses sing, one of them
on the mountain (Pelion), the other in seven-gated Thebes.'

other excellent qualities, and which they very much admire. No doubt there are plainer things in Mr Tennyson's poetry than the three lines I quoted; in choosing them, as in choosing a specimen of ballad-poetry, I wished to bring out clearly, by a strong instance, the qualities of thought and style to which I was calling attention; but, when Mr Spedding talks of a plainness of thought *like Homer's*, of a plainness of speech *like Homer's*, and says that he finds these constantly in Mr Tennyson's poetry, I answer that these I do not find there at all. Mr Tennyson is a most distinguished and charming poet; but the very essential characteristic of his poetry is, it seems to me, an extreme sublety and curious elaborateness of thought, an extreme subtlety and curious elaborateness of expression. In the best and most characteristic productions of his genius, these characteristics are most prominent. They are marked characteristics, as we have seen, of the Elizabethan poets; they are marked, though not the essential, characteristics of Shakespeare himself. Under the influences of the nineteenth century, under wholly new conditions of thought and culture, they manifest themselves in Mr Tennyson's poetry in a wholly new way. But they are still there. The essential bent of his poetry is towards such expressions as

Now lies the Earth all Danaë to the stars . . .

or

O'er the sun's bright eye
Drew the vast eyelid of an inky cloud . . .

or

When the cairn'd mountain was a shadow, sunn'd
The world to peace again . . .

or

The fresh young captains flash'd their glittering teeth,
The huge bush-bearded barons heaved and blew . . .

or

> He bared the knotted column of his throat,
> The massive square of his heroic breast,
> The arms on which the standing muscle sloped
> As slopes a wild brook o'er a little stone,
> Running too vehemently to break upon it . . .[9]

And this way of speaking is the least *plain*, the most *unHomeric*, which can possibly be conceived. Homer presents his thought to you just as it wells from the source of his mind: Mr Tennyson carefully distils his thought before he will part with it. Hence comes, in the expression of the thought, a heightened and elaborate air. In Homer's poetry it is all natural thoughts in natural words; in Mr Tennyson's poetry it is all distilled thoughts in distilled words. Exactly this heightening and elaboration may be observed in Mr Spedding's

> While the steeds *mouth'd their corn aloof* . . .

(an expression which might have been Mr Tennyson's), on which I have already commented; and to one who is penetrated with a sense of the real simplicity of Homer, this subtle sophistication of the thought is, I think, very perceptible even in such lines as these,

> And drunk delight of battle with my peers,
> Far on the ringing plains of windy Troy . . .[10]

which I have seen quoted as perfectly Homeric. Perfect simplicity can be obtained only by a genius of which perfect simplicity is an essential characteristic.

So true is this, that when a genius essentially subtle, or a genius which, from whatever cause, is in its essence not truly and broadly simple, determines to be perfectly plain, determines not to admit a shade of subtlety or curiosity into its expression, it cannot even then attain real simplicity; it can

only attain a semblance of simplicity.* French criticism, richer
in its vocabulary than ours, has invented a useful word to distinguish this semblance (often very beautiful and valuable)
from the real quality. The real quality it calls *simplicité*, the
semblance *simplesse*. The one is natural simplicity, the other is
artificial simplicity. What is called simplicity in the productions
of a genius essentially not simple, is in truth *simplesse*. The two
are distinguishable from one another the moment they appear
in company. For instance, let us take the opening of the narrative in Wordsworth's Michael:

> Upon the forest-side in Grasmere Vale
> There dwelt a shepherd, Michael was his name;
> An old man, stout of heart, and strong of limb.
> His bodily frame had been from youth to age
> Of an unusual strength; his mind was keen,
> Intense, and frugal, apt for all affairs;
> And in his shepherd's calling he was prompt
> And watchful more than ordinary men.

Now let us take the opening of the narrative in Mr Tennyson's
Dora:

> With Farmer Allan at the farm abode
> William and Dora. William was his son,
> And she his niece. He often look'd at them,
> And often thought, 'I'll make them man and wife.'

The simplicity of the first of these passages is *simplicité*; that of
the second, *simplesse*. Let us take the end of the same two
poems; first, of Michael: –

---

* I speak of poetic genius as employing itself upon narrative or dramatic
poetry, – poetry in which the poet has to go out of himself and to create. In
lyrical poetry, in the direct expression of personal feeling, the most subtle
genius may, under the momentary pressure of passion, express itself simply.
Even here, however, the native tendency will generally be discernible.

> The cottage which was named the Evening Star
> Is gone – the ploughshare has been through the ground
> On which it stood; great changes have been wrought
> In all the neighbourhood: yet the oak is left
> That grew beside their door: and the remains
> Of the unfinish'd sheepfold may be seen
> Beside the boisterous brook of Green-head Ghyll.

And now, of Dora:

> So those four abode
> Within one house together; and as years
> Went forward, Mary took another mate;
> But Dora lived unmarried till her death.

A heedless critic may call both of these passages simple if he will. Simple, in a certain sense, they both are; but between the simplicity of the two there is all the difference that there is between the simplicity of Homer and the simplicity of Moschus . . .[11]

'A. H. Clough'

It is for the future translator that one must work. The successful translator of Homer will have (or he cannot succeed) that true sense for his subject, and that disinterested love of it, which are, both of them, so rare in literature, and so precious; he will not be led off by any false scent; he will have an eye for the real matter, and, where he thinks he may find any indication of this, no hint will be too slight for him, no shade will be too fine, no imperfections will turn him aside, – he will go before his adviser's thought, and help it out with his own. This is the sort of student that a critic of Homer should always have in his thoughts; but students of this sort are, indeed, rare.

And how, then, can I help being reminded what a student of this sort we have just lost in Mr Clough,[12] whose name I have already mentioned in these lectures? He, too, was busy with Homer; but it is not on that account that I now speak of him.

Nor do I speak of him in order to call attention to his qualities and powers in general, admirable as these were. I mention him because, in so eminent a degree, he possessed these two invaluable literary qualities, – a true sense for his object of study, and a singlehearted care for it. He had both; but he had the second even more eminently than the first. He greatly developed the first through means of the second. In the study of art, poetry, or philosophy, he had the most undivided and disinterested love for his object in itself, the greatest aversion to mixing up with it anything accidental or personal. His interest was in literature itself; and it was this which gave so rare a stamp to his character, which kept him so free from all taint of littleness. In the saturnalia of ignoble personal passions, of which the struggle for literary success, in old and crowded communities, offers so sad a spectacle, he never mingled. He had not yet traduced his friends, nor flattered his enemies, nor disparaged what he admired, or praised what he despised. Those who knew him well had the conviction that, even with time, these literary arts would never be his. His poem, of which I before spoke, has some admirable Homeric qualities; – out-of-doors freshness, life, naturalness, buoyant rapidity. Some of the expressions in that poem, – '*Dangerous Corrievreckan . . . Where roads are unknown to Loch Nevish,*'[13] – come back now to my ear with the true Homeric ring. But that in him of which I think oftenest, is the Homeric simplicity of his literary life.

THE POPULAR EDUCATION
OF FRANCE

Democracy

In giving an account of education in certain countries of the Continent, I have often spoken of the State and its action in such a way as to offend, I fear, some of my readers, and to surprise others. With many Englishmen, perhaps with the majority, it is a maxim that the State, the executive power, ought to be entrusted with no more means of action than those which it is impossible to withhold from it; that the State neither would nor could make a safe use of any more extended liberty; would not, because it has in itself a natural instinct of despotism, which, if not jealously checked, would become outrageous; could not, because it is, in truth, not at all more enlightened, or fit to assume a lead, than the mass of this enlightened community.

No sensible man will lightly go counter to an opinion firmly held by a great body of his countrymen. He will take for granted, that for any opinion which has taken deep root among a people so powerful, so successful, and so well worthy of respect as the people of this country, there certainly either are, or have been, good and sound reasons. He will venture to impugn such an opinion with real hesitation, and only when he thinks he perceives that the reasons which once supported it exist no longer, or at any rate seem about to disappear very soon. For undoubtedly there arrive periods, when, the circumstances and conditions of government having changed, the guiding maxims of government ought to change also. *J'ai dit souvent*, says Mirabeau, admonishing the Court of France of 1790, *qu'on devait changer de manière de gouverner, lorsque le gouvernement n'est plus le même.* And these decisive changes in the political situation of a people happen gradually as well as violently. 'In the silent lapse of events,' says Burke, writing in England twenty years before the French Revolution, 'as material alterations have been insensibly brought about in the policy and character of governments and nations, as those which have been marked by the tumult of public revolutions.'

I propose to submit to those who have been accustomed to regard all State-action with jealousy, some reasons for thinking that the circumstances which once made that jealousy prudent and natural have undergone an essential change. I desire to lead them to consider with me, whether, in the present altered conjuncture, that State-action, which was once dangerous, may not become, not only without danger in itself, but the means of helping us against dangers from another quarter. To combine and present the considerations upon which these two propositions are based, is a task of some difficulty and delicacy. My aim is to invite impartial reflection upon the subject, not to make a hostile attack against old opinions, still less to set on foot and fully equip a new theory. In offering, therefore, the thoughts which have suggested themselves to me, I shall studiously avoid all particular applications of them likely to give offence, and shall use no more illustration and development than may be indispensable to enable the reader to seize and appreciate them.

The dissolution of the old political parties which have governed this country since the Revolution of 1688 has long been remarked. It was repeatedly declared to be happening long before it actually took place, while the vital energy of these parties still subsisted in full vigour, and was threatened only by some temporary obstruction. It has been eagerly deprecated long after it had actually begun to take place, when it was in full progress, and inevitable. These parties, differing in so much else, were yet alike in this, that they were both, in a certain broad sense, *aristocratical* parties. They were combinations of persons considerable, either by great family and estate, or by Court favour, or, lastly, by eminent abilities and popularity; this last body, however, attaining participation in public affairs only through a conjunction with one or other of the former. These connections, though they contained men of very various degrees of birth and property, were still wholly leavened with the feelings and habits of the upper class of the nation. They had the bond of a common culture; and, however their political opinions and acts might differ, what they said and did had the stamp and style imparted by this culture, and by a common and elevated social condition.

Aristocratical bodies have no taste for a very imposing executive, or for a very active and penetrating domestic administration. They have a sense of equality among themselves, and of constituting in themselves what is greatest and most dignified in the realm, which makes their pride revolt against the overshadowing greatness and dignity of a commanding executive. They have a temper of independence, and a habit of uncontrolled action, which makes them impatient of encountering, in the management of the interior concerns of the country, the machinery and regulations of a superior and peremptory power. The different parties among them, as they successively get possession of the government, respect this jealous disposition in their opponents, because they share it themselves. It is a disposition proper to them as great personages, not as ministers; and as they are great personages for their whole life, while they may probably be ministers but for a very short time, the instinct of their social condition avails more with them than the instinct of their official function. To administer as little as possible, to make its weight felt in foreign affairs rather than in domestic, to see in ministerial station rather the means of power and dignity than a means of searching and useful administrative activity, is the natural tendency of an aristocratic executive. It is a tendency which is creditable to the good sense of aristocracies, honourable to their moderation, and at the same time fortunate for their country, of whose internal development they are not fitted to have the full direction.

One strong and beneficial influence, however, the administration of a vigorous and high-minded aristocracy is calculated to exert upon a robust and sound people. I have had occasion, in speaking of Homer, to say very often, and with much emphasis, that he is *in the grand style*.[1] It is the chief virtue of a healthy and uncorrupted aristocracy, that it is, in general, in this grand style. That elevation of character, that noble way of thinking and behaving, which is an eminent gift of nature to some individuals, is also often generated in whole classes of men (at least when these come of a strong and good race) by the possession of power, by the importance and responsibility of high station, by habitual dealing with great things, by being placed above the necessity of constantly struggling for little things. And it is the source of great virtues. It may go along with a not very quick or open intelligence; but it cannot well go along with a conduct vulgar and ignoble. A governing class imbued with it may not be capable of intelligently leading the masses of a people to the highest pitch of welfare for them; but it sets them an invaluable example of qualities without which no really high welfare can exist. This has been done for their nation by the best aristocracies. The Roman aristocracy did it; the English aristocracy has done it. They each fostered in the mass of the peoples they governed, – peoples of sturdy moral constitution and apt to learn such lessons, – a greatness of spirit, the natural growth of the condition of magnates and rulers, but not the natural growth of the condition of the common people. They made, the one of the Roman, the other of the English people, in spite of all the shortcomings of each, great peoples, peoples *in the grand style*. And this they did, while wielding the people according to their own notions, and in the direction which seemed good to them; not as servants and instruments of the people, but as its commanders and heads; solicitous for the good of their country, indeed, but taking for granted that of that good they themselves were the supreme judges, and were to fix the conditions.

The time has arrived, however, when it is becoming impossible for the aristocracy of England to conduct and wield the English nation any longer. It still, indeed, administers public affairs; and it is a great error to suppose, as many persons in England suppose, that it administers but does not govern. He who administers, governs,* because he infixes his own mark and stamps his own character on all public affairs as they pass

---

* *Administrer, c'est gouverner*, says Mirabeau; *gouverner, c'est régner; tout se réduit là.*

through his hands; and, therefore, so long as the English aristocracy administers the commonwealth, it still governs it. But signs not to be mistaken show that its headship and leadership of the nation, by virtue of the substantial acquiescence of the body of the nation in its predominance and right to lead, is nearly over. That acquiescence was the tenure by which it held its power; and it is fast giving way. The superiority of the upper class over all others is no longer so great; the willingness of the others to recognize that superiority is no longer so ready.

This change has been brought about by natural and inevitable causes, and neither the great nor the multitude are to be blamed for it. The growing demands and audaciousness of the latter, the encroaching spirit of democracy, are, indeed, matters of loud complaint with some persons. But these persons are complaining of human nature itself, when they thus complain of a manifestation of its native and ineradicable impulse. Life itself consists, say the philosophers, in the effort *to affirm one's own essence*; meaning by this, to develop one's own existence fully and freely, to have ample light and air, to be neither cramped nor overshadowed. Democracy is trying to *affirm its own essence*; to live, to enjoy, to possess the world, as aristocracy has tried, and successfully tried, before it. Ever since Europe emerged from barbarism, ever since the condition of the common people began a little to improve, ever since their minds began to stir, this effort of democracy has been gaining strength; and the more their condition improves, the more strength this effort gains. So potent is the charm of life and expansion upon the living; the moment men are aware of them, they begin to desire them, and the more they have of them, the more they crave.

This movement of democracy, like other operations of nature, merits properly neither blame nor praise. Its partisans are apt to give it credit which it does not deserve, while its enemies are apt to upbraid it unjustly. Its friends celebrate it as the author of all freedom. But political freedom may very well be established by aristocratic founders; and, certainly, the political freedom of England owes more to the grasping English barons than to democracy. Social freedom, – equality, – that is rather the field of the conquests of democracy. And here what I must call the injustice of its enemies comes in. For its seeking after equality, democracy is often, in this country above all, vehemently and scornfully blamed; its temper contrasted with that worthier temper which can magnanimously endure social distinctions; its operations all referred, as of course, to the stirrings of a base and malignant envy. No doubt there is a gross and vulgar spirit of envy, prompting the hearts of many of those who cry for equality. No doubt there are ignoble natures which prefer equality to liberty. But what we have to ask is, when the life of democracy is admitted as something natural and inevitable, whether this or that product of democracy is a necessary growth from its parent stock, or merely an excrescence upon it. If it be the latter, certainly it may be due to the meanest and most culpable passions. But if it be the former, then this product, however base and blameworthy the passions which it may sometimes be made to serve, can in itself be no more reprehensible than the vital impulse of democracy is in itself reprehensible; and this impulse is, as has been shown, identical with the ceaseless vital effort of human nature itself.

Now, can it be denied, that a certain approach to equality, at any rate a certain reduction of signal inequalities, is a natural, instinctive demand of that impulse which drives society as a whole, – no longer individuals and limited classes only, but the mass of a community, – to develop itself with the utmost possible fulness and freedom? Can it be denied, that to live in a society of equals tends in general to make a man's spirits expand, and his faculties work easily and actively; while, to live in a society of superiors, although it may occasionally be a very good discipline, yet in general tends to tame the spirits and to make the play of the faculties less secure and active? Can it be denied, that to be heavily overshadowed, to be profoundly insignificant, has, on the whole, a depressing and benumbing effect on the character? I know that some individuals react against the strongest impediments, and owe success and greatness to the efforts which they are thus forced to make. But the question is not about individuals. The question is about the common bulk of mankind, persons without extraordinary gifts or exceptional energy, and who will ever require, in order to make the best of themselves, encouragement and directly favouring circumstances. Can any one deny, that for these the spectacle, when they would rise, of a condition of splendour, grandeur, and culture, which they cannot possibly reach, has the effect of making them flag in spirit, and of disposing them to sink despondingly back into their own condition? Can any one deny, that the knowledge how poor and insignificant the best condition of improvement and culture attainable by them must be esteemed by a class incomparably richer-endowed, tends to cheapen this modest possible amelioration in the account of those classes also for whom it would be relatively a real progress, and to disenchant their imaginations with it? It seems to me impossible to deny this. And therefore a philo-sophic observer,* with no love for democracy, but rather with a terror of it, has been constrained to remark, that 'the common people is more uncivilized in aristocratic countries than in any others;' because there 'the lowly and the poor feel themselves, as it were, overwhelmed with the weight of their own inferior-ity.' He has been constrained to remark, that 'there is such a thing as a manly and legitimate passion for equality, prompting men to desire to be, *all* of them, in the enjoyment of power and consideration.' And, in France, that very equality, which is by us so impetuously decried, while it has by no means improved (it is said) the upper classes of French society, has undoubtedly given to the lower classes, to the body of the common people, a self-respect, an enlargement of spirit, a consciousness of counting for something in their country's action, which has raised them in the scale of humanity. The common people, in France, seems to me the soundest part of the French nation. They seem to me more free from the two opposite degradations

---

* M. de Tocqueville. See his *Démocratie en Amérique* (edit. of 1835); vol. i, p. 11. 'Le peuple est plus grossier dans les pays aristocratiques que partout ail-leurs. Dans ces lieux, où se rencontrent des hommes si forts et si riches, les faibles et les pauvres se sentent comme accablés de leur bassesse; ne décou-vrant aucun point par lequel ils puissent regagner l'égalité, ils désespèrent entièrement d'eux-mêmes, et se laissent tomber au-dessous de la dignité humaine.'

of multitudes, brutality and servility, to have a more developed human life, more of what distinguishes elsewhere the cultured classes from the vulgar, than the common people in any other country with which I am acquainted.

I do not say that grandeur and prosperity may not be attained by a nation divided into the most widely distinct classes, and presenting the most signal inequalities of rank and fortune. I do not say that great national virtues may not be developed in it. I do not even say that a popular order, accepting this demarcation of classes as an eternal providential arrangement, not questioning the natural right of a superior order to lead it, content within its own sphere, admiring the grandeur and high-mindedness of its ruling class, and catching on its own spirit some reflex of what it thus admires, may not be a happier body, as to the eye of the imagination it is certainly a more beautiful body, than a popular order, pushing, excited, and presumptuous; a popular order, jealous of recognizing fixed superiorities, petulantly claiming to be as good as its betters, and tastelessly attiring itself with the fashions and designations which have become unalterably associated with a wealthy and refined class, and which, tricking out those who have neither wealth nor refinement, are ridiculous. But a popular order of that old-fashioned stamp exists now only for the imagination. It is not the force with which modern society has to reckon. Such a body may be a sturdy, honest, and sound-hearted lower class; but it is not a democratic people. It is not that power, which at the present day in all nations is to be found existing; in some, has obtained the mastery; in others, is yet in a state of expectation and preparation.

The power of France in Europe is at this day mainly owing to the completeness with which she has organized democratic institutions. The action of the French State is excessive; but it is too little understood in England that the French people has adopted this action for its own purposes, has in great measure attained those purposes by it, and owes to its having done so the chief part of its influence in Europe. The growing power in Europe is democracy; and France has organized democracy with a certain indisputable grandeur and success. The ideas of

1789 were working everywhere in the eighteenth century; but it was because in France the State adopted them that the French Revolution became an historic epoch for the world, and France the lode-star of Continental democracy. Her airs of superiority and overweening pretensions come from her sense of the power which she derives from this cause. Everyone knows how Frenchmen proclaim France to be the head of civilization, the French army to be the soldier of God, Paris to be the brain of Europe, and so on. All this is, no doubt, in a vein of sufficient fatuity and bad taste; but it means, at bottom, that France believes she has so organized herself as to facilitate for all members of her society full and free expansion; that she believes herself to have remodelled her institutions with an eye to reason rather than custom, and to right rather than fact; it means, that she believes the other peoples of Europe to be preparing themselves, more or less rapidly, for a like achievement, and that she is conscious of her power and influence upon them as an initiatress and example. In this belief there is a part of truth and a part of delusion. I think it is more profitable for a Frenchman to consider the part of delusion contained in it; for an Englishman, the part of truth.

It is because aristocracies almost inevitably fail to appreciate justly, or even to take into their mind, the instinct pushing the masses towards expansion and fuller life, that they lose their hold over them. It is the old story of the incapacity of aristocracies for ideas; the secret of their want of success in modern epochs. The people treats them with flagrant injustice, when it denies all obligation to them. They can, and often do, impart a high spirit, a fine ideal of grandeur, to the people; thus they lay the foundations of a great nation. But they leave the people still the multitude, the crowd; they have small belief in the power of the ideas which are its life. Themselves a power reposing on all which is most solid, material, and visible, they are slow to attach any great importance to influences impalpable, spiritual, and viewless. Although, therefore, a disinterested looker-on might often be disposed, seeing what has actually been achieved by aristocracies, to wish to retain or replace them in their preponderance, rather than commit a nation to the hazards of a new and untried future; yet the masses instinctively feel that they can never consent to this without renouncing the inmost impulse of their being; and that they should make such a renunciation cannot seriously be expected of them. Except on conditions which make its expansion, in the sense understood by itself, fully possible, democracy will never frankly ally itself with aristocracy; and on these conditions perhaps no aristocracy will ever frankly ally itself with it. Even the English aristocracy, so politic, so capable of compromises, has shown no signs of being able to transform itself as to render such an alliance possible. The reception given by the Peers to the bill for establishing life-peerages was, in this respect, of ill omen.[2] The separation between aristocracy and democracy will probably, therefore, go on still widening.

And it must in fairness be added, that as in one most important part of general human culture, – openness to ideas and ardour for them, – aristocracy is less advanced than democracy, to replace or keep the latter under the tutelage of the former would in some respects be actually unfavourable to the progress of the world. At epochs when new ideas are powerfully fermenting in a society, and profoundly changing its spirit, aristocracies, as they are in general not long suffered to guide it without question, so are they by nature not well fitted to guide it intelligently.

In England, democracy has been slow in developing itself, having met with much to withstand it, not only in the worth of the aristocracy, but also in the fine qualities of the common people. The aristocracy has been more in sympathy with the common people than perhaps any other aristocracy. It has rarely given them great umbrage; it has neither been frivolous, so as to provoke their contempt, nor impertinent, so as to provoke their irritation. Above all, it has in general meant to act with justice, according to its own notions of justice. Therefore the feeling of admiring deference to such a class was more deep-rooted in the people of this country, more cordial, and more persistent, than in any people of the Continent. But, besides this, the vigour and high spirit of the English common people bred in them a self-reliance which disposed each man to

act individually and independently; and so long as this disposition prevails through a nation divided into classes, the
predominance of an aristocracy, of the class containing the
greatest and strongest individuals of the nation, is secure.
Democracy is a force in which the concert of a great number of
men makes up for the weakness of each man taken by himself;
democracy accepts a certain relative rise in their condition,
obtainable by this concert for a great number, as something
desirable in itself, because though this is undoubtedly far below
grandeur, it is yet a good deal above insignificance. A very
strong, self-reliant people neither easily learns to act in concert,
nor easily brings itself to regard any middling good, any good
short of the best, as an object ardently to be coveted and striven
for. It keeps its eye on the grand prizes, and these are to be won
only by distancing competitors, by getting before one's comrades, by succeeding all by one's self; and so long as a people
works thus individually, it does not work democratically. The
English people has all the qualities which dispose a people to
work individually; may it never lose them! A people without
the salt of these qualities, relying wholly on mutual co-operation,
and proposing to itself second-rate ideals, would arrive at the
pettiness and stationariness of China. But the English people is
no longer so entirely ruled by them as not to show visible beginnings of democratic action; it becomes more and more sensible
to the irresistible seduction of democratic ideas, promising to
each individual of the multitude increased self-respect and
expansion with the increased importance and authority of the
multitude to which he belongs, with the diminished preponderance of the aristocratic class above him.

While the habit and disposition of deference are thus dying
out among the lower classes of the English nation, it seems to
me indisputable that the advantages which command deference,
that eminent superiority in high feeling, dignity, and culture,
tend to diminish among the highest class. I shall not be sus-
pected of any inclination to underrate the aristocracy of this
country. I regard it as the worthiest, as it certainly has been the
most successful, aristocracy of which history makes record. If
it has not been able to develop excellences which do not belong

to the nature of an aristocracy, yet it has been able to avoid defects to which the nature of an aristocracy is peculiarly prone. But I cannot read the history of the flowering time of the English aristocracy, the eighteenth century, and then look at this aristocracy in our own century, without feeling that there has been a change. I am not now thinking of private and domestic virtues, of morality, of decorum. Perhaps with respect to these there has in this class, as in society at large, been a change for the better. I am thinking of those public and conspicuous virtues by which the multitude is captivated and led, – lofty spirit, commanding character, exquisite culture. It is true that the advance of all classes in culture and refinement may make the culture of one class, which, isolated, appeared remarkable, appear so no longer; but exquisite culture and great dignity are always something rare and striking, and it is the distinction of the English aristocracy, in the eighteenth century, that not only was their culture something rare by comparison with the rawness of the masses, it was something rare and admirable in itself. It is rather that this rare culture of the highest class has actually somewhat declined,* than that it has come to look less by juxtaposition with the augmented culture of other classes.

Probably democracy has something to answer for in this falling off of her rival. To feel itself raised on high, venerated, followed, no doubt stimulates a fine nature to keep itself worthy to be followed, venerated, raised on high; hence that lofty maxim, *noblesse oblige*. To feel its culture something precious and singular, makes such a nature zealous to retain and extend it. The elation and energy thus fostered by the sense of its advantages, certainly enhances the worth, strengthens the behaviour, and quickens all the active powers of the class enjoying it. *Possunt quia posse videntur.*[3] The removal of the stimulus

---

* This will appear doubtful to no one well acquainted with the literature and memoirs of the last century. To give but two illustrations out of a thousand. Let the reader refer to the anecdote told by Robert Wood in his *Essay on the Genius of Homer* (London, 1775), p. vii, and to Lord Chesterfield's *Letters* (edit. of 1845), vol. i, pp. 115, 143, vol. ii, p. 54; and then say, whether the culture there indicated as the culture of a *class* has maintained itself at that level.

a little relaxes their energy. It is not so much that they sink to be somewhat less than themselves, as that they cease to be somewhat more than themselves. But, however this may be, whencesoever the change may proceed, I cannot doubt that in the aristocratic virtue, in the intrinsic commanding force of the English upper class, there is a diminution. Relics of a great generation are still, perhaps, to be seen among them, surviving exemplars of noble manners and consummate culture; but they disappear one after the other, and no one of their kind takes their place. At the very moment when democracy becomes less and less disposed to follow and to admire, aristocracy becomes less and less qualified to command and to captivate.

On the one hand, then, the masses of the people in this country are preparing to take a much more active part than formerly in controlling its destinies; on the other hand, the aristocracy (using this word in the widest sense, to include not only the nobility and landed gentry, but also those reinforcements from the classes bordering upon itself, which this class constantly attracts and assimilates), while it is threatened with losing its hold on the rudder of government, its power to give to public affairs its own bias and direction, is losing also that influence on the spirit and character of the people which it long exercised.

I know that this will be warmly denied by some persons. Those who have grown up amidst a certain state of things, those whose habits, and interests, and affections, are closely concerned with its continuance, are slow to believe that it is not a part of the order of nature, or that it can ever come to an end. But I think that what I have here laid down will not appear doubtful either to the most competent and friendly foreign observers of this country, or to those Englishmen who, clear of all influences of class or party, have applied themselves steadily to see the tendencies of their nation as they really are. Assuming it to be true, a great number of considerations are suggested by it; but it is my purpose here to insist upon one only.

That one consideration is: On what action may we rely to replace, for some time at any rate, that action of the aristocracy upon the people of this country, which we have seen exercise an influence in many respects elevating and beneficial, but which is rapidly, and from inevitable causes, ceasing? In other words, and to use a short and significant modern expression which everyone understands, what influence may help us to prevent the English people from becoming, with the growth of democracy, *Americanized*?[4] I confess I am disposed to answer: On the action of the State.

I know what a chorus of objectors will be ready. One will say: Rather repair and restore the influence of aristocracy. Another will say: It is not a bad thing, but a good thing, that the English people should be Americanized. But the most formidable and the most widely entertained objection, by far, will be that which founds itself upon the present actual state of things in another country; which says: Look at France! there you have a signal example of the alliance of democracy with a powerful State-action, and see how it works.

This last and principal objection I will notice at once. I have had occasion to touch upon the first already, and upon the second I shall touch presently. It seems to me, then, that one may save one's self from much idle terror at names and shadows if one will be at the pains to remember what different conditions the different character of two nations must necessarily impose on the operation of any principle. That which operates noxiously in one, may operate wholesomely in the other; because the unsound part of the one's character may be yet further inflamed and enlarged by it, the unsound part of the other's may find in it a corrective and an abatement. This is the great use which two unlike characters may find in observing each other. Neither is likely to have the other's faults, so each may safely adopt as much as suits him of the other's qualities. If I were a Frenchman I should never be weary of admiring the independent, individual, local habits of action in England, of directing attention to the evils occasioned in France by the excessive action of the State; for I should be very sure that, say what I might, the part of the State would never be too small in France, nor that of the individual too large. Being an Englishman, I see nothing but good in freely recognizing the coherence, rationality, and efficaciousness which characterize the strong State-action of France, of acknowledging the want of method, reason, and result which attend the feeble State-action of England; because I am very sure that, strengthen in England the action of the State as one may, it will always find itself sufficiently controlled. But when either the *Constitutionnel*[5] sneers at the do-little talkativeness of parliamentary government, or when the *Morning Star*[6] inveighs against the despotism of a centralized administration, it seems to me that they lose their labour, because they are hardening themselves against dangers to which they are neither of them liable. Both the one and the other, in plain truth,

> Compound for sins they are inclined to,
> By damning those they have no mind to.[7]

They should rather exchange doctrines one with the other, and each might thus, perhaps, be profited.

So that the exaggeration of the action of the State, in France, furnishes no reason for absolutely refusing to enlarge the action of the State in England; because the genius and temper of the people of this country are such as to render impossible that exaggeration which the genius and temper of the French rendered easy. There is no danger at all that the native independence and individualism of the English character will ever belie itself, and become either weakly prone to lean on others, or blindly confiding in them.

English democracy runs no risk of being over-mastered by the State; it is almost certain that it will throw off the tutelage of aristocracy. Its real danger is, that it will have far too much its own way, and be left far too much to itself. 'What harm will there be in that?' say some; 'are we not a self-governing people?' I answer: 'We have never yet been a *self-governing democracy,* or anything like it.' The difficulty for democracy is, how to find and keep high ideals. The individuals who compose it are, the bulk of them, persons who need to follow an ideal, not to set one; and one ideal of greatness, high feeling, and fine culture, which an aristocracy once supplied to them, they lose by the very fact of ceasing to be a lower order and becoming a democracy. Nations are not truly great solely because the individuals composing them are numerous, free, and active; but they are great when these numbers, this freedom, and this activity are employed in the service of an ideal higher than that of an ordinary man, taken by himself. Our society is probably destined to become much more democratic; who or what will give a high tone to the nation then? That is the grave question.

The greatest men of America, her Washingtons, Hamiltons, Madisons, well understanding that aristocratical institutions are not in all times and places possible; well perceiving that in their Republic there was no place for these; comprehending, therefore, that from these that security for national dignity and greatness, an ideal commanding popular reverence, was not to be obtained, but knowing that this ideal was indispensable, would have been rejoiced to found a substitute for it in the dignity and authority of the State. They deplored the weakness and insignificance of the executive power as a calamity. When the inevitable course of events has made our self-government something really like that of America, when it has removed or weakened that security for national dignity, which we possessed in *aristocracy*, will the substitute of the *State* be equally wanting to us? If it is, then the dangers of America will really be ours; the dangers which come from the multitude being in power, with no adequate ideal to elevate or guide the multitude.

It would really be wasting time to contend at length, that to give more prominence to the idea of the State is now possible in this country, without endangering liberty. In other countries the habits and dispositions of the people may be such that the State, if once it acts, may be easily suffered to usurp exorbitantly; here they certainly are not. Here the people will always sufficiently keep in mind that any public authority is a trust delegated by themselves, for certain purposes, and with certain limits; and if that authority pretends to an absolute, independent character, they will soon enough (and very rightly) remind it of its error. Here there can be no question of a paternal government, of an irresponsible executive power, professing to act for the people's good, but without the people's consent, and, if necessary, against the people's wishes; here no one dreams of removing a single constitutional control, of abolishing a single safe-guard for securing a correspondence between the acts of government and the will of the nation. The question is, whether, retaining all its power of control over a government which should abuse its trust, the nation may not now find advantage in voluntarily allowing to it purposes somewhat ampler, and limits somewhat wider within which to execute them, than formerly; whether the nation may not thus acquire in the State an ideal of high reason and right feeling, representing its best self, commanding general respect, and forming a rallying-point for the intelligence and for the worthiest instincts of the community, which will herein find a true bond of union.

I am convinced that if the worst mischiefs of democracy ever happen in England, it will be, not because a new condition of things has come upon us unforeseen, but because, though we all foresaw it, our efforts to deal with it went in the wrong direction. At the present time, almost everyone believes in the growth of democracy, almost everyone talks of it, almost everyone laments it; but the last thing people can be brought to do is to make timely preparation for it. Many of those who, if they would, could do most to forward this work of preparation, are made slack and hesitating by the belief that, after all, in England, things may probably never go very far; that it will be possible to keep much more of the past than speculators say. Others, with a more robust faith, think that all democracy wants is vigorous putting-down; and that, with a good will and strong hand, it is perfectly possible to retain or restore the whole system of the Middle Ages.[8] Others, free from the prejudices of class and position which warp the judgment of these, and who would, I believe, be the first and greatest gainers by strengthening the hands of the State, are averse from doing so by reason of suspicions and fears, once perfectly well-grounded, but, in this age and in the present circumstances, well-grounded no longer.

I speak of the middle classes. I have already shown how it is the natural disposition of an aristocratical class to view with jealousy the development of a considerable State-power. But this disposition has in England found extraordinary favour and support in regions not aristocratical, – from the middle classes;

and, above all, from the kernel of these classes, the Protestant Dissenters. And for a very good reason. In times when passions ran high, even an aristocratical executive was easily stimulated into using, for the gratification of its friends and the abasement of its enemies, those administrative engines which, the moment it chose to stretch its hand forth, stood ready for its grasp. Matters of domestic concern, matters of religious profession and religious exercise, offered a peculiar field for an intervention gainful and agreeable to friends, injurious and irritating to enemies. Such an intervention was attempted and practised. Government lent its machinery and authority to the aristocratical and ecclesiastical party, which it regarded as its best support. The party which suffered comprised the flower and strength of that middle class of society, always very flourishing and robust in this country. That powerful class, from this specimen of the administrative activity of government, conceived a strong antipathy against all intervention of the State in certain spheres. An active, stringent administration in those spheres, meant at that time a High Church and Prelatic administration in them, an administration galling to the Puritan party and to the middle class; and this aggrieved class had naturally no proneness to draw nice philosophical distinctions between State-action in these spheres, as a thing for abstract consideration, and State-action in them as they practically felt it and supposed themselves likely long to feel it, guided by their adversaries. In the minds of the English middle class, therefore, State-action in social and domestic concerns became inextricably associated with the idea of a Conventicle Act, a Five-Mile Act, an Act of Uniformity.[9] Their abhorrence of such a State-action as this they extended to State-action in general; and, having never known a beneficent and just State-power, they enlarged their hatred of a cruel and partial State-power, the only one they had ever known, into a maxim that no State-power was to be trusted, that the least action, in certain provinces, was rigorously to be denied to the State, whenever this denial was possible.

Thus that jealousy of an important, sedulous, energetic executive, natural to grandees unwilling to suffer their personal authority to be circumscribed, their individual grandeur to be eclipsed, by the authority and grandeur of the State, became reinforced in this country by a like sentiment among the middle classes, who had no such authority or grandeur to lose, but who, by a hasty reasoning, had theoretically condemned for ever an agency which they had practically found at times oppressive. *Leave us to ourselves!* magnates and middle classes alike cried to the State. Not only from those who were full and abounded went up this prayer, but also from those whose condition admitted of great amelioration. Not only did the whole repudiate the physician, but also those who were sick.[10]

For it is evident, that the action of a diligent, an impartial, and a national government, while it can do little to better the condition, already fortunate enough, of the highest and richest class of its people, can really do much, by institution and regulation, to better that of the middle and lower classes. The State can bestow certain broad collective benefits, which are, indeed, not much if compared with the advantages already possessed by individual grandeur, but which are rich and valuable if compared with the make-shifts of mediocrity and poverty. A good thing meant for the many cannot well be so exquisite as the good things of the few; but it can easily, if it comes from a donor of great resources and wide power, be incomparably better than what the many could, unaided, provide for themselves.

In all the remarks which I have been making, I have hitherto abstained from any attempt to suggest a positive application of them. I have limited myself to simply pointing out in how changed a world of ideas we are living; I have not sought to go further, and to discuss in what particular manner the world of facts is to adapt itself to this changed world of ideas. This has been my rule so far; but from this rule I shall here venture to depart, in order to dwell for a moment on a matter of practical institution, designed to meet new social exigencies: on the intervention of the State in public education.

The public secondary schools of France, decreed by the Revolution and established under the Consulate, are said by many good judges to be inferior to the old colleges. By means of the old colleges and of private tutors, the French aristocracy could procure for its children (so it is said, and very likely with truth) a better training than that which is now given in the lyceums. Yes; but the boon conferred by the State, when it founded the lyceums, was not for the aristocracy; it was for the vast middle class of Frenchmen. This class, certainly, had not already the means of a better training for its children, before the State interfered. This class, certainly, would not have succeeded in procuring by its own efforts a better training for its children if the State had not interfered. Through the intervention of the State this class enjoys better schools for its children, not than the great and rich enjoy (that is not the question), but than the same class enjoys in any country where the State had not interfered to found them. The lyceums may not be so good as Eton or Harrow; but they are a great deal better than a *Classical and Commercial Academy.*[11]

The aristocratic classes in England may, perhaps, be well content to rest satisfied with their Eton and Harrow. The State is not likely to do better for them. Nay, the superior confidence, spirit, and style, engendered by a training in the great public schools, constitute for these classes a real privilege, a real engine of command, which they might, if they were selfish, be sorry to lose by the establishment of schools great enough to beget a like spirit in the classes below them. But the middle classes in England have every reason not to rest content with their private schools; the State can do a great deal better for them. By giving to schools for these classes a public character, it can bring the instruction in them under a criticism which the stock of knowledge and judgment in our middle classes is not of itself at present able to supply. By giving to them a national character, it can confer on them a greatness and a noble spirit, which the tone of these classes is not of itself at present adequate to impart. Such schools would soon prove notable competitors with the existing public schools; they would do these a great service by stimulating them, and making them look into their own weak points more closely. Economical, because with charges uniform and under severe revision, they would do a great service to that large body of persons who, at present, seeing that on the whole the best secondary instruction to be found is that of the existing public schools, obtain it for their children from a sense of duty, although they can ill afford it, and although its cost is certainly exorbitant. Thus the middle classes might, by the aid of the State, better their instruction, while still keeping its cost moderate. This in itself would be a gain; but this gain would be slight in comparison with that of acquiring the sense of belonging to great and honourable seats of learning, and of breathing in their youth the air of the best culture of their nation. This sense would be an educational influence for them of the highest value. It would really augment their self-respect and moral force; it would truly fuse them with the class above, and tend to bring about for them the equality which they are entitled to desire.

So it is not State-action in itself which the middle and lower classes of a nation ought to deprecate; it is State-action exercised by a hostile class, and for their oppression. From a State-action reasonably, equitably, and nationally exercised, they may derive great benefit; greater, by the very nature and necessity of things, than can be derived from this source by the class above them. For the middle or lower classes to obstruct such a State-action, to repel its benefits, is to play the game of their enemies, and to prolong for themselves a condition of real inferiority.

This, I know, is rather dangerous ground to tread upon. The great middle classes of this country are conscious of no weakness, no inferiority; they do not want any one to provide anything for them. Such as they are, they believe that the freedom and prosperity of England are their work, and that the future belongs to them. No one esteems them more than I do; but those who esteem them most, and who most believe in their capabilities, can render them no better service than by pointing out in what they underrate their deficiencies, and how their deficiencies, if unreminded, may impair their future. They want culture and dignity; they want ideas. Aristocracy has culture and dignity; democracy has readiness for new ideas, and ardour for what ideas it possesses. Of these, our middle class has the last only: ardour for the ideas it already possesses. It believes ardently in liberty, it believes ardently in industry; and, by its zealous belief in these two ideas, it has accomplished great things. What it has accomplished by its belief in industry is patent to all the world. The liberties of England are less its exclusive work than it supposes; for these, aristocracy has achieved nearly as much. Still, of one inestimable part of liberty, liberty of thought, the middle class has been (without precisely intending it) the principal champion. The intellectual action of the Church of England upon the nation has been insignificant; its social action has been great. The social action of Protestant Dissent, that genuine product of the English middle class, has not been civilizing; its positive intellectual action has been insignificant; its negative intellectual action, – in so far as by strenuously maintaining for itself, against persecution, liberty of conscience and the right of free opinion, it at the same time maintained and established this right as a universal principle, – has been invaluable. But the actual results of this negative intellectual service rendered by Protestant Dissent, – by the middle class, – to the whole community, great as they undoubtedly are, must not be taken for something which they are not. It is a very great thing to be able to think as you like; but, after all, an important question remains: *what* you think. It is a fine thing to secure a free stage and no favour; but, after all, the part which you play on that stage will have to be criticized. Now, all the liberty and industry in the world will not ensure these two things: a high reason and a fine culture. They may favour them, but they will not of themselves produce them; they may exist without them. But it is by the appearance of these two things, in some shape or other, in the life of a nation, that it becomes something more than an independent, an energetic, a successful nation, – that it becomes a great nation.

In modern epochs the part of a high reason, of ideas, acquires constantly increasing importance in the conduct of the world's affairs. A fine culture is the complement of a high reason, and it is in the conjunction of both with character, with energy, that the ideal for men and nations is to be placed. It is common to hear remarks on the frequent divorce between culture and character, and to infer from this that culture is a mere varnish, and that character only deserves any serious attention. No error can be more fatal. Culture without character is, no doubt, something frivolous, vain, and weak; but character without culture is, on the other hand, something raw, blind, and dangerous. The most interesting, the most truly glorious peoples, are those in which the alliance of the two has been effected most successfully, and its result spread most widely. This is why the spectacle of ancient Athens has such profound interest for a rational man; that it is the spectacle of the culture of a *people*. It is not an aristocracy, leavening with its own high spirit the multitude which it wields, but leaving it the unformed multitude still; it is not a democracy, acute and energetic, but tasteless, narrow-minded, and ignoble; it is the middle and lower classes in the highest development of their humanity that these classes have yet reached. It was the *many* who relished those arts, who were not satisfied with less than those monuments. In the conversations recorded by Plato, or even by the matter-of-fact Xenophon, which for the free yet refined discussion of ideas have set the tone for the whole cultivated world, shopkeepers and tradesmen of Athens mingle as speakers. For any one but a pedant, this is why a handful of Athenians of two thousand years ago are more interesting than the millions of most nations our contemporaries. Surely, if they knew this, those friends of progress, who have confidently pronounced the remains of the ancient world to be so much lumber, and a classical education an aristocratic impertinence, might be inclined to reconsider their sentence.

The course taken in the next fifty years by the middle classes of this nation will probably give a decisive turn to its history. If they will not seek the alliance of the State for their own elevation, if they go on exaggerating their spirit of individualism, if they persist in their jealousy of all governmental action, if they cannot learn that the antipathies and the Shibboleths of a past age are now an anachronism for them, – that will not prevent them, probably, from getting the rule of their country for a season, but they will certainly *Americanize* it. They will rule it by their energy, but they will deteriorate it by their low ideals and want of culture. In the decline of the aristocratical element, which in some sort supplied an ideal to ennoble the spirit of the nation and to keep it together, there will be no other element present to perform this service. It is of itself a serious calamity for a nation that its tone of feeling and grandeur of spirit should be lowered or dulled. But the calamity appears far more serious still, when we consider that the middle classes, remaining as they are now, with their narrow, harsh, unintelligent, and unattractive spirit and culture, will almost certainly fail to mould or assimilate the masses below them, whose sympathies are at the present moment actually wider and more liberal than theirs. They arrive, these masses, eager to enter into possession of the world, to gain a more vivid sense of their own life and activity. In this their irrepressible development, their natural educators and initiators are those immediately above them, the middle classes. If these classes cannot win their sympathy or give them their direction, society is in danger of falling into anarchy.

Therefore, with all the force I can, I wish to urge upon the middle classes of this country, both that they might be very greatly profited by the action of the State, and also that they are continuing their opposition to such action out of an unfounded fear. But at the same time I say that the middle classes have the right, in admitting the action of government, to make the condition that this government shall be one of their own adoption, one that they can trust. To ensure this is now in their own power. If they do not as yet ensure this, they ought to do so, they have the means of doing so. Two centuries ago they had not; now they have. Having this security, let them now show themselves jealous to keep the action of the State equitable and rational, rather than to exclude the action of the State altogether. If the State acts amiss, let them check it; but let them no longer take for granted that the State cannot possibly act usefully.

The State, – but what is the State? cry many. Speculations on the idea of a State abound, but these do not satisfy them; of that which is to have practical effect and power they require a plain account. The full force of the term, *the State,* as the full force of any other important term, no one will master without going a little deeply, without resolutely entering the world of ideas; but it is possible to give in very plain language an account of it sufficient for all practical purposes. The State is properly just what Burke called it: *the nation in its collective and corporate character.*[12] The State is the representative acting-power of the nation; the action of the State is the representative action of the nation. Nominally emanating from the Crown, as the ideal unity in which the nation concentrates itself, this action, by the constitution of our country, really emanates from the Ministers of the Crown. It is common to hear the deprecators of State-action run through a string of Ministers' names, and then say: 'Here is really your *State*; would you accept the action of these men as your own representative action? in what respect is their judgment on national affairs likely to be any better than that of the rest of the world?' In the first place I answer: Even supposing them to be originally no better or wiser than the rest of the world, they have two great advantages from their position: access to almost boundless means of information, and the enlargement of mind which the habit of dealing with great affairs tends to produce. Their position itself, therefore, if they are men of only average honesty and capacity, tends to give them a fitness for acting on behalf of the nation superior to that of other men of equal honesty and capacity who are not in the same position. This fitness may be yet further increased by treating them as persons on whom, indeed, a very grave responsibility has fallen, and from whom very much will be expected; – nothing less than the representing, each of them in his own department, under the control of Parliament, and aided by the suggestions of public opinion, the collective energy and intelligence of his nation. By treating them as men on whom all this devolves to do, to their honour if they do it well, to their shame if they do it ill, one probably augments their faculty of well-doing; as it is excellently said: 'To treat men as if they were better than they are, is the surest way to *make* them better than they are.' But to treat them as if they had been shuffled into their places by a lucky accident, were most likely soon to be shuffled out of them again, and meanwhile ought to magnify themselves and their office as little as possible; to treat them as if they and their functions could without much inconvenience be quite dispensed with, and they ought perpetually to be admiring their own inconceivable good fortune in being permitted to discharge them; – this is the way to paralyse all high effort in the executive government, to extinguish all lofty sense of responsibility; to make its members either merely solicitous for the gross advantages, the emolument and self-importance, which they derive from their offices, or else timid, apologetic, and self-mistrustful in filling them; in either case, formal and inefficient.

But in the second place I answer: If the executive government is really in the hands of men no wiser than the bulk of mankind, of men whose action an intelligent man would be unwilling to accept as representative of his own action, whose fault is that? It is the fault of the nation itself, which, not being in the hands of a despot or an oligarchy, being free to control the choice of those who are to sum up and concentrate its action, controls it in such a manner that it allows to be chosen agents so little in its confidence, or so mediocre, or so incompetent, that it thinks the best thing to be done with them is to reduce their action as near as possible to a nullity. Hesitating, blundering, unintelligent, inefficacious, the action of the State may be; but, such as it is, it is the collective action of the nation itself, and the nation is responsible for it. It is our own action which we suffer to be thus unsatisfactory. Nothing can free us from this responsibility. The conduct of our affairs is in our own power. To carry on into its executive proceedings the indecision, conflict, and discordance of its parliamentary debates, may be a natural defect of a free nation, but it is certainly a defect; it is a dangerous error to call it, as some do, a perfection. The want of concert, reason, and organization in the State, is the want of concert, reason, and organization in the collective nation.

Inasmuch, therefore, as collective action is more efficacious than isolated individual efforts, a nation having great and complicated matters to deal with must greatly gain by employing the action of the State. Only, the State-power which it employs should be a power which really represents its best self, and whose action its intelligence and justice can heartily avow and adopt; not a power which reflects its inferior self, and of whose action, as of its own second-rate action, it has perpetually to be ashamed. To offer a worthy initiative, and to set a standard of rational and equitable action, – this is what the nation should expect of the State; and the more the State fulfils this expectation, the more will it be accepted in practice for what in idea it must always be. People will not then ask the State, what title it has to commend or reward genius and merit, since commendation and reward imply an attitude of superiority, for it will then be felt that the State truly acts for the English nation; and the genius of the English nation is greater than the genius of any individual, greater even than Shakespeare's genius, for it includes the genius of Newton also.

I will not deny that to give a more prominent part to the State would be a considerable change in this country; that maxims once very sound, and habits once very salutary, may be appealed to against it. The sole question is, whether those maxims and habits are sound and salutary at this moment. A yet graver and more difficult change, – to reduce the all-effacing prominence of the State, to give a more prominent part to the individual, – is imperiously presenting itself to other countries. Both are the suggestions of one irresistible force, which is gradually making its way everywhere, removing old conditions and imposing new, altering long-fixed habits, undermining venerable institutions, even modifying national character: *the modern spirit.*

Undoubtedly we are drawing on towards great changes; and for every nation the thing most needful is to discern clearly its own condition, in order to know in what particular way it may best meet them. Openness and flexibility of mind are at such a time the first of virtues. *Be ye perfect,* said the Founder of Christianity; *I count not myself to have apprehended,*[13] said its greatest Apostle. Perfection will never be reached; but to recognize a period of transformation when it comes, and to adapt themselves honestly and rationally to its laws, is perhaps the nearest approach to perfection of which men and nations are capable. No habits or attachments should prevent their trying to do this; nor indeed, in the long run, can they. Human thought, which made all institutions, inevitably saps them, resting only in that which is absolute and eternal.

ESSAYS IN CRITICISM

Preface

Several of the Essays which are here collected and reprinted had the good or the bad fortune to be much criticized at the time of their first appearance. I am not now going to inflict upon the reader a reply to those criticisms; for one or two explanations which are desirable, I shall elsewhere, perhaps, be able some day to find an opportunity; but, indeed, it is not in my nature – some of my critics would rather say, not in my power – to dispute on behalf of any opinion, even my own, very obstinately. To try and approach truth on one side after another, not to strive or cry, nor to persist in pressing forward, on any one side, with violence and self-will – it is only thus, it seems to me, that mortals may hope to gain any vision of the mysterious Goddess, whom we shall never see except in outline, but only thus even in outline. He who will do nothing but fight impetuously towards her on his own, one, favourite, particular line, is inevitably destined to run his head into the folds of the black robe in which she is wrapped.

So it is not to reply to my critics that I write this preface, but to prevent a misunderstanding, of which certain phrases that some of them use make me apprehensive. Mr Wright, one of the many translators of Homer, has published a Letter to the Dean of Canterbury, complaining of some remarks of mine, uttered now a long while ago, on his version of the Iliad.[1] One cannot be always studying one's own works, and I was really under the impression, till I saw Mr Wright's complaint, that I had spoken of him with all respect. The reader may judge of my astonishment, therefore, at finding, from Mr Wright's pamphlet, that I had 'declared with much solemnity that there is not any proper reason for his existing'. That I never said; but, on looking back at my Lectures on translating Homer, I find that I did say, not that Mr Wright, but that Mr Wright's version of the Iliad, repeating in the main the merits and defects of Cowper's version, as Mr Sotheby's repeated those of Pope's version, had, if I might be pardoned for saying so, no proper reason for existing. Elsewhere I expressly spoke of the merit of his version; but I confess that the phrase, qualified as I have shown, about its want of a proper reason for existing, I used. Well, the phrase had, perhaps, too much vivacity; we have all of us a right to exist, we and our works; an unpopular author should be the last person to call in question this right. So I gladly withdraw the offending phrase, and I am sorry for having used it; Mr Wright, however, would perhaps be more indulgent to my vivacity, if he considered that we are none of us likely to be lively much longer. My vivacity is but the last sparkle of flame before we are all in the dark, the last glimpse of colour before we all go into drab, – the drab of the earnest, prosaic, practical, austerely literal future. Yes, the world will soon be the Philistines'! and then, with every voice, not of thunder, silenced, and the whole earth filled and ennobled every morning by the magnificent roaring of the young lions of the *Daily Telegraph,* we shall all yawn in one another's faces with the dismallest, the most unimpeachable gravity.

But I return to my design in writing this Preface. That design was, after apologizing to Mr Wright for my vivacity of five years ago, to beg him and others to let me bear my own burdens, without saddling the great and famous University to which I have the honour to belong with any portion of them. What I mean to deprecate is such phrases as, 'his professorial assault,' 'his assertions issued *ex cathedrâ,*' 'the sanction of his name as the representative of poetry,' and so on. Proud as I am of my connection with the University of Oxford, I can truly say, that knowing how unpopular a task one is undertaking when one tries to pull out a few more stops in that powerful but at present somewhat narrow-toned organ, the modern Englishman,

I have always sought to stand by myself, and to compromise others as little as possible. Besides this, my native modesty is such, that I have always been shy of assuming the honourable style of Professor, because this is a title I share with so many distinguished men, – Professor Pepper, Professor Anderson, Professor Frickel,[2] and others, – who adorn it, I feel, much more than I do.

However, it is not merely out of modesty that I prefer to stand alone, and to concentrate on myself, as a plain citizen of the republic of letters, and not as an office-bearer in a hierarchy, the whole responsibility for all I write; it is much more out of genuine devotion to the University of Oxford, for which I feel, and always must feel, the fondest, the most reverential attachment. In an epoch of dissolution and transformation, such as that on which we are now entered, habits, ties, and associations are inevitably broken up, the action of individuals becomes more distinct, the shortcomings, errors, heats, disputes, which necessarily attend individual action, are brought into greater prominence. Who would not gladly keep clear, from all these passing clouds, an august institution which was there before they arose, and which will be there when they have blown over?

It is true, the *Saturday Review* maintains that our epoch of transformation is finished; that we have found our philosophy; that the British nation has searched all anchorages for the spirit, and has finally anchored itself, in the fulness of perfected knowledge, on Benthamism.[3] This idea at first made a great impression on me; not only because it is so consoling in itself, but also because it explained a phenomenon which in the summer of last year had, I confess, a good deal troubled me. At that time my avocations led me to travel almost daily on one of the Great Eastern Lines, – the Woodford Branch. Everyone knows that the murderer, Müller, perpetrated his detestable act on the North London Railway, close by.[4] The English middle class, of which I am myself a feeble unit, travel on the Woodford Branch in large numbers. Well, the demoralization of our class, – the class which (the newspapers are constantly saying it, so I may repeat it without vanity) has done all the great things which have ever been done in England, – the demoralization, I say, of

our class, caused by the Bow tragedy, was something bewildering. Myself a transcendentalist (as the *Saturday Review* knows),
I escaped the infection; and, day after day, I used to ply my
agitated fellow-travellers with all the consolations which my
transcendentalism would naturally suggest to me. I reminded
them how Caesar refused to take precautions against assassina-
tion, because life was not worth having at the price of an
ignoble solicitude for it. I reminded them what insignificant
atoms we all are in the life of the world. 'Suppose the worst to
happen,' I said, addressing a portly jeweller from Cheapside;
'suppose even yourself to be the victim; *il n'y a pas d'homme
nécessaire*. We should miss you for a day or two upon the
Woodford Branch; but the great mundane movement would
still go on, the gravel walks of your villa would still be rolled,
dividends would still be paid at the Bank, omnibuses would
still run, there would still be the old crush at the corner of Fen-
church Street.' All was of no avail. Nothing could moderate, in
the bosom of the great English middle class, their passionate,
absorbing, almost blood-thirsty clinging to life. At the moment
I thought this over-concern a little unworthy; but the *Saturday
Review* suggests a touching explanation of it. What I took for
the ignoble clinging to life of a comfortable worldling, was,
perhaps, only the ardent longing of a faithful Benthamite, tra-
versing an age still dimmed by the last mists of transcendentalism,
to be spared long enough to see his religion in the full and final
blaze of its triumph. This respectable man, whom I imagined to
be going up to London to serve his shop, or to buy shares, or
to attend an Exeter Hall meeting,[5] or to assist at the delibera-
tions of the Marylebone Vestry,[6] was even, perhaps, in real
truth, on a pious pilgrimage, to obtain from Mr Bentham's
executors a sacred bone of his great, dissected master.[7]

And yet, after all, I cannot but think that the *Saturday
Review* has here, for once, fallen a victim to an idea, – a beautiful but deluding idea, – and that the British nation has not yet,
so entirely as the reviewer seems to imagine, found the last
word of its philosophy. No, we are all seekers still! Seekers
often make mistakes, and I wish mine to redound to my own
discredit only, and not to touch Oxford. Beautiful city! so

venerable, so lovely, so unravaged by the fierce intellectual life of our century, so serene!

'There are our young barbarians, all at play!'[8]

And yet, steeped in sentiment as she lies, spreading her gardens to the moonlight, and whispering from her towers the last enchantments of the Middle Age, who will deny that Oxford, by her ineffable charm, keeps ever calling us nearer to the true goal of all of us, to the ideal, to perfection, – to beauty, in a word, which is only truth seen from another side? – nearer, perhaps, than all the science of Tübingen.[9] Adorable dreamer, whose heart has been so romantic! who hast given thyself so prodigally, given thyself to sides and to heroes not mine, only never to the Philistines! home of lost causes, and forsaken beliefs, and unpopular names, and impossible loyalties! what example could ever so inspire us to keep down the Philistine in ourselves, what teacher could ever so save us from that bondage to which we are all prone, that bondage which Goethe, in his incomparable lines on the death of Schiller, makes it his friend's highest praise (and nobly did Schiller deserve the praise) to have left miles out of sight behind him; – the bondage of *'was uns alle bändigt, DAS GEMEINE!'*[10] She will forgive me, even if I have unwittingly drawn upon her a shot or two aimed at her unworthy son; for she is generous, and the cause in which I fight is, after all, hers. Apparitions of a day, what is our puny warfare against the Philistines, compared with the warfare which this queen of romance has been waging against them for centuries, and will wage after we are gone?

The Function of Criticism
at the Present Time

Many objections have been made to a proposition which, in some remarks of mine on translating Homer, I ventured to put forth; a proposition about criticism, and its importance at the present day. I said: 'Of the literature of France and Germany, as of the intellect of Europe in general, the main effort, for now many years, has been a critical effort; the endeavour, in all branches of knowledge, theology, philosophy, history, art, science, to see the object as in itself it really is.' I added, that owing to the operation in English literature of certain causes, 'almost the last thing for which one would come to English literature is just that very thing which now Europe most desires, – criticism', and that the power and value of English literature was thereby impaired. More than one rejoinder declared that the importance I here assigned to criticism was excessive, and asserted the inherent superiority of the creative effort of the human spirit over its critical effort. And the other day, having been led by a Mr Shairp's excellent notice of Wordsworth* to turn again to his biography, I found, in the words of this great man, whom I, for one, must always listen to with the profoundest respect, a sentence passed on the critic's business, which seems to justify every possible disparagement of it. Wordsworth says in one of his letters: –

'The writers in these publications' (the Reviews), 'while they prosecute their inglorious employment, can not be supposed to be in a state of mind very favourable for being affected by the finer influences of a thing so pure as genuine poetry.'

And a trustworthy reporter of his conversation quotes a more elaborate judgment to the same effect: –

'Wordsworth holds the critical power very low, infinitely lower than the inventive; and he said today that if the quantity of time consumed in writing critiques on the works of others were given to original composition, of whatever kind it might

* I cannot help thinking that a practice, common in England during the last century, and still followed in France, of printing a notice of this kind – a notice by a competent critic – to serve as an introduction to an eminent author's works, might be revived among us with advantage. To introduce all succeeding editions of Wordsworth, Mr Shairp's notice might, it seems to me, excellently serve; it is written from the point of view of an admirer, nay, of a disciple, and that is right; but then the disciple must be also, as in this case he is, a critic, a man of letters, not, as too often happens, some relation or friend with no qualification for his task except affection for his author.

be, it would be much better employed; it would make a man find out sooner his own level, and it would do infinitely less mischief. A false or malicious criticism may do much injury to the minds of others; a stupid invention, either in prose or verse, is quite harmless.'

It is almost too much to expect of poor human nature, that a man capable of producing some effect in one line of literature, should, for the greater good of society, voluntarily doom himself to impotence and obscurity in another. Still less is this to be expected from men addicted to the composition of the 'false or malicious criticism,' of which Wordsworth speaks. However, everybody would admit that a false or malicious criticism had better never have been written. Everybody, too, would be willing to admit, as a general proposition, that the critical faculty is lower than the inventive. But is it true that criticism is really, in itself, a baneful and injurious employment; is it true that all time given to writing critiques on the works of others would be much better employed if it were given to original composition, of whatever kind this may be? Is it true that Johnson had better have gone on producing more *Irenes* instead of writing his *Lives of the Poets*; nay, is it certain that Wordsworth himself was better employed in making his Ecclesiastical Sonnets, than when he made his celebrated Preface, so full of criticism, and criticism of the works of others? Wordsworth was himself a great critic, and it is to be sincerely regretted that he has not left us more criticism; Goethe was one of the greatest of critics, and we may sincerely congratulate ourselves that he has left us so much criticism. Without wasting time over the exaggeration which Wordsworth's judgment on criticism clearly contains, or over an attempt to trace the causes, – not difficult I think to be traced, – which may have led Wordsworth to this exaggeration, a critic may with advantage seize an occasion for trying his own conscience, and for asking himself of what real service, at any given moment, the practice of criticism either is, or may be made, to his own mind and spirit, and to the minds and spirits of others.

The critical power is of lower rank than the creative. True; but in assenting to this proposition, one or two things are to be kept in mind. It is undeniable that the exercise of a creative power, that a free creative activity, is the highest function of man; it is proved to be so by man's finding in it his true happiness. But it is undeniable, also, that men may have the sense of exercising this free creative activity in other ways than in producing great works of literature or art; if it were not so, all but a very few men would be shut out from the true happiness of all men. They may have it in well-doing, they may have it in learning, they may have it even in criticizing. This is one thing to be kept in mind. Another is, that the exercise of the creative power in the production of great works of literature or art, however high this exercise of it may rank, is not at all epochs and under all conditions possible; and that, therefore; labour may be vainly spent in attempting it, which might with more fruit be used in preparing for it, in rendering it possible. This creative power works with elements, with materials; what if it has not those materials, those elements, ready for its use? In that case it must surely wait till they are ready. Now in literature, – I will limit myself to literature, for it is about literature that the question arises, – the elements with which the creative power works are ideas; the best ideas, on every matter which literature touches, current at the time. At any rate we may lay it down as certain that in modern literature no manifestation of the creative power not working with these can be very important or fruitful. And I say *current* at the time, not merely accessible at the time; for creative literary genius does not principally show itself in discovering new ideas; that is rather the business of the philosopher. The grand work of literary genius is a work of synthesis and exposition, not of analysis and discovery; its gift lies in the faculty of being happily inspired by a certain intellectual and spiritual atmosphere, by a certain order of ideas, when it finds itself in them; of dealing divinely with these ideas, presenting them in the most effective and attractive combinations, – making beautiful works with them, in short. But it must have the atmosphere, it must find itself amidst the order of ideas, in order to work freely; and these it is not so easy to command. This is why great creative epochs in literature are so rare, this is why there is so much that is unsatisfactory in the productions of many men of real genius; – because, for the creation of a master-work of literature two powers must concur, the power of the man and the power of the moment, and the man is not enough without the moment; the creative power has, for its happy exercise, appointed elements, and those elements are not in its own control.

Nay, they are more within the control of the critical power. It is the business of the critical power, as I said in the words already quoted, 'in all branches of knowledge, theology, philosophy, history, art, science, to see the object as in itself it really is.' Thus it tends, at last, to make an intellectual situation of which the creative power can profitably avail itself. It tends to establish an order of ideas, if not absolutely true, yet true by comparison with that which it displaces; to make the best ideas prevail. Presently these new ideas reach society, the touch of truth is the touch of life, and there is a stir and growth everywhere; out of this stir and growth come the creative epochs of literature.

Or, to narrow our range, and quit these considerations of the general march of genius and of society, considerations which are apt to become too abstract and impalpable, – everyone can see that a poet, for instance, ought to know life and the world before dealing with them in poetry; and life and the world being, in modern times, very complex things, the creation of a modern poet, to be worth much, implies a great critical effort behind it; else it must be a comparatively poor, barren, and short-lived affair. This is why Byron's poetry had so little endurance in it, and Goethe's so much; both Byron and Goethe had a great productive power, but Goethe's was nourished by a great critical effort providing the true materials for it, and Byron's was not; Goethe knew life and the world, the poet's necessary subjects, much more comprehensively and thoroughly than Byron. He knew a great deal more of them, and he knew them much more as they really are.

It has long seemed to me that the burst of creative activity in our literature, through the first quarter of this century, had about it, in fact, something premature; and that from this cause its productions are doomed, most of them, in spite of the sanguine hopes which accompanied and do still accompany them, to prove hardly more lasting than the productions of far less splendid epochs. And this prematureness comes from its having proceeded without having its proper data, without sufficient materials to work with. In other words, the English poetry of the first quarter of this century, with plenty of energy, plenty of creative force, did not know enough. This makes Byron so empty of matter, Shelley so incoherent, Wordsworth even, profound as he is, yet so wanting in completeness and variety. Wordsworth cared little for books, and disparaged Goethe. I admire Wordsworth, as he is, so much that I cannot wish him different; and it is vain, no doubt, to imagine such a man different from what he is, to suppose that he *could* have been different. But surely the one thing wanting to make Wordsworth an even greater poet than he is, – his thought richer, and his influence of wider application, – was that he should have read more books, among them, no doubt, those of that Goethe whom he disparaged without reading him.

But to speak of books and reading may easily lead to a misunderstanding here. It was not really books and reading that lacked to our poetry, at this epoch; Shelley had plenty of reading, Coleridge had immense reading. Pindar and Sophocles – as we all say so glibly, and often with so little discernment of the real import of what we are saying – had not many books; Shakespeare was no deep reader. True; but in the Greece of Pindar and Sophocles, in the England of Shakespeare, the poet lived in a current of ideas in the highest degree animating and nourishing to the creative power; society was, in the fullest measure, permeated by fresh thought, intelligent and alive. And this state of things is the true basis for the creative power's exercise, in this it finds its data, its materials, truly ready for its hand; all the books and reading in the world are only valuable as they are helps to this. Even when this does not actually exist, books and reading may enable a man to construct a kind of semblance of it in his own mind, a world of knowledge and intelligence in which he may live and work. This is by no means an equivalent, to the artist, for the nationally diffused life and thought of the epochs of Sophocles or Shakespeare; but, besides that it may be a means of preparation for such epochs, it does really constitute, if many share in it, a quickening and sustaining atmosphere of great value. Such an atmosphere the many-sided learning and the long and widely-combined critical effort of Germany formed for Goethe, when he lived and worked. There was no national glow of life and thought there, as in the Athens of Pericles, or the England of Elizabeth. That was the poet's weakness. But there was a sort of equivalent for it in the complete culture and unfettered thinking of a large body of Germans. That was his strength. In the England of the first quarter of this century, there was neither a national glow of life and thought, such as we had in the age of Elizabeth, nor yet a culture and a force of learning and criticism, such as were to be found in Germany. Therefore, the creative power of poetry wanted, for success in the highest sense, materials and a basis; a thorough interpretation of the world was necessarily denied to it.

At first sight it seems strange that out of the immense stir of the French Revolution and its age should not have come a crop of works of genius equal to that which came out of the stir of the great productive time of Greece, or out of that of the Renascence with its powerful episode the Reformation. But the truth is that the stir of the French Revolution took a character which essentially distinguished it from such movements as these. These were, in the main, disinterestedly intellectual and spiritual movements; movements in which the human spirit looked for its satisfaction in itself and in the increased play of its own activity. The French Revolution took a political, practical character. The movement which went on in France under the old *régime*, from 1700 to 1789, was far more really akin than that of the Revolution itself to the movement of the Renascence; the France of Voltaire and Rousseau told far more powerfully upon the mind of Europe than the France of the Revolution. Goethe reproached this last expressly with having 'thrown quiet culture back.' Nay, and the true key to how much in our Byron, even in our Wordsworth, is this! – that they had their source in a great movement of feeling, not in a great movement of mind. The French Revolution, however, – that object of so much blind love and so much blind hatred, – found undoubtedly its motive-power in the intelligence of men and not in their practical sense; – this is what distinguishes it from the English Revolution of Charles the First's time. This is what makes it a more spiritual event than our Revolution, an event of much more powerful and world-wide interest, though practically less successful; – it appeals to an order of ideas which are universal, certain, permanent. 1789 asked of a thing, Is it rational? 1642 asked of a thing, Is it legal? or, when it went furthest, Is it according to conscience? This is the English fashion; a fashion to be treated, within its own sphere, with the highest respect; for its success, within its own sphere, has been prodigious. But what is law in one place, is not law in another; what is law here today, is not law even here tomorrow; and as for conscience, what is binding on one man's conscience is not binding on another's. The old woman who threw her stool at the head of the surpliced minister in St Giles's Church at Edinburgh[1] obeyed an impulse to which millions of the human race may be permitted to remain strangers. But the prescriptions of reason are absolute, unchanging, of universal validity; *to count by tens is the easiest way of counting*, – that is a proposition of which everyone, from here to the Antipodes, feels the force; at least, I should say so, if we did not live in a country where it is not impossible that any morning we may find a letter in the *Times* declaring that a decimal coinage is an absurdity.[2] That a whole nation should have been penetrated with an enthusiasm for pure reason, and with an ardent zeal for making its prescriptions triumph, is a very remarkable thing, when we consider how little of mind, or anything so worthy and quickening as mind, comes into the motives which alone, in general, impel great masses of men. In spite of the extravagant direction given to this enthusiasm, in spite of the crimes and follies in which it lost itself, the French Revolution derives from the force, truth, and universality of the ideas which it took for its law, and from the passion with which it could inspire a multitude for these ideas, a unique and still living power; it is, – it will probably long remain, – the greatest, the most animating event in history. And, as no sincere passion for the things of the mind, even though it turn out in many respects an unfortunate passion, is ever quite thrown away and quite barren of good, France has reaped from hers one fruit, – the natural and legitimate fruit, though not precisely the grand fruit she expected: she is the country in Europe where *the people* is most alive.

But the mania for giving an immediate political and practical application to all these fine ideas of the reason was fatal. Here an Englishman is in his element: on this theme we can all go on for hours. And all we are in the habit of saying on it has undoubtedly a great deal of truth. Ideas cannot be too much prized in and for themselves, cannot be too much lived with; but to transport them abruptly into the world of politics and practice, violently to revolutionize this world to their bidding, – that is quite another thing. There is the world of ideas and there is the world of practice; the French are often for suppressing the one and the English the other; but neither is to be suppressed. A member of the House of Commons said to me the other day: 'That a thing is an anomaly, I consider to be no objection to it whatever.' I venture to think he was wrong; that a thing is an anomaly *is* an objection to it, but absolutely and in the sphere of ideas: it is not necessarily, under such and such circumstances, or at such and such a moment, an objection to it in the sphere of politics and practice. Joubert has said beautifully: 'C'est la force et le droit qui règlent toutes choses dans le monde; la force en attendant le droit.' (Force and right are the governors of this world; force till right is ready.) *Force till right is ready*; and till right is ready, force, the existing order of things, is justified, is the legitimate ruler. But right is something moral, and implies inward recognition, free assent of the will; we are not ready for right, – *right,* so far as we are concerned, *is not ready,* – until we have attained this sense of seeing it and willing it. The way in which for us it may change and transform force, the existing order of things, and become, in its turn, the legitimate ruler of the world, should depend on the way in which, when our time comes, we see it and will it. Therefore, for other people enamoured of their own newly discerned right, to attempt to impose it upon us as ours, and violently to substitute their right for our force, is an act of tyranny, and to be resisted. It sets at nought the second great half of our maxim, *force till right is ready*. This was the grand error of the French Revolution; and its movement of ideas, by quitting the intellectual sphere and rushing furiously into the political sphere, ran, indeed, a prodigious and memorable course, but produced no such intellectual fruit as the movement of ideas of the Renascence, and created, in opposition to itself, what I may call an *epoch of concentration*. The great force of that epoch of concentration was England; and the great voice of that epoch of concentration was Burke. It is the fashion to treat Burke's writings on the French Revolution as superannuated and conquered by the event; as the eloquent but unphilosophical tirades of bigotry and prejudice. I will not deny that they are often disfigured by the violence and passion of the moment, and that in some directions Burke's view was bounded, and his observation, therefore, at fault. But on the whole, and for those who can make the needful corrections, what distinguishes these writings is their profound, permanent, fruitful, philosophical truth. They contain the true philosophy of an epoch of concentration, dissipate the heavy atmosphere which its own nature is apt to engender round it, and make its resistance rational instead of mechanical.

But Burke is so great because, almost alone in England, he brings thought to bear upon politics, he saturates politics with thought. It is his accident that his ideas were at the service of an epoch of concentration, not of an epoch of expansion; it is his characteristic that he so lived by ideas, and had such a source of them welling up within him, that he could float even an epoch of concentration and English Tory politics with them. It does not hurt him that Dr Price[3] and the Liberals were enraged with him; it does not even hurt him that George the Third and the Tories were enchanted with him. His greatness is that he lived in a world which neither English Liberalism nor English Toryism is apt to enter; – the world of ideas, not the world of catchwords and party habits. So far is it from being really true of him that he 'to party gave up what was meant for mankind,'[4] that at the very end of his fierce struggle with the French Revolution, after all his invectives against its false pretensions, hollowness, and madness, with his sincere conviction of its mischievousness, he can close a memorandum on the best means of combating it, some of the last pages he ever wrote, – the *Thoughts on French Affairs,* in December 1791, – with these striking words: –

'The evil is stated, in my opinion, as it exists. The remedy must be where power, wisdom, and information, I hope, are more united with good intentions than they can be with me. I have done with this subject, I believe, for ever. It has given me many anxious moments for the last two years. *If a great change is to be made in human affairs, the minds of men will be fitted to it; the general opinions and feelings will draw that way. Every fear, every hope will forward it; and then they who persist in opposing this mighty current in human affairs, will appear rather to resist the decrees of Providence itself, than the mere designs of men. They will not be resolute and firm, but perverse and obstinate.*'

That return of Burke upon himself has always seemed to me one of the finest things in English literature, or indeed in any literature. That is what I call living by ideas: when one side of a question has long had your earnest support, when all your feelings are engaged, when you hear all round you no language but one, when your party talks this language like a steam-engine and can imagine no other, – still to be able to think, still to be irresistibly carried, if so it be, by the current of thought to the opposite side of the question, and, like Balaam, to be unable to speak anything *but what the Lord has put in your mouth.*[5] I know nothing more striking, and I must add that I know nothing more un-English.

For the Englishman in general is like my friend the Member of Parliament, and believes, point-blank, that for a thing to be an anomaly is absolutely no objection to it whatever. He is like the Lord Auckland of Burke's day, who, in a memorandum on the French Revolution, talks of 'certain miscreants, assuming the name of philosophers, who have presumed themselves capable of establishing a new system of society.' The Englishman has been called a political animal, and he values what is political and practical so much that ideas easily become objects of dislike in his eyes, and thinkers 'miscreants,' because ideas and thinkers have rashly meddled with politics and practice. This would be all very well if the dislike and neglect confined themselves to ideas transported out of their own sphere, and meddling rashly with practice; but they are inevitably extended to ideas as such, and to the whole life of intelligence; practice is everything, a free play of the mind is nothing. The notion of the free play of the mind upon all subjects being a pleasure in itself, being an object of desire, being an essential provider of elements without which a nation's spirit, whatever compensations it may have for them, must, in the long run, die of inanition, hardly enters into an Englishman's thoughts. It is noticeable that the word *curiosity*, which in other languages is used in a good sense, to mean, as a high and fine quality of man's nature, just this disinterested love of a free play of the mind on all subjects, for its own sake, – it is noticeable, I say, that this word has in our language no sense of the kind, no sense but a rather bad and disparaging one. But criticism, real criticism, is essentially the exercise of this very quality. It obeys an instinct prompting it to try to know the best that is known and thought in the world, irrespectively of practice, politics, and everything of the kind; and to value knowledge and thought as they approach this best, without the intrusion of any other considerations whatever. This is an instinct for which there is, I think, little original sympathy in the practical English nature, and what there was of it has undergone a long benumbing period of blight and suppression in the epoch of concentration which followed the French Revolution.

But epochs of concentration cannot well endure for ever; epochs of expansion, in the due course of things, follow them. Such an epoch of expansion seems to be opening in this country. In the first place all danger of a hostile forcible pressure of foreign ideas upon our practice has long disappeared; like the traveller in the fable, therefore, we begin to wear our cloak a little more loosely.[6] Then, with a long peace, the ideas of Europe steal gradually and amicably in, and mingle, though in infinitesimally small quantities at a time, with our own notions. Then, too, in spite of all that is said about the absorbing and brutalizing influence of our passionate material progress, it seems to me indisputable that this progress is likely, though not certain, to lead in the end to an apparition of intellectual life; and that man, after he has made himself perfectly comfortable and has now to determine what to do with himself next, may begin to remember that he has a mind, and that the mind may be made the source of great pleasure. I grant it is mainly the privilege of faith, at present, to discern this end to our railways, our business, and our fortune-making; but we shall see if, here as elsewhere, faith is not in the end the true prophet. Our ease, our travelling, and our unbounded liberty to hold just as hard and securely as we please to the practice to which our notions have given birth, all tend to beget an inclination to deal a little more freely with these notions themselves, to canvass them a little, to penetrate a little into their real nature. Flutterings of curiosity, in the foreign sense of the word, appear among us, and it is in these that criticism must look to find its account. Criticism first; a time of true creative activity, perhaps, – which, as I have said, must inevitably be preceded among us by a time of criticism, – hereafter, when criticism has done its work.

It is of the last importance that English criticism should clearly discern what rule for its course, in order to avail itself of the field now opening to it, and to produce fruit for the future, it ought to take. The rule may be summed up in one word, – *disinterestedness*. And how is criticism to show disinterestedness? By keeping aloof from what is called 'the practical view of things;' by resolutely following the law of its own nature, which is to be a free play of the mind on all subjects which it touches. By steadily refusing to lend itself to any of those ulterior, political, practical considerations about ideas, which plenty of people will be sure to attach to them, which perhaps ought often to be attached to them, which in this country at any rate are certain to be attached to them quite sufficiently, but which criticism has really nothing to do with. Its business is, as I have said, simply to know the best that is known and thought in the world, and by in its turn making this known, to create a current of true and fresh ideas. Its business is to do this with inflexible honesty, with due ability; but its business is to do no more, and to leave alone all questions of practical consequences and applications, questions which will never fail to have due prominence given to them. Else criticism, besides being really false to its own nature, merely continues in the old rut which it has hitherto followed in this country, and will certainly miss the chance now given to it. For what is at present the bane of criticism in this country? It is that practical considerations cling to it and stifle it. It subserves interests not its own. Our organs of criticism are organs of men and parties having practical ends to serve, and with them those practical ends are the first thing and the play of mind the second; so much play of mind as is compatible with the prosecution of those practical ends is all that is wanted. An organ like the *Revue des Deux Mondes,* having for its main function to understand and utter the best that is known and thought in the world, existing, it may be said, as just an organ for a free play of the mind, we have not. But we have the *Edinburgh Review,* existing as an organ of the old Whigs, and for as much play of the mind as may suit its being that; we have the *Quarterly Review,* existing as an organ of the Tories, and for as much play of mind as may suit its being that; we have the *British Quarterly Review,* existing as an organ of the political Dissenters, and for as much play of mind as may suit its being that; we have the *Times,* existing as an organ of the common, satisfied, well-to-do Englishman, and for as much play of mind as may suit its being that. And so on through all the various fractions, political and religious, of our society; every fraction has, as such, its organ of criticism, but the notion of combining all fractions in the common pleasure of a free disinterested play of mind meets with no favour. Directly this play of mind wants to have more scope, and to forget the pressure of practical considerations a little, it is checked, it is made to feel the chain. We saw this the other day in the extinction, so much to be regretted, of the *Home and Foreign Review.* Perhaps in no organ of criticism in this country was there so much knowledge, so much play of mind; but these could not save it. The *Dublin Review* subordinates play of mind to the practical business of English and Irish Catholicism, and lives. It must needs be that men should act in sects and parties, that each of these sects and parties should have its organ, and should make this organ subserve the interests of its action; but it would be well, too, that there should be a criticism, not the minister of these interests, not their enemy, but absolutely and entirely independent of them. No other criticism will ever attain any real authority or make any real way towards its end, – the creating a current of true and fresh ideas.

It is because criticism has so little kept in the pure intellectual sphere, has so little detached itself from practice, has been so directly polemical and controversial, that it has so ill accomplished, in this country, its best spiritual work; which is to keep man from a self-satisfaction which is retarding and vulgarizing, to lead him towards perfection, by making his mind dwell upon what is excellent in itself, and the absolute beauty and fitness of things. A polemical practical criticism makes men blind even to the ideal imperfection of their practice, makes them willingly assert its ideal perfection, in order the better to secure it against attack; and clearly this is narrowing and baneful for them. If they were reassured on the practical side, speculative considerations of ideal perfection they might be brought to entertain, and their spiritual horizon would thus gradually widen. Sir Charles Adderley[7] says to the Warwickshire farmers: –

'Talk of the improvement of breed! Why, the race we ourselves represent, the men and women, the old Anglo-Saxon race, are the best breed in the whole world . . . The absence of a too enervating climate, too unclouded skies, and a too luxurious nature, has produced so vigorous a race of people, and has rendered us so superior to all the world.'

Mr Roebuck[8] says to the Sheffield cutlers: –

'I look around me and ask what is the state of England? Is not property safe? Is not every man able to say what he likes? Can you not walk from one end of England to the other in perfect security? I ask you whether, the world over or in past history, there is anything like it? Nothing. I pray that our unrivalled happiness may last.'

Now obviously there is a peril for poor human nature in words and thoughts of such exuberant self-satisfaction, until we find ourselves safe in the streets of the Celestial City.

'Das wenige verschwindet leicht dem Blicke
Der vorwärts sieht, wie viel noch übrig bleibt –'

says Goethe; 'the little that is done seems nothing when we
look forward and see how much we have yet to do.' Clearly
this is a better line of reflection for weak humanity, so long as
it remains on this earthly field of labour and trial.

But neither Sir Charles Adderley nor Mr Roebuck are by
nature inaccessible to considerations of this sort. They only
lose sight of them owing to the controversial life we all lead,
and the practical form which all speculation takes with us.
They have in view opponents whose aim is not ideal, but practical; and in their zeal to uphold their own practice against
these innovators, they go so far as even to attribute to this
practice an ideal perfection. Somebody has been wanting to
introduce a six-pound franchise, or to abolish church-rates, or
to collect agricultural statistics by force, or to diminish local
self-government. How natural, in reply to such proposals, very
likely improper or ill-timed, to go a little beyond the mark, and
to say stoutly, 'Such a race of people as we stand, so superior to
all the world! The old Anglo-Saxon race, the best breed in the
whole world! I pray that our unrivalled happiness may last! I
ask you whether, the world over or in past history, there is anything like it!' And so long as criticism answers this dithyramb
by insisting that the old Anglo-Saxon race would be still more
superior to all others if it had no church-rates, or that our
unrivalled happiness would last yet longer with a six-pound
franchise, so long will the strain, 'The best breed in the whole
world!' swell louder and louder, everything ideal and refining
will be lost out of sight, and both the assailed and their critics
will remain in a sphere, to say the truth, perfectly unvital, a
sphere in which spiritual progression is impossible. But let criticism leave church-rates and the franchise alone, and in the
most candid spirit, without a single lurking thought of practical innovation, confront with our dithyramb this paragraph
on which I stumbled in a newspaper immediately after reading
Mr Roebuck: –

'A shocking child murder has just been committed at

Nottingham. A girl named Wragg left the workhouse there on Saturday morning with her young illegitimate child. The child was soon afterwards found dead on Mapperly Hills, having been strangled. Wragg is in custody.'

Nothing but that; but, in juxtaposition with the absolute eulogies of Sir Charles Adderley and Mr Roebuck, how eloquent, how suggestive are those few lines! 'Our old Anglo-Saxon breed, the best in the whole world!' – how much that is harsh and ill-favoured there is in this best! *Wragg!* If we are to talk of ideal perfection, of 'the best in the whole world,' has any one reflected what a touch of grossness in our race, what an original shortcoming in the more delicate spiritual perceptions, is shown by the natural growth among us of such hideous names, – Higginbottom, Stiggins, Bugg! In Ionia and Attica they were luckier in this respect than 'the best race in the world;' by the Ilissus there was no Wragg, poor thing! And 'our unrivalled happiness;' – what an element of grimness, bareness, and hideousness mixes with it and blurs it; the workhouse, the dismal Mapperly Hills, – how dismal those who have seen them will remember; – the gloom, the smoke, the cold, the strangled illegitimate child! 'I ask you whether, the world over or in past history, there is anything like it?' Perhaps not, one is inclined to answer; but at any rate, in that case, the world is very much to be pitied. And the final touch, – short, bleak, and inhuman: *Wragg is in custody.* The sex lost in the confusion of our unrivalled happiness; or (shall I say?) the superfluous Christian name lopped off by the straightforward vigour of our old Anglo-Saxon breed! There is profit for the spirit in such contrasts as this; criticism serves the cause of perfection by establishing them. By eluding sterile conflict, by refusing to remain in the sphere where alone narrow and relative conceptions have any worth and validity, criticism may diminish its momentary importance, but only in this way has it a chance of gaining admittance for those wider and more perfect conceptions to which all its duty is really owed. Mr Roebuck will have a poor opinion of an adversary who replies to his defiant songs of triumph only by murmuring under his breath, *Wragg is in custody*; but in no other way will these songs of triumph be induced gradually to moderate themselves, to get rid of what in them is excessive and offensive, and to fall into a softer and truer key.

It will be said that it is a very subtle and indirect action which I am thus prescribing for criticism, and that by embracing in this manner the Indian virtue of detachment and abandoning the sphere of practical life, it condemns itself to a slow and obscure work. Slow and obscure it may be, but it is the only proper work of criticism. The mass of mankind will never have any ardent zeal for seeing things as they are; very inadequate ideas will always satisfy them. On these inadequate ideas reposes, and must repose, the general practice of the world. That is as much as saying that whoever sets himself to see things as they are will find himself one of a very small circle; but it is only by this small circle resolutely doing its own work that adequate ideas will ever get current at all. The rush and roar of practical life will always have a dizzying and attracting effect upon the most collected spectator, and tend to draw him into its vortex; most of all will this be the case where that life is so powerful as it is in England. But it is only by remaining collected, and refusing to lend himself to the point of view of the practical man, that the critic can do the practical man any service; and it is only by the greatest sincerity in pursuing his own course, and by at last convincing even the practical man of his sincerity, that he can escape misunderstandings which perpetually threaten him.

For the practical man is not apt for fine distinctions, and yet in these distinctions truth and the highest culture greatly find their account. But it is not easy to lead a practical man, – unless you reassure him as to your practical intentions, you have no chance of leading him, – to see that a thing which he has always been used to look at from one side only, which he greatly values, and which, looked at from that side, quite deserves, perhaps, all the prizing and admiring which he bestows upon it, – that this thing, looked at from another side, may appear much less beneficent and beautiful, and yet retain all its claims to our practical allegiance. Where shall we find language inno-cent enough, how shall we make the spotless purity of our intentions evident enough, to enable us to say to the political

Englishman that the British Constitution itself, which, seen from the practical side, looks such a magnificent organ of progress and virtue, seen from the speculative side, – with its compromises, its love of facts, its horror of theory, its studied avoidance of clear thoughts, – that, seen from this side, our august Constitution sometimes looks, – forgive me, shade of Lord Somers[9]! – a colossal machine for the manufacture of Philistines? How is Cobbett to say this and not be misunderstood, blackened as he is with the smoke of a life-long conflict in the field of political practice?[10] how is Mr Carlyle to say it and not be misunderstood, after his furious raid into this field with his *Latter-day Pamphlets*?[11] how is Mr Ruskin, after his pugnacious political economy?[12] I say, the critic must keep out of the region of immediate practice in the political, social, humanitarian sphere, if he wants to make a beginning for that more free speculative treatment of things, which may perhaps one day make its benefits felt even in this sphere, but in a natural and thence irresistible manner.

Do what he will, however, the critic will still remain exposed to frequent misunderstandings, and nowhere so much as in this country. For here people are particularly indisposed even to comprehend that without this free disinterested treatment of things, truth and the highest culture are out of the question. So immersed are they in practical life, so accustomed to take all their notions from this life and its processes, that they are apt to think that truth and culture themselves can be reached by the processes of this life, and that it is an impertinent singularity to think of reaching them in any other. 'We are all *terræ filii*,'[13] cries their eloquent advocate; 'all Philistines together. Away with the notion of proceeding by any other course than the course dear to the Philistines; let us have a social movement, let us organize and combine a party to pursue truth and new thought, let us call it *the liberal party,* and let us all stick to each other, and back each other up. Let us have no nonsense about independent criticism, and intellectual delicacy, and the few and the many. Don't let us trouble ourselves about foreign thought; we shall invent the whole thing for ourselves as we go along. If one of us speaks well, applaud him; if one of us speaks ill, applaud him, too; we are all in the same movement, we are all liberals, we are all in pursuit of truth.' In this way the pursuit of truth becomes really a social, practical, pleasurable affair, almost requiring a chairman, a secretary, and advertisements; with the excitement of an occasional scandal, with a little resistance to give the happy sense of difficulty overcome; but, in general, plenty of bustle and very little thought. To act is so easy, as Goethe says; to think is so hard! It is true that the critic has many temptations to go with the stream, to make one of the party movement, one of these *terræ filii*; it seems ungracious to refuse to be a *terræ filius*, when so many excellent people are; but the critic's duty is to refuse, or, if resistance is vain, at least to cry with Obermann:[14] *Périssons en résistant*.

How serious a matter it is to try and resist, I had ample opportunity of experiencing when I ventured some time ago to criticize the celebrated first volume of Bishop Colenso.*[15] The echoes of the storm which was then raised I still, from time to time, hear grumbling round me. That storm arose out of a misunderstanding almost inevitable. It is a result of no little culture to attain to a clear perception that science and religion are two wholly different things. The multitude will for ever confuse them; but happily that is of no great real importance, for while the multitude imagines itself to live by its false science, it does really live by its true religion. Dr Colenso, however, in his first volume did all he could to strengthen the confusion,† and to make it dangerous. He did this with the best intentions, I freely

* So sincere is my dislike to all personal attack and controversy, that I abstain from reprinting, at this distance of time from the occasion which called them forth, the essays in which I criticized Dr Colenso's book; I feel bound, however, after all that has passed, to make here a final declaration of my sincere impenitence for having published them. Nay, I cannot forbear repeating yet once more, for his benefit and that of his readers, this sentence from my original remarks upon him: *There is truth of science and truth of religion; truth of science does not become truth of religion till it is made religious.* And I will add: Let us have all the science there is from the men of science; from the men of religion let us have religion.

† It has been said I make it 'a crime against literary criticism and the higher culture to attempt to inform the ignorant.' Need I point out that the ignorant are not informed by being confirmed in a confusion?

admit, and with the most candid ignorance that this was the natural effect of what he was doing; but, says Joubert, 'Ignorance, which in matters of morals extenuates the crime, is itself, in intellectual matters, a crime of the first order.' I criticized Bishop Colenso's speculative confusion. Immediately there was a cry raised: 'What is this? here is a liberal attacking a liberal. Do not you belong to the movement? are not you a friend of truth? Is not Bishop Colenso in pursuit of truth? then speak with proper respect of his book. Dr Stanley is another friend of truth, and you speak with proper respect of his book;[16] why make these invidious differences? both books are excellent, admirable, liberal; Bishop Colenso's perhaps the most so, because it is the boldest, and will have the best practical consequences for the liberal cause. Do you want to encourage to the attack of a brother liberal his, and your, and our implacable enemies, the *Church and State Review* or the *Record*, – the High Church rhinoceros and the Evangelical hyæna? Be silent, therefore; or rather speak, speak as loud as ever you can! and go into ecstasies over the eighty and odd pigeons.'[17]

But criticism cannot follow this coarse and indiscriminate method. It is unfortunately possible for a man in pursuit of truth to write a book which reposes upon a false conception. Even the practical consequences of a book are to genuine criticism no recommendation of it, if the book is, in the highest sense, blundering. I see that a lady who herself, too, is in pursuit of truth, and who writes with great ability, but a little too much, perhaps, under the influence of the practical spirit of the English liberal movement, classes Bishop Colenso's book and M. Renan's together, in her survey of the religious state of Europe, as facts of the same order, works, both of them, of 'great importance'; 'great ability, power, and skill'; Bishop Colenso's, perhaps, the most powerful; at least, Miss Cobbe gives special expression to her gratitude that to Bishop Colenso 'has been given the strength to grasp, and the courage to teach, truths of such deep import.' In the same way, more than one popular writer has compared him to Luther. Now it is just this kind of false estimate which the critical spirit is, it seems to me, bound to resist. It is really the strongest possible proof of the low ebb

at which, in England, the critical spirit is, that while the critical
hit in the religious literature of Germany is Dr Strauss's book,[18]
in that of France M. Renan's book,[19] the book of Bishop
Colenso is the critical hit in the religious literature of England.
Bishop Colenso's book reposes on a total misconception of the
essential elements of the religious problem, as that problem is
now presented for solution. To criticism, therefore, which seeks
to have the best that is known and thought on this problem, it
is, however well meant, of no importance whatever. M. Renan's
book attempts a new synthesis of the elements furnished to us
by the Four Gospels. It attempts, in my opinion, a synthesis,
perhaps premature, perhaps impossible, certainly not successful. Up to the present time at any rate, we must acquiesce in
Fleury's sentence on such recastings of the Gospel story: *Qui-
conque s'imagine la pouvoir mieux écrire, ne l'entend pas*. M.
Renan had himself passed by anticipation a like sentence on his
own work, when he said: 'If a new presentation of the character of Jesus were offered to me, I would not have it; its very
clearness would be, in my opinion, the best proof of its insufficiency.' His friends may with perfect justice rejoin that at the
sight of the Holy Land, and of the actual scene of the Gospel-story,
all the current of M. Renan's thoughts may have naturally
changed, and a new casting of that story irresistibly suggested
itself to him; and that this is just a case for applying Cicero's
maxim: Change of mind is not inconsistency – *nemo doctus
unquam mutationem consilii inconstantiam dixit esse*. Nevertheless, for criticism, M. Renan's first thought must still be the truer
one, as long as his new casting so fails more fully to commend
itself, more fully (to use Coleridge's happy phrase about the
Bible) to *find* us. Still M. Renan's attempt is, for criticism, of the
most real interest and importance, since, with all its difficulty, a
fresh synthesis of the New Testament *data*, – not a making war
on them, in Voltaire's fashion, not a leaving them out of mind, in
the world's fashion, but the putting a new construction upon
them, the taking them from under the old, traditional, conventional point of view and placing them under a new one, – is the
very essence of the religious problem, as now presented; and
only by efforts in this direction can it receive a solution.

Again, in the same spirit in which she judges Bishop Colenso, Miss Cobbe, like so many earnest liberals of our practical race, both here and in America, herself sets vigorously about a positive reconstruction of religion, about making a religion of the future out of hand, or at least setting about making it. We must not rest, she and they are always thinking and saying, in negative criticism, we must be creative and constructive; hence we have such works as her recent *Religious Duty,* and works still more considerable, perhaps, by others, which will be in every one's mind. These works often have much ability; they often spring out of sincere convictions, and a sincere wish to do good; and they sometimes, perhaps, do good. Their fault is (if I may be permitted to say so) one which they have in common with the British College of Health, in the New Road.[20] Everyone knows the British College of Health; it is that building with the lion and the statue of the Goddess Hygeia before it; at least, I am sure about the lion, though I am not absolutely certain about the Goddess Hygeia. This building does credit, perhaps, to the resources of Dr Morrison and his disciples; but it falls a good deal short of one's idea of what a British College of Health ought to be. In England, where we hate public interference and love individual enterprise, we have a whole crop of places like the British College of Health; the grand name without the grand thing. Unluckily, creditable to individual enterprise as they are, they tend to impair our taste by making us forget what more grandiose, noble, or beautiful character properly belongs to a public institution. The same may be said of the religions of the future of Miss Cobbe and others. Creditable, like the British College of Health, to the resources of their authors, they yet tend to make us forget what more grandiose, noble, or beautiful character properly belongs to religious constructions. The historic religions, with all their faults, have had this; it certainly belongs to the religious sentiment, when it truly flowers, to have this; and we impoverish our spirit if we allow a religion of the future without it. What then is the duty of criticism here? To take the practical point of view, to applaud the liberal movement and all its works, – its New Road religions of the future into the bargain, – for their general utility's sake? By no means; but to be perpetually dissatisfied with these works, while they perpetually fall short of a high and perfect ideal.

For criticism, these are elementary laws; but they never can be popular, and in this country they have been very little followed, and one meets with immense obstacles in following them. That is a reason for asserting them again and again. Criticism must maintain its independence of the practical spirit and its aims. Even with well-meant efforts of the practical spirit it must express dissatisfaction, if in the sphere of the ideal they seem impoverishing and limiting. It must not hurry on to the goal because of its practical importance. It must be patient, and know how to wait; and flexible, and know how to attach itself to things and how to withdraw from them. It must be apt to study and praise elements that for the fulness of spiritual perfection are wanted, even though they belong to a power which in the practical sphere may be maleficent. It must be apt to discern the spiritual shortcomings or illusions of powers that in the practical sphere may be beneficent. And this without any notion of favouring or injuring, in the practical sphere, one power or the other; without any notion of playing off, in this sphere, one power against the other. When one looks, for instance, at the English Divorce Court,[21] – an institution which perhaps has its practical conveniences, but which in the ideal sphere is so hideous; an institution which neither makes divorce impossible nor makes it decent, which allows a man to get rid of his wife, or a wife of her husband, but makes them drag one another first, for the public edification, through a mire of unutterable infamy, – when one looks at this charming institution, I say, with its crowded trials, its newspaper-reports, and its money-compensations, this institution in which the gross unregenerate British Philistine has, indeed, stamped an image of himself, – one may be permitted to find the marriage-theory of Catholicism refreshing and elevating. Or when Protestantism, in virtue of its supposed rational and intellectual origin, gives the law to criticism too magisterially, criticism may and must remind it that its pretensions, in this respect, are illusive and do it harm; that the Reformation was a moral rather than an intellectual event; that Luther's theory of grace no more exactly reflects the mind of the spirit than Bossuet's philosophy of history reflects it; and that there is no more antecedent probability of the Bishop of Durham's stock of ideas being agreeable to perfect reason than of Pope Pius the Ninth's. But criticism will not on that account forget the achievements of Protestantism in the practical and moral sphere; nor that, even in the intellectual sphere, Protestantism, though in a blind and stumbling manner, carried forward the Renascence, while Catholicism threw itself violently across its path.

I lately heard a man of thought and energy contrasting the want of ardour and movement which he now found among young men in this country with what he remembered in his own youth, twenty years ago. 'What reformers we were then!' he exclaimed; 'what a zeal we had! how we canvassed every institution in Church and State, and were prepared to remodel them all on first principles!' He was inclined to regret, as a spiritual flagging, the lull which he saw. I am disposed rather to regard it as a pause in which the turn to a new mode of spiritual progress is being accomplished. Everything was long seen, by the young and ardent among us, in inseparable connection with politics and practical life. We have pretty well exhausted the benefits of seeing things in this connection, we have got all that can be got by so seeing them. Let us try a more disinterested mode of seeing them; let us betake ourselves more to the serener life of the mind and spirit. This life, too, may have its excesses and dangers; but they are not for us at present. Let us think of quietly enlarging our stock of true and fresh ideas, and not, as soon as we get an idea or half an idea, be running out with it into the street, and trying to make it rule there. Our ideas will, in the end, shape the world all the better for maturing a little. Perhaps in fifty years' time it will in the English House of Commons be an objection to an institution that it is an anomaly, and my friend the Member of Parliament will shudder in his grave. But let us in the meanwhile rather endeavour that in twenty years' time it may, in English literature, be an objection to a proposition that it is absurd. That will be a change so vast, that the imagination almost fails to grasp it. *Ab integro sæclorum nascitur ordo.*[22]

If I have insisted so much on the course which criticism must take where politics and religion are concerned, it is because, where these burning matters are in question, it is most likely to go astray. I have wished, above all, to insist on the attitude which criticism should adopt towards things in general; on its right tone and temper of mind. But then comes another question as to the subject-matter which literary criticism should most seek. Here, in general, its course is determined for it by the idea which is the law of its being; the idea of a disinterested endeavour to learn and propagate the best that is known and thought in the world, and thus to establish a current of fresh and true ideas. By the very nature of things, as England is not all the world, much of the best that is known and thought in the world cannot be of English growth, must be foreign; by the nature of things, again, it is just this that we are least likely to know, while English thought is streaming in upon us from all sides, and takes excellent care that we shall not be ignorant of its existence. The English critic of literature, therefore, must dwell much on foreign thought, and with particular heed on any part of it, which, while significant and fruitful in itself, is for any reason specially likely to escape him. Again, judging is often spoken of as the critic's one business; and so in some sense it is; but the judgment which almost insensibly forms itself in a fair and clear mind, along with fresh knowledge, is the valuable one; and thus knowledge, and ever fresh knowledge, must be the critic's great concern for himself. And it is by communicating fresh knowledge, and letting his own judgment pass along with it, – but insensibly, and in the second place, not the first, as a sort of companion and clue, not as an abstract lawgiver, – that the critic will generally do most good to his readers. Sometimes, no doubt, for the sake of establishing an author's place in literature, and his relation to a central standard (and if this is not done, how are we to get at our *best in the world?*) criticism may have to deal with a subject-matter so familiar that fresh knowledge is out of the question, and then it must be all judgment; an enunciation and detailed application of principles. Here the great safeguard is never to let oneself become abstract, always to retain an intimate and lively consciousness of the truth of what one is saying, and, the moment this fails us, to be sure that something is wrong. Still, under all circumstances, this mere judgment and application of principles is, in itself, not the most satisfactory work to the critic; like mathematics, it is tautological, and cannot well give us, like fresh learning, the sense of creative activity.

But stop, some one will say; all this talk is of no practical use to us whatever; this criticism of yours is not what we have in our minds when we speak of criticism; when we speak of critics and criticism, we mean critics and criticism of the current English literature of the day; when you offer to tell criticism its function, it is to this criticism that we expect you to address yourself. I am sorry for it, for I am afraid I must disappoint these expectations. I am bound by my own definition of criticism: *a disinterested endeavour to learn and propagate the best that is known and thought in the world*. How much of current English literature comes into this 'best that is known and thought in the world'? Not very much, I fear; certainly less, at this moment, than of the current literature of France or Germany. Well, then, am I to alter my definition of criticism, in order to meet the requirements of a number of practising English critics, who, after all, are free in their choice of a business? That would be making criticism lend itself just to one of those alien practical considerations, which, I have said, are so fatal to it. One may say, indeed, to those who have to deal with the mass – so much better disregarded – of current English literature, that they may at all events endeavour, in dealing with this, to try it, so far as they can, by the standard of the best that is known and thought in the world; one may say, that to get anywhere near this standard, every critic should try and possess one great literature, at least, besides his own; to the more unlike his own, the better. But, after all, the criticism I am really concerned with, – the criticism which alone can much help us for the future, the criticism which, throughout Europe, is at the present day meant, when so much stress is laid on the importance of criticism and the critical spirit, – is a criticism which regards Europe as being, for intellectual and spiritual purposes, one great confederation, bound to a joint action and working to a common result; and whose members have, for their proper outfit, a knowledge of Greek, Roman, and Eastern antiquity, and of one another. Special, local, and temporary advantages being put out of account, that modern nation will in the intellectual and spiritual sphere make most progress, which most thoroughly carries out this programme. And what is that but saying that we too, all of us, as individuals, the more thoroughly we carry it out, shall make the more progress?

There is so much inviting us! – what are we to take? what will nourish us in growth towards perfection? That is the question which, with the immense field of life and of literature lying before him, the critic has to answer; for himself first, and afterwards for others. In this idea of the critic's business the essays brought together in the following pages have had their origin; in this idea, widely different as are their subjects, they have, perhaps, their unity.

I conclude with what I said at the beginning: to have the sense of creative activity is the great happiness and the great proof of being alive, and it is not denied to criticism to have it; but then criticism must be sincere, simple, flexible, ardent, ever widening its knowledge. Then it may have, in no contemptible measure, a joyful sense of creative activity; a sense which a man of insight and conscience will prefer to what he might derive from a poor, starved, fragmentary, inadequate creation. And at some epochs no other creation is possible.

Still, in full measure, the sense of creative activity belongs only to genuine creation; in literature we must never forget that. But what true man of letters ever can forget it? It is no such common matter for a gifted nature to come into possession of a current of true and living ideas, and to produce amidst the inspiration of them, that we are likely to underrate it. The epochs of Æschylus and Shakespeare make us feel their preeminence. In an epoch like those is, no doubt, the true life of a literature; there is the promised land, towards which criticism can only beckon. That promised land it will not be ours to enter, and we shall die in the wilderness: but to have desired to enter it, to have saluted it from afar, is already, perhaps, the best distinction among contemporaries; it will certainly be the best title to esteem with posterity.

From MAURICE DE GUÉRIN

'The Grand Power of Poetry'

... The grand power of poetry is its interpretative power; by which I mean, not a power of drawing out in black and white an explanation of the mystery of the universe, but the power of so dealing with things as to awaken in us a wonderfully full, new, and intimate sense of them, and of our relations with them. When this sense is awakened in us, as to objects without us, we feel ourselves to be in contact with the essential nature of those objects, to be no longer bewildered and oppressed by them, but to have their secret, and to be in harmony with them; and this feeling calms and satisfies us as no other can. Poetry, indeed, interprets in another way besides this; but one of its two ways of interpreting, of exercising its highest power, is by awakening this sense in us. I will not now inquire whether this sense is illusive, whether it can be proved not to be illusive, whether it does absolutely make us possess the real nature of things; all I say is, that poetry can awaken it in us, and that to awaken it is one of the highest powers of poetry. The interpretations of science do not give us this intimate sense of objects as the interpretations of poetry give it; they appeal to a limited faculty, and not to the whole man. It is not Linnæus, or Cavendish, or Cuvier[1] who gives us the true sense of animals, or water, or plants, who seizes their secret for us, who makes us participate in their life; it is Shakespeare, with his

> 'daffodils
> That come before the swallow dares, and take
> The winds of March with beauty;'[2]

it is Wordsworth, with his

> 'voice ... heard
> In spring-time from the cuckoo-bird,
> Breaking the silence of the seas
> Among the farthest Hebrides;'[3]

it is Keats, with his

> 'moving waters at their priestlike task
> Of cold ablution round Earth's human shores;'[4]

it is Chateaubriand, with his *'cîme indéterminée des forêts;'*[5] it is Senancour,[6] with his mountain birch-tree: *'Cette écorce blanche, lisse et crevassée; cette tige agreste; ces branches qui s'inclinent vers la terre; la mobilité des feuilles, et tout cet abandon, simplicité de la nature, attitude des déserts.'*

Eminent manifestations of this magical power of poetry are very rare and very precious: the compositions of Guérin manifest it. I think, in singular eminence. Not his poems, strictly so called – his verse – so much as his prose; his poems in general take for their vehicle that favourite metre of French poetry, the Alexandrine; and, in my judgment, I confess they have thus, as compared with his prose, a great disadvantage to start with. In prose, the character of the vehicle for the composer's thoughts is not determined beforehand; every composer has to make his own vehicle; and who has ever done this more admirably than the great prose-writers of France, – Pascal, Bossuet, Fénelon, Voltaire? But in verse the composer has (with comparatively narrow liberty of modification) to accept his vehicle ready-made; it is, therefore, of vital importance to him that he should find at his disposal a vehicle adequate to convey the highest matters of poetry . . .

From HEINRICH HEINE

'Philistinism and the Modern Spirit'

. . . Modern times find themselves with an immense system of institutions, established facts, accredited dogmas, customs, rules, which have come to them from times not modern. In this system their life has to be carried forward; yet they have a sense that this system is not of their own creation, that it by no means corresponds exactly with the wants of their actual life, that, for them, it is customary, not rational. The awakening of this sense is the awakening of the modern spirit. The modern spirit is now awake almost everywhere; the sense of want of correspondence between the forms of modern Europe and its spirit, between the new wine of the eighteenth and nineteenth centuries, and the old bottles of the eleventh and twelfth centuries, or even of the sixteenth and seventeeth, almost everyone now perceives; it is no longer dangerous to affirm that this want of correspondence exists; people are even beginning to be shy of denying it. To remove this want of correspondence is beginning to be the settled endeavour of most persons of good sense. Dissolvents of the old European system of dominant ideas and facts we must all be, all of us who have any power of working; what we have to study is that we may not be acrid dissolvents of it.

And how did Goethe, that grand dissolvent in an age when there were fewer of them than at present, proceed in his task of dissolution, of liberation of the modern European from the old routine? He shall tell us himself. 'Through me the German poets have become aware that, as man must live from within outwards, so the artist must work from within outwards, seeing that, make what contortions he will, he can only bring to light his own individuality. I can clearly mark where this influence of mine has made itself felt; there arises out of it a kind of poetry of nature, and only in this way is it possible to be original.'

My voice shall never be joined to those which decry Goethe, and if it is said that the foregoing is a lame and impotent conclusion to Goethe's declaration that he had been the liberator of the Germans in general, and of the young German poets in particular, I say it is not. Goethe's profound, imperturbable naturalism is absolutely fatal to all routine thinking; he puts the standard, once for all, inside every man instead of outside him; when he is told, such a thing must be so, there is immense authority and custom in favour of its being so, it has been held to be so for a thousand years, he answers with Olympian politeness, 'But *is* it so? is it so to *me*?' Nothing could be more really subversive of the foundations on which the old European order rested; and it may be remarked that no persons are so radically detached from this order, no persons so thoroughly modern, as those who have felt Goethe's influence most deeply. If it is said that Goethe professes to have in this way deeply influenced but a few persons, and those persons poets, one may answer that he could have taken no better way to secure, in the end, the ear of the world; for poetry is simply the most beautiful, impressive, and widely effective mode of saying things, and hence its importance. Nevertheless the process of liberation, as Goethe worked it, though sure, is undoubtedly slow; he came, as Heine says, to be eighty years old in thus working it, and at the end of that time the old Middle-Age machine was still creaking on, the thirty German courts and their chamberlains subsisted in all their glory; Goethe himself was a minister, and the visible triumph of the modern spirit over prescription and routine seemed as far off as ever. It was the year 1830; the German sovereigns had passed the preceding fifteen years in breaking the promises of freedom they had made to their subjects when they wanted their help in the final struggle with Napoleon. Great events were happening in France; the revolution, defeated in 1815, had arisen from its defeat, and was wresting from its adversaries the power. Heinrich Heine, a young man of genius, born at Hamburg, and with all the culture of Germany, but by race a Jew; with warm sympathies for France, whose Revolution had given to his race the rights of citizenship, and whose rule had been, as is well known, popular in the Rhine provinces, where he passed his youth; with a passionate admiration for the great French Emperor, with a passionate contempt for the sovereigns who had overthrown him, for their agents, and for their policy, – Heinrich Heine was in 1830 in no humour for any such gradual process of liberation from the old order of things as that which Goethe had followed. His counsel was for open war. Taking that terrible modern weapon, the pen, in his hand, he passed the remainder of his life in one fierce battle. What was that battle? the reader will ask. It was a life and death battle with Philistinism.

Philistinism! – we have not the expression in English.

Perhaps we have not the word because we have so much of the thing. At Soli,[1] I imagine, they did not talk of solecisms; and here, at the very head-quarters of Goliath, nobody talks of Philistinism.[2] The French have adopted the term *épicier* (grocer), to designate the sort of being whom the Germans designate by the term Philistine; but the French term, – besides that it casts a slur upon a respectable class, composed of living and susceptible members, while the original Philistines are dead and buried long ago, – is really, I think, in itself much less apt and expressive than the German term. Efforts have been made to obtain in English some term equivalent to *Philister* or *épicier*; Mr Carlyle has made several such efforts: 'respectability with its thousand gigs,'[3] he says; – well, the occupant of every one of these gigs is, Mr Carlyle means, a Philistine. However, the word *respectable* is far too valuable a word to be thus perverted from its proper meaning; if the English are ever to have a word for the thing we are speaking of, – and so prodigious are the changes which the modern spirit is introducing, that even we English shall perhaps one day come to want such a word, – I think we had much better take the term *Philistine* itself.

Philistine must have originally meant, in the mind of those who invented the nickname, a strong, dogged, unenlightened opponent of the chosen people, of the children of the light. The party of change, the would-be remodellers of the old traditional European order, the invokers of reason against custom, the representatives of the modern spirit in every sphere where it is applicable, regarded themselves, with the robust self-confidence natural to reformers as a chosen people, as children of the light. They regarded their adversaries as humdrum people, slaves to routine, enemies to light; stupid and oppressive, but at the same time very strong. This explains the love which Heine, that Paladin of the modern spirit, has for France; it explains the preference which he gives to France over Germany: 'the French,' he says, 'are the chosen people of the new religion, its first gospels and dogmas have been drawn up in their language; Paris is the new Jerusalem, and the Rhine is the Jordan which divides the consecrated land of freedom from the land of the Philistines.' He means that the French, as a people, have shown more accessibility to ideas than any other people; that prescription and routine have had less hold upon them than upon any other people; that they have shown most readiness to move and to alter at the bidding (real or supposed) of reason. This explains, too, the detestation which Heine had for the English: 'I might settle in England,' he says, in his exile, 'if it were not that I should find there two things, coal-smoke and Englishmen; I cannot abide either.' What he hated in the English was the 'äch-brittische Beschränktheit,' as he calls it, – the *genuine British narrowness*. In truth, the English, profoundly as they have modified the old Middle-Age order, great as is the liberty which they have secured for themselves, have in all their changes proceeded, to use a familiar expression, by the rule of thumb; what was intolerably inconvenient to them they have suppressed, and as they have suppressed it, not because it was irrational, but because it was practically inconvenient, they have seldom in suppressing it appealed to reason, but always, if possible, to some precedent, or form, or letter, which served as a convenient instrument for their purpose, and which saved them from the necessity of recurring to general principles. They have thus become, in a certain sense, of all people the most inaccessible to ideas and the most impatient of them; inaccessible to them, because of their want of familiarity with them; and impatient of them because they have got on so well without them, that they despise those who, not having got on as well as themselves, still make a fuss for what they themselves have done so well without. But there has certainly followed from hence, in this country, somewhat of a general depression of pure intelligence: Philistia has come to be thought by us the true Land of Promise, and it is anything but that; the born lover of ideas, the born hater of commonplaces, must feel in this country, that the sky over his head is of brass and iron. The enthusiast for the idea, for reason, values reason, the idea, in and for themselves; he values them, irrespectively of the practical conveniences which their triumph may obtain for him; and the man who regards the possession of these practical conveniences as something sufficient in itself, something which compensates for the absence or surrender of the idea, of reason, is, in his eyes, a

Philistine. This is why Heine so often and so mercilessly attacks the liberals; much as he hates conservatism he hates Philistinism even more, and whoever attacks conservatism itself ignobly, not as a child of light, not in the name of the idea, is a Philistine. Our Cobbett is thus for him, much as he disliked our clergy and aristocracy whom Cobbett attacked, a Philistine with six fingers on every hand and on every foot six toes, four-and-twenty in number: a Philistine, the staff of whose spear is like a weaver's beam. Thus he speaks of him: –

'While I translate Cobbett's words, the man himself comes bodily before my mind's eye, as I saw him at that uproarious dinner at the Crown and Anchor Tavern, with his scolding red face and his radical laugh, in which venomous hate mingles with a mocking exultation at his enemies' surely approaching downfall. He is a chained cur, who falls with equal fury on everyone whom he does not know, often bites the best friend of the house in his calves, barks incessantly, and just because of this incessantness of his barking cannot get listened to, even when he barks at a real thief. Therefore, the distinguished thieves who plunder England do not think it necessary to throw the growling Cobbett a bone to stop his mouth. This makes the dog furiously savage, and he shows all his hungry teeth. Poor old Cobbett! England's dog! I have no love for thee, for every vulgar nature my soul abhors: but thou touchest me to the inmost soul with pity, as I see how thou strainest in vain to break loose and to get at those thieves, who make off with their booty before thy very eyes, and mock at thy fruitless springs and thine impotent howling.'

There is balm in Philistia as well as in Gilead.[4] A chosen circle of children of the modern spirit, perfectly emancipated from prejudice and commonplace, regarding the ideal side of things in all its efforts for change, passionately despising half-measures and condescension to human folly and obstinacy, – with a bewildered, timid, torpid multitude behind, – conducts a country to the government of Herr von Bismarck.[5] A nation regarding the practical side of things in its efforts for change, attacking not what is irrational, but what is pressingly inconvenient, and attacking this as one body, 'moving altogether if it move at all,'[6] and treating children of light like the very harshest of step-mothers, comes to the prosperity and liberty of modern England. For all that, however, Philistia (let me say it again) is not the true promised land, as we English commonly imagine it to be; and our excessive neglect of the idea, and consequent inaptitude for it, threatens us, at a moment when the idea is beginning to exercise a real power in human society, with serious future inconvenience, and, in the meanwhile, cuts us off from the sympathy of other nations, which feel its power more than we do . . .

'The Defects of English Romanticism'

We in England, in our great burst of literature during the first thirty years of the present century, had no manifestation of the modern spirit, as this spirit manifests itself in Goethe's works or Heine's. And the reason is not far to seek. We had neither the German wealth of ideas, nor the French enthusiasm for applying ideas. There reigned in the mass of the nation that inveterate inaccessibility to ideas, that Philistinism – to use the German nickname – which reacts even on the individual genius that is exempt from it. In our greatest literary epoch, that of the Elizabethan age, English society at large was accessible to ideas, was permeated by them, was vivified by them, to a degree which has never been reached in England since. Hence the unique greatness in English literature of Shakespeare and his contemporaries. They were powerfully upheld by the intellectual life of their nation; they applied freely in literature the then modern ideas, – ideas of the Renascence and the Reformation. A few years afterwards the great English middle class, the kernel of the nation, the class whose intelligent sympathy had upheld a Shakespeare, entered the prison of Puritanism, and had the key turned on its spirit there for two hundred years. *He enlargeth a nation,* says Job, *and straiteneth it again.*[7]

In the literary movement of the beginning of the nineteenth century the signal attempt to apply freely the modern spirit was made in England by two members of the aristocratic class, Byron and Shelley. Aristocracies are, as such, naturally impenetrable by ideas; but their individual members have a high courage and a turn for breaking bounds; and a man of genius, who is the born child of the idea, happening to be born in the aristocratic ranks, chafes against the obstacles which prevent him from freely developing it. But Byron and Shelley did not succeed in their attempt freely to apply the modern spirit in English literature; they could not succeed in it; the resistance to baffle them, the want of intelligent sympathy to guide and uphold them, were too great. Their literary creation, compared with the literary creation of Shakespeare and Spenser, compared with the literary creation of Goethe and Heine, is a failure. The best literary creation of that time in England proceeded from men who did not make the same bold attempt as Byron and Shelley. What, in fact, was the career of the chief English men of letters, their contemporaries? The gravest of them, Wordsworth, retired (in Middle-Age phrase) into a monastery. I mean, he plunged himself in the inward life, he voluntarily cut himself off from the modern spirit. Coleridge took to opium. Scott became the historiographer royal of feudalism. Keats passionately gave himself up to a sensuous genius, to his faculty for interpreting nature; and he died of consumption at twenty-five. Wordsworth, Scott, and Keats have left admirable works; far more solid and complete works than those which Byron and Shelley have left. But their works have this defect; – they do not belong to that which is the main current of the literature of modern epochs, they do not apply modern ideas to life; they constitute, therefore, *minor currents,* and all other literary work of our day, however popular, which has the same defect, also constitutes but a minor current. Byron and Shelley will long be remembered, long after the inadequacy of their actual work is clearly recognized, for their passionate, their Titanic effort to flow in the main stream of modern literature; their names will be greater than their writings; *stat magni nominis umbra.*[8]

Heine's literary good fortune was superior to that of Byron and Shelley. His theatre of operations was Germany, whose Philistinism does not consist in her want of ideas, or in her inaccessibility to ideas, for she teems with them and loves them, but, as I have said, in her feeble and hesitating application of modern ideas to life. Heine's intense modernism, his absolute freedom, his utter rejection of stock classicism and stock romanticism, his bringing all things under the point of view of the nineteenth century, were understood and laid to heart by Germany, through virtue of her immense, tolerant intellectualism, much as there was in all Heine said to affront and wound Germany. The wit and ardent modern spirit of France Heine joined to the culture, the sentiment, the thought of Germany. This is what makes him so remarkable; his wonderful clearness, lightness, and freedom, united with such power of feeling, and width of range . . .

From JOUBERT

'Joubert and Coleridge'

. . . I have likened Joubert to Coleridge; and indeed the points of resemblance between the two men are numerous. Both of them great and celebrated talkers, Joubert attracting pilgrims to his upper chamber in the Rue St-Honoré, as Coleridge attracted pilgrims to Mr Gilman's at Highgate; both of them desultory and incomplete writers, – here they had an outward likeness with one another. Both of them passionately devoted to reading in a class of books, and to thinking on a class of subjects, out of the beaten line of the reading and thought of their day; both of them ardent students and critics of old literature, poetry, and the metaphysics of religion; both of them curious explorers of words, and of the latent significance hidden under the popular use of them; both of them, in a certain sense, conservative in religion and politics, by antipathy to the narrow and shallow foolishness of vulgar modern liberalism; – here they had their inward and real likeness. But that in which the essence of their likeness consisted is this, – that they both had from nature an ardent impulse for seeking the genuine truth on all matters they thought about, and a gift for finding it and recognizing it when it was found. To have the impulse for

seeking this truth is much rarer than most people think; to have
the gift for finding it is, I need not say, very rare indeed. By this
they have a spiritual relationship of the closest kind with one
another, and they become, each of them, a source of stimulus
and progress for all of us.

Coleridge had less delicacy and penetration than Joubert, but
more richness and power; his production, though far inferior to
what his nature at first seemed to promise, was abundant and
varied. Yet in all his production how much is there to dissatisfy
us! How many reserves must be made in praising either his
poetry, or his criticism, or his philosophy! How little either of
his poetry, or of his criticism, or of his philosophy, can we expect
permanently to stand! But that which will stand of Coleridge is
this: the stimulus of his continual effort, – not a moral effort, for
he had no morals, – but of his continual instinctive effort,
crowned often with rich success, to get at and to lay bare the
real truth of his matter in hand, whether that matter were literary, or philosophical, or political, or religious; and this in
a country where at that moment such an effort was almost
unknown; where the most powerful minds threw themselves upon
poetry, which conveys truth, indeed, but conveys it indirectly; and
where ordinary minds were so habituated to do without thinking
altogether, to regard considerations of established routine and
practical convenience as paramount, that any attempt to introduce within the domain of these the disturbing element of thought,
they were prompt to resent as an outrage. Coleridge's great usefulness lay in his supplying in England, for many years and under
critical circumstances, by the spectacle of this effort of his, a stimulus to all minds capable of profiting by it; in the generation which
grew up around him.[1] His action will still be felt as long as the need
for it continues. When, with the cessation of the need, the action
too has ceased, Coleridge's memory, in spite of the disesteem –
nay, repugnance – which his character may and must inspire, will
yet for ever remain invested with that interest and gratitude which
invests the memory of founders . . .

. . . There is, however, in France a sympathy with intellectual activity for its own sake, and for the sake of its inherent

pleasurableness and beauty, keener than any which exists in England; and Joubert had more effect in Paris, – though his conversation was his only weapon, and Coleridge wielded besides his conversation his pen, – than Coleridge had or could have in London. I mean, a more immediate, appreciable effect; an effect not only upon the young and enthusiastic, to whom the future belongs, but upon formed and important personages to whom the present belongs, and who are actually moving society. He owed this partly to his real advantages over Coleridge. If he had, as I have already said, less power and richness than his English parallel, he had more tact and penetration. He was more *possible* than Coleridge; his doctrine was more intelligible than Coleridge's, more receivable . . .

'The Power of Common Words'

. . . And yet with Joubert, the striving after a consummate and attractive clearness of expression came from no mere frivolous dislike of labour and inability for going deep, but was a part of his native love of truth and perfection. The delight of his life he found in truth, and in the satisfaction which the enjoying of truth gives to the spirit; and he thought the truth was never really and worthily said, so long as the least cloud, clumsiness, and repulsiveness hung about the expression of it.

Some of his best passages are those in which he upholds this doctrine. Even metaphysics he would not allow to remain difficult and abstract: so long as they spoke a professional jargon, the language of the schools, he maintained, – and who shall gainsay him? – that metaphysics were imperfect; or, at any rate, had not yet reached their ideal perfection.

'The true science of metaphysics,' he says, 'consists not in rendering abstract that which is sensible, but in rendering sensible that which is abstract; apparent that which is hidden; imaginable, if so it may be, that which is only intelligible; and intelligible, finally, that which an ordinary attention fails to seize.'

And therefore: –

'Distrust, in books on metaphysics, words which have not

been able to get currency in the world, and are only calculated to form a special language.'

Nor would he suffer common words to be employed in a special sense by the schools: –

'Which is the best, if one wants to be useful and to be really understood, to get one's words in the world, or to get them in the schools? I maintain that the good plan is to employ words in their popular sense rather than in their philosophical sense; and the better plan still, to employ them in their natural sense rather than in their popular sense. By their natural sense, I mean the popular and universal acceptation of them brought to that which in this is essential and invariable. To prove a thing by definition proves nothing, if the definition is purely philo-sophical; for such definitions only bind him who makes them. To prove a thing by definition, when the definition expresses the necessary, inevitable, and clear idea which the world at large attaches to the object, is, on the contrary, all in all; because then what one does is simply to show people what they do really think, in spite of themselves and without knowing it. The rule that one is free to give to words what sense one will, and that the only thing needful is to be agreed upon the sense one gives them, is very well for the mere purposes of argumenta-tion, and may be allowed in the schools where this sort of fencing is to be practised; but in the sphere of the true-born and noble science of metaphysics, and in the genuine world of lit-erature, it is good for nothing. One must never quit sight of realities, and one must employ one's expressions simply as media, – as glasses, through which one's thoughts can be best made evident. I know, by my own experience, how hard this rule is to follow; but I judge of its importance by the failure of every system of metaphysics. Not one of them has succeeded; for the simple reason, that in every one ciphers have been con-stantly used instead of values, artificial ideas instead of native ideas, jargon instead of idiom.'

I do not know whether the metaphysician will ever adopt Joubert's rules; but I am sure that the man of letters, whenever he has to speak of metaphysics, will do well to adopt them. He, at any rate, must remember: –

'It is by means of familiar words that style takes hold of the reader and gets possession of him. It is by means of these that great thoughts get currency and pass for true metal, like gold and silver which have had a recognized stamp put upon them. They beget confidence in the man who, in order to make his thoughts more clearly perceived, uses them; for people feel that such an employment of the language of common human life betokens a man who knows that life and its concerns, and who keeps himself in contact with them. Besides, these words make a style frank and easy. They show that an author has long made the thought or the feeling expressed his mental food; that he has so assimilated them and familiarized them, that the most common expressions suffice him in order to express ideas which have become every-day ideas to him by the length of time they have been in his mind. And lastly, what one says in such words looks more true; for, of all the words in use, none are so clear as those which we call common words; and clearness is so eminently one of the characteristics of truth, that often it even passes for truth itself.'

These are not, in Joubert, mere counsels of rhetoric; they come from his accurate sense of perfection, from his having clearly seized the fine and just idea that beauty and light are properties of truth, and that truth is incompletely exhibited if it is exhibited without beauty and light: –

'Be profound with clear terms and not with obscure terms. What is difficult will at last become easy; but as one goes deep into things, one must still keep a charm, and one must carry into these dark depths of thought, into which speculation has only recently penetrated, the pure and antique clearness of centuries less learned than ours, but with more light in them.'

And elsewhere he speaks of those 'spirits, lovers of light, who, when they have an idea to put forth, brood long over it first, and wait patiently till it *shines*, as Buffon enjoined, when he defined genius to be the aptitude for patience; spirits who know by experience that the driest matter and the dullest words hide within them the germ and spark of some brightness, like those fairy nuts in which were found diamonds if one broke the shell and was the right person; spirits who maintain that, to see and exhibit things in beauty, is to see and show things as in their essence they really are, and not as they exist for the eye of the careless, who do not look beyond the outside; spirits hard to satisfy, because of a keen-sightedness in them, which makes them discern but too clearly both the models to be followed and those to be shunned; spirits active though meditative, who cannot rest except in solid truths, and whom only beauty can make happy; spirits far less concerned for glory than for perfection, who, because their art is long and life is short, often die without leaving a monument, having had their own inward sense of life and fruitfulness for their best reward.'

No doubt there is something a little too ethereal in all this, something which reminds one of Joubert's physical want of body and substance; no doubt, if a man wishes to be a great author, it is to consider too curiously, to consider as Joubert did; it is a mistake to spend so much of one's time in setting up one's ideal standard of perfection, and in contemplating it. Joubert himself knew this very well: 'I cannot build a house for my ideas,' said he; 'I have tried to do without words, and words take their revenge on one by their difficulty . . .'

'Literature, a Criticism of Life'

Joubert was not famous while he lived, and he will not be famous now that he is dead. But, before we pity him for this, let us be sure what we mean, in literature, by *famous*. There are the famous men of genius in literature, – the Homers, Dantes, Shakespeares: of them we need not speak; their praise is for ever and ever. Then there are the famous men of ability in literature: their praise is in their own generation. And what makes this difference? The work of the two orders of men is at the bottom the same, – *a criticism of life*. The end and aim of all literature, if one considers it attentively, is, in truth, nothing but that. But the criticism which the men of genius pass upon human life is permanently acceptable to mankind; the criticism which the men of ability pass upon human life is transitorily acceptable. Between Shakespeare's criticism of human life and Scribe's[2] the difference is there; – the one is permanently acceptable, the other transitorily. Whence then, I repeat, this difference? It is that the acceptableness of Shakespeare's criticism depends upon its inherent truth: the acceptableness of Scribe's upon its suiting itself, by its subject-matter, ideas, mode of treatment, to the taste of the generation that hears it. But the taste and ideas of one generation are not those of the next. This next generation in its turn arrives; – first its sharpshooters, its quick-witted, audacious light troops; then the elephantine main body. The imposing array of its predecessor it confidently assails, riddles it with bullets, passes over its body. It goes hard then with many once popular reputations, with many authorities once oracular. Only two kinds of authors are safe in the general havoc. The first kind are the great abounding fountains of truth, whose criticism of life is a source of illumination and joy to the whole human race for ever, – the Homers, the Shakespeares. These are the sacred personages, whom all civilized warfare respects. The second are those whom the out-skirmishers of the new generation, its forerunners, – quick-witted soldiers, as I have said, the select of the army, – recognize, though the bulk of their comrades behind might not, as of the same family and character with the sacred personages, exercising like them an immortal function, and like them inspiring a permanent interest. They snatch them up, and set them in a place of shelter, where the on-coming multitude may not overwhelm them. These are the Jouberts. They will never, like the Shakespeares, command the homage of the multitude; but they are safe; the multitude will not trample them down. Except these two kinds, no author is safe. Let us consider, for example, Joubert's famous contemporary, Lord Jeffrey.[3] All his vivacity and accomplishment avail him nothing; of the true critic he had in an eminent degree no quality, except one, – curiosity. Curiosity he had, but he had no gift for truth; he cannot illuminate and rejoice us; no intelligent out-skirmisher of the new generation cares about him, cares to put him in safety; at this moment we are all passing over his body. Let us consider a greater than Jeffrey, a critic whose reputation still stands firm, – will stand, many people think, for ever, – the great apostle of the Philistines, Lord Macaulay.[4] Lord Macaulay was, as I have already said, a born rhetorician; a splendid rhetorician doubtless, and, beyond that, an *English* rhetorician also, an *honest* rhetorician; still, beyond the apparent rhetorical truth of things he never could pene- trate; for their vital truth, for what the French call the *vraie vérité*, he had absolutely no organ; therefore, his reputation, brilliant as it is, is not secure. Rhetoric so good as his excites and gives pleasure; but by pleasure alone you cannot perman- ently bind men's spirits to you. Truth illuminates and gives joy, and it is by the bond of joy, not of pleasure, that men's spirits are indissolubly held. As Lord Macaulay's own generation dies out, as a new generation arrives, without those ideas and ten- dencies of its predecessor which Lord Macaulay so deeply shared and so happily satisfied, will he give the same pleasure? and, if he ceases to give this, has he enough of light in him to make him last? Pleasure the new generation will get from its own novel ideas and tendencies; but light is another and a rarer thing, and must be treasured wherever it can be found. Will Macaulay be saved, in the sweep and pressure of time, for his light's sake, as Johnson has already been saved by two genera- tions, Joubert by one? I think it very doubtful. But for a spirit of any delicacy and dignity, what a fate, if he could foresee it! to be an oracle for one generation, and then of little or no account for ever. How far better, to pass with scant notice through one's own generation, but to be singled out and pre- served by the very iconoclasts of the next, then in their turn by those of the next, and so, like the lamp of life itself, to be handed on from one generation to another in safety! This is Joubert's lot, and it is a very enviable one. The new men of the new generations, while they let the dust deepen on a thousand Laharpes,[5] will say of him: 'He lived in the Philistine's day, in a place and time when almost every idea current in literature had the mark of Dagon[6] upon it, and not the mark of the children of light. Nay, the children of light were as yet hardly so much as heard of: the Canaanite was then in the land. Still, there were even then a few, who, nourished on some secret tradition, or illumined, perhaps, by a divine inspiration, kept aloof from the reigning superstitions, never bowed the knee to the gods of Canaan; and one of these few was called *Joubert*.'

My Countrymen

About a year ago the *Saturday Review* published an article which gave me, as its articles often do give me, much food for reflection. The article was about the unjust estimate which, says the *Saturday Review,* I form of my countrymen, and about the indecency of talking of 'British Philistines.' It appears that I assume the truth of the transcendental system of philosophy,* and then lecture my wiser countrymen because they will not join me in recognizing as eternal truths a set of platitudes which may be proved to be false. 'Now there is in England a school of philosophy which thoroughly understands, and, on theoretical grounds, deliberately rejects, the philosophical theory which Mr Arnold accuses the English nation of neglecting; and the practical efforts of the English people, especially their practical efforts in the way of criticism, are for the most part strictly in accordance with the principles of that philosophy.'

I do not quite know what to say about the transcendental system of philosophy, for I am a mere dabbler in these great matters, and to grasp and hold a system of philosophy is a feat much beyond my strength; but I certainly did talk about British Philistines, and to call people Philistines when they are doing just what the wisest men in the country have settled to be quite right, does seem unreasonable, not to say indecent. Being really the most teachable man alive, I could not help making, after I had read the article in the *Saturday Review,* a serious return, as the French say, upon myself;[1] and I resolved never to call my

* Philosophy has always been bringing me into trouble. – ED.

countrymen Philistines again till I had thought more about it, and could be quite sure I was not committing an indecency.

I was very much fortified in this good resolution by something else which happened about the same time. Everyone knows that the heart of the English nation is its middle class; there had been a good deal of talk, a year ago, about the education of this class, and I, among others, had imagined it was not good, and that the middle class suffered by its not being better. But Mr Bazley,*² the member for Manchester, who is a kind of representative of this class, made a speech last year at Manchester, the middle-class metropolis, which shook me a good deal. 'During the last few months,' said Mr Bazley, 'there had been a cry that middle-class education ought to receive more attention. He confessed himself very much surprised by the clamour that was raised. He did not think that class need excite the sympathy either of the legislature or the public.' Much to the same effect spoke Mr Miall, another middle-class leader, in the *Nonconformist*:³ 'Middle-class education seems to be the favourite topic of the hour, and we must confess to a feeling of shame at the nonsense which is being uttered on the subject. It might be thought from what is said, that this section of the community, which has done everything else so well, – which has astonished the world by its energy, enterprise, and self-reliance, which is continually striking out new paths of industry and subduing the forces of nature, – cannot, from some mysterious reason, get their children properly educated.' Still more strong were the words of the *Daily News* (I love to range all the evidence in black and white before me, though it tends to my own discomfiture) about the blunder some of us were making: 'All the world knows that the great middle class of this country supplies the mind, the will, and the power for all the great and good things that have to be done, and it is not likely that that class should surrender its powers and privileges in the one case of the training of its own children. How the idea of such a scheme can have occurred to anybody, how it can have been imagined that parents and schoolmasters in the most

* Now Sir Thomas Bazley, Bart. – ED.

independent, and active, and enlightened class of English society,* how it can have been supposed that the class which has done all the great things that have been done in all departments, will beg the Government to send inspectors through its schools, when it can itself command whatever advantages exist, might seem unintelligible but for two or three considerations.' These considerations do not much matter just now; but it is clear how perfectly Mr Bazley's stand was a stand such as it becomes a representative man like Mr Bazley to make, and how well the *Daily Telegraph* might say of the speech: 'It was at once grand, genial, national, and distinct;' and the *Morning Star* of the speaker: 'He talked to his constituents as Manchester people like to be talked to, in the language of clear, manly intelligence, which penetrates through sophisms, ignores commonplaces, and gives to conventional illusions their true value. His speech was thoroughly instinct with that earnest good sense which characterizes Manchester, and which, indeed, may be fairly set down as the general characteristic of England and Englishmen everywhere.'

Of course if Philistinism is characteristic of the British nation just now, it must in a special way be characteristic of the representative part of the British nation, the part by which the British nation is what it is, and does all its best things, the middle class. And the newspapers, who have so many more means than I of knowing the truth, and who have that trenchant authoritative style for communicating it which makes so great an impression, say that the British middle class is characterized, not by Philistinism, but by enlightenment; by a passion for penetrating through sophisms, ignoring commonplaces, and giving to conventional illusions their true value. Evidently it is nonsense, as the *Daily News* says, to think that this great middle class which supplies the mind, the will, and the power for all the great and good things that have to be done, should want its schools, the nurseries of its admirable intelligence, meddled with. It may

---

* How very fine and striking is this language! Eloquent as is the homage which our newspapers still pay in the same quarter, it seems as if, in 1866, their eulogy had a ring and fulness which it has since in some measure lost. – ED.

easily be imagined that all this, coming on the top of the *Satur-day Review*'s rebuke of me for indecency, was enough to set me meditating; and after a long and painful self-examination, I saw that I had been making a great mistake. Instead of confin-ing myself to what alone I had any business with, – the slow and obscure work of trying to understand things, to see them as they are, – I had been meddling with practice, proposing this and that, saying how it might be if we established this or that. So I was suffering deservedly in being taunted with hawking about my nostrums of State schools for a class much too wise to want them, and of an Academy for people who have an inimitable style already. To be sure, I had said that schools ought to be things of local, not State, institution and manage-ment, and that we ought not to have an Academy;[4] but that makes no difference. I saw what danger I had been running by thus intruding into a sphere where I have no business, and I resolved to offend in this way no more.

This I say as a sincere penitent; but I do not see that there is any harm in my still trying to know and understand things, if I keep humbly to that, and do not meddle with greater matters, which are out of my reach. So having once got into my head this notion of British Philistinism and of the want of clear and large intelligence in our middle class, I do not consider myself bound at once to put away and crush such a notion, as people are told to do with their religious doubts; nor, when the *Satur-day Review* tells me that no nation in the world is so logical as the English nation, and the *Morning Star,* that our grand national characteristic is a clear intelligence which penetrates through sophisms, ignores commonplaces, and gives to con-ventional illusions their true value, do I feel myself compelled to receive these propositions with absolute submission as articles of faith, transcending reason; indeed, this would be transcendentalism, which the *Saturday Review* condemns. Canvass them, then, as mere matters of speculation, I may; and having lately had occasion to travel on the Continent for many months,[5] during which I was thrown in company with a great variety of people, I remembered what Burns says of the profita-bleness of trying to see ourselves as others see us,[6] and I kept on the watch for anything to confirm or contradict my old notion, in which, without absolutely giving it up, I had begun certainly to be much shaken and staggered.

I must say that the foreign opinion about us is not at all like that of the *Saturday Review* and the *Morning Star.* I know how madly the foreigners envy us, and that this must warp their judgment;[7] I know, too, that this test of foreign opinion can never be decisive; I only take it for what it is worth, and as a contribution to our study of the matter in question. But I do really think that the admirers of our great middle class, which has, as its friends and enemies both agree, risen into such preponderating importance of late years, and now returns the House of Commons, dictates the policy of Ministers, makes the newspapers speak with its voice, and in short governs the country, – I do think, I say, the admirers of this great class would be astounded if they could hear how cavalierly a foreigner treats this country of their making and managing. 'It is not so much that we dislike England,' a Prussian official,* with the graceful tact of his nation, said to me the other day, 'as that we think little of her.' The *Cologne Gazette,* perhaps the chief newspaper of Germany, published in the summer a series of letters, much esteemed, I believe, by military men, on the armies of the leading Continental powers. The writer was a German officer, but not a Prussian. Speaking of the false military system followed by the Emperor Nicholas, whose great aim was to turn his soldiers into perfectly drilled machines, and contrasting this with the free play left to the individual soldier in the French system: 'In consequence of their purely mechanical training,' says this writer, 'the Russians, in spite of their splendid courage, were in the Crimean war constantly beaten by the French, nay, decidedly beaten *even by the English and the Turks.*'† Hardly a German newspaper can discuss territorial changes in Europe but it will add, after its remarks on the probable policy of France in this or that event: 'England will probably make a fuss, but what England thinks is of no importance.' I believe

* Not Arminius. – ED.
† 'Ja, selbst von den Engländern und Türkern entschieden geschlagen.'

the German newspapers must keep a phrase of that kind stereotyped, they use it so often. France is our very good friend
just now,[8] but at bottom our 'clear intelligence penetrating
through sophisms,' and so on, is not held in much more esteem
there than in Germany. One of the gravest and most moderate
of French newspapers, – a newspaper, too, our very good friend,
like France herself, into the bargain, – broke out lately, when
some jealousy of the proposed Cholera Commission in the East
was shown on this side the water, in terms which, though less
rough than the 'great fool' of the *Saturday Review,* were still
far from flattering.[9] 'Let us speak to these English the only
language they can comprehend. England lives for her trade;
Cholera interrupts trade; therefore it is for England's interest
to join in precautions against Cholera.'*

Compliments of this sort are displeasing to remember, displeasing to repeat; but their abundance strikes the attention;
and then the happy unconsciousness of those at whom they are
aimed, their state of imperturbable self-satisfaction, strikes the
attention too, and makes an inquisitive mind quite eager to see
its way clearly in this apparent game of cross purposes. For
never, surely, was there such a game of cross purposes played.
It came to its height when Lord Palmerston died the other day.[10]
Lord Palmerston was England; 'the best type of our age and
country,' the *Times* well called him; he was 'a great representative man, emphatically the English Minister;' the interpreter of
the wishes of that great middle class of this country which supplies the mind, the will, and the power requisite for all the great
and good things that have to be done, and therefore 'acknow-
ledged by a whole people as their best impersonation.' Monsieur
Thiers says of Pitt, that though he used and abused the strength
of England, she was the second country in the world at the time
of his death, and the first eight years afterwards. That was
after Waterloo and the triumphs of Wellington. And that era of
primacy and triumphs, Lord Palmerston, say the English newspapers, has carried on to this hour. 'What Wellington was as a

* Poor France! As Mr Bottles says, neither her favourable nor her unfavourable criticisms are of much consequence just now. – ED.

soldier, this was Palmerston as a statesman.' When I read these words in some foreign city or other, I could not help rubbing my eyes and asking myself if I was dreaming. Why, taking Lord Palmerston's career from 1830 (when he first became Foreign Secretary) to his death, there cannot be a shadow of doubt, for any one with eyes and ears in his head, that he found England the first Power in the world's estimation, and that he leaves her the third, after France* and the United States. I am no politician; I mean no disparagement at all to Lord Palmerston, to whose talents and qualities I hope I can do justice; and indeed it is not Lord Palmerston's policy, or any minister's policy, that is in question here, it is the policy of all of us, it is the policy of England; for in a government such as ours is at present, it is only, as we are so often reminded, by interpreting public opinion, by being 'the best type of his age and country,' that a minister governs; and Lord Palmerston's greatness lay precisely in our all 'acknowledging him as our best impersonation.' Well, then, to this our logic, our practical efforts in the way of criticism, our clear manly intelligence penetrating through sophisms and ignoring commonplaces, and above all, our redoubtable phalanx possessing these advantages in the highest degree, our great middle class, which makes Parliament, and which supplies the mind, the will, and the power requisite for all the great and good things that have to be done, have brought us; to the third place in the world's estimation, instead of the first. He who disbelieves it, let him go round to every embassy in Europe and ask if it is not true.

The foreigners, indeed, are in no doubt as to the real authors of the policy of modern England; they know that ours is no longer a policy of Pitts and aristocracies,† disposing of every movement of the hoodwinked nation to whom they dictate it; they know that our policy is now dictated by the strong middle part of England, – England happy, as Mr Lowe,[12] quoting Aristotle, says, in having her middle part strong and her extremes weak; and that, though we are administered by one of our

---

* Heu incredibiles humanarum rerum mutationes! – ED.[11]
† Arminius; he says it over again in his last letter but one. – ED.

weak extremes, the aristocracy, these managers administer us, as a weak extreme naturally must, with a nervous attention to the wishes of the strong middle part, whose agents they are. It was not the aristocracy which made the Crimean war; it was the strong middle part – the constituencies. It was the strong middle part which showered abuse and threats on Germany for mishandling Denmark;[13] and when Germany gruffly answered, *Come and stop us,* slapped its pockets, and vowed that it had never had the slightest notion of pushing matters so far as this. It was the strong middle part which, by the voice of its favourite newspapers, kept threatening Germany, after she had snapped her fingers at us, with a future chastisement from France, just as a smarting school-boy threatens his bully with a drubbing to come from some big boy in the background. It was the strong middle part, speaking through the same newspapers, which was full of coldness, slights, and sermons for the American Federals during their late struggle;[14] and as soon as they had succeeded, discovered that it had always wished them well, and that nothing was so much to be desired as that the United States, and we, should be the fastest friends possible. Some people will say that the aristocracy was an equal offender in this respect: very likely: but the behaviour of the strong middle part makes more impression than the behaviour of a weak extreme; and the more so, because from the middle class, their fellows in numberless ways, the Americans expected sympathy, while from the aristocracy they expected none. And, in general, the faults with which foreigners reproach us in the matters named, – rash engagement, intemperate threatening, undignified retreat, ill-timed cordiality, – are not the faults of an aristocracy, by nature in such concerns prudent, reticent, dignified, sensitive on the point of honour; they are rather the faults of a rich middle class, – testy, absolute, ill-acquainted with foreign matters, a little ignoble, very dull to perceive when it is making itself ridiculous.

I know the answer one gets at home when one says that England is not very highly considered just now on the Continent. There is first of all the envy to account for it, – that of course; and then our clear intelligence is making a radical change in

our way of dealing with the Continent; the old, bad, aristocratical policy of incessantly intermeddling with the affairs of
the Continent, – this it is getting rid of; it is leaving the miserable
foreigners to themselves, to their wars, despotisms, bureaucracy,
and hatred of free, prosperous England. A few inconveniences
may arise before the transition from our old policy to our
new is fairly accomplished, and we quite leave off the habit of
meddling where our own interests are not at stake. We may be
exposed to a little mortification in the passage, but our clear
intelligence will discern any occasion where our interests are
really at stake. Then we shall come forward and prove ourselves
as strong as ever; and the foreigners, in spite of their envy,
know it. But what strikes me so much in all which these foreigners say is, that it is just this clear intelligence of ours that
they appear at the present moment to hold cheap. Englishmen
are often heard complaining of the little gratitude foreign
nations show them for their sympathy, their good-will. The
reason is, that the foreigners think that an Englishman's good-
will to a foreign cause, or dislike to it, is never grounded in a
perception of its real merits and bearings, but in some chance
circumstance. They say the Englishman never, in these cases,
really comprehends the situation, and so they can never feel
him to be in living sympathy with them. I have got into much
trouble for calling my countrymen Philistines, and all through
these remarks I am determined never to use that word; but I
wonder if there can be anything offensive in calling one's countryman a young man from the country. I hope not; and if not, I
should say, for the benefit of those who have seen Mr John
Parry's amusing entertainment,[15] that England and Englishmen,
holding forth on some great crisis in a foreign country, – Poland,
say, or Italy, – are apt to have on foreigners very much the effect
of the young man from the country who talks to the nursemaid
after she has upset the perambulator. There is a terrible crisis,
and the discourse of the young man from the country, excellent
in itself, is felt not to touch the crisis vitally. Nevertheless, on he
goes; the perambulator lies a wreck, the child screams, the
nursemaid wrings her hands, the old gentleman storms, the
policeman gesticulates, the crowd thickens; still, that astonishing

young man talks on, serenely unconscious that he is not at the centre of the situation.

Happening to be much thrown with certain foreigners, who criticized England in this sort of way, I used often to think what a short and ready way one of our hard-hitting English newspapers would take with these scorners, if they fell into its hands. But being myself a meer seeker for truth, with nothing trenchant or authoritative about me, I could do more than look shocked and begin to ask questions. 'What!' I said, 'you hold the England of today cheap, and declare that we do not comprehend the situation; yet you rate the England of 1815 so high, and call our fathers and grandfathers the foremost people in Europe. Did they comprehend the situation better than we?' 'Yes,' replied my foreign friends, 'the situation as they had it, a great deal better. Their time was a time for energy, and they succeeded in it, perfectly. Our time is a time for intelligence, and you are not succeeding in it at all.'

Though I could not hear without a shudder this insult to the earnest good sense which, as the *Morning Star* says, may be fairly set down as the general characteristic of England and Englishmen everywhere, yet I pricked up my ears when my companions talked of energy, and England's success in a time for energy, because I have always had a notion myself that energy, – energy with honesty, – is England's great force; a greater force to her, even, than her talent for penetrating through sophisms and ignoring commonplaces; so I begged my acquaintances to explain a little more fully to me what they meant. 'Nothing can be clearer,' they answered. 'Your *Times* was telling you the other day, with the enlightenment it so often shows at present, that instead of being proud of Waterloo and the great war which was closed by it, it really seemed as if you ought rather to feel embarrassed at the recollection of them, since the policy for which they were fought is grown obsolete; the world has taken a turn which was not Lord Castlereagh's, and to look back on the great Tory war is to look back upon an endless account of blood and treasure wasted. Now, that is not so at all. What France had in her head, from the Convention, "faithful to the principles of the sovereignty of the people, which will not permit them to acknowledge anywhere the institutions militating against it," to Napoleon, with his "immense projects for assuring to France the empire of the world," – what she had in her head, along with many better and sounder notions destined to happier fortune, was *supremacy*. She had always a vision of a sort of federation of the States of Europe under the primacy of France. Now to this the world, whose progress no doubt lies in the direction of more conflict and common purpose among nations, but these nations free, self-impelled, and living each its own life, was not moving. Whoever knocks to pieces a scheme of this sort does the world a service. In antiquity, Roman empire had a scheme of this sort, and much more. The barbarians knocked it to pieces; – honour to the barbarians. In the Middle Ages Frederick the Second had a scheme of this sort. The Papacy knocked it to pieces, – honour to the Papacy. In our own century, France had a scheme of this sort. Your fathers knocked it to pieces; – honour to your fathers. They were just the people to do it. They had a vigorous lower class, a vigorous middle class, and a vigorous aristocracy. The lower class worked and fought, the middle class found the money, and the aristocracy wielded the whole. This aristocracy was high-spirited, reticent, firm, despising frothy declamation. It had all the qualities useful for its task and time; Lord Grenville's words, as early as 1793: "England will never consent that France shall arrogate the power of annulling at her pleasure, and under the pretence of a pretended natural right, the political system of Europe," – these few words, with their lofty strength, contain, as one may say, the prophecy of future success; you hear the very voice of an aristocracy standing on sure ground, and with the stars in its favour. Well, you succeeded, and in 1815, after Waterloo, you were the first power in Europe. "These people have a secret," we all said; "they have discerned the way the world was going, and therefore they have prevailed; while, on the other hand, the 'stars in their courses fought against Sisera."[16] We held you in the greatest respect; we tried to copy your constitutional government; we read your writers. "After the peace,'" says George Sand, "the literature of Great Britain crossed the straits, and came to reign amongst us." It reigned in

Byron and Scott, voices of the great aristocratical spirit which had just won the victory: Scott expressing its robust, genial conservatism, holding by a thousand roots to the past; Byron its defiant force and indomitable pride.

'We believed in you for a good while; but gradually it began to dawn upon us that the era for which you had had the secret was over, and that a new era, for which you had not the secret, was beginning. The work of the old era was to prevent the formation of a second Roman empire, and to maintain a store of free, rich, various national lives for the future to work with and bring to harmony. This was a work of force, of energy: it was a work for an aristocratical power, since, as you yourself are always saying, aristocracies, poor in ideas, are rich in energy. You were a great aristocratical power, and did it. But then came an era with another work, a work of which it is the great glory of the French Revolution (pardon us for saying so, we know it makes some of your countrymen angry to hear it,) passionately to have embraced the idea: the work of making human life, hampered by a past which it has outgrown, natural and rational. This is a work of intelligence, and in intelligence an aristocratic power, as you know, does not so much shine. Accordingly, since the world has been steadily moving this way, you seem to have lost your secret, and we are gradually ceasing to believe in you. You will say, perhaps, that England is no longer an aristocratical power, but a middle-class power, wielded by an industrial middle class, as the England of your fathers was wielded by a territorial aristocracy. This may be so; and indeed, as the style, carriage, and policy of England have of late years been by no means those of an aristocratical power, it probably is so. But whatever class dictates it, your course, allow us to say, has not of late years been intelligent; has not, at any rate, been successful. And depend upon it, a nation who has the secret of her era, who discerns which way the world is going, is successful, keeps rising. Can you yourselves, with all your powers of self-satisfaction, suppose that the Crimean war raised you, or that your Indian mutiny raised you, or that your attitude in the Italian war raised you, as your performances at the beginning of the century raised you? Surely you cannot. You held your own, if you will; you showed tenacity; you saved yourselves from disaster; but you did not raise yourselves, did not advance one jot. Can you, on the other hand, suppose that your attitude in the Danish business, in the American business, has not lowered you? You are losing the instinct which tells people how the world is going; you are beginning to make mistakes; you are falling out of the front rank. The era of aristocracies is over; nations must now stand or fall by the intelligence of their middle class and their people. The people with you is still an embryo; no one can yet quite say what it will come to. You lean, therefore, with your whole weight upon the intelligence of your middle class. And intelligence, in the true sense of the word, your middle class has absolutely none.'

I was aghast. I thought of this great class, every morning and evening extolled for its clear, manly intelligence by a hundred vigorous influential writers; and though the fine enthusiasm of these writers had always seemed to me to be carrying them a little too far, and I had even been guilty of the indecency of now and then calling my countrymen Philistines, these foreign critics struck me as passing all bounds, and quite out-Heroding Herod. Fortunately I had just received from England a copy of Mr Lowe's powerful and much-admired speech against Reform.[17] I took it out of my pocket. 'Now,' said I to my envious, carping foreigners, 'just listen to me. You say that the early years of this century were a time for energy, and we did well in them; you say that the last thirty or forty years have been a time for intelligence, and we have done ill in them. Mr Lowe shall answer you. Here is his reading of our last thirty or forty years' history, as made by our middle-class Parliament, as he calls it; by a Parliament, therefore, filled by the mind and will of this great class whose rule you disparage. Mr Lowe says: "The seven Houses of Commons that have sate since the Reform Bill have performed exploits unrivalled, not merely in the six centuries during which Parliament has existed, but in the whole history of representative assemblies." He says: "Look at the noble work, the heroic work which the House of Commons has performed within these thirty-five years. It has gone through and revised every institution of the country; it has scanned our trade, our colonies, our laws, and our municipal institutions; everything that was complained of, everything that had grown distasteful, has been touched with success and moderation by the amending hand. And to such a point have these amendments been carried, that when gentlemen come to argue this question, and do all in their power to get up a practical grievance, they fail in suggesting even one." There is what Mr Lowe says. You see we have nothing left to desire, absolutely nothing. As Mr Lowe himself goes on: "With all this continued peace, contentment, happiness, and prosperity, – England in its present state of development and civilization, – the mighty fabric of English prosperity, – what can we want more?" Evidently nothing! therefore to propose "for England to make a step in the direction of democracy is the strangest and wildest proposition ever broached by man." People talk of America. "In America the working classes are the masters; does anybody doubt that?" And compare, Mr Lowe means, England, as the middle class is making her, with America, as the working classes are making her. How entirely must the comparison turn to the advantage of the English middle class! Then, finally, as to the figure we cut in the eyes of the world, our grandeur and our future, here is a crowning sentence, worthy of Lord Macaulay himself, whose style Mr Lowe enthusiastically admires: "*The destiny of England is in the great heart of England!*" '

Mr Bright[18] had not then made his famous speech about the misdeeds of the Tories, but, if he had, I should certainly have added that our middle class, by these unrivalled exploits of theirs, had not only raised their country to an unprecedented height of greatness, but had also saved our foolish and obstructive aristocracy from being emptied into the Thames.[19]

As it was, however, what I had urged, or rather what I had borrowed from Mr Lowe, seemed to me exceedingly forcible, and I looked anxiously for its effect on my hearers. They did not appear so much disconcerted as I had hoped. 'Undoubtedly,' they said, 'the coming of your middle class to power was a natural, salutary event, to be blessed, not anathematized. Aristocracies cannot deal with a time for intelligence; their sense is for facts, not ideas. The world of ideas is the possible, the future; the world of aristocracies is the established, the past, which has made their fortune, and which they hope to prolong. No doubt, too, your middle class found a great deal of commercial and social business waiting to be done, which your aristocratic governments had left undone, and had no talents for doing. Their talents were for other times and tasks; for curbing the power of the Crown when other classes were too inconsiderable to do it; for managing (if one compares them with other aristocracies) their affairs and their dependants with vigour, prudence, and moderation, during the feudal and patriarchal stage of society; for wielding the force of their country against foreign powers with energy, firmness, and dignity. But then came the modern spirit, the modern time; the notion, as we say, of making human life more natural and rational, – or, as your philosophers say, of getting the greatest happiness for the greatest number. Have you succeeded, are you succeeding, in this hour of the many, as your aristocracy succeeded in the hour of the few? You say you are: you point to "the noble work, the heroic work which the House of Commons has performed within these last thirty-five years; everything that was complained of, everything that had grown distasteful, has been touched with success and moderation by the amending hand." Allow us to set clap-trap on one side; we are not at one of your public meetings. What is the modern problem? to make human life, the life of society, all through, more natural and rational; to have the greatest possible number of one's nation happy. Here is the standard by which we are to try ourselves and one another now, as national grandeur, in the old regal and aristocratical conception of it, was the standard formerly. Every nation must have wished to be in England in 1815, tried by the old standard: must we all wish to be in England, in 1865, tried by the new standard? Your aristocracy, you say, is as splendid, as fortunate, an enviable as ever: very likely; but all the world cannot be aristocracy. What do you make of the mass of your society, of its vast middle and lower portion? Are we to envy you your common people; is our common people to wish to change places with yours; are we to say that you, more than we, have the modern secret here? Without insisting too much

on the stories of misery and degradation which are perpetually
reaching us, we will say that no one can mix with a great crowd
in your country, no one can walk with his eyes and ears open
through the poor quarters of your large towns, and not feel
that your common people, as it meets one's eyes, is at present
more raw, to say the very least, less enviable-looking, further
removed from civilized and humane life, than the common
people almost anywhere. Well, then, you are not a success,
according to the modern standard, with your common people.
Are you a success with your middle class? They have the power
now; what have they made of themselves? what sort of a life is
theirs? A life more natural, more rational, fuller of happiness,
more enviable, therefore, than the life of the middle classes on
the Continent? Yes, you will say, because the English middle
class is the most industrious and the richest. But it is just here
that you go a great deal too fast, and so deceive yourselves.
What brings about, or rather tends to bring about, a natural,
rational life, satisfying the modern spirit? This: the growth of a
love of industry, trade, and wealth; the growth of a love of the
things of the mind; and the growth of a love of beautiful things.
There are body, intelligence, and soul all taken care of. Of these
three factors of modern life, your middle class has no notion of
any but one, the first. Their love of industry, trade, and wealth,
is certainly prodigious; and their example has done us a great
deal of good; we, too, are beginning to get this love, and we
wanted it. But what notion have they of anything else? Do but
look at them, look at their lives. Some of us know your middle
class very well; a great deal better than your own upper class in
general knows them. Your middle class is educated, to begin
with, in the worst schools of your country, and our middle class
is educated in the best of ours. What becomes of them after
that? The fineness and capacity of a man's spirit is shown by his
enjoyments; your middle class has an enjoyment in its business,
we admit, and gets on well in business, and makes money; but
beyond that? Drugged with business, your middle class seems
to have its sense blunted for any stimulus besides, except religion; it has a religion narrow, unintelligent, repulsive. All
sincere religion does something for the spirit, raises a man out

of the bondage of his merely bestial part, and saves him; but the religion of your middle class is the very lowest form of intelligential life which one can imagine as saving. What other enjoyments have they? The newspapers, a sort of eating and drinking which are not to our taste, a literature of books almost entirely religious or semi-religious, books utterly unreadable by an educated class anywhere, but which your middle class consumes, they say, by the hundred thousand; and in their evenings, for a great treat, a lecture on teetotalism or nunneries. Can any life be imagined more hideous, more dismal, more unenviable? Compare it with the life of our middle class as you have seen it on the Rhine this summer, or at Lausanne, or Zurich. The world of enjoyment, so liberalizing and civilizing, belongs to the middle classes there, as well as the world of business; the whole world is theirs, they possess life; in England the highest class seems to have the monopoly of the world of enjoyment, the middle class enjoys itself, as your Shakespeare would say, in hugger-mugger,[20] and possesses life only by reading in the newspapers, which it does devoutly, the doings of great people. Well then, we do not at all want to be as your middle class; we want to learn from it to do business and to get rich, and this we are learning a great deal faster than you think; but we do not, like your middle class, fix our consummation here: we have a notion of a whole world besides, not dreamed of in your middle class's philosophy; so they, too, like your common people, seem to us no success. They may be the masters of the modern time with you, but they are not solving its problem. They cannot see the way the world is going, and the future does not belong to them. Talk of the present state of development and civilization of England, meaning England as they represent it to us! Why, the capital, pressing danger of England, is the barbarism of her middle class; the civilization of her middle class is England's capital, pressing want.'

'Well, but,' said I, still catching at Mr Lowe's powerful help, 'the Parliament of this class has performed exploits unrivalled not merely in the six centuries during which Parliament has existed, but in the whole history of representative assemblies. The exploits are there; all the reforms we have made in the last five-and-thirty years.'

'Let us distinguish,' replied the envious foreigners, 'let us distinguish. We named three powers, – did we not? – which go to spread that rational humane life which is the aim of modern society: the love of wealth, the love of intelligence, the love of beauty. Your middle class, we agreed, has the first; its commercial legislation, accordingly, has been very good, and in advance of that of foreign countries. Not that free trade was really brought about by your middle class: it was brought about, as important reforms always are, by two or three great men. However, let your middle class, which had the sense to accept free trade, have the credit of it. But this only brings us a certain way. The legislation of your middle class in all that goes to give human life more intelligence and beauty, is no better than was to be expected from its own want of both. It is nothing to say that its legislation in these respects is an improvement upon what you had before; that is not the question; you are holding up its achievements as absolutely admirable, as unrivalled, as a model to us. You may have done, – for you, – much for religious toleration, social improvement, public instruction, municipal reform, law reform; but the French Revolution and its consequences have done, upon the Continent, a great deal more. Such a spectacle as your Irish Church Establishment* you cannot find in France or Germany. Your Irish land-question you hardly dare to face,† – Stein settled as threatening a land-question in Prussia.[21] Of the schools for your middle class we have already spoken; while these schools are what they are, while the schools for your poor are maintained in the expensive, unjust, irrational way they are, England is full of endowments and foundations, capable by themselves, if properly applied, of putting your public education on a much better footing. In France and Germany all similar funds are thus employed, having been brought under public responsible management; in England they are left to private irresponsible management, and are, in nine cases out of ten, wasted. You talk of municipal reform; and cities and the manner of life in them have, for the modern

* It is gone, thanks to Anti-State-Church-ism! – ED.
† We have faced it! – ED.

business of promoting a more rational and humane life in the great body of the community, incalculable importance. Do you suppose we should tolerate in France, Germany, Switzerland, Italy, your London corporation and London vestries, and London as they make it? In your provincial towns you do better; but even there, do the municipalities show a tenth part either of the intelligence or the care for the ends, as we have laid them down, of modern society, that our municipalities show? Your middle-class man thinks it the highest pitch of development and civilization when his letters are carried twelve times a day from Islington to Camberwell, and from Camberwell to Islington, and if railway-trains run to and fro between them every quarter of an hour. He thinks it is nothing that the trains only carry him from an illiberal, dismal life at Islington to an illiberal, dismal life at Camberwell; and the letters only tell him that such is the life there. A Swiss burgher takes heaven knows how many hours to go from Berne to Geneva, and his trains are very few; this is an extreme on the other side; but compare the life the Swiss burgher finds or leaves at Berne or Geneva with the life of the middle class in your English towns. Or else you think to cover everything by saying: "We are free! we are free! Our newspapers can say what they like!" Freedom, like Industry, is a very good horse to ride; – but to ride somewhere. You seem to think that you have only got to get on the back of your horse Freedom, or your horse Industry, and to ride away as hard as you can, to be sure of coming to the right destination. If your newspapers can say what they like, you think you are sure of being well advised. That comes of your inaptitude for ideas, and aptitude for clap-trap; you can never see the two sides of a question; never perceive that every human state of things, even a good one, has its inconveniences. We can see the conveniences of your state well enough; and the inconveniences of ours, of newspapers not free, and prefects over-busy; and there are plenty of us who proclaim them. You eagerly repeat after us all we say that redounds to your own honour and glory; but you never follow our example yourselves. You are full of acuteness to perceive the ill influence of our prefects on us; but if any one says to you, in your turn: "The English system of a great landed aristocracy* keeps your lower class a lower class for ever, and materializes and vulgarizes your whole middle class," – you stare vacantly at the speaker, you cannot even take in his ideas; you can only blurt forth, in reply, some clap-trap or other about a "system of such tried and tested efficiency as no other country was ever happy enough to possess since the world was a world."'

I have observed in my travels, that most young gentlemen of our highest class go through Europe, from Calais to Constantinople, with one sentence on their lips, and one idea in their minds, which suffices, apparently, to explain all that they see to them: *Foreigners don't wash.* No doubt, thought I to myself, my friends have fallen in with some distinguished young Britons of this sort, and had their feelings wounded by them; hence their rancour against our aristocracy. And as to our middle class, foreigners have no notion how much this class, with us, contains; how many shades and gradations in it there are, and how little what is said of one part of it will apply to another. Something of this sort I could not help urging aloud. 'You do not know,' I said, 'that there is broken off, as one may say, from the top of our middle class, a large fragment, which receives the best education the country can give, the same education as our aristocracy; which is perfectly intelligent and which enjoys life perfectly. These men do the main part of our intellectual work, write all our best newspapers; and cleverer people, I assure you, are nowhere to be found.'

'Clever enough,' was the answer, 'but they show not much intelligence, in the true sense of the word, – not much intelligence of the way the world is going. Whether it is that they must try to hit your current public opinion, which is not intelligent; whether it is that, having been, as you say, brought up

---

* What a contrast between this Jacobinism and the noble sentiments of Barrow: 'Men will never be heartily loyal and submissive to authority till they become really good; nor will they ever be very good, till they see their leaders such.' I remember once quoting this passage to Arminius at the time when we were all full of the Mordaunt trial. 'Yes,' remarked Arminius, in his thoughtful manner, 'that is what makes your Lord Coles so inexpressibly precious!' But was this an answer? I say, not. – ED.

with your aristocracy, they have been too much influenced by it, have taken, half insensibly, an aristocracy's material standard, and do not believe in ideas; certain it is that their intelligence has no ardour, no plan, leads them nowhere; it is ineffectual. Your intellect is at this moment, to an almost unexampled degree, without influence on the intellect of Europe.'

While this was being said, I noticed an Italian,*[22] who was one of our party, fumbling with his pocket-book, from whence he presently produced a number of grey newspaper slips, which I could see were English. 'Now just listen to me for a moment,' he cried, 'and I will show you what makes us say, on the Continent, that you English have no sense for logic, for ideas, and that your praise and blame, having no substantial foundation, are worth very little. You remember the famous French pamphlet before our war began in 1859: *Napoleon the Third and Italy*. The pamphlet appealed, in the French way, to reason and first principles; the upshot of it was this: "The treaties which bind governments would be invariable only if the world was immovable. A power which should intrench itself behind treaties in order to resist modifications demanded by general feeling would have doubtless on her side an acquired right, but she would have against her moral right and universal conscience." You English, on the other hand, took your stand on things as they were: "If treaties are made," said your *Times*, "they must be respected. Tear one, and all are waste paper." Very well; this is a policy, at any rate, an aristocratical policy; much may be said for it. The *Times* was full of contempt for the French pamphlet, an essay, as it called it, "conveying the dreams of an agitator expressed in the language of an academician." It said: "No one accustomed to the pithy comments with which liberty notices passing history, can read such a production without complacency that he does not live in the country which produces it. To see the heavy apparatus of an essay brought out to solve a question on which men have corresponded and talked and speculated in the funds, and acted in the most practical manner possible for a month past, is as strange as if we beheld

* Little Pompeo Pococurante. Almost all the rest is Arminius.

some spectral review," and so on. Still very well; there is the strong practical man despising theories and reveries. "The sentiment of race is just now threatening to be exceedingly troublesome. It is to a considerable extent in our days a literary revival." That is all to the same effect. Then came a hitch in our affairs, and fortune seemed as if she was going to give, as she often does give, the anti-theorists a triumph. "The Italian plot," cried the *Times,* "has failed. The Emperor and his familiars knew not the moral strength which is still left in the enlightened communities of Europe. To the unanimous and indignant reprobation of English opinion is due the failure of the imperial plots. While silence and fear reign everywhere abroad, the eyes and ears of the Continent are turned continually to these Islands. English opinion has been erected into a kind of Areopagus."[23] Our business went forward again, and your English opinion grew very stern indeed. "Sardinia," said the *Times,* "is told very plainly that she has deserted the course by which alone she could hope either to be happy or great, and abandoned herself to the guidance of fatal delusions, which are luring her on to destruction. By cultivating the arts of peace she would have been solving, in the only possible way, the difficult problem of Italian independence. She has been taught by France to look instead to the acquisition of fresh territory by war and conquest. She has now been told with perfect truth by the warning voice of the British Parliament that she has not a moment to lose in retracing her steps, if indeed her penitence be not too late." Well, to make a long story short, we did not retrace our steps; we went on, as you know; we succeeded; and now let us make a jump from the spring to the autumn. Here is your unanimous English opinion, here is your Areopagus, here is your *Times,* in October: "It is very irregular (Sardinia's course),[24] it is contrary to all diplomatic forms. Francis the Second can show a thousand texts of international law against it. Yes; but there are extremities beyond all law, and there are laws which existed before even society was formed. There are laws which are implanted in our nature, and which form part of the human mind," and so on. Why, here you have entirely boxed the compass and come round from the aristocratical programme to the programme of the French pamphlet, "the dreams of an agitator in the language of an academician!" And you approved not only our present but our past, and kindly took off your ban of reprobation issued in February. "How great a change has been effected by the wisely courageous policy of Sardinia! The firmness and boldness which have raised Italy from degradation form the enduring character of a ten years' policy. King Victor Emmanuel and his sagacious counsellor have achieved success by remembering that fortune favours the bold." There you may see why the mind of France influences the Continent so much and the mind of England so little. France has intelligence enough to perceive the ideas that are moving, or are likely to move, the world; she believes in them, sticks to them, and shapes her course to suit them. You neither perceive them nor believe in them, but you play with them like counters, taking them up and laying them down at random, and following really some turn of your imagination, some gust of liking or disliking. When I heard of your countrymen complaining of Italy and her ingratitude for English sympathy, I made, to explain it, the collection of those extracts and of a good many more. They are all at your service; I have some here from the *Saturday Review,* which you will find exactly follow suit with those from the *Times.*' 'No, thank you,' I answered. 'The *Times* is enough. My relations with the *Saturday Review* are rather tight-stretched, as you say here, already; make me a party to none of your quarrels with them.'[25]

After this my original tormentor* once more took up his parable. 'You see now what I meant,' he said, 'by saying that you did better in the old time, in the day of aristocracies. An aristocracy has no ideas, but it has a policy, – to resist change. In this policy it believes, it sticks to it; when it is beaten in it, it holds its tongue. This is respectable, at any rate. But your great middle class, as you call it, your present governing power, having no policy, except that of doing a roaring trade, does not know what to be at in great affairs, – blows hot and cold by turns, – makes itself ridiculous, in short. It was a good

---

* Arminius, of course.

aristocratical policy to have helped Austria in the Italian war; it was a good aristocratical policy to have helped the South in the American war. The days of aristocratical policy are over for you; with your new middle-class public opinion you cut, in Italy, the figure our friend here has just shown you; in America you scold right and left, you get up a monster-memorial to deprecate the further effusion of blood; you lament over the abridgement of civil liberty by people engaged in a struggle for life and death, and meaning to win; and when they turn a deaf ear to you and win, you say, "Oh, now let us be one great united Anglo-Saxon family and astonish the world!" This is just of a piece with your threatening Germany with the Emperor of the French. Do you not see that all these blunders dispose the Americans, who are very shrewd, and who have been succeeding as steadily as you have been failing, to answer: "We have got the lead, no thanks to you, and we mean to astonish the world without you"? Unless you change, unless your middle class grows more intelligent, you will tell upon the world less and less, and end by being a second Holland. We do not hold you cheap for saying you will wash your hands of all concerns but your own, that you do not care a rush for influence in Europe; though this sentence of your Lord Bolingbroke is true: "The opinion of mankind, which is fame after death, is superior strength and power in life." We hold you cheap because you show so few signs, except in the one department of industry, of understanding your time and its tendencies, and of exhibiting a modern life which shall be a signal success. And the reaction is the stronger, because, after 1815, we believed in you as now-a-days we are coming to believe in America. You had won the last game, and we thought you had your hand full of trumps, and were going to win the next. Now the game has begun to be played, and we have an inkling of what your cards are; we shrewdly suspect you have scarcely any trumps at all.'

I am no arguer, as is well known, 'and every puny whipster gets my sword.'*[26] So, instead of making bad worse by a lame

* And this is why it was peculiarly unlucky for me to be thrown so much with Arminius, who loved arguing. – ED.

answer, I held my tongue, consoling myself with the thought that these foreigners get from us, at any rate, plenty of Rolands for any stray Oliver[27] they may have the luck to give us. I have since meditated a good deal on what was then said, but I cannot profess to be yet quite clear about it. However, all due deductions made for envy, exaggeration, and injustice, enough stuck by me of these remarks on our logic, criticism, and love of intelligence, to determine me to go on trying (taking care, of course, to steer clear of indecency) to keep my mind fixed on these, instead of singing hosannahs to our actual state of development and civilization. The old recipe, to think a little more and bustle a little less, seemed to me still the best recipe to follow. So I take comfort when I find the *Guardian* reproaching me with having no influence; for I know what influence means, – a party, practical proposals, action; and I say to myself: 'Even suppose I could get some followers, and assemble them, brimming with affectionate enthusiasm, in a committee-room at some inn; what on earth should I say to them? what resolutions could I propose? I could only propose the old Socratic commonplace, *Know thyself*; and how black they would all look at that!' No; to inquire, perhaps too curiously, what that present state of English development and civilization is, which according to Mr Lowe is so perfect that to give votes to the working class is stark madness; and, on the other hand, to be less sanguine about the divine and saving effect of a vote on its possessor than my friends in the committee-room at the 'Spotted Dog,' – that is my inevitable portion. To bring things under the light of one's intelligence, to see how they look there, to accustom oneself simply to regard the Marylebone Vestry, or the Educational Home, or the Irish Church Establishment, or our railway management, or our Divorce Court, or our gin-palaces open on Sunday and the Crystal Palace shut, as absurdities, – that is, I am sure, invaluable exercise for us just at present. Let all persist in it who can, and steadily set their desires on introducing, with time, a little more soul and spirit into the too, too solid flesh of English society.

I have a friend who is very sanguine, in spite of the dismal, croakings of these foreigners, about the turn things are even now taking among us. 'Mean and ignoble as our middle class looks,' he says, 'it has this capital virtue, it has seriousness. With frivolity, cultured or uncultured, you can do nothing; but with seriousness there is always hope. Then, too, the present bent of the world towards amusing itself, so perilous to the highest class, is curative and good for our middle class. A piano in a Quaker's drawing-room is a step for him to more humane life; nay, perhaps, even the penny gaff[28] of the poor East-Londoner is a step for him to more humane life; it is, – what example shall we choose? it is *Strathmore,* let us say, – it is the one-pound-eleven-and-sixpenny gaff[29] of the young gentlemen of the clubs and the young ladies of Belgravia, that is for them but a step in the primrose path to the everlasting bonfire. Besides, say what you like of the idealessness of aristocracies, the vulgarity of our middle class, the immaturity of our lower, and the poor chance which a happy type of modern life has between them, consider this: Of all that makes life liberal and humane, – of light, of ideas, of culture, – every man in every class of society who has a dash of genius in him is the born friend. By his bringing up, by his habits, by his interest, he may be their enemy; by the primitive, unalterable complexion of his nature, he is their friend. Therefore, the movement of the modern spirit will be more and more felt among us, it will spread, it will prevail. Nay,' this enthusiast often continues, getting excited as he goes on, 'the *Times* itself, which so stirs some people's indignation, – what is the *Times* but a gigantic Sancho Panza, to borrow a phrase of your friend Heine; – a gigantic Sancho Panza, following by an attraction he cannot resist that poor, mad, scorned, suffering, sublime enthusiast, the modern spirit; following it, indeed, with constant grumbling, expostulation, and opposition, with airs of protection, of compassionate superiority, with an incessant byplay of nods, shrugs, and winks addressed to the spectators; following it, in short, with all the incurable recalcitrancy of a lower nature, but still following it?' When my friend talks thus, I always shake my head, and say that this sounds very like the transcendentalism which has already brought me into so many scrapes.

I have another friend again (and I am grown so cowed by all

the rebuke my original speculations have drawn upon me that I find myself more and more filling the part of a mere listener), who calls himself Anglo-Saxon rather than English,* and this is what he says: 'We are a small country,' he says, 'and our middle class has, as you say, not much gift for anything but making money. Our freedom and wealth have given us a great start, our capital will give us for a long time an advantage; but as other countries grow better-governed and richer, we must necessarily sink to the position to which our size, and our want of any eminent gift for telling upon the world spiritually, doom us. But look at America; it is the same race; whether we are first or they, Anglo-Saxonism triumphs. You used to say that they had all the Philistinism of the English middle class from which they spring, and a great many faults of their own besides. But you noticed, too, that, blindly as they seemed following in general the star of their god Buncombe,[30] they showed, at the same time, a feeling for ideas, a vivacity and play of mind, which our middle class has not, and which comes to the Americans, probably, from their democratic life, with its ardent hope, its forward stride, its gaze fixed on the future. Well, since these great events have lately come to purge and form them, how is this intelligence of theirs developing itself? Now they are manifesting a quick sense to see how the world is really going, and a sure faith, indispensable to all nations that are to be great, that greatness is only to be reached by going that way and no other. And then, if you talk of culture, look at the culture their middle, and even their working class is getting, as compared with the culture ours are getting. The trash which circulates by the hundred thousand among our middle class has no readers in America; our rubbish is for home-consumption; all our best books, books which are read here only by the small educated class, are in America the books of the great reading public. So over there they will advance spiritually as well as materially; and if our race at last flowers to modern life there, and not here, does it so much matter?' So says my friend, who is, as I

---

* Not the talented author of 'Greater Britain,' though the reader might be inclined to suppose so. – ED.

premised, a devotee of Anglo-Saxonism; I, who share his pious
frenzy but imperfectly, do not feel quite satisfied with these
plans of vicarious greatness, and have a longing for this old and
great country of ours to be always great in herself, not only in
her progeny. So I keep looking at her, and thinking of her; and
as often as I consider how history is a series of waves, coming
gradually to a head and then breaking, and that, as the successive waves come up, one nation is seen at the top of this wave,
and then another of the next, I ask myself, counting all the waves
which have come up with England at the top of them: When
the great wave which is now mounting has come up, will she be
at the top of it? *Illa nihil, nec me quærentem vana moratur!*[31] –

> Yes, we arraign her; but she,
> The weary Titan, with deaf
> Ears, and labour-dimm'd eyes,
> Regarding neither to right
> Nor left, goes passively by,
> Staggering on to her goal;
> Bearing, on shoulders immense,
> Atlantéan, the load,
> Wellnigh not to be borne,
> Of the too vast orb of her fate.[32]

CULTURE AND ANARCHY

Introduction

In one of his speeches a short time ago, that fine speaker and famous Liberal, Mr Bright,[1] took occasion to have a fling at the friends and preachers of culture. 'People who talk about what they call *culture!*' said he contemptuously; 'by which they mean a smattering of the two dead languages of Greek and Latin.' And he went on to remark, in a strain with which modern speakers and writers have made us very familiar, how poor a thing this culture is, how little good it can do to the world, and how absurd it is for its possessors to set much store by it. And the other day a younger Liberal than Mr Bright, one of a school whose mission it is to bring into order and system that body of truth with which the earlier Liberals merely fumbled, a member of the University of Oxford, and a very clever writer, Mr Frederic Harrison,[2] developed, in the systematic and stringent manner of his school, the thesis which Mr Bright had propounded in only general terms. 'Perhaps the very silliest cant of the day,' said Mr Frederic Harrison, 'is the cant about culture. Culture is a desirable quality in a critic of new books, and sits well on a professor of *belles lettres*; but as applied to politics, it means simply a turn for small fault-finding, love of selfish ease, and indecision in action. The man of culture is in politics one of the poorest mortals alive. For simple pedantry and want of good sense no man is his equal. No assumption is too unreal, no end is too unpractical for him. But the active exercise of politics requires common sense, sympathy, trust, resolution, and enthusiasm, qualities which your man of culture has carefully rooted up, lest they damage the delicacy of his critical olfactories. Perhaps they are the only class of responsible beings in the community who cannot with safety be entrusted with power.'

Now for my part I do not wish to see men of culture asking to be entrusted with power; and, indeed, I have freely said, that in my opinion the speech most proper, at present, for a man of culture to make to a body of his fellow-countrymen who gets him into a committee-room, is Socrates's: *Know thyself!* and this is not a speech to be made by men wanting to be entrusted with power. For this very indifference to direct political action I have been taken to task by the *Daily Telegraph,* coupled, by a strange perversity of fate, with just that very one of the Hebrew prophets whose style I admire the least, and called 'an elegant Jeremiah.'³ It is because I say (to use the words which the *Daily Telegraph* puts in my mouth): – 'You mustn't make a fuss because you have no vote, – that is vulgarity; you mustn't hold big meetings to agitate for reform bills and to repeal corn laws, – that is the very height of vulgarity,' – it is for this reason that I am called, sometimes an elegant Jeremiah, sometimes a spurious Jeremiah, a Jeremiah about the reality of whose mission the writer in the *Daily Telegraph* has his doubts. It is evident, therefore, that I have so taken my line as not to be exposed to the whole brunt of Mr Frederic Harrison's censure. Still, I have often spoken in praise of culture, I have striven to make all my works and ways serve the interests of culture. I take culture to be something a great deal more than what Mr Frederic Harrison and others call it: 'a desirable quality in a critic of new books.' Nay, even though to a certain extent I am disposed to agree with Mr Frederic Harrison, that men of culture are just the class of responsible beings in this community of ours who cannot properly, at present, be entrusted with power, I am not sure that I do not think this the fault of our community rather than of the men of culture. In short, although, like Mr Bright and Mr Frederic Harrison, and the editor of the *Daily Telegraph,* and a large body of valued friends of mine, I am a Liberal, yet I am a Liberal tempered by experience, reflection, and renouncement, and I am, above all, a believer in culture. Therefore, I

propose now to try and enquire, in the simple unsystematic
way which best suits both my taste and my powers, what culture really is, what good it can do, what is our own special need
of it; and I shall seek to find some plain grounds on which
a faith in culture, – both my own faith in it and the faith of
others, – may rest securely.

CHAPTER I
Sweetness and Light

The disparagers of culture make its motive curiosity; sometimes, indeed, they make its motive mere exclusiveness and
vanity. The culture which is supposed to plume itself on a smattering of Greek and Latin is a culture which is begotten by
nothing so intellectual as curiosity; it is valued either out of
sheer vanity and ignorance, or else as an engine of social and
class distinction, separating its holder, like a badge or title,
from other people who have not got it. No serious man would
call this *culture,* or attach any value to it, as culture, at all. To
find the real ground for the very differing estimate which serious people will set upon culture, we must find some motive for
culture in the terms of which may lie a real ambiguity; and such
a motive the word *curiosity* gives us.

I have before now pointed out that we English do not, like
the foreigners, use the word in a good sense as well as in a bad
sense.[1] With us the word is always used in a somewhat disap-
proving sense. A liberal and intelligent eagerness about the
things of the mind may be meant by a foreigner when he speaks
of curiosity, but with us the word always conveys a certain
notion of frivolous and unedifying activity. In the *Quarterly
Review,* some little time ago, was an estimate of the celebrated
French critic, M. Sainte-Beuve,[2] and a very inadequate estimate
it in my judgment was. And its inadequacy consisted chiefly in
this: that in our English way it left out of sight the double sense
really involved in the word *curiosity,* thinking enough was said

to stamp M. Sainte-Beuve with blame if it was said that he was impelled in his operations as a critic by curiosity, and omitting either to perceive that M. Sainte-Beuve himself, and many other people with him, would consider that this was praiseworthy and not blameworthy, or to point out why it ought really to be accounted worthy of blame and not of praise. For as there is a curiosity about intellectual matters which is futile, and merely a disease, so there is certainly a curiosity, – a desire after the things of the mind simply for their own sakes and for the pleasure of seeing them as they are, – which is, in an intelligent being, natural and laudable. Nay, and the very desire to see things as they are, implies a balance and regulation of mind which is not often attained without fruitful effort, and which is the very opposite of the blind and diseased impulse of mind which is what we mean to blame when we blame curiosity. Montesquieu says: – 'The first motive which ought to impel us to study is the desire to augment the excellence of our nature, and to render an intelligent being yet more intelligent.' This is the true ground to assign for the genuine scientific passion, however manifested, and for culture, viewed simply as a fruit of this passion; and it is a worthy ground, even though we let the term *curiosity* stand to describe it.

But there is of culture another view, in which not solely the scientific passion, the sheer desire to see things as they are, natural and proper in an intelligent being, appears as the ground of it. There is a view in which all the love of our neighbour, the impulses towards action, help, and beneficence, the desire for removing human error, clearing human confusion, and diminishing human misery, the noble aspiration to leave the world better and happier than we found it, – motives eminently such as are called social, – come in as part of the grounds of culture, and the main and pre-eminent part. Culture is then properly described not as having its origin in curiosity, but as having its origin in the love of perfection; it is *a study of perfection*. It moves by the force, not merely or primarily of the scientific passion for pure knowledge, but also of the moral and social passion for doing good. As, in the first view of it, we took for its worthy motto Montesquieu's words: 'To render an intelligent being yet more intelligent!' so, in the second view of it, there is no better motto which it can have than these words of Bishop Wilson:[3] 'To make reason and the will of God prevail!'

Only, whereas the passion for doing good is apt to be over-hasty in determining what reason and the will of God say, because its turn is for acting rather than thinking and it wants to be beginning to act; and whereas it is apt to take its own conceptions, which proceed from its own state of development and share in all the imperfections and immaturities of this, for a basis of action; what distinguishes culture is, that it is pos-sessed by the scientific passion as well as by the passion of doing good; that it demands worthy notions of reason and the will of God, and does not readily suffer its own crude concep-tions to substitute themselves for them. And knowing that no action or institution can be salutary and stable which are not based on reason and the will of God, it is not so bent on acting and instituting, even with the great aim of diminishing human error and misery ever before its thoughts, but that it can remem-ber that acting and instituting are of little use, unless we know how and what we ought to act and to institute.

This culture is more interesting and more far-reaching than that other, which is founded solely on the scientific passion for knowing. But it needs times of faith and ardour, times when the intellectual horizon is opening and widening all round us, to flourish in. And is not the close and bounded intellectual hori-zon within which we have long lived and moved now lifting up, and are not new lights finding free passage to shine in upon us? For a long time there was no passage for them to make their way in upon us, and then it was of no use to think of adapting the world's action to them. Where was the hope of making rea-son and the will of God prevail among people who had a routine which they had christened reason and the will of God, in which they were inextricably bound, and beyond which they had no power of looking? But now the iron force of adhesion to the old routine, – social, political, religious, – has wonder-fully yielded; the iron force of exclusion of all which is new has wonderfully yielded. The danger now is, not that people should obstinately refuse to allow anything but their old routine to pass for reason and the will of God, but either that they should allow some novelty or other to pass for these too easily, or else that they should underrate the importance of them altogether, and think it enough to follow action for its own sake, without troubling themselves to make reason and the will of God prevail therein. Now, then, is the moment for culture to be of service, culture which believes in making reason and the will of God prevail, believes in perfection, is the study and pursuit of perfection, and is no longer debarred, by a rigid invincible exclusion of what ever is new, from getting acceptance for its ideas, simply because they are new.

The moment this view of culture is seized, the moment it is regarded not solely as the endeavour to see things as they are, to draw towards a knowledge of the universal order which seems to be intended and aimed at in the world, and which it is a man's happiness to go along with or his misery to go counter to, – to learn, in short, the will of God, – the moment, I say, culture is considered not merely as the endeavour to *see* and *learn* this, but as the endeavour, also, to make it *prevail,* the moral, social, and beneficent character of culture becomes manifest. The mere endeavour to see and learn the truth for our own personal satisfaction is indeed a commencement for making it prevail, a preparing the way for this, which always serves this, and is wrongly, therefore, stamped with blame absolutely in itself and not only in its caricature and degeneration. But perhaps it has got stamped with blame, and disparaged with the dubious title of curiosity, because in comparison with this wider endeavour of such great and plain utility it looks selfish, petty, and unprofitable.

And religion, the greatest and most important of the efforts by which the human race has manifested its impulse to perfect itself, – religion, that voice of the deepest human experience, – does not only enjoin and sanction the aim which is the great aim of culture, the aim of setting ourselves to ascertain what perfection is and to make it prevail; but also, in determining generally in what human perfection consists, religion comes to a conclusion identical with that which culture, – culture seeking the determination of this question through *all* the voices of

human experience which have been heard upon it, of art, science, poetry, philosophy, history, as well as of religion, in order
to give a greater fulness and certainty to its solution, – likewise
reaches. Religion says: *The kingdom of God is within you;*[4] and
culture, in like manner, places human perfection in an *internal*
condition, in the growth and predominance of our humanity
proper, as distinguished from our animality. It places it in the
ever-increasing efficacy and in the general harmonious expansion of those gifts of thought and feeling, which make the
peculiar dignity, wealth, and happiness of human nature. As I
have said on a former occasion: 'It is in making endless additions to itself, in the endless expansion of its powers, in endless
growth in wisdom and beauty, that the spirit of the human race
finds its ideal. To reach this ideal, culture is an indispensable
aid, and that is the true value of culture.'[5] Not a having and
a resting, but a growing and a becoming, is the character of
perfection as culture conceives it; and here, too, it coincides
with religion.

And because men are all members of one great whole, and
the sympathy which is in human nature will not allow one
member to be indifferent to the rest or to have a perfect welfare
independent of the rest, the expansion of our humanity, to suit
the idea of perfection which culture forms, must be a *general*
expansion. Perfection, as culture conceives it, is not possible
while the individual remains isolated. The individual is required,
under pain of being stunted and enfeebled in his own development if he disobeys, to carry others along with him in his march
towards perfection, to be continually doing all he can to enlarge
and increase the volume of the human stream sweeping thither-
ward. And here, once more, culture lays on us the same obligation
as religion, which says, as Bishop Wilson has admirably put it,
that 'to promote the kingdom of God is to increase and hasten
one's own happiness.'

But, finally, perfection, – as culture from a thorough disinterested study of human nature and human experience learns
to conceive it, – is a harmonious expansion of *all* the powers
which make the beauty and worth of human nature, and is not
consistent with the over-development of any one power at the

expense of the rest. Here culture goes beyond religion, as religion is generally conceived by us.

If culture, then, is a study of perfection, and of harmonious perfection, general perfection, and perfection which consists in becoming something rather than in having something, in an inward condition of the mind and spirit, not in an outward set of circumstances, – it is clear that culture, instead of being the frivolous and useless thing which Mr Bright, and Mr Frederic Harrison, and many other Liberals are apt to call it, has a very important function to fulfil for mankind. And this function is particularly important in our modern world, of which the whole civilization is, to a much greater degree than the civilization of Greece and Rome, mechanical and external, and tends constantly to become more so.[6] But above all in our own country has culture a weighty part to perform, because here that mechanical character, which civilization tends to take everywhere, is shown in the most eminent degree. Indeed nearly all the characters of perfection, as culture teaches us to fix them, meet in this country with some powerful tendency which thwarts them and sets them at defiance. The idea of perfection as an *inward* condition of the mind and spirit is at variance with the mechanical and material civilization in esteem with us, and nowhere, as I have said, so much in esteem as with us. The idea of perfection as a *general* expansion of the human family is at variance with our strong individualism, our hatred of all limits to the unrestrained swing of the individual's personality, our maxim of 'every man for himself.' Above all, the idea of perfection as a *harmonious* expansion of human nature is at variance with our want of flexibility, with our inaptitude for seeing more than one side of a thing, with our intense energetic absorption in the particular pursuit we happen to be following. So culture has a rough task to achieve in this country. Its preachers have, and are likely long to have, a hard time of it, and they will much oftener be regarded, for a great while to come, as elegant or spurious Jeremiahs, than as friends and benefactors. That, however, will not prevent their doing in the end good service if they persevere. And meanwhile, the mode of action they have to pursue, and the sort of habits they must fight against, ought to be made quite clear for everyone to see, who may be willing to look at the matter attentively and dispassionately.

Faith in machinery is, I said, our besetting danger; often in machinery most absurdly disproportioned to the end which this machinery, if it is to do any good at all, is to serve; but always in machinery, as if it had a value in and for itself. What is freedom but machinery? what is population but machinery? what is coal but machinery? what are railroads but machinery? what is wealth but machinery? what are, even, religious organizations but machinery? Now almost every voice in England is accustomed to speak of these things as if they were precious ends in themselves, and, therefore, had some of the characters of perfection indisputably joined to them. I have before now noticed Mr Roebuck's stock argument for proving the greatness and happiness of England as she is, and for quite stopping the mouths of all gainsayers.[7] Mr Roebuck is never weary of reiterating this argument of his, so I do not know why I should be weary of noticing it. 'May not every man in England say what he likes?' – Mr Roebuck perpetually asks; and that, he thinks, is quite sufficient, and when every man may say what he likes, our aspirations ought to be satisfied. But the aspirations of culture, which is the study of perfection, are not satisfied, unless what men say, when they say what they like, is worth saying, – has good in it, and more good than bad. In the same way the *Times* replying to some foreign strictures on the dress, looks, and behaviour of the English abroad, urges that the English ideal is that everyone should be free to do and to look just as he likes. But culture indefatigably tries, not to make what each raw person may like, the rule by which he fashions himself; but to draw ever nearer to a sense of what is indeed beautiful, graceful, and becoming, and to get the raw person to like that.

And in the same way with respect to railroads and coal. Everyone must have observed the strange language current during the late discussions as to the possible failure of our supplies of coal. Our coal, thousands of people were saying, is the real basis of our national greatness; if our coal runs short, there is an end of the greatness of England. But what *is* greatness? – culture makes us ask. Greatness is a spiritual condition worthy to excite love, interest, and admiration; and the outward proof of possessing greatness is that we excite love, interest, and admiration. If England were swallowed up by the sea tomorrow, which of the two, a hundred years hence, would most excite the love, interest, and admiration of mankind, – would most, therefore, show the evidences of having possessed greatness, – the England of the last twenty years, or the England of Elizabeth, of a time of splendid spiritual effort, but when our coal, and our industrial operations depending on coal, were very little developed? Well, then, what an unsound habit of mind it must be which makes us talk of things like coal or iron as constituting the greatness of England, and how salutary a friend is culture, bent on seeing things as they are, and thus dissipating delusions of this kind and fixing standards of perfection that are real!

Wealth, again, that end to which our prodigious works for material advantage are directed, – the commonest of commonplaces tells us how men are always apt to regard wealth as a precious end in itself; and certainly they have never been so apt thus to regard it as they are in England at the present time. Never did people believe anything more firmly, than nine Englishmen out of ten at the present day believe that our greatness and welfare are proved by our being so very rich. Now, the use of culture is that it helps us, by means of its spiritual standard of perfection, to regard wealth as but machinery, and not only to say as a matter of words that we regard wealth as but machinery, but really to perceive and feel that it is so. If it were not for this purging effect wrought upon our minds by culture, the whole world, the future as well as the present, would inevitably belong to the Philistines. The people who believe most that our greatness and welfare are proved by our being very rich, and who most give their lives and thoughts to becoming rich, are just the very people whom we call Philistines. Culture says: 'Consider these people, then, their way of life, their habits, their manners, the very tones of their voice; look at them attentively; observe the literature they read, the things which give them pleasure, the words which come forth out of their mouths, the thoughts which make the furniture of their minds;

would any amount of wealth be worth having with the condition that one was to become just like these people by having it?' And thus culture begets a dissatisfaction which is of the highest possible value in stemming the common tide of men's thoughts in a wealthy and industrial community, and which saves the future, as one may hope, from being vulgarized, even if it cannot save the present.

Population, again, and bodily health and vigour, are things which are nowhere treated in such an unintelligent, misleading, exaggerated way as in England. Both are really machinery; yet how many people all around us do we see rest in them and fail to look beyond them! why, one has heard people, fresh from reading certain articles of the *Times* on the Registrar-General's returns of marriages and births in this country, who would talk of our large English families in quite a solemn strain, as if they had something in itself beautiful, elevating, and meritorious in them; as if the British Philistine would have only to present himself before the Great Judge with his twelve children, in order to be received among the sheep as a matter of right!

But bodily health and vigour, it may be said, are not to be classed with wealth and population as mere machinery; they have a more real and essential value. True; but only as they are more intimately connected with a perfect spiritual condition than wealth or population are. The moment we disjoin them from the idea of a perfect spiritual condition, and pursue them, as we do pursue them, for their own sake and as ends in themselves, our worship of them becomes as mere worship of machinery, as our worship of wealth or population, and as unintelligent and vulgarizing a worship as that is. Everyone with anything like an adequate idea of human perfection has distinctly marked this subordination to higher and spiritual ends of the cultivation of bodily vigour and activity. 'Bodily exercise profiteth little; but godliness is profitable unto all things,' says the author of the Epistle to Timothy. And the utilitarian Franklin says just as explicitly: – 'Eat and drink such an exact quantity as suits the constitution of thy body, *in reference to the services of the mind*.' But the point of view of culture, keeping the mark of human perfection simply and broadly in view, and not assigning to this perfection, as religion or utilitarianism assign to it, a special and limited character, – this point of view, I say, of culture is best given by these words of Epictetus: – 'It is a sign of ἀφυΐα,' says he, – that is, of a nature not finely tempered, – 'to give yourselves up to things which relate to the body; to make, for instance, a great fuss about exercise, a great fuss about eating, a great fuss about drinking, a great fuss about walking, a great fuss about riding. All these things ought to be done merely by the way: the formation of the spirit and character must be our real concern.' This is admirable; and, indeed, the Greek word εὐφυΐα, a finely tempered nature, gives exactly the notion of perfection as culture brings us to conceive it: a harmonious perfection, a perfection in which the characters of beauty and intelligence are both present, which unites 'the two noblest of things,' – as Swift, who of one of the two, at any rate, had himself all too little, most happily calls them in his *Battle of the Books,* – 'the two noblest of things, *sweetness and light.*'[8] The εὐφυής is the man who tends towards sweetness and light; the ἀφυής, on the other hand, is our Philistine. The immense spiritual significance of the Greeks is due to their having been inspired with this central and happy idea of the essential character of human perception; and Mr Bright's misconception of culture, as a smattering of Greek and Latin, comes itself, after all, from this wonderful significance of the Greeks having affected the very machinery of our education, and is in itself a kind of homage to it.

In thus making sweetness and light to be characters of perfection, culture is of like spirit with poetry, follows one law with poetry. Far more than on our freedom, our population, and our industrialism, many among us rely upon our religious organizations to save us. I have called religion a yet more important manifestation of human nature than poetry, because it has worked on a broader scale for perfection, and with greater masses of men. But the idea of beauty and of a human nature perfect on all its sides, which is the dominant idea of poetry, is a true and invaluable idea, though it has not yet had the success that the idea of conquering the obvious faults of our animality, and of a human nature perfect on the moral

side, – which is the dominant idea of religion, – has been enabled to have; and it is destined, adding to itself the religious
idea of a devout energy, to transform and govern the other.

The best art and poetry of the Greeks, in which religion and
poetry are one, in which the idea of beauty and of a human
nature perfect on all sides adds to itself a religious and devout
energy, and works in the strength of that, is on this account of
such surpassing interest and instructiveness for us, though it
was, – as, having regard to the human race in general, and,
indeed, having regard to the Greeks themselves, we must own, –
a premature attempt, an attempt which for success needed the
moral and religious fibre in humanity to be more braced and
developed than it had yet been. But Greece did not err in having
the idea of beauty, harmony, and complete human perfection,
so present and paramount. It is impossible to have this idea too
present and paramount; only, the moral fibre must be braced,
too. And we, because we have braced the moral fibre, are not
on that account in the right way, if at the same time the idea of
beauty, harmony, and complete human perfection, is wanting
or misapprehended among us; and evidently it *is* wanting or
misapprehended at present. And when we rely as we do on our
religious organizations, which in themselves do not and cannot
give us this idea, and think we have done enough if we make
them spread and prevail, then, I say, we fall into our common
fault of overvaluing machinery.

Nothing is more common than for people to confound the
inward peace and satisfaction which follows the subduing of
the obvious faults of our animality with what I may call absolute inward peace and satisfaction, – the peace and satisfaction
which are reached as we draw near to complete spiritual perfection, and not merely to moral perfection, or rather to relative
moral perfection. No people in the world have done more and
struggled more to attain this relative moral perfection than our
English race has. For no people in the world has the command
to *resist the devil,* to *overcome the wicked one,* in the nearest
and most obvious sense of those words, had such a pressing
force and reality. And we have had our reward, not only in the
great worldly prosperity which our obedience to this command

has brought us, but also, and far more, in great inward peace and satisfaction. But to me few things are more pathetic than to see people, on the strength of the inward peace and satisfaction which their rudimentary efforts towards perfection have brought them, employ, concerning their incomplete perfection and the religious organizations within which they have found it, language which properly applies only to complete perfection, and is a far-off echo of the human soul's prophecy of it. Religion itself, I need hardly say, supplies them in abundance with this grand language. And very freely do they use it; yet it is really the severest possible criticism of such an incomplete perfection as alone we have yet reached through our religious organizations.

The impulse of the English race towards moral development and self-conquest has nowhere so powerfully manifested itself as in Puritanism. Nowhere has Puritanism found so adequate an expression as in the religious organization of the Independents. The modern Independents have a newspaper, the *Nonconformist*,[9] written with great sincerity and ability. The motto, the standard, the profession of faith which this organ of theirs carries aloft, is: 'The Dissidence of Dissent and the Protestation of the Protestant religion.' There is sweetness and light, and an ideal of complete harmonious human perfection! One need not go to culture and poetry to find language to judge it. Religion, with its instinct for perfection, supplies language to judge it, language, too, which is in our mouths every day. 'Finally, be of one mind, united in feeling,' says St Peter.[10] There is an ideal which judges the Puritan ideal: 'The Dissidence of Dissent and the Protestation of the Protestant religion!' And religious organizations like this are what people believe in, rest in, would give their lives for! Such, I say, is the wonderful virtue of even the beginnings of perfection, of having conquered even the plain faults of our animality, that the religious organization which has helped us to do it can seem to us something precious, salutary, and to be propagated, even when it wears such a brand of imperfection on its forehead as this. And men have got such a habit of giving to the language of religion a special application, of making it a mere jargon, that for the condemnation which religion itself passes on the shortcomings of their religious organizations they have no ear; they are sure to cheat themselves and to explain this condemnation away. They can only be reached by the criticism which culture, like poetry, speaking a language not to be sophisticated, and resolutely testing these organizations by the ideal of a human perfection complete on all sides, applies to them.

But men of culture and poetry, it will be said, are again and again failing, and failing conspicuously, in the necessary first stage to a harmonious perfection, in the subduing of the great obvious faults of our animality, which it is the glory of these religious organizations to have helped us to subdue. True, they do often so fail. They have often been without the virtues as well as the faults of the Puritan; it has been one of their dangers that they so felt the Puritan's faults that they too much neglected the practice of his virtues. I will not, however, exculpate them at the Puritan's expense. They have often failed in morality, and morality is indispensable. And they have been punished for their failure, as the Puritan has been rewarded for his performance. They have been punished wherein they erred; but their ideal of beauty, of sweetness and light, and a human nature complete on all its sides, remains the true ideal of perfection still; just as the Puritan's ideal of perfection remains narrow and inadequate, although for what he did well he has been richly rewarded. Notwithstanding the mighty results of the Pilgrim Fathers' voyage, they and their standard of perfection are rightly judged when we figure to ourselves Shakespeare or Virgil, – souls in whom sweetness and light, and all that in human nature is most humane, were eminent, – accompanying them on their voyage, and think what intolerable company Shakespeare and Virgil would have found them! In the same way let us judge the religious organizations which we see all around us. Do not let us deny the good and the happiness which they have accomplished; but do not let us fail to see clearly that their idea of human perfection is narrow and inadequate, and that the Dissidence of Dissent and the Protestantism of the Protestant religion will never bring humanity to its true goal. As I said with regard to wealth: Let us look at the life of those who live in and for it, – so I say with regard to the religious organizations. Look at the life imaged in such a newspaper as the *Nonconformist*, – a life of jealousy of the Establishment, disputes, tea-meetings, openings of chapels, sermons; and then think of it as an ideal of a human life completing itself on all sides, and aspiring with all its organs after sweetness, light, and perfection!

Another newspaper, representing, like the *Nonconformist*, one of the religious organizations of this country, was a short time ago giving an account of the crowd at Epsom on the Derby day, and of all the vice and hideousness which was to be seen in that crowd; and then the writer turned suddenly round upon Professor Huxley, and asked him how he proposed to cure all this vice and hideousness without religion.[11] I confess I felt disposed to ask the asker this question: and how do you propose to cure it with such a religion as yours? How is the ideal of a life so unlovely, so unattractive, so incomplete, so narrow, so far removed from a true and satisfying ideal of human perfection, as is the life of your religious organization as you yourself reflect it, to conquer and transform all this vice and hideousness? Indeed, the strongest plea for the study of perfection as pursued by culture, the clearest proof of the actual inadequacy of the idea of perfection held by the religious organizations, – expressing, as I have said, the most widespread effort which the human race has yet made after perfection, – is to be found in the state of our life and society with these in possession of it, and having been in possession of it I know not how many hundred years. We are all of us included in some religious organization or other; we all call ourselves, in the sublime and aspiring language of religion which I have before noticed, *children of God*. Children of God; – it is an immense pretension! – and how are we to justify it? By the works which we do, and the words which we speak. And the work which we collective children of God do, our grand centre of life, our *city* which we have builded for us to dwell in, is London ! London, with its unutterable external hideousness, and with its internal canker of *publicè egestas, privatim opulentia*,[12] – to use the words which Sallust puts into Cato's mouth about Rome, – unequalled in the world! The word, again, which we children of God speak, the voice which most hits our collective thought, the newspaper with the largest circulation in England, nay, with the largest circulation in the whole world, is the *Daily Telegraph*! I say that when our religious organizations, – which I admit to express the most considerable effort after perfection that our race has yet made, – land us in no better result than this, it is high time to examine carefully their idea of perfection, to see whether it does not leave out of account sides and forces of human nature which we might turn to great use; whether it would not be more operative if it were more complete. And I say that the English reliance on our religious organizations and on their ideas of human perfection just as they stand, is like our reliance on freedom, on muscular Christianity,[13] on population, on coal, on wealth, – mere belief in machinery, and unfruitful; and that it is wholesomely counteracted by culture, bent on seeing things as they are, and on drawing the human race onwards to a more complete, a harmonious perfection.

Culture, however, shows its single-minded love of perfection, its desire simply to make reason and the will of God prevail, its freedom from fanaticism, by its attitude towards all this machinery, even while it insists that it *is* machinery. Fanatics, seeing the mischief men do themselves by their blind belief in some machinery or other, – whether it is wealth and industrialism, or whether it is the cultivation of bodily strength and activity, or whether it is a political organization, – or whether it is a religious organization, – oppose with might and main the tendency to this or that political and religious organization, or to games and athletic exercises, or to wealth and industrialism, and try violently to stop it. But the flexibility which sweetness and light give, and which is one of the rewards of culture pursued in good faith, enables a man to see that a tendency may be necessary, and even, as a preparation for something in the future, salutary, and yet that the generations or individuals who obey this tendency are sacrificed to it, that they fall short of the hope of perfection by following it; and that its mischiefs are to be criticized, lest it should take too firm a hold and last after it has served its purpose.

Mr Gladstone well pointed out, in a speech at Paris, – and others have pointed out the same thing, – how necessary is the present great movement towards wealth and industrialism, in order to lay broad foundations of material well-being for the society of the future. The worst of these justifications is, that they are generally addressed to the very people engaged, body and soul, in the movement in question; at all events, that they are always seized with the greatest avidity by these people, and taken by them as quite justifying their life; and that thus they tend to harden them in their sins. Now, culture admits the necessity of the movement towards fortune-making and exaggerated industrialism, readily allows that the future may derive benefit from it; but insists, at the same time, that the passing generations of industrialists, – forming, for the most part, the stout main body of Philistinism, – are sacrificed to it. In the same way, the result of all the games and sports which occupy the passing generation of boys and young men may be the establishment of a better and sounder physical type for the future to work with. Culture does not set itself against the games and sports; it congratulates the future, and hopes it will make a good use of its improved physical basis; but it points out that our passing generation of boys and young men is, meantime, sacrificed. Puritanism was perhaps necessary to develop the moral fibre of the English race, Nonconformity to break the yoke of ecclesiastical domination over men's minds and to prepare the way for freedom of thought in the distant future; still, culture points out that the harmonious perfection of generations of Puritans and Nonconformists has been, in consequence, sacrificed. Freedom of speech may be necessary for the society of the future, but the young lions of the *Daily Telegraph* in the meanwhile are sacrificed. A voice for every man in his country's government may be necessary for the society of the future, but meanwhile Mr Beales and Mr Bradlaugh are sacrificed.[14]

Oxford, the Oxford of the past, has many faults; and she has heavily paid for them in defeat, in isolation, in want of hold upon the modern world. Yet we in Oxford, brought up amidst the beauty and sweetness of that beautiful place, have not failed to seize one truth: – the truth that beauty and sweetness are

essential characters of a complete human perfection. When I
insist on this, I am all in the faith and tradition of Oxford. I say
boldly that this our sentiment for beauty and sweetness, our
sentiment against hideousness and rawness, has been at the
bottom of our attachment to so many beaten causes, of our
opposition to so many triumphant movements. And the sentiment is true, and has never been wholly defeated, and has
shown its power even in its defeat. We have not won our political battles, we have not carried our main points, we have not
stopped our adversaries' advance, we have not marched victo-
riously with the modern world; but we have told silently upon
the mind of the country, we have prepared currents of feeling
which sap our adversaries' position when it seems gained, we
have kept up our own communications with the future. Look
at the course of the great movement which shook Oxford to its
centre some thirty years ago![15] It was directed, as anyone who
reads Dr Newman's *Apology* may see, against what in one
word may be called 'Liberalism.'[16] Liberalism prevailed; it was
the appointed force to do the work of the hour; it was necessary, it was inevitable that it should prevail. The Oxford
movement was broken, it failed; our wrecks are scattered on
every shore: –

Quæ regio in terris nostri non plena laboris?[17]

But what was it, this liberalism, as Dr Newman saw it, and as
it really broke the Oxford movement? It was the great
middle-class liberalism, which had for the cardinal points of its
belief the Reform Bill of 1832, and local self-government, in
politics; in the social sphere, free trade, unrestricted competition, and the making of large industrial fortunes; in the religious
sphere, the Dissidence of Dissent and the Protestantism of the
Protestant religion. I do not say that other and more intelligent
forces than this were not opposed to the Oxford movement:
but this was the force which really beat it; this was the force
which Dr Newman felt himself fighting with; this was the
force which till only the other day seemed to be the paramount
force in this country, and to be in possession of the future; this

was the force whose achievements fill Mr Lowe with such inexpressible admiration, and whose rule he was so horror-struck to see threatened.[18] And where is this great force of Philistinism now? It is thrust into the second rank, it is become a power of yesterday, it has lost the future. A new power has suddenly appeared, a power which it is impossible yet to judge fully, but which is certainly a wholly different force from middle-class liberalism; different in its cardinal points of belief, different in its tendencies in every sphere. It loves and admires neither the legalization of middle-class Parliaments, nor the local self-government of middle-class vestries, nor the unrestricted competition of middle-class industrialists, nor the dissidence of middle-class Dissent and the Protestantism of middle-class Protestant religion. I am not now praising this new force, or saying that its own ideals are better; all I say is, that they are wholly different. And who will estimate how much the currents of feeling created by Dr Newman's movements, the keen desire for beauty and sweetness which it nourished, the deep aversion it manifested to the hardness and vulgarity of middle-class liberalism, the strong light it turned on the hideous and grotesque illusions of middle-class Protestantism, – who will estimate how much all these contributed to swell the tide of secret dissatisfaction which has mined the ground under the self-confident liberalism of the last thirty years, and has prepared the way for its sudden collapse and supersession? It is in this manner that the sentiment of Oxford for beauty and sweetness conquers, and in this manner long may it continue to conquer!

In this manner it works to the same end as culture, and there is plenty of work for it yet to do. I have said that the new and more democratic force which is now superseding our middle-class liberalism cannot yet be rightly judged. It has its main tendencies still to form. We hear promises of its giving us administrative reform, law reform, reform of education, and I know not what; but those promises come rather from its advocates, wishing to make a good plea for it and to justify it for superseding middle-class liberalism, than from clear tendencies which it has itself yet developed. But meanwhile it has plenty of well-maintained friends against whom culture may with

advantage continue to uphold steadily its ideal of human perfection; that this is *an inward spiritual activity, having for its
characters increased sweetness, increased light, increased life,
increased sympathy.* Mr Bright, who has a foot in both worlds,
the world of middle-class liberalism and the world of democracy, but who brings most of his ideas from the world of
middle-class liberalism in which he was bred, always inclines
to inculcate that faith in machinery to which, as we have seen,
Englishmen are so prone, and which has been the bane of
middle-class liberalism. He complains with a sorrowful indignation of people who 'appear to have no proper estimate of the
value of the franchise'; he leads his disciples to believe, – what
the Englishman is always too ready to believe, – that the having
a vote, like the having a large family, or a large business, or
large muscles, has in itself some edifying and perfecting effect
upon human nature. Or else he cries out to the democracy, – 'the
men,' as he calls them, 'upon whose shoulders the greatness of
England rests,' – he cries out to them: 'See what you have done!
I look over this country and see the cities you have built, the
railroads you have made, the manufactures you have produced,
the cargoes which freight the ships of the greatest mercantile
navy the world has ever seen! I see that you have converted by
your labours what was once a wilderness, these islands, into a
fruitful garden; I know that you have created this wealth, and
are a nation whose name is a word of power throughout all the
world.' Why, this is just the very style of laudation with which
Mr Roebuck or Mr Lowe debauch the minds of the middle
classes, and make such Philistines of them. It is the same fashion of teaching a man to value himself not on what he *is,* not
on his progress in sweetness and light, but on the number of the
railroads he has constructed, or the bigness of the tabernacle he
has built. Only the middle classes are told they have done it all
with their energy, self-reliance, and capital, and the democracy
are told they have done it all with their hands and sinews. But
teaching the democracy to put its trust in achievements of this
kind is merely training them to be Philistines to take the place
of the Philistines whom they are superseding; and they too, like
the middle class, will be encouraged to sit down at the banquet

of the future without having on a wedding garment, and nothing excellent can then come from them. Those who know their besetting faults, those who have watched them and listened to them, or those who will read the instructive account recently given of them by one of themselves, the *Journeyman Engineer,*[19] will agree that the idea which culture sets before us of perfection, – an increased spiritual activity, having for its characters increased sweetness, increased light, increased life, increased sympathy, – is an idea which the new democracy needs far more than the idea of the blessedness of the franchise, or the wonderfulness of its own industrial performances.

Other well-meaning friends of this new power are for leading it, not in the old ruts of middle-class Philistinism, but in ways which are naturally alluring to the feet of democracy, though in this country they are novel and untried ways. I may call them the ways of Jacobinism. Violent indignation with the past, abstract systems of renovation applied wholesale, a new doctrine drawn up in black and white for elaborating down to the very smallest details a rational society for the future, – these are the ways of Jacobinism. Mr Frederic Harrison and other disciples of Comte, – one of them, Mr Congreve, is an old friend of mine, and I am glad to have an opportunity of publicly expressing my respect for his talents and character, – are among the friends of democracy who are for leading it in paths of this kind. Mr Frederic Harrison is very hostile to culture, and from a natural enough motive; for culture is the eternal opponent of the two things which are the signal marks of Jacobinism, – its fierceness, and its addiction to an abstract system. Culture is always assigning to system-makers and systems a smaller share in the bent of human destiny than their friends like. A current in people's minds sets towards new ideas; people are dissatisfied with their old narrow stock of Philistine ideas, Anglo-Saxon ideas, or any other; and some man, some Bentham or Comte, who has the real merit of having early and strongly felt and helped the new current, but who brings plenty of narrowness and mistakes of his own into his feeling and help of it, is credited with being the author of the whole current, the fit person to be entrusted with its regulation and to guide the human race.

The excellent German historian of the mythology of Rome, Preller, relating the introduction at Rome under the Tarquins of the worship of Apollo, the god of light, healing and reconcili-ation, will have us observe that it was not so much the Tarquins who brought to Rome the new worship of Apollo, as a current in the mind of the Roman people which set powerfully at that time towards a new worship of this kind, and away from the old run of Latin and Sabine religious ideas. In a similar way, culture directs our attention to the natural current there is in human affairs, and to its continual working, and will not let us rivet our faith upon any one man and his doings. It makes us see, not only his good side, but also how much in him was of necessity limited and transient; nay, it even feels a pleasure, a sense of an increased freedom and of an ampler future, in so doing.

I remember, when I was under the influence of a mind to which I feel the greatest obligations, the mind of a man who was the very incarnation of sanity and clear sense, a man the most considerable, it seems to me, whom America has yet pro-duced, – Benjamin Franklin, – I remember the relief with which, after long feeling the sway of Franklin's imperturbable com-monsense, I came upon a project of his for a new version of the Book of Job, to replace the old version, the style of which, says Franklin, has become obsolete, and thence less agreeable. 'I give,' he continues, 'a few verses, which may serve as a sample of the kind of version I would recommend.' We all recollect the famous verse in our translation: 'Then Satan answered the Lord and said: "Doth Job fear God for nought?"' Franklin makes this: 'Does Your Majesty imagine that Job's good con-duct is the effect of mere personal attachment and affection?' I well remember how when first I read that, I drew a deep breath of relief, and said to myself: 'After all, there is a stretch of humanity beyond Franklin's victorious good sense!' So, after hearing Bentham cried loudly up as the renovator of modern society, and Bentham's mind and ideas proposed as the rulers of our future, I open the *Deontology*. There I read: 'While Xen-ophon was writing his history and Euclid teaching geometry, Socrates and Plato were talking nonsense under pretence of talking wisdom and morality. This morality of theirs consisted in words; this wisdom of theirs was the denial of matters known to every man's experience.' From the moment of reading that, I am delivered from the bondage of Bentham! the fanaticism of his adherents can touch me no longer. I feel the inadequacy of his mind and ideas for supplying the rule of human society, for perfection.

Culture tends always thus to deal with the men of a system, of disciples, of a school; with men like Comte, or the late Mr Buckle, or Mr Mill.[20] However much it may find to admire in these personages, or in some of them, it nevertheless remembers the text: 'Be not ye called Rabbi!' and it soon passes on from any Rabbi.[21] But Jacobinism loves a Rabbi; it does not want to pass on from its Rabbi in pursuit of a future and still unreached perfection; it wants its Rabbi and his ideas to stand for perfection, that they may with the more authority recast the world; and for Jacobinism, therefore, culture, – eternally passing onwards and seeking, – is an impertinence and an offence. But culture, just because it resists this tendency of Jacobinism to impose on us a man with limitations and errors of his own along with the true ideas of which he is the organ, really does the world and Jacobinism itself a service.

So, too, Jacobinism, in its fierce hatred of the past and of those whom it makes liable for the sins of the past, cannot away with the inexhaustible indulgence proper to culture, the consideration of circumstances, the severe judgment of actions joined to the merciful judgment of persons. 'The man of culture is in politics,' cries Mr Frederic Harrison, 'one of the poorest mortals alive!' Mr Frederic Harrison wants to be doing business, and he complains that the man of culture stops him with a 'turn for small fault-finding, love of selfish ease, and indecision in action.' Of what use is culture, he asks, except for 'a critic of new books or a professor of *belles lettres*?' Why, it is of use because, in presence of the fierce exasperation which breathes, or rather, I may say, hisses, through the whole production in which Mr Frederic Harrison asks that question, it reminds us that the perfection of human nature is sweetness and light. It is of use because, like religion, – that other effort after perfection, – it testifies that, where bitter envying and strife are, there is confusion and every evil work.

The pursuit of perfection, then, is the pursuit of sweetness and light. He who works for sweetness and light, works to make reason and the will of God prevail. He who works for machinery, he who works for hatred, works only for confusion. Culture looks beyond machinery, culture hates hatred; culture has one great passion, the passion for sweetness and light. It has one even yet greater! – the passion for making them *prevail*. It is not satisfied till we *all* come to a perfect man; it knows that the sweetness and light of the few must be imperfect until the raw and unkindled masses of humanity are touched with sweetness and light. If I have not shrunk from saying that we must work for sweetness and light, so neither have I shrunk from saying that we must have a broad basis, must have sweetness and light for as many as possible. Again and again I have insisted how those are the happy moments of humanity, how those are the marking epochs of a people's life, how those are the flowering times for literature and art and all the creative power of genius, when there is a *national* glow of life and thought, when the whole of society is in the fullest measure permeated by thought, sensible to beauty, intelligent and alive.[22] Only it must be *real* thought and *real* beauty; *real* sweetness and *real* light. Plenty of people will try to give the masses, as they call them, an intellectual food prepared and adapted in the way they think proper for the actual condition of the masses. The ordinary popular literature is an example of this way of working on the masses. Plenty of people will try to indoctrinate the masses with the set of ideas and judgments constituting the creed of their own profession or party. Our religious and political organizations give an example of this way of working on the masses. I condemn neither way; but culture works differently. It does not try to teach down to the level of inferior classes; it does not try to win them for this or that sect of its own, with ready-made judgments and watchwords. It seeks to do away with classes; to make the best that has been thought and known in the world current everywhere; to make all men live in an atmosphere of sweetness and light, where they may use ideas, as it uses them itself, freely, – nourished, and not bound by them.

This is the *social idea*; and the men of culture are the true apostles of equality. The great men of culture are those who have had a passion for diffusing, for making prevail, for carrying from one end of society to the other, the best knowledge, the best ideas of their time; who have laboured to divest knowledge of all that was harsh, uncouth, difficult, abstract, professional, exclusive; to humanize it, to make it efficient outside the clique of the cultivated and learned, yet still remaining the *best* knowledge and thought of the time, and a true source, therefore, of sweetness and light. Such a man was Abelard in the Middle Ages, in spite of all his imperfections; and thence the boundless emotion and enthusiasm which Abelard excited.[23] Such were Lessing and Herder in Germany, at the end of the last century; and their services to Germany were in this way inestimably precious.[24] Generations will pass, and literary monuments will accumulate, and works far more perfect than the works of Lessing and Herder will be produced in Germany; and yet the names of these two men will fill a German with a reverence and enthusiasm such as the names of the most gifted masters will hardly awaken. And why? Because they *humanized* knowledge; because they broadened the basis of life and intelligence; because they worked powerfully to diffuse sweetness and light, to make reason and the will of God prevail. With Saint Augustine they said: 'Let us not leave Thee alone to make in the secret of thy knowledge, as thou didst before the creation of the firmament, the division of light from darkness; let the children of thy spirit, placed in their firmament, make their light shine upon the earth, mark the division of night and day, and announce the revolution of the times; for the old order is passed, and the new arises; the night is spent, the day is come forth; and thou shalt crown the year with thy blessing, when thou shalt send forth labourers into thy harvest sown by other hands than theirs; when thou shalt send forth new labourers to new seed-times, whereof the harvest shall be not yet.'

CHAPTER 2
Doing as One Likes

I have been trying to show that culture is, or ought to be, the study and pursuit of perfection; and that of perfection as pursued by culture, beauty and intelligence, or, in other words, sweetness and light, are the main characters. But hitherto I have been insisting chiefly on beauty, or sweetness, as a character of perfection. To complete rightly my design, it evidently remains to speak also of intelligence, or light, as a character of perfection.

First, however, I ought perhaps to notice that, both here and on the other side of the Atlantic, all sorts of objections are raised against the 'religion of culture,' as the objectors mockingly call it, which I am supposed to be promulgating. It is said to be a religion proposing parmaceti, or some scented salve or other, as a cure for human miseries; a religion breathing a spirit of cultivated inaction, making its believer refuse to lend a hand at uprooting the definite evils on all sides of us, and filling him with antipathy against the reforms and reformers which try to extirpate them. In general, it is summed up as being not practical, or, – as some critics familiarly put it, – all moonshine. That Alcibiades, the editor of the *Morning Star*,[1] taunts me, as its promulgator, with living out of the world and knowing nothing of life and men. That great austere toiler, the editor of the *Daily Telegraph*, upbraids me, – but kindly, and more in sorrow than in anger, – for trifling with æsthetics and poetical fancies, while he himself, in that arsenal of his in Fleet Street, is bearing the burden and heat of the day. An intelligent American newspaper, the *Nation*, says that it is very easy to sit in one's study and find fault with the course of modern society, but the thing is to propose practical improvements for it. While, finally, Mr Frederic Harrison, in a very good-tempered and witty satire, which makes me quite understand his having apparently achieved such a conquest of my young Prussian friend, Arminius, at last gets moved to an almost stern moral impatience, to behold, as he says, 'Death, sin, cruelty stalk among us, filling their maws with innocence and youth,' and me, in the midst of the general tribulation, handing out my pouncet-box.[2]

It is impossible that all these remonstrances and reproofs should not affect me, and I shall try my very best, in completing my design and in speaking of light as one of the characters of perfection, and of culture as giving us light, to profit by the objections I have heard and read, and to drive at practice as much as I can, by showing the communications and passages into practical life from the doctrine which I am inculcating.

It is said that a man with my theories of sweetness and light is full of antipathy against the rougher or coarser movements going on around him, that he will not lend a hand to the humble operation of uprooting evil by their means, and that, therefore, the believers in action grow impatient with him. But what if rough and coarse action, ill-calculated action, action with insufficient light, is, and has for a long time been, our bane? What if our urgent want now is, not to act at any price, but rather to lay in a stock of light for our difficulties? In that case, to refuse to lend a hand to the rougher and coarser movements going on round us, to make the primary need, both for oneself and others, to consist in enlightening ourselves and qualifying ourselves to act less at random, is surely the best and in real truth the most practical line our endeavours can take. So that if I can show what my opponents call rough or coarse action, but what I would rather call random and ill-regulated action, – action with insufficient light, action pursued because we like to be doing something and doing it as we please, and do not like the trouble of thinking and the severe constraint of any kind of rule, – if I can show this to be, at the present moment, a practical mischief and dangerous to us, then I have found a practical use for light in correcting this state of things, and have only to exemplify how, in cases which fall under everybody's observation, it may deal with it.

When I began to speak of culture, I insisted on our bondage to machinery, on our proneness to value machinery as an end in itself, without looking beyond it to the end for which alone, in truth, it is valuable. Freedom, I said, was one of those things which we thus worshipped in itself, without enough regarding the ends for which freedom is to be desired. In our common notions and talk about freedom, we eminently show our idolatry of machinery. Our prevalent notion is, – and I quoted a number of instances to prove it, – that it is a most happy and important thing for a man merely to be able to do as he likes. On what he is to do when he is thus free to do as he likes, we do not lay so much stress. Our familiar praise of the British Constitution under which we live, is that it is a system of checks, – a system which stops and paralyses any power in interfering with the free action of individuals.[3] To this effect Mr Bright, who loves to walk in the old ways of the Constitution, said forcibly in one of his great speeches, what many other people are every day saying less forcibly, that the central idea of English life and politics is the *assertion of personal liberty*. Evidently this is so; but evidently, also, as feudalism, which with its ideas and habits of subordination was for many centuries silently behind the British Constitution, dies out, and we are left with nothing but our system of checks, and our notion of its being the great right and happiness of an Englishman to do as far as possible what he likes, we are in danger of drifting towards anarchy. We have not the notion, so familiar on the Continent and to antiquity, of *the State*, – the nation in its collective and corporate character,[4] entrusted with stringent powers for the general advantage, and controlling individual wills in the name of an interest wider than that of individuals. We say, what is very true, that this notion is often made instrumental to tyranny; we say that a State is in reality made up of the individuals who compose it, and that every individual is the best judge of his own interests. Our leading class is an aristocracy, and no aristocracy likes the notion of a State-authority greater than itself, with a stringent administrative machinery superseding the decorative inutilities of lord-lieutenancy, deputy-lieutenancy, and the *posse comitatus,* which are all in its own hands. Our middle class, the great representative of trade and Dissent, with its maxims of every man for himself in business, every man for himself in religion, dreads a powerful administration which might somehow interfere with it; and besides, it has its own decorative inutilities of vestrymanship and guardianship, which are to this class what lord-lieutenancy and the county magistracy are to the aristocratic class, and a stringent administration might either take these functions out of its hands, or prevent its exercising them in its own comfortable, independent manner, as at present.

Then as to our working class. This class, pressed constantly by the hard daily compulsion of material wants, is naturally the very centre and stronghold of our national idea, that it is man's ideal right and felicity to do as he likes. I think I have somewhere related how M. Michelet said to me of the people of France, that it was 'a nation of barbarians civilized by the conscription.'[5] He meant that through their military service the idea of public duty and of discipline was brought to the mind of these masses, in other respects so raw and uncultivated. Our masses are quite as raw and uncultivated as the French; and so far from their having the idea of public duty and of discipline, superior to the individual's self-will, brought to their mind by a universal obligation of military service, such as that of the conscription, – so far from their having this, the very idea of a conscription is so at variance with our English notion of the prime right and blessedness of doing as one likes, that I remember the manager of the Clay Cross works in Derbyshire told me during the Crimean War, when our want of soldiers was much felt and some people were talking of a conscription, that sooner than submit to a conscription the population of that district would flee to the mines, and lead a sort of Robin Hood life under ground.

For a long time, as I have said, the strong feudal habits of subordination and deference continued to tell upon the working class. The modern spirit has now almost entirely dissolved those habits, and the anarchical tendency of our worship of freedom in and for itself, of our superstitious faith, as I say, in machinery, is becoming very manifest. More and more, because of this our blind faith in machinery, because of our want of light to enable us to look beyond machinery to the end for which machinery is valuable, this and that man, and this and that body of men, all over the country, are beginning to assert and put in practice an Englishman's right to do what he likes; his right to march where he likes, meet where he likes, enter where he likes, hoot as he likes, threaten as he likes, smash as he likes. All this, I say, tends to anarchy; and though a number of excellent people, and particularly my friends of the Liberal or progressive party, as they call themselves, are kind enough to reassure us by saying that these are trifles, that a few transient outbreaks of rowdyism signify nothing, that our system of liberty is one which itself cures all the evils which it works, that the educated and intelligent classes stand in overwhelming strength and majestic repose, ready, like our military force in riots, to act at a moment's notice, – yet one finds one's Liberal friends generally say this because they have such faith in themselves and their nostrums, when they shall return, as the public welfare requires, to place and power. But this faith of theirs one cannot exactly share, when one has so long had them and their nostrums at work, and sees that they have not prevented our coming to our present embarrassed condition. And one finds, also, that the outbreaks of rowdyism tend to become less and less of trifles, to become more frequent rather than less frequent; and that meanwhile our educated and intelligent classes remain in their majestic repose, and somehow or other, whatever happens, their overwhelming strength, like our military force in riots, never does act.

How, indeed, *should* their overwhelming strength act, when the man who gives an inflammatory lecture, or breaks down the park railings,[6] or invades a Secretary of State's office,[7] is only following an Englishman's impulse to do as he likes; and our own conscience tells us that we ourselves have always regarded this impulse as something primary and sacred? Mr Murphy lectures at Birmingham,[8] and showers on the Catholic population of that town 'words,' says the Home Secretary, 'only fit to be addressed to thieves or murderers.' What then? Mr Murphy has his own reasons of several kinds. He suspects the Roman Catholic Church of designs upon Mrs Murphy; and he says, if mayors and magistrates do not care for their wives and daughters, he does. But, above all, he is doing as he likes;

or in worthier language, asserting his personal liberty. 'I will carry out my lectures if they walk over my body as a dead corpse; and I say to the Mayor of Birmingham that he is my servant while I am in Birmingham, and as my servant he must do his duty and protect me.' Touching and beautiful words, which find a sympathetic chord in every British bosom! The moment it is plainly put before us that a man is asserting his personal liberty, we are half disarmed; because we are believers in freedom, and not in some dream of a right reason to which the assertion of our freedom is to be subordinated. Accordingly, the Secretary of State had to say that although the lecturer's language was 'only fit to be addressed to thieves or murderers,' yet, 'I do not think he is to be deprived, I do not think that anything I have said could justify the inference that he is to be deprived, of the right of protection in a place built by him for the purpose of these lectures; because the language was not language which afforded grounds for a criminal prosecution.' No, nor to be silenced by Mayor, or Home Secretary, or any administrative authority on earth, simply on their notion of what is discreet and reasonable! This is in perfect consonance with our public opinion, and with our national love for the assertion of personal liberty.

In quite another department of affairs, an experienced and distinguished Chancery Judge relates an incident which is just to the same effect as this of Mr Murphy. A testator bequeathed 300l. a year, to be for ever applied as a pension to some person who had been unsuccessful in literature, and whose duty should be to support and diffuse, by his writings, the testator's own views, as enforced in the testator's publications. The views were not worth a straw, and the bequest was appealed against in the Court of Chancery on the ground of its absurdity; but, being only absurd, it was upheld, and the so-called charity was established. Having, I say, at the bottom of our English hearts a very strong belief in freedom, and a very weak belief in right reason, we are soon silenced when a man pleads the prime right to do as he likes, because this is the prime right for ourselves, too; and even if we attempt now and then to mumble something about reason, yet we have ourselves thought so little about this and so much about liberty, that we are in conscience forced, when our brother Philistine with whom we are meddling turns boldly round upon us and asks: *Have you any light?* – to shake our heads ruefully, and to let him go his own way after all.

There are many things to be said on behalf of this exclusive attention of ours to liberty, and of the relaxed habits of government which it has engendered. It is very easy to mistake or to exaggerate the sort of anarchy from which we are in danger through them. We are not in danger from Fenianism,[9] fierce and turbulent as it may show itself; for against this our conscience is free enough to let us act resolutely and put forth our overwhelming strength the moment there is any real need for it. In the first place, it never was any part of our creed that the great right and blessedness of an Irishman, or, indeed, anybody on earth except an Englishman, is to do as he likes; and we can have no scruple at all about abridging, if necessary, a non-Englishman's assertion of personal liberty. The British Constitution, its checks, and its prime virtues, are for Englishmen. We may extend them to others out of love and kindness; but we find no real divine law written on our hearts constraining us so to extend them. And then the difference between an Irish Fenian and an English rough is so immense, and the case, in dealing with the Fenian, so much more clear! He is so evidently desperate and dangerous, a man of a conquered race, a Papist, with centuries of ill-usage to inflame him against us, with an alien religion established in his country by us at his expense, with no admiration of our institutions, no love of our virtues, no talents for our business, no turn for our comfort! Show him our symbolical Truss Manufactory on the finest site in Europe,[10] and tell him that British industrialism and individualism can bring a man to that, and he remains cold! Evidently, if we deal tenderly with a sentimentalist like this, it is out of pure philanthropy.

But with the Hyde Park rioter how different! He is our own flesh and blood; he is a Protestant; he is framed by nature to do as we do, hate what we hate, love what we love; he is capable of feeling the symbolical force of the Truss Manufactory; the question of questions, for him, is a wages question. That beautiful sentence Sir Daniel Gooch[11] quoted to the Swindon workmen, and which I treasure as Mrs Gooch's Golden Rule, or the Divine Injunction 'Be ye Perfect' done into British, – the sentence Sir Daniel Gooch's mother repeated to him every morning when he was a boy going to work: *'Ever remember, my dear Dan, that you should look forward to being some day manager of that concern!'* – this fruitful maxim is perfectly fitted to shine forth in the heart of the Hyde Park rough also, and to be his guiding-star through life. He has no visionary schemes of revolution and transformation, though of course he would like his class to rule, as the aristocratic class like their class to rule, and the middle class theirs. But meanwhile our social machine is a little out of order; there are a good many people in our paradisiacal centres of industrialism and individualism taking the bread out of one another's mouths. The rough has not yet quite found his groove and settled down to his work, and so he is just asserting his personal liberty a little, going where he likes, assembling where he likes, bawling as he likes, hustling as he likes. Just as the rest of us, – as the country squires in the aristocratic class, as the political dissenters in the middle class, – he has no idea of a *State,* of the nation in its collective and corporate character controlling, as government, the free swing of this or that one of its members in the name of the higher reason of all of them, his own as well as that of others. He sees the rich, the aristocratic class, in occupation of the executive government, and so if he is stopped from making Hyde Park a bear-garden or the streets impassable, he says he is being butchered by the aristocracy.

His apparition is somewhat embarrassing, because too many cooks spoil the broth; because, while the aristocratic and middle classes have long been doing as they like in great vigour, he has been too undeveloped and submissive hitherto to join in the game; and now, when he does come, he comes in immense numbers, and is rather raw and rough. But he does not break many laws, or not many at one time; and, as our laws were made for very different circumstances from our present (but always with an eye to Englishmen doing as they like), and as the clear letter of the law must be against our Englishman who does as he likes and not only the spirit of the law and public policy, and as Government must neither have any discretionary power nor act resolutely on its own interpretation of the law if any one disputes it, it is evident our laws give our playful giant, in doing as he likes, considerable advantage. Besides, even if he can be clearly proved to commit an illegality in doing as he likes, there is always the resource of not putting the law in force, or of abolishing it. So he has his way, and if he has his way he is soon satisfied for the time. However, he falls into the habit of taking it oftener and oftener, and at last begins to create by his operations a confusion of which mischievous people can take advantage, and which at any rate, by troubling the common course of business throughout the country, tends to cause distress, and so to increase the sort of anarchy and social disintegration which had previously commenced. And thus that profound sense of settled order and security, without which a society like ours cannot live and grow at all, sometimes seems to be beginning to threaten us with taking its departure.

Now, if culture, which simply means trying to perfect oneself, and one's mind as part of oneself, brings us light, and if light shows us that there is nothing so very blessed in merely doing as one likes, that the worship of the mere freedom to do as one likes is worship of machinery, that the really blessed thing is to like what right reason ordains, and to follow her authority, then we have got a practical benefit out of culture. We have got a much wanted principle, a principle of authority, to counteract the tendency to anarchy which seems to be threatening us.

But how to organize this authority, or to what hands to entrust the wielding of it? How to get your *State,* summing up the right reason of the community, and giving effect to it, as circumstances may require, with vigour? And here I think I see my enemies waiting for me with a hungry joy in their eyes. But I shall elude them.

The *State,* the power most representing the right reason of the nation, and most worthy, therefore, of ruling, – of exercising, when circumstances require it, authority over us all, – is for Mr Carlyle the aristocracy.[12] For Mr Lowe, it is the middle class with its incomparable Parliament. For the Reform League, it is the working class, the class with 'the brightest powers of sympathy and readiest powers of action.' Now culture, with its disinterested pursuit of perfection, culture, simply trying to see things as they are in order to seize on the best and to make it prevail, is surely well fitted to help us to judge rightly, by all the aids of observing, reading, and thinking, the qualifications and titles to our confidence of these three candidates for authority, and can thus render us a practical service of no mean value.

So when Mr Carlyle, a man of genius to whom we have all at one time or other been indebted for refreshment and stimulus, says we should give rule to the aristocracy, mainly because of its dignity and politeness, surely culture is useful in reminding us, that in our idea of perfection the characters of beauty and intelligence are both of them present, and sweetness and light, the two noblest of things, are united. Allowing, therefore, with Mr Carlyle, the aristocratic class to possess sweetness, culture insists on the necessity of light also, and shows us that aristocracies, being by the very nature of things inaccessible to ideas, unapt to see how the world is going, must be somewhat wanting in light, and must, therefore, be, at a moment when light is our great requisite, inadequate to our needs. Aristocracies, those children of the established fact, are for epochs of concentration. In epochs of expansion, epochs such as that in which we now live, epochs when always the warning voice is again heard: *Now is the judgment of this world*,[13] – in such epochs aristocracies with their natural clinging to the established fact, their want of sense for the flux of things, for the inevitable transitoriness of all human institutions, are bewildered and helpless. Their serenity, their high spirit, their power of haughty resistance, – the great qualities of an aristocracy, and the secret of its distinguished manners and dignity, – these very qualities, in an epoch of expansion, turn against their possessors. Again and again I have said how the refinement of an aristocracy may be precious and educative to a raw nation as a kind of shadow of true refinement; how its serenity and dignified freedom from petty cares may serve as a useful foil to set off the vulgarity and hideousness of that type of life which a hard middle class tends to establish, and to help people to see this vulgarity and hideousness in their true colours.[14] But the true grace and serenity is that of which Greece and Greek art suggest the admirable ideals of perfection, – a serenity which comes from having made order among ideas and harmonized them; whereas the serenity of aristocracies, at least the peculiar serenity of aristocracies of Teutonic origin, appears to come from their never having had any ideas to trouble them. And so, in a time of expansion like the present, a time for ideas, one gets, perhaps, in regarding an aristocracy, even more than the idea of serenity, the idea of futility and sterility.

One has often wondered whether upon the whole earth there is anything so unintelligent, so unapt to perceive how the world is really going, as an ordinary young Englishman of our upper class. Ideas he has not, and neither has he that serious-ness of our middle class which is, as I have often said, the great strength of this class, and may become its salvation. Why, a man may hear a young Dives of the aristocratic class,[15] when the whim takes him to sing the praises of wealth and material comfort, sing them with a cynicism from which the conscience of the veriest Philistine of our industrial middle class would recoil in affright. And when, with the natural sympathy of aris-tocracies for firm dealing with the multitude, and his uneasiness at our feeble dealing with it at home, an unvarnished young Englishman of our aristocratic class applauds the absolute rulers on the Continent, he in general manages completely to miss the grounds of reason and intelligence which alone can give any colour of justification, and possibility of existence, to those rulers, and applauds them on grounds which it would make their own hair stand on end to listen to.

And all this time we are in an epoch of expansion; and the essence of an epoch of expansion is a movement of ideas, and the one salvation of an epoch of expansion is a harmony of ideas. The very principle of the authority which we are seeking as a defence against anarchy is right reason, ideas, light. The more, therefore, an aristocracy calls to its aid its innate forces, – its impenetrability, its high spirit, its power of haughty resistance, – to deal with an epoch of expansion, the graver is the danger, the greater the certainty of explosion, the surer the aristocracy's defeat; for it is trying to do violence to nature instead of working along with it. The best powers shown by the best men of an aristocracy at such an epoch are, it will be observed, non-aristocratical powers, powers of industry, powers of intelligence; and these powers thus exhibited, tend really not to strengthen the aristocracy, but to take their owners out of it, to expose them to the dissolving agencies of thought and change, to make them men of the modern spirit and of the future. If, as sometimes happens, they add to their non-aristocratical qualities of labour and thought, a strong dose of aristocratical qualities also, – of pride, defiance, turn for resistance, – this truly aristocratical side of them, so far from adding any strength to them, really neutralizes their force and makes them impracticable and ineffective.

Knowing myself to be indeed sadly to seek, as one of my many critics says, in 'a philosophy with coherent, interdependent, subordinate and derivative principles,' I continually have recourse to a plain man's expedient of trying to make what few simple notions I have, clearer and more intelligible to myself by means of example and illustration. And having been brought up at Oxford in the bad old times,[16] when we were stuffed with Greek and Aristotle, and thought nothing of preparing ourselves by the study of modern languages, – as after Mr Lowe's great speech at Edinburgh we shall do, – to fight the battle of life with the waiters in foreign hotels,[17] my head is still full of a number of phrases we learnt at Oxford from Aristotle, about virtue being in a mean, and about excess and defect and so on.[18] Once when I had had the advantage of listening to the Reform debates in the House of Commons, having heard a number of interesting speakers, and among them a well-known lord and a well-known baronet,[19] I remember it struck me, applying Aristotle's machinery of the mean to my ideas about our aristocracy, that the lord was exactly the perfection, or happy mean, or virtue, of aristocracy, and the baronet the excess. And I fancied that by observing these two we might see both the inadequacy of aristocracy to supply the principle of authority needful for our present wants, and the danger of its trying to supply it when it was not really competent for the business. On the one hand, in the brilliant lord, showing plenty of high spirit, but remarkable, far above and beyond his gift of high spirit, for the fine tempering of his high spirit, for ease, serenity, politeness, – the great virtues, as Mr Carlyle says, of aristocracy, – in this beautiful and virtuous mean, there seemed evidently some insufficiency of light; while, on the other hand, the worthy baronet, in whom the high spirit of aristocracy, its impenetrability, defiant courage, and pride of resistance, were developed even in excess, was manifestly capable, if he had his way given him, of causing us great danger, and, indeed, of throwing the whole commonwealth into confusion. Then I reverted to that old fundamental notion of mine about the grand merit of our race being really our honesty. And the very helplessness of our aristocratic or governing class in dealing with our perturbed social condition, their jealousy of entrusting too much power to the State as it now actually exists – that is to themselves – gave me a sort of pride and satisfaction; because I saw they were, as a whole, too honest to try and manage a business for which they did not feel themselves capable.

Surely, now, it is no inconsiderable boon which culture confers upon us, if in embarrassed times like the present it enables us to look at the ins and the outs of things in this way, without hatred and without partiality, and with a disposition to see the good in everybody all round. And I try to follow just the same course with our middle class as with our aristocracy. Mr Lowe talks to us of this strong middle part of the nation, of the unrivalled deeds of our Liberal middle-class Parliament, of the noble, the heroic work it has performed in the last thirty years; and I begin to ask myself if we shall not, then, find in our middle class the principle of authority we want, and if we had not better take administration as well as legislation away from the weak extreme which now administers for us, and commit both to the strong middle part. I observe, too, that the heroes of middle-class liberalism, such as we have hitherto known it, speak with a kind of prophetic anticipation of the great destiny which awaits them, and as if the future was clearly theirs. The advanced party, the progressive party, the party in alliance with the future, are the names they like to give themselves. 'The principles which will obtain recognition in the future,' says Mr Miall,[20] a personage of deserved eminence among the political Dissenters, as they are called, who have been the backbone of middle-class liberalism – 'the principles which will obtain recognition in the future are the principles for which I have long and zealously laboured. I qualified myself for joining in the work of harvest by doing to the best of my ability the duties of seedtime.' These duties, if one is to gather them from the works of the great Liberal party in the last thirty years, are, as I have elsewhere summed them up, the advocacy of free trade, of Parliamentary reform, of abolition of church-rates, of voluntaryism in religion and education, of non-interference of the State between employers and employed, and of marriage with one's deceased wife's sister.

Now I know, when I object that all this is machinery, the great Liberal middle class has by this time grown cunning enough to answer that it always meant more by these things than meets the eye; that it has had that within which passes show, and that we are soon going to see, in a Free Church and all manner of good things, what it was. But I have learned from Bishop Wilson (if Mr Frederic Harrison will forgive my again quoting that poor old hierophant of a decayed superstition): 'If we would really know our heart let us impartially view our actions'; and I cannot help thinking that if our Liberals had had so much sweetness and light in their inner minds as they allege, more of it must have come out in their sayings and doings.

An American friend of the English Liberals says, indeed, that their Dissidence of Dissent has been a mere instrument of the political Dissenters for making reason and the will of God prevail (and no doubt he would say the same of marriage with one's deceased wife's sister); and that the abolition of a State Church is merely the Dissenter's means to this end, just as culture is mine. Another American defender of theirs says just the same of their industrialism and free trade; indeed, this gentleman, taking the bull by the horns, proposes that we should for the future call industrialism culture, and the industrialists the men of culture, and then of course there can be no longer any misapprehension about their true character; and besides the pleasure of being wealthy and comfortable, they will have authentic recognition as vessels of sweetness and light.

All this is undoubtedly specious; but I must remark that the culture of which I talked was an endeavour to come at reason and the will of God by means of reading, observing, and thinking; and that whoever calls anything else culture, may, indeed, call it so if he likes, but then he talks of something quite different from what I talked of. And, again, as culture's way of working for reason and the will of God is by directly trying to know more about them, while the Dissidence of Dissent is evidently in itself no effort of this kind, nor is its Free Church, in fact, a Church with worthier conceptions of God and the ordering of the world than the State Church professes, but with mainly the same conceptions of these as the State Church has, only that every man is to comport himself as he likes in professing them, – this being so, I cannot at once accept the Nonconformity any more than the industrialism and the other great works of our Liberal middle class as proof positive that this class is in possession of light, and that here is the true seat of authority for which we are in search; but I must try a little further, and seek for other indications which may enable me to make up my mind.

Why should we not do with the middle class as we have done with the aristocratic class, – find in it some representative men who may stand for the virtuous mean of this class, for the perfection of its present qualities and mode of being, and also for the excess of them. Such men must clearly not be men of genius like Mr Bright; for, as I have formerly said, so far as a man has genius he tends to take himself out of the category of class altogether, and to become simply a man. Some more ordinary man would be more to the purpose, – would sum up better in himself, without disturbing influences, the general liberal force of the middle class, the force by which it has done its great works of free trade, Parliamentary reform, voluntaryism, and so on, and the spirit in which it has done them. Now it happens that a typical middle-class man,[21] the member for one of our chief industrial cities, has given us a famous sentence which bears directly on the resolution of our present question: whether there is light enough in our middle class to make it the proper seat of the authority we wish to establish. When there was a talk some little while ago about the state of middle-class education, our friend, as the representative of that class, spoke some memorable words: – 'There had been a cry that middle-class education ought to receive more attention. He confessed himself very much surprised by the clamour that was raised. He did not think that class need excite the sympathy either of the legislature or the public.' Now this satisfaction of our middle-class member of Parliament with the mental state of the middle class was truly representative, and makes good his claim to stand as the beautiful and virtuous mean of that class. But it is obviously at variance with our definition of culture, or the pursuit of light and perfection, which made light and perfection consist, not in resting and being, but in growing and becoming, in a perpetual advance in beauty and wisdom. So the middle class is by its essence, as one may say, by its incomparable self-satisfaction decisively expressed through its beautiful and virtuous mean, self-excluded from wielding an authority of which light is to be the very soul.

Clear as this is, it will be made clearer still if we take some representative man as the excess of the middle class, and remember that the middle class, in general, is to be conceived as a body swaying between the qualities of its mean and of its excess, and on the whole, of course, as human nature is constituted, inclining rather towards the excess than the mean. Of its excess no better representative can possibly be imagined than a Dissenting minister from Walsall,[22] who came before the public in connection with the proceedings at Birmingham of Mr Murphy, already mentioned. Speaking in the midst of an irritated population of Catholics, this Walsall gentleman exclaimed: – 'I say, then, away with the Mass! It is from the bottomless pit; and in the bottomless pit shall all liars have their part, in the lake that burneth with fire and brimstone.' And again: 'When all the praties were black in Ireland, why didn't the priests say the hocus-pocus over them, and make them all good again?' He shared, too, Mr Murphy's fears of some invasion of his domestic happiness: 'What I wish to say to you as Protestant husbands is, *Take care of your wives!*' And, finally, in the true vein of an Englishman doing as he likes, a vein of which I have at some length pointed out the present dangers, he recommended for imitation the example of some church-wardens at Dublin, among whom, said he, 'there was a Luther and also a Melanchthon,'[23] who had made very short work with some ritualist or other, hauled him down from his pulpit, and kicked him out of church. Now it is manifest, as I said in the case of our aristocratical baronet, that if we let this excess of the sturdy English middle class, this conscientious Protestant Dissenter, so strong, so self-reliant, so fully persuaded in his own mind, have his way, he would be capable, with his want of light, – or, to use the language of the religious world, with his zeal without knowledge, – of stirring up strife which neither he nor anyone else could easily compose.

And then comes in, as it did also with the aristocracy, the honesty of our race, and by the voice of another middle-class man, Alderman of the City of London and Colonel of the City of London Militia, proclaims that it has twinges of conscience, and that it will not attempt to cope with our social disorders, and to deal with a business which it feels to be too high for it. Everyone remembers how this virtuous Alderman-Colonel, or Colonel-Alderman, led his militia through the London streets; how the bystanders gathered to see him pass; how the London roughs, asserting an Englishman's best and most blissful right of doing what he likes, robbed and beat the bystanders; and how the blameless warrior-magistrate refused to let his troops interfere.[24] 'The crowd,' he touchingly said afterwards, 'was mostly composed of fine healthy strong men, bent on mischief; if he had allowed his soldiers to interfere they might have been over-powered, their rifles taken from them and used against them by the mob; a riot, in fact, might have ensued, and been attended with bloodshed, compared with which the assaults and loss of property that actually occurred would have been as nothing.' Honest and affecting testimony of the English middle class to its own inadequacy for the authoritative part one's admiration would sometimes incline one to assign to it! 'Who are we,' they say by the voice of their Alderman-Colonel, 'that we should not be overpowered if we attempt to cope with social anarchy, our rifles taken from us and used against us by the mob, and we, perhaps, robbed and beaten ourselves? Or what light have we, beyond a free-born Englishman's impulse to do as he likes, which could justify us in preventing, at the cost of bloodshed, other free-born Englishmen from doing as they like, and robbing and beating us as much as they please?'

This distrust of themselves as an adequate centre of authority does not mark the working class, as was shown by their readiness the other day in Hyde Park to take upon themselves all the functions of government. But this comes from the working class being, as I have often said, still an embryo, of which no one can yet quite foresee the final development; and from its not having the same experience and self-knowledge as the aristocratic and middle classes. Honesty it no doubt has, just like the other classes of Englishmen, but honesty in an inchoate and untrained state; and meanwhile its powers of action, which are, as Mr Frederic Harrison says, exceedingly ready, easily run away with it. That it cannot at present have a sufficiency of light which comes by culture, – that is, by reading, observing, and thinking, – is clear from the very nature of its condition; and, indeed, we saw that Mr Frederic Harrison, in seeking to make a free stage for its bright powers of sympathy and ready powers of action, had to begin by throwing overboard culture, and flouting it as only fit for a professor of *belles lettres*. Still, to make it perfectly manifest that no more in the working class than in the aristocratic and middle classes can one find an adequate centre of authority, – that is, as culture teaches us to conceive our required authority, of light, – let us again follow, with this class, the method we have followed with the aristocratic and middle classes, and try to bring before our minds representative men, who may figure to us its virtue and its excess.

We must not take, of course, men like the chiefs of the Hyde Park demonstration, Colonel Dickson or Mr Beales; because Colonel Dickson, by his martial profession and dashing exterior, seems to belong properly, like Julius Cæsar and Mirabeau and other great popular leaders, to the aristocratic class, and to be carried into the popular ranks only by his ambition or his genius; while Mr Beales belongs to our solid middle class, and, perhaps, if he had not been a great popular leader, would have been a Philistine. But Mr Odger,[25] whose speeches we have all read, and of whom his friends relate, besides, much that is favourable, may very well stand for the beautiful and virtuous mean of our present working class; and I think everybody will admit that in Mr Odger there is manifestly, with all his good points, some insufficiency of light. The excess of the working class, in its present state of development, is perhaps best shown in Mr Bradlaugh, the inconoclast, who seems to be almost for baptizing us all in blood and fire into his new social dispensation, and to whose reflections, now that I have once been set going on Bishop Wilson's track, I cannot forbear commending this maxim of the good old man: 'Intemperance in talk makes a dreadful havoc in the heart.' Mr Bradlaugh, like our types of excess in the aristocratic and middle classes, is evidently capable, if he had his head given him, of running us all into great dangers and confusion. I conclude, therefore, – what indeed, few of those who do me the honour to read this disquisition are likely to dispute, – that we can as little find in the working class as in the aristocratic or in the middle class our much-wanted source of authority, as culture suggests it to us.

Well, then, what if we tried to rise above the idea of class to the idea of the whole community, *the State,* and to find our centre of light and authority there? Everyone of us has the idea of country, as a sentiment; hardly anyone of us has the idea of *the State,* as a working power. And why? Because we habitually live in our ordinary selves, which do not carry us beyond the ideas and wishes of the class to which we happen to belong. And we are all afraid of giving to the State too much power, because we only conceive of the State as something equivalent to the class in occupation of the executive government, and are afraid of that class abusing power to its own purposes. If we strengthen the State with the aristocratic class in occupation of the executive government, we imagine we are delivering ourselves up captive to the ideas and wishes of our fierce aristocratical baronet; if with the middle class in occupation of the executive government, to those of our truculent middle-class Dissenting minister; if with the working class, to those of its notorious tribune, Mr Bradlaugh. And with much justice; owing to the exaggerated notion which we English, as I have said, entertain of the right and blessedness of the mere doing as one likes, of the affirming oneself, and oneself just as it is. People of the aristocratic class want to affirm their ordinary selves, their likings and dislikings; people of the middle class the same, people of the working class the same. By our every-day selves, however, we are separate, personal, at war; we are only safe from one another's tyranny when no one has any power; and this safety, in its turn, cannot save us from anarchy. And when, therefore, anarchy presents itself as a danger to us, we know not where to turn.

But by our *best self* we are united, impersonal, at harmony. We are in no peril from giving authority to this, because it is the truest friend we all of us have; and when anarchy is a danger to us, to this authority we may turn with sure trust. Well, and this is the very self which culture, or the study of perfection, seeks to develop in us; at the expense of our old untransformed self, taking pleasure only in doing what it likes or is used to do, and exposing us to the risk of clashing with everyone else who is doing the same! So that our poor culture, which is flouted as so unpractical, leads us to the very ideas capable of meeting the great want of our present embarrassed times! We want an authority, and we find nothing but jealous classes, checks, and a deadlock; culture suggests the idea of *the State*. We find no basis for a firm State-power in our ordinary selves; culture suggests one to us in our *best self*.

It cannot but acutely try a tender conscience to be accused, in a practical country like ours, of keeping aloof from the work and hope of a multitude of earnest-hearted men, and of merely toying with poetry and æsthetics. So it is with no little sense of relief that I find myself thus in the position of one who makes a contribution in aid of the practical necessities of our times. The great thing, it will be observed, is to find our *best* self, and to seek to affirm nothing but that; not, – as we English with our over-value for merely being free and busy have been so accustomed to do, – resting satisfied with a self which comes uppermost long before our best self, and affirming that with blind energy. In short, – to go back yet once more to Bishop Wilson, – of these two excellent rules of Bishop Wilson's for a man's guidance: 'Firstly, never go against the best light you have; secondly, take care that your light be not darkness,' we English have followed with praiseworthy zeal the first rule, but we have not given so much heed to the second. We have gone manfully according to the best light we have; but we have not taken enough care that this should be really the best light possible for us, that it should not be darkness. And, our honesty being very great, conscience has whispered to us that the light we were following, our ordinary self, was, indeed, perhaps, only an inferior self, only darkness; and that it would not do to impose this seriously on all the world.

But our best self inspires faith, and is capable of affording a serious principle of authority. For example. We are on our way to what the late Duke of Wellington, with his strong sagacity, foresaw and admirably described as 'a revolution by due course of law.'[26] This is undoubtedly, – if we are still to live and grow, and this famous nation is not to stagnate and dwindle away on the one hand, or, on the other, to perish miserably in mere anarchy and confusion, – what we are on the way to. Great changes there must be, for a revolution cannot accomplish itself without great changes; yet order there must be, for without order a revolution cannot accomplish itself by due course of law. So whatever brings risk of tumult and disorder, multitudinous processions in the streets of our crowded towns, multitudinous meetings in their public places and parks, – demonstrations perfectly unnecessary in the present course of our affairs, – our best self, or right reason, plainly enjoins us to set our faces against. It enjoins us to encourage and uphold the occupants of the executive power, whoever they may be, in firmly prohibiting them. But it does this clearly and resolutely, and is thus a real principle of authority, because it does it with a free conscience; because in thus provisionally strengthening the executive power, it knows that it is not doing this merely to enable our aristocratical baronet to affirm himself as against our working men's tribune, or our middle-class Dissenter to affirm himself as against both. It knows that it is establishing *the State,* or organ of our collective best self, of our national right reason. And it has the testimony of conscience that it is establishing the State on behalf of whatever great changes are needed, just as much as on behalf of order; establishing it to deal just as stringently, when the time comes, with our baronet's aristocratical prejudices, or with the fanaticism of our middle-class Dissenter, as it deals with Mr Bradlaugh's street-processions.

CHAPTER 3

Barbarians, Philistines, Populace

From a man without a philosophy no one can expect philo-sophical completeness. Therefore, I may observe without shame, that in trying to get a distinct notion of our aristocratic, our middle, and our working class, with a view of testing the claims of each of these classes to become a centre of authority, I have omitted, I find, to complete the old-fashioned analysis which I had the fancy of applying, and have not shown in these classes, as well as the virtuous mean and the excess, the defect also. I do not know that the omission very much matters. Still as clear-ness is the one merit which a plain, unsystematic writer, without a philosophy, can hope to have, and as our notion of the three great English classes may perhaps be made clearer if we see their distinctive qualities in the defect, as well as in the excess and in the mean, let us try, before proceeding further, to remedy this omission.

It is manifest, if the perfect and virtuous mean of that fine spirit which is the distinctive quality of aristocracies, is to be found in a high, chivalrous style, and its excess in a fierce turn for resistance, that its defect must lie in a spirit not bold and high enough, and in an excessive and pusillanimous unaptness for resistance. If, again, the perfect and virtuous mean of that force by which our middle class has done its great works, and of that self-reliance with which it contemplates itself and them, is to be seen in the performances and speeches of our commercial member of Parliament, and the excess of that force and of that self-reliance in the performances and speeches of our fanatical Dissenting minister, then it is manifest that their defect must lie in a helpless inaptitude for the great works of the middle class, and in a poor and despicable lack of its self-satisfaction.

To be chosen to exemplify the happy mean of a good quality, or set of good qualities, is evidently a praise to a man; nay, to be chosen to exemplify even their excess, is a kind of praise. Therefore, I could have no hesitation in taking actual personages to exemplify, respectively, the mean and the excess of aristocratic and middle-class qualities. But perhaps there might be a want of urbanity in singling out this or that personage as the representative of defect. Therefore, I shall leave the defect of aristocracy unillustrated by any representative man. But with oneself one may always, without impropriety, deal quite freely; and, indeed, this sort of plain-dealing with oneself has in it, as all the moralists tell us, something very wholesome. So I will venture to humbly offer myself as an illustration of defect in those forces and qualities which make our middle class what it is. The too well-founded reproaches of my opponents declare how little I have lent a hand to the great works of the middle class; for it is evidently these works, and my slackness at them, which are meant, when I am said to 'refuse to lend a hand to the humble operation of uprooting certain definite evils' (such as church-rates and others), and that, therefore, 'the believers in action grow impatient' with me. The line, again, of a still unsatisfied seeker which I have followed, the idea of self-transformation, of growing towards some measure of sweetness and light not yet reached, is evidently at clean variance with the perfect self-satisfaction current in my class, the middle class, and may serve to indicate in me, therefore, the extreme defect of this feeling. But these confessions, though salutary, are bitter and unpleasant.

To pass, then, to the working class. The defect of this class would be the falling short in what Mr Frederic Harrison calls those 'bright powers of sympathy and ready powers of action,' of which we saw in Mr Odger the virtuous mean, and in

Mr Bradlaugh the excess. The working class is so fast growing and rising at the present time, that instances of this defect cannot well be now very common. Perhaps Canning's 'Needy Knife-Grinder'[1] (who is dead, and, therefore, cannot be pained at my taking him for an illustration) may serve to give us the notion of defect in the essential quality of a working class; or I might even cite (since, though he is alive in the flesh, he is dead to all heed of criticism) my poor old poaching friend, Zephaniah Diggs,[2] who, between his hare-snaring and his gin-drinking, has got his powers of sympathy quite dulled and his powers of action in any great movement of his class hopelessly impaired. But examples of this defect belong, as I have said, to a bygone age rather than to the present.

The same desire for clearness, which has led me thus to extend a little my first analysis of the three great classes of English society, prompts me also to improve my nomenclature for them a little, with a view to making it thereby more manageable. It is awkward and tiresome to be always saying the aristocratic class, the middle class, the working class. For the middle class, for that great body which, as we know, 'has done all the great things that have been done in all departments,' and which is to be conceived as moving between its two cardinal points of our commercial member of Parliament and our fanatical Protestant Dissenter, – for this class we have a designation which now has become pretty well known, and which we may as well still keep for them, the designation of Philistines. What this term means I have so often explained that I need not repeat it here.[3] For the aristocratic class, conceived mainly as a body moving between the two cardinal points of our chivalrous lord and our defiant baronet, we have as yet got no special designation. Almost all my attention has naturally been concentrated on my own class, the middle class, with whom I am in closest sympathy, and which has been, besides, the great power of our day, and has had its praises sung by all speakers and newspapers.

Still the aristocratic class is so important in itself, and the weighty functions which Mr Carlyle proposes at the present critical time to commit to it must add so much to its importance, that it seems neglectful and a strong instance of that want of coherent philosophic method for which Mr Frederic Harrison blames me, to leave the aristocratic class so much without notice and denomination. It may be thought that the characteristic which I have occasionally mentioned as proper to aristocracies, – their natural inaccessibility, as children of the established fact, to ideas, – points to our extending to this class also the designation of Philistines; the Philistine being, as is well known, the enemy of the children of light or servants of the idea. Nevertheless, there seems to be an inconvenience in thus giving one and the same designation to two very different classes; and besides, if we look into the thing closely, we shall find that the term Philistine conveys a sense which makes it more peculiarly appropriate to our middle class than to our aristocratic. For *Philistine* gives the notion of something particularly stiff-necked and perverse in the resistance to light and its children; and therein it specially suits our middle class, who not only do not pursue sweetness and light, but who even prefer to them that sort of machinery of business, chapels, tea-meetings, and addresses from Mr Murphy, which makes up the dismal and illiberal life on which I have so often touched. But the aristocratic class has actually, as we have seen, in its well-known politeness, a kind of image or shadow of sweetness; and as for light, if it does not pursue light, it is not that it perversely cherishes some dismal and illiberal existence in preference to light, but it is lured off from following light by those mighty and eternal seducers of our race which weave for this class their most irresistible charms, – by worldly splendour, security, power, and pleasure. These seducers are exterior goods, but in a way they are goods; and he who is hindered by them from caring for light and ideas, is not so much doing what is perverse as what is too natural.

Keeping this in view, I have in my own mind often indulged myself with the fancy of employing, in order to designate our aristocratic class, the name of *The Barbarians*.[4] The Barbarians, to whom we all owe so much, and who reinvigorated and renewed our worn-out Europe, had, as is well known, eminent merits; and in this country, where we are for the most part sprung from the Barbarians, we have never had the prejudice against them which prevails among the races of Latin origin. The Barbarians brought with them that staunch individualism, as the modern phrase is, and that passion for doing as one likes, for the assertion of personal liberty, which appears to Mr Bright the central idea of English life, and of which we have, at any rate, a very rich supply. The stronghold and natural seat of this passion was in the nobles of whom our aristocratic class are the inheritors; and this class, accordingly, have signally manifested it, and have done much by their example to recommend it to the body of the nation, who already, indeed, had it in their blood. The Barbarians, again, had the passion for field-sports; and they have handed it on to our aristocratic class, who of this passion too, as of the passion for asserting one's personal liberty, are the great natural stronghold. The care of the Barbarians for the body, and for all manly exercises; the vigour, good looks, and fine complexion which they acquired and perpetuated in their families by these means, – all this may be observed still in our aristocratic class. The chivalry of the Barbarians, with its characteristics of high spirit, choice manners, and distinguished bearing, – what is this but the attractive commencement of the politeness of our aristocratic class? In some Barbarian noble, no doubt, one would have admired, if one could have been then alive to see it, the rudiments of our politest peer. Only, all this culture (to call it by that name) of the Barbarians was an exterior culture mainly. It consisted principally in outward gifts and graces, in looks, manners, accomplishments, prowess. The chief inward gifts which had part in it were the most exterior, so to speak, of inward gifts, those which come nearest to outward ones; they were courage, a high spirit, self-confidence. Far within, and unawakened, lay a whole range of powers of thought and feeling, to which these interesting productions of nature had, from the circumstances of their life, no access. Making allowances for the difference of the times, surely we can observe precisely the same thing now in our aristocratic class. In general its culture is exterior chiefly; all the exterior graces and accomplishments, and the more external of the inward virtues, seem to be principally its portion. It now, of course, cannot but be often in contact with those studies by which, from the world of thought and feeling, true culture teaches us to fetch sweetness and light; but its hold upon these very studies appears remarkably external, and unable to exert any deep power upon its spirit. Therefore, the one insufficiency which we noted in the perfect mean of this class was an insufficiency of light. And owing to the same causes, does not a subtle criticism lead us to make, even on the good looks and politeness of our aristocratic class, and of even the most fascinating half of that class, the feminine half, the one qualifying remark, that in these charming gifts there should perhaps be, for ideal perfection, a shade more *soul*?

I often, therefore, when I want to distinguish clearly the aristocratic class from the Philistines proper, or middle class, name the former, in my own mind, *the Barbarians*. And when I go through the country, and see this and that beautiful and imposing seat of theirs crowning the landscape, 'There,' I say to myself, 'is a great fortified post of the Barbarians.'

It is obvious that that part of the working class which, working diligently by the light of Mrs Gooch's Golden Rule, looks forward to the happy day when it will sit on thrones with commercial members of Parliament and other middle-class potentates, to survey, as Mr Bright beautifully says, 'the cities it has built, the railroads it has made, the manufactures it has produced, the cargoes which freight the ships of the greatest mercantile navy the world has ever seen,' – it is obvious, I say, that this part of the working class is, or is in a fair way to be, one in spirit with the industrial middle class. It is notorious that our middle-class Liberals have long looked forward to this consummation, when the working class shall join forces with them, aid them heartily to carry forward their great works, go in a body to their tea-meetings, and, in short, enable them to bring about their millennium. That part of the working class, therefore, which does really seem to lend itself to these great aims, may, with propriety, be numbered by us among the Philistines. That part of it, again, which so much occupies the attention of philanthropists at present, – the part which gives all its energies to organizing itself, through trades' unions and other means, so as to constitute, first, a great working-class power independent of the middle and aristocratic classes, and then, by dint of numbers, give the law to them and itself reign absolutely, – this lively and promising part must also, according to our definition, go with the Philistines; because it is its class and its class instinct which it seeks to affirm, its ordinary self not its best self; and it is a machinery, an industrial machinery, and power and pre-eminence and other external goods, which fill its thoughts, and not an inward perfection. It is wholly occupied, according to Plato's subtle expression, with the things of itself and not its real self, with the things of the State and not the real State. But that vast portion, lastly, of the working class which, raw and half-developed, has long lain half-hidden amidst its poverty and squalor, and is now issuing from its hiding-place to assert an Englishman's heaven-born privilege of doing as he likes, and is beginning to perplex us by marching where it likes, meeting where it likes, bawling what it likes, breaking what it likes, – to this vast residuum we may with great propriety give the name of *Populace*.

Thus we have got three distinct terms, *Barbarians, Philistines, Populace,* to denote roughly the three great classes into which our society is divided; and though this humble attempt at a scientific nomenclature falls, no doubt, very far short in precision of what might be required from a writer equipped with a complete and coherent philosophy, yet, from a notoriously unsystematic and unpretending writer, it will, I trust, be accepted as sufficient.

But in using this new, and, I hope, convenient division of English society, two things are to be borne in mind. The first is, that since, under all our class divisions, there is a common basis of human nature, therefore, in every one of us, whether we be properly Barbarians, Philistines, or Populace, there exists, sometimes only in germ and potentially, sometimes more or less developed, the same tendencies and passions which have made our fellow-citizens of other classes what they are. This consideration is very important, because it has great influence in begetting that spirit of indulgence which is a necessary part of sweetness, and which, indeed, when our culture is complete, is, as I have said, inexhaustible. Thus, an English Barbarian who examines himself will, in general, find himself to be not so entirely a Barbarian but that he has in him, also, something of the Philistine, and even something of the Populace as well. And the same with Englishmen of the two other classes.

This is an experience which we may all verify every day. For instance, I myself (I again take myself as a sort of *corpus vile* to serve for illustration in a matter where serving for illustration may not by everyone be thought agreeable), I myself am properly a Philistine, – Mr Swinburne would add, the son of a Philistine.[5] And although, through circumstances which will perhaps one day be known if ever the affecting history of my conversion comes to be written, I have, for the most part, broken with the ideas and the tea-meetings of my own class, yet I have not, on that account, been brought much the nearer to the ideas and works of the Barbarians or of the Populace. Nevertheless, I never take a gun or a fishing-rod in my hands without feeling that I have in the ground of my nature the self-same seeds which, fostered by circumstances, do so much to make the Barbarian; and that, with the Barbarian's advantages, I might have rivalled him.[6] Place me in one of his great fortified posts, with these seeds of a love for field-sports sown in my nature, with all the means of developing them, with all pleasures at my command, with most whom I met deferring to me, everyone I met smiling on me, and with every appearance of permanence and security before me and behind me, – then I, too, might have grown, I feel, into a very passable child of the established fact, of commendable spirit and politeness, and, at the same time, a little inaccessible to ideas and light; not, of course, with either the eminent fine spirit of our type of aristocratic perfection, or the eminent turn for resistance of our type of aristocratic excess, but, according to the measure of the common run of mankind, something between the two. And as to the Populace, who, whether he be Barbarian or Philistine, can look at them without sympathy, when he remembers how often, – every time that we snatch up a vehement opinion in ignorance and passion, every time that we long to crush an adversary by sheer violence, every time that we are envious, every time that we are brutal, every time that we adore mere power or success, every time that we add our voice to swell a blind clamour against some unpopular personage, every time that we trample savagely on the fallen, – he has found in his own bosom the eternal spirit of the Populace, and that there needs only a little help from circumstances to make it triumph in him untameably.

The second thing to be borne in mind I have indicated several times already. It is this. All of us, so far as we are Barbarians, Philistines, or Populace, imagine happiness to consist in doing what one's ordinary self likes. What one's ordinary self likes differs according to the class to which one belongs, and has its severer and its lighter side; always, however, remaining machinery, and nothing more. The graver self of the Barbarian likes honours and consideration; his more relaxed self, field-sports and pleasure. The graver self of one kind of Philistine likes fanaticism, business, and money-making; his more relaxed self, comfort and tea-meetings. Of another kind of Philistine, the graver self likes rattening;[7] the relaxed self, deputations, or hearing Mr Odger speak. The sterner self of the Populace likes bawling, hustling, and smashing; the lighter self, beer. But in each class there are born a certain number of natures with a curiosity about their best self, with a bent for seeing things as they are, for disentangling themselves from machinery, for simply concerning themselves with reason and the will of God, and doing their best to make these prevail; – for the pursuit, in a word, of perfection. To certain manifestations of this love for perfection mankind have accustomed themselves to give the name of genius; implying, by this name, something original and heaven-bestowed in the passion. But the passion is to be found far beyond those manifestations of it to which the world usually gives the name of genius, and in which there is, for the most part, a *talent* of some kind or other, a special and striking faculty of execution, informed by the heaven-bestowed ardour, or genius. It is to be found in many manifestations besides these, and may best be called, as we have called it, the love and pursuit of perfection; culture being the true nurse of the pursuing love, and sweetness and light the true character of the pursued perfection. Natures with this bent emerge in all classes, – among the Barbarians, among the Philistines, among the Populace. And this bent always tends to take them out of their class, and to make their distinguishing characteristic not their Barbarianism or their Philistinism, but their *humanity*. They have, in general, a rough time of it in their lives; but they are sown more abundantly than one might think, they appear where and when one least expects it, they set up a fire which enfilades, so to speak, the class with which they are ranked; and, in general, by the extrication of their best self as the self to develop, and by the simplicity of the ends fixed by them as paramount, they hinder the unchecked predominance of that class-life which is the affirmation of our ordinary self, and seasonably disconcert mankind in their worship of machinery.

Therefore, when we speak of ourselves as divided into Barbarians, Philistines, and Populace, we must be understood always to imply that within each of these classes there are a certain number of *aliens,* if we may so call them, – persons who are mainly led, not by their class spirit, but by a general *humane* spirit, by the love of human perfection; and that this number is capable of being diminished or augmented. I mean, the number of those who will succeed in developing this happy instinct will be greater or smaller, in proportion both to the force of the original instinct within them, and to the hindrance or encouragement which it meets with from without. In almost all who have it, it is mixed with some infusion of the spirit of an ordinary self, some quantity of class-instinct, and even, as has been shown, of more than one class-instinct at the same time; so that, in general, the extrication of the best self, the predominance of the *humane* instinct, will very much depend upon its meeting, or not, with what is fitted to help and elicit it. At a moment, therefore, when it is agreed that we want a source of authority, and when it seems probable that the right source is our best self, it becomes of vast importance to see whether or not the things around us are, in general, such as to help and elicit our best self, and if they are not, to see why they are not, and the most promising way of mending them.

Now, it is clear that the very absence of any powerful authority among us, and the prevalent doctrine of the duty and happiness of doing as one likes, and asserting our personal liberty, must tend to prevent the erection of any very strict standard of excellence, the belief in any very paramount authority of right reason, the recognition of our best self as anything very recondite and hard to come at. It may be, as I have said, a proof of our honesty that we do not attempt to give to our ordinary self, as we have it in action, predominant authority, and to impose its rule upon other people. But it is evident, also, that it is not easy, with our style of proceeding, to get beyond the notion of an ordinary self at all, or to get the paramount authority of a commanding best self, or right reason, recognized. The learned Martinus Scriblerus[8] well says: – 'the taste of the bathos is implanted by nature itself in the soul of man; till, perverted by custom or example, he is taught, or rather compelled, to relish the sublime.' But with us everything seems directed to prevent any such perversion of us by custom or example as might compel us to relish the sublime; by all means we are encouraged to keep our natural taste for the bathos unimpaired.

I have formerly pointed out how in literature the absence of any authoritative centre, like an Academy, tends to do this. Each section of the public has its own literary organ, and the mass of the public is without any suspicion that the value of these organs is relative to their being nearer a certain ideal centre of correct information, taste, and intelligence, or farther away from it. I have said that within certain limits, which any-one who is likely to read this will have no difficulty in drawing for himself, my old adversary, the *Saturday Review,* may, on matters of literature and taste, be fairly enough regarded, rela-tively to the mass of newspapers which treat these matters, as a kind of organ of reason.[9] But I remember once conversing with a company of Nonconformist admirers of some lecturer who had let off a great firework, which the *Saturday Review* said was all noise and false lights, and feeling my way as tenderly as I could about the effect of this unfavourable judgment upon those with whom I was conversing. 'Oh,' said one who was their spokesman, with the most tranquil air of conviction, 'it is true the *Saturday Review* abuses the lecture, but the *British*

Banner' (I am not quite sure it was the *British Banner,* but it was some newspaper of that stamp)[10] 'says that the *Saturday Review* is quite wrong.' The speaker had evidently no notion that there was a scale of value for judgments on these topics, and that the judgments of the *Saturday Review* ranked high on this scale, and those of the *British Banner* low; the taste of the bathos implanted by nature in the literary judgments of man had never, in my friend's case, encountered any let or hindrance.

Just the same in religion as in literature. We have most of us little idea of a high standard to choose our guides by, of a great and profound spirit which is an authority while inferior spirits are none. It is enough to give importance to things that this or that person says them decisively, and has a large following of some strong kind when he says them. This habit of ours is very well shown in that able and interesting work of Mr Hepworth Dixon's, which we were all reading lately, *The Mormons, by One of Themselves.*[11] Here, again, I am not quite sure that my memory serves me as to the exact title, but I mean the well-known book in which Mr Hepworth Dixon described the Mormons, and other similar religious bodies in America, with so much detail and such warm sympathy. In this work it seems enough for Mr Dixon that this or that doctrine has its Rabbi, who talks big to him, has a staunch body of disciples, and, above all, has plenty of rifles. That there are any further stricter tests to be applied to a doctrine, before it is pronounced important, never seems to occur to him. 'It is easy to say,' he writes of the Mormons, 'that these saints are dupes and fanatics, to laugh at Joe Smith and his church,[12] but what then? *The great facts remain.* Young and his people are at Utah; a church of 200,000 souls; an army of 20,000 rifles.' But if the followers of a doctrine are really dupes, or worse, and its promulgators are really fanatics, or worse, it gives the doctrine no seriousness or authority the more that there should be found 200,000 souls, – 200,000 of the innumerable multitude with a natural taste for the bathos, – to hold it, and 20,000 rifles to defend it. And again, of another religious organization in America: 'A fair and open field is not to be refused when hosts so mighty throw down wager of battle on behalf of what they hold to be true,

however strange their faith may seem.' A fair and open field is
not to be refused to any speaker; but this solemn way of herald-
ing him is quite out of place, unless he has, for the best reason
and spirit of man, some significance. 'Well, but,' says Mr Hepworth Dixon, 'a theory which has been accepted by men like
Judge Edmonds, Dr Hare, Elder Frederick, and Professor
Bush!' And again: 'Such are, in brief, the bases of what Newman Weeks, Sarah Horton, Deborah Butler, and the associated
brethren, proclaimed in Rolt's Hall as the new covenant!' If he
was summing up an account of the doctrine of Plato, or of
St Paul, and of its followers, Mr Hepworth Dixon could not be
more earnestly reverential. But the question is, Have personages like Judge Edmonds, and Newman Weeks, and Elderess
Polly, and Elderess Antoinette, and the rest of Mr Hepworth
Dixon's heroes and heroines, anything of the weight and significance for the best reason and spirit of man that Plato and
St Paul have? Evidently they, at present, have not; and a very
small taste of them and their doctrines ought to have convinced
Mr Hepworth Dixon that they never could have. 'But,' says he,
'the magnetic power which Shakerism[13] is exercising on American thought would of itself compel us,' – and so on. Now as
far as real thought is concerned, – thought which affects the
best reason and spirit of man, the scientific or the imaginative
thought of the world, the only thought which deserves speaking of in this solemn way, – America has up to the present time
been hardly more than a province of England, and even now
would not herself claim to be more than abreast of England;
and of this only real human thought, English thought itself is
not just now, as we must all admit, the most significant factor.
Neither, then, can American thought be; and the magnetic power
which Shakerism exercises on American thought is about as
important, for the best reason and spirit of man, as the magnetic
power which Mr Murphy exercises on Birmingham Protestantism. And as we shall never get rid of our natural taste for the
bathos in religion, – never get access to a best self and right
reason which may stand as a serious authority, – by treating
Mr Murphy as his own disciples treat him, seriously, and as if
he was as much an authority as anyone else: so we shall never

get rid of it while our able and popular writers treat their Joe
Smiths and Deborah Butlers, with their so many thousand
souls and so many thousand rifles, in the like exaggerated and
misleading manner, and so do their best to confirm us in a bad
mental habit to which we are already too prone.

If our habits make it hard for us to come at the idea of a high
best self, of a paramount authority, in literature or religion,
how much more do they make this hard in the sphere of politics!
In other countries the governors, not depending so immediately
on the favour of the governed, have everything to urge them, if
they know anything of right reason (and it is at least supposed
that governors should know more of this than the mass of the
governed), to set it authoritatively before the community. But
our whole scheme of government being representative, every
one of our governors has all possible temptation, instead of
setting up before the governed who elect him, and on whose
favour he depends, a high standard of right reason, to accom-
modate himself as much as possible to their natural taste for
the bathos; and even if he tries to go counter to it, to proceed
in this with so much flattering and coaxing, that they shall not
suspect their ignorance and prejudices to be anything very
unlike right reason, or their natural taste for the bathos to differ much from a relish for the sublime. Everyone is thus in
every possible way encouraged to trust in his own heart; but 'he
that trusteth in his own heart,' says the Wise Man, 'is a fool';[14]
and at any rate this, which Bishop Wilson says, is undeniably
true: 'The number of those who need to be awakened is far
greater than that of those who need comfort.'

But in our political system everybody is comforted. Our
guides and governors who have to be elected by the influence
of the Barbarians, and who depend on their favour, sing the
praises of the Barbarians, and say all the smooth things that
can be said of them. With Mr Tennyson, they celebrate 'the
great broad-shouldered genial Englishman,' with his 'sense of
duty,' his 'reverence for the laws,' and his 'patient force,' who
saves us from the 'revolts, republics, revolutions, most no
graver than a schoolboy's barring out,' which upset other and
less broad-shouldered nations.[15] Our guides who are chosen by

the Philistines and who have to look to their favour, tell the Philistines how 'all the world knows that the great middle class of this country supplies the mind, the will, and the power requisite for all the great and good things that have to be done,' and congratulate them on their 'earnest good sense, which penetrates through sophisms, ignores commonplaces, and gives to conventional illusions their true value.' Our guides who look to the favour of the Populace, tell them that 'theirs are the brightest powers of sympathy, and the readiest powers of action.'

Harsh things are said, too, no doubt, against all the great classes of the community; but these things so evidently come from a hostile class, and are so manifestly dictated by the passions and prepossessions of a hostile class, and not by right reason, that they make no serious impression on those at whom they are launched, but slide easily off their minds. For instance, when the Reform League orators inveigh against our cruel and bloated aristocracy, these invectives so evidently show the passions and point of view of the Populace, that they do not sink into the minds of those at whom they are addressed, or awaken any thought or self-examination in them. Again, when our aristocratical baronet describes the Philistines and the Populace as influenced with a kind of hideous mania for emasculating the aristocracy, that reproach so clearly comes from the wrath and excited imagination of the Barbarians, that it does not much set the Philistines and the Populace thinking. Or when Mr Lowe calls the Populace drunken and venal,[16] he so evidently calls them this in an agony of apprehension for his Philistine or middle-class Parliament, which has done so many great and heroic works, and is now threatened with mixture and debasement, that the Populace do not lay his words seriously to heart.

So the voice which makes a permanent impression on each of our classes is the voice of its friends, and this is from the nature of things, as I have said, a comforting voice. The Barbarians remain in the belief that the great broad-shouldered genial Englishman may be well satisfied with himself; the Philistines remain in the belief that the great middle class of this country, with its earnest common sense penetrating through sophisms and ignoring commonplaces, may be well satisfied with itself; the Populace, that the working man with his bright powers of sympathy and ready powers of action, may be well satisfied with himself. What hope, at this rate, of extinguishing the taste of the bathos implanted by nature itself in the soul of man, or of inculcating the belief that excellence dwells among high and deep rocks, and can only be reached by those who sweat blood to reach her?

But it will be said, perhaps, that candidates for political influence and leadership, who thus caress the self-love of those whose suffrages they desire, know quite well that they are not saying the sheer truth as reason sees it, but that they are using a sort of conventional language, or what we call clap-trap, which is essential to the working of representative institutions. And, therefore, I suppose, we ought rather to say with Figaro: *Qui est-ce qu'on trompe ici?* Now, I admit that often, but not always, when our governors say smooth things to the self-love of the class whose political support they want, they know very well that they are overstepping, by a long stride, the bounds of truth and soberness; and while they talk, they in a manner, no doubt, put their tongue in their cheek. Not always; because, when a Barbarian appeals to his own class to make him their representative and give him political power, he, when he pleases their self-love by extolling broad-shouldered genial Englishmen with their sense of duty, reverence for the laws, and patient force, pleases his own self-love and extols himself, and is, therefore, himself ensnared by his own smooth words. And so, too, when a Philistine wants to be sent to Parliament by his brother Philistines, and extols the earnest good sense which character-izes Manchester and supplies the mind, the will, and the power, as the *Daily News* eloquently says, requisite for all the great and good things that have to be done, he intoxicates and deludes himself as well as his brother Philistines who hear him.

But it is true that a Barbarian often wants the political sup-port of the Philistines; and he unquestionably, when he flatters the self-love of Philistinism, and extols, in the approved fash-ion, its energy, enterprise, and self-reliance, knows that he is talking clap-trap, and so to say, puts his tongue in his cheek. On all matters where Nonconformity and its catchwords are concerned, this insincerity of Barbarians needing Nonconformist support, and, therefore, flattering the self-love of Nonconformity and repeating its catchwords without the least real belief in them, is very noticeable. When the Nonconformists, in a transport of blind zeal, threw out Sir James Graham's useful Education Clauses in 1843,[17] one-half of their Parliamentary advocates, no doubt, who cried aloud against 'trampling on the religious liberty of the Dissenters by taking the money of Dissenters to teach the tenets of the Church of England,' put their tongue in their cheek while they so cried out. And perhaps there is even a sort of motion of Mr Frederic Harrison's tongue towards his cheek when he talks of 'the shriek of superstition,' and tells the working class that 'theirs are the brightest powers of sympathy and the readiest powers of action.' But the point on which I would insist is, that this involuntary tribute to truth and soberness on the part of certain of our governors and guides never reaches at all the mass of us governed, to serve as a lesson to us, to abate our self-love, and to awaken in us a suspicion that our favourite prejudices may be, to a higher reason, all nonsense. Whatever by-play goes on among the more intelligent of our leaders, we do not see it; and we are left to believe that, not only in our own eyes, but in the eyes of our representative and ruling men, there is nothing more admirable than our ordinary self, whatever our ordinary self happens to be, Barbarian, Philistine, or Populace.

Thus everything in our political life tends to hide from us that there is anything wiser than our ordinary selves, and to prevent our getting the notion of a paramount right reason. Royalty itself, in its idea the expression of the collective nation, and a sort of constituted witness to its best mind, we try to turn into a kind of grand advertising van, meant to give publicity and credit to the inventions, sound or unsound, of the ordinary self of individuals.

I remember, when I was in North Germany, having this very strongly brought to my mind in the matter of schools and their institution. In Prussia, the best schools are Crown patronage schools, as they are called; schools which have been established and endowed (and new ones are to this day being established

and endowed) by the Sovereign himself out of his own reve-
nues, to be under the direct control and management of him or
of those representing him, and to serve as types of what schools
should be. The Sovereign, as his position raises him above
many prejudices and littlenesses, and as he can always have at
his disposal the best advice, has evident advantages over private founders in well planning and directing a school; while at
the same time his great means and his great influence secure, to
a well-planned school of his, credit and authority. This is what,
in North Germany, the governors do in the matter of education
for the governed; and one may say that they thus give the governed a lesson, and draw out in them the idea of a right reason
higher than the suggestions of an ordinary man's ordinary self.

But in England how different is the part which in this matter
our governors are accustomed to play! The Licensed Victuallers or the Commercial Travellers propose to make a school for
their children; and I suppose, in the matter of schools, one may
call the Licensed Victuallers or the Commercial Travellers ordinary men, with their natural taste for the bathos still strong; and
a Sovereign with the advice of men like Wilhelm von Humboldt or Schleiermacher[18] may, in this matter, be a better judge,
and nearer to right reason. And it will be allowed, probably,
that right reason would suggest that, to have a sheer school of
Licensed Victuallers' children, or a sheer school of Commercial
Travellers' children, and to bring them all up, not only at home
but at school, too, in a kind of odour of licensed victualism or
of bagmanism, is not a wise training to give to these children.
And in Germany, I have said, the action of the national guides
or governors is to suggest and provide a better. But, in England,
the action of the national guides or governors is, for a Royal
Prince or a great Minister to go down to the opening of the
Licensed Victuallers' or of the Commercial Travellers' school,
to take the chair, to extol the energy and self-reliance of the
Licensed Victuallers or the Commercial Travellers, to be all of
their way of thinking, to predict full success to their schools,
and never so much as to hint to them that they are probably
doing a very foolish thing, and that the right way to go to work
with their children's education is quite different. And it is the

same in almost every department of affairs. While, on the Continent, the idea prevails that it is the business of the heads and representatives of the nation, by virtue of their superior means, power, and information, to set an example and to provide suggestions of right reason, among us the idea is that the business of the heads and representatives of the nation is to do nothing of the kind, but to applaud the natural taste for the bathos showing itself vigorously in any part of the community, and to encourage its works.

Now I do not say that the political system of foreign countries has not inconveniences which may outweigh the inconveniences of our own political system; nor am I the least proposing to get rid of our own political system and to adopt theirs. But a sound centre of authority being what, in this disquisition, we have been led to seek, and right reason, or our best self, appearing alone to offer such a sound centre of authority, it is necessary to take note of the chief impediments which hinder, in this country, the extrication or recognition of this right reason as a paramount authority, with a view to afterwards trying in what way they can best be removed.

This being borne in mind, I proceed to remark how not only do we get no suggestions of right reason, and no rebukes of our ordinary self, from our governors, but a kind of philosophical theory is widely spread among us to the effect that there is no such thing at all as a best self and a right reason having claim to paramount authority, or, at any rate, no such thing ascertainable and capable of being made use of; and that there is nothing but an infinite number of ideas and works of our ordinary selves, and suggestions of our natural taste for the bathos, pretty nearly equal in value, which are doomed either to an irreconcilable conflict, or else to a perpetual give and take; and that wisdom consists in choosing the give and take rather than the conflict, and in sticking to our choice with patience and good humour.

And, on the other hand, we have another philosophical theory rife among us, to the effect that without the labour of perverting ourselves by custom or example to relish right reason, but by continuing all of us to follow freely our natural taste for the bathos, we shall, by the mercy of Providence, and by a kind of natural tendency of things, come in due time to relish and follow right reason.

The great promoters of these philosophical theories are our newspapers, which, no less than our Parliamentary representatives, may be said to act the part of guides and governors to us; and these favourite doctrines of theirs I call, – or should call, if the doctrines were not preached by authorities I so much respect, – the first, a peculiarly British form of Atheism, the second, a peculiarly British form of Quietism. The first-named melancholy doctrine is preached in the *Times* with great clearness and force of style; indeed, it is well known, from the example of the poet Lucretius and others, what great masters of style the atheistic doctrine has always counted among its promulgators. 'It is of no use,' says the *Times*, 'for us to attempt to force upon our neighbours our several likings and dislikings. We must take things as they are. Everybody has his own little vision of religious or civil perfection. Under the evident impossibility of satisfying everybody, we agree to take our stand on equal laws and on a system as open and liberal as is possible. The result is that everybody has more liberty of action and of speaking here than anywhere else in the Old World.' We come again here upon Mr Roebuck's celebrated definition of happiness, on which I have so often commented: 'I look around me and ask what is the state of England? Is not every man able to say what he likes? I ask you whether the world over, or in past history, there is anything like it? Nothing. I pray that our unrivalled happiness may last.' This is the old story of our system of checks and every Englishman doing as he likes, which we have already seen to have been convenient enough so long as there were only the Barbarians and the Philistines to do what they liked, but to be getting inconvenient, and productive of anarchy, now that the Populace wants to do what it likes, too.

But for all that, I will not at once dismiss this famous doctrine, but will first quote another passage from the *Times*, applying the doctrine to a matter of which we have just been speaking, – education. 'The difficulty here' (in providing a national system of education), says the *Times*, 'does not reside in any removable arrangements. It is inherent and native in the actual and inveterate state of things in this country. All these powers and personages, all these conflicting influences and varieties of character, exist, and have long existed among us; they are fighting it out, and will long continue to fight it out, without coming to that happy consummation when some one element of the British character is to destroy or to absorb all the rest.' There it is! the various promptings of the natural taste for the bathos in this man and that among us are fighting it out; and the day will never come (and, indeed, why should we wish it to come?) when one man's particular sort of taste for the bathos shall tyrannize over another man's; nor when right reason (if that may be called an element of the British character) shall absorb and rule them all. 'The whole system of this country, like the constitution we boast to inherit, and are glad to uphold, is made up of established facts, prescriptive authorities, existing usages, powers that be, persons in possession, and communities or classes that have won dominion for themselves, and will hold it against all comers.' Every force in the world, evidently, except the one reconciling force, right reason! Barbarian here, Philistine there, Mr Bradlaugh and Populace striking in! – pull devil, pull baker! Really, presented with the mastery of style of our leading journal, the sad picture, as one gazes upon it, assumes the iron and inexorable solemnity of tragic Destiny.

After this, the milder doctrine of our other philosophical teacher, the *Daily News*,[19] has, at first, something very attractive and assuaging. The *Daily News* begins, indeed, in appearance, to weave the iron web of necessity round us like the *Times*. 'The alternative is between a man's doing what he likes and his doing what some one else, probably not one whit wiser than himself, likes.' This points to the tacit compact, mentioned in my last paper, between the Barbarians and the Philistines, and into which it is hoped that the Populace will one day enter; the compact, so creditable to English honesty, that since each class has only the ideas and aims of its ordinary self to give effect to, none of them shall, if it exercise power, treat its ordinary self too seriously, or attempt to impose it on others; but shall let these others, – the fanatical Protestant, for instance, in his

Papist-baiting, and the popular tribune in his Hyde Park anarchy-mongering, – have their fling. But then the *Daily News* suddenly lights up the gloom of necessitarianism with bright beams of hope. 'No doubt,' it says, 'the common reason of society ought to check the aberrations of individual eccentricity.' This common reason of society looks very like our best self or right reason, to which we want to give authority, by making the action of the *State*, or nation in its collective character, the expression of it. But of this project of ours, the *Daily News*, with its subtle dialectics, makes havoc. 'Make the State the organ of the common reason?' – it says. 'You make it the organ of something or other, but how can you be certain that reason will be the quality which will be embodied in it?' You cannot be certain of it, undoubtedly, if you never try to bring the thing about; but the question is, the action of the State being the action of the collective nation, and the action of the collective nation carrying naturally great publicity, weight, and force of example with it, whether we should not try to put into the action of the State as much as possible of right reason or our best self, which may, in this manner, come back to us with new force and authority; may have visibility, form, and influence; and help to confirm us, in the many moments when we are tempted to be our ordinary selves merely, in resisting our natural taste of the bathos rather than in giving way to it?

But no! says our teacher: 'It is better there should be an infinite variety of experiments in human action; the common reason of society will in the main check the aberrations of individual eccentricity well enough, if left to its natural operation.' This is what I call the specially British form of Quietism, or a devout, but excessive reliance on an over-ruling Providence. Providence, as the moralists are careful to tell us, generally works in human affairs by human means; so when we want to make right reason act on individual inclination, our best self on our ordinary self, we seek to give it more power of doing so by giving it public recognition and authority, and embodying it, so far as we can, in the State. It seems too much to ask of Providence, that while we, on our part, leave our congenital taste for the bathos to its natural operation and its infinite variety of experiments, Providence should mysteriously guide it into the true track, and compel it to relish the sublime. At any rate, great men and great institutions have hitherto seemed necessary for producing any considerable effect of this kind. No doubt we have an infinite variety of experiments, and an ever-multiplying multitude of explorers. Even in these few chapters I have enumerated many: the *British Banner*, Judge Edmonds, Newman Weeks, Deborah Butler, Elderess Polly, Brother Noyes, Mr Murphy, the Licensed Victuallers, the Commercial Travellers, and I know not how many more; and the members of the noble army are swelling every day. But what a depth of Quietism, or rather, what an over-bold call on the direct interposition of Providence, to believe that these interesting explorers will discover the true track, or at any rate, 'will do so in the main well enough' (whatever that may mean) if left to their natural operation; that is, by going on as they are! Philosophers say, indeed, that we learn virtue by performing acts of virtue; but to say that we shall learn virtue by performing any acts to which our natural taste for the bathos carries us, that the fanatical Protestant comes at his best self by Papist-baiting, or Newman Weeks and Deborah Butler at right reason by following their noses, this certainly does appear over-sanguine.

It is true, what we want is to make right reason act on individual reason, the reason of individuals; all our search for authority has that for its end and aim. The *Daily News* says, I observe, that all my argument for authority 'has a non-intellectual root;' and from what I know of my own mind and its poverty I think this so probable, that I should be inclined easily to admit it, if it were not that, in the first place, nothing of this kind, perhaps, should be admitted without examination; and, in the second, a way of accounting for the charge being made, in this particular instance, without good grounds, appears to present itself. What seems to me to account here, perhaps, for the charge, is the want of flexibility of our race, on which I have so often remarked. I mean, it being admitted that the conformity of the individual reason of the fanatical Protestant or the popular rioter with right reason is our true object, and not the mere restraining them, by the strong arm of the State, from

Papist-baiting or railing-breaking, – admitting this, we English have so little flexibility that we cannot readily perceive that the State's restraining them from these indulgences may yet fix clearly in their minds that, to the collective nation, these indulgences appear irrational and unallowable, may make them pause and reflect, and may contribute to bringing, with time, their individual reason into harmony with right reason. But in no country, owing to the want of intellectual flexibility above mentioned, is the leaning which is our natural one, and, therefore, needs no recommending to us, so sedulously recommended, and the leaning which is not our natural one, and, therefore, does not need dispraising to us, so sedulously dispraised, as in ours. To rely on the individual being, with us, the natural leaning, we will hear of nothing but the good of relying on the individual; to act through the collective nation on the individual being not our natural leaning, we will hear nothing in recommendation of it. But the wise know that we often need to hear most of that to which we are least inclined, and even to learn to employ, in certain circumstances, that which is capable, if employed amiss, of being a danger to us.

Elsewhere this is certainly better understood than here. In a recent number of the *Westminster Review*, an able writer, but with precisely our national want of flexibility of which I have been speaking, has unearthed, I see, for our present needs, an English translation, published some years ago, of Wilhelm von Humboldt's book, *The Sphere and Duties of Government*. Humboldt's object in this book is to show that the operation of government ought to be severely limited to what directly and immediately relates to the security of person and property. Wilhelm von Humboldt, one of the most beautiful souls that have ever existed, used to say that one's business in life was first to perfect oneself by all the means in one's power, and secondly to try and create in the world around one an aristocracy, the most numerous that one possibly could, of talents and characters. He saw, of course, that, in the end, everything comes to this, – that the individual must act for himself, and must be perfect in himself; and he lived in a country, Germany, where people were disposed to act too little for themselves, and to rely too much on the Government. But even thus, such was his flexibility, so little was he in bondage to a mere abstract maxim, that he saw very well that for his purpose itself, of enabling the individual to stand perfect on his own foundations and to do without the State, the action of the State would for long, long years be necessary. And soon after he wrote his book on *The Sphere and Duties of Government*, Wilhelm von Humboldt became Minister of Education in Prussia; and from his ministry all the great reforms which give the control of Prussian education to the State, – the transference of the management of public schools from their old boards of trustees to the State, the obligatory State-examination for schoolmasters, and the foundation of the great State-University of Berlin, – take their origin. This his English reviewer says not a word of. But, writing for a people whose dangers lie, as we have seen, on the side of their unchecked and unguided individual action, whose dangers none of them lie on the side of an over-reliance on the State, he quotes just so much of Wilhelm von Humboldt's example as can flatter them in their propensities, and do them no good; and just what might make them think, and be of use to them, he leaves on one side. This precisely recalls the manner, it will be observed, in which we have seen that our royal and noble personages proceed with the Licensed Victuallers.

In France the action of the State on individuals is yet more preponderant than in Germany; and the need which friends of human perfection feel for what may enable the individual to stand perfect on his own foundations is all the stronger. But what says one of the staunchest of these friends, M. Renan,[20] on State-action; and even State-action in that very sphere where in France it is most excessive, the sphere of education? Here are his words: – 'A Liberal believes in liberty, and liberty signifies the non-intervention of the State. *But such an ideal is still a long way off from us, and the very means to remove it to an indefinite distance would be precisely the State's withdrawing its action too soon.*' And this, he adds, is even truer of education than of any other department of public affairs.

We see, then, how indispensable to that human perfection which we seek is, in the opinion of good judges, some public recognition and establishment of our best self, of right reason. We see how our habits and practice oppose themselves to such a recognition, and the many inconveniences which we therefore suffer. But now let us try to go a little deeper, and to find, beneath our actual habits and practice, the very ground and cause out of which they spring.

CHAPTER 4

Hebraism and Hellenism

This fundamental ground is our preference of doing to thinking. Now this preference is a main element in our nature, and as we study it we find ourselves opening up a number of large questions on every side.

Let me go back for a moment to Bishop Wilson, who says: – 'First, never go against the best light you have; secondly, take care that your light be not darkness.' We show, as a nation, laudable energy and persistence in walking according to the best light we have, but are not quite careful enough, perhaps, to see that our light be not darkness. This is only another version of the old story that energy is our strong point and favourable characteristic, rather than intelligence. But we may give to this idea a more general form still, in which it will have a yet larger range of application. We may regard this energy driving at practice, this paramount sense of the obligation of duty, self-control, and work, this earnestness in going manfully with the best light we have, as one force. And we may regard the intelligence driving at those ideas which are, after all, the basis of right practice, the ardent sense for all the new and changing combinations of them which man's development brings with it, the indomitable impulse to know and adjust them perfectly, as another force. And these two forces we may regard as in some sense rivals, – rivals not by the necessity of their own nature, but as exhibited in man and his history, – and rivals dividing the empire of the world between them. And to give these forces names from the two races of men who have supplied the most signal and splendid manifestations of them, we may call them respectively the forces of Hebraism and Hellenism. Hebraism and Hellenism, – between these two points of influence moves our world. At one time it feels more powerfully the attraction of one of them, at another time of the other; and it ought to be, though it never is, evenly and happily balanced between them.

The final aim of both Hellenism and Hebraism, as of all great spiritual disciplines, is no doubt the same: man's perfection or salvation. The very language which they both of them use in schooling us to reach this aim is often identical. Even when their language indicates by variation, – sometimes a broad variation, often a but slight and subtle variation, – the different courses of thought which are uppermost in each discipline, even then the unity of the final end and aim is still apparent. To employ the actual words of that discipline with which we ourselves are all of us most familiar, and the words of which, therefore, come most home to us, that final end and aim is 'that we might be partakers of the divine nature.'[1] These are the words of a Hebrew apostle, but of Hellenism and Hebraism alike this is, I say, the aim. When the two are confronted, as they very often are confronted, it is nearly always with what I may call a rhetorical purpose; the speaker's whole design is to exalt and enthrone one of the two, and he uses the other only as a foil and to enable him the better to give effect to his purpose. Obviously, with us, it is usually Hellenism which is thus reduced to minister to the triumph of Hebraism. There is a sermon on Greece and the Greek spirit by a man never to be mentioned without interest and respect, Frederick Robertson,[2] in which this rhetorical use of Greece and the Greek spirit, and the inadequate exhibition of them necessarily consequent upon this, is almost ludicrous, and would be censurable if it were not to be explained by the exigencies of a sermon. On the other hand, Heinrich Heine,[3] and other writers of his sort, give us the spectacle of the tables completely turned, and of Hebraism brought in just as a foil and contrast to Hellenism, and to make the superiority of Hellenism more manifest. In both these cases there is injustice and misrepresentation. The aim and end of both Hebraism and Hellenism is, as I have said, one and the same, and this aim and end is august and admirable.

Still, they pursue this aim by very different courses. The uppermost idea with Hellenism is to see things as they really are; the uppermost idea with Hebraism is conduct and obedience. Nothing can do away with this ineffaceable difference. The Greek quarrel with the body and its desires is, that they hinder right thinking, the Hebrew quarrel with them is, that they hinder right acting. 'He that keepeth the law, happy is he;' 'Blessed is the man that feareth the Eternal, that delighteth greatly in his commandments;'[4] – that is the Hebrew notion of felicity; and, pursued with passion and tenacity, this notion would not let the Hebrew rest till, as is well known, he had at last got out of the law a network of prescriptions to enwrap his whole life, to govern every moment of it, every impulse, every action. The Greek notion of felicity, on the other hand, is perfectly conveyed in these words of a great French moralist: '*C'est le bonheur des hommes*,' – when? when they abhor that which is evil? – no; when they exercise themselves in the law of the Lord day and night? – no; when they die daily? – no; when they walk about the New Jerusalem with palms in their hands? – no; but when they think aright, when their thought hits: '*quand ils pensent juste*.' At the bottom of both the Greek and the Hebrew notion is the desire, native in man, for reason and the will of God, the feeling after the universal order, – in a word, the love of God. But, while Hebraism seizes upon certain plain, capital intimations of the universal order, and rivets itself, one may say, with unequalled grandeur of earnestness and intensity on the study and observance of them, the bent of Hellenism is to follow, with flexible activity, the whole play of the universal order, to be apprehensive of missing any part of it, of sacrificing one part to another, to slip away from resting in this or that intimation of it, however capital. An unclouded clearness of mind, an unimpeded play of thought, is what this bent drives at. The governing idea of Hellenism is *spontaneity of consciousness*; that of Hebraism, *strictness of conscience*.

Christianity changed nothing in this essential bent of Hebraism to set doing above knowing. Self-conquest, self-devotion, the following not our own individual will, but the will of God, *obedience*, is the fundamental idea of this form, also, of the discipline to which we have attached the general name of Hebraism. Only, as the old law and the network of prescriptions with which it enveloped human life were evidently a motive-power not driving and searching enough to produce the result aimed at, – patient continuance in well doing, self-conquest, – Christianity substituted for them boundless devotion to that inspiring and affecting pattern of self-conquest offered by Jesus Christ; and by the new motive-power, of which the essence was this, though the love and admiration of Christian Churches have for centuries been employed in varying, amplifying, and adorning the plain description of it, Christianity, as St Paul truly says, 'establishes the law,'[5] and in the strength of the ampler power which she has thus supplied to fulfil it, has accomplished the miracles, which we all see, of her history.

So long as we do not forget that both Hellenism and Hebraism are profound and admirable manifestations of man's life, tendencies, and powers, and that both of them aim at a like final result, we can hardly insist too strongly on the divergence of line and of operation with which they proceed. It is a divergence so great that it most truly, as the prophet Zechariah says, 'has raised up thy sons, O Zion, against thy sons, O Greece!' The difference whether it is by doing or by knowing that we set most store, and the practical consequences which follow from this difference, leave their mark on all the history of our race and of its development. Language may be abundantly quoted from both Hellenism and Hebraism to make it seem that one follows the same current as the other towards the same goal. They are, truly, borne towards the same goal; but the currents, which bear them are infinitely different. It is true, Solomon will praise knowing: 'Understanding is a well-spring of life unto him that hath it.' And in the New Testament, again, Jesus Christ is a 'light,' and 'truth makes us free.' It is true, Aristotle will undervalue knowing: 'In what concerns virtue,' says he, 'three things are necessary – knowledge, deliberate will, and perseverance; but, whereas the two last are all-important, the first is a

matter of little importance.'[6] It is true that with the same impatience with which St James enjoins a man to be not a forgetful
hearer, but a *doer of the work*, Epictetus exhorts us to *do* what
we have demonstrated to ourselves we ought to do; or he taunts
us with futility, for being armed at all points to prove that lying
is wrong, yet all the time continuing to lie. It is true, Plato, in
words which are almost the words of the New Testament or the
Imitation, calls life a learning to die. But underneath the super-
ficial agreement the fundamental divergence still subsists. The
understanding of Solomon is 'the walking in the way of the
commandments;' this is 'the way of peace,' and it is of this that
blessedness comes. In the New Testament, the truth which
gives us the peace of God and makes us free, is the love of
Christ constraining us to crucify, as he did, and with a like purpose of moral regeneration, the flesh with its affections and
lusts, and thus establishing, as we have seen, the law. The moral
virtues, on the other hand, are with Aristotle but the porch and
access to the intellectual, and with these last is blessedness.
That partaking of the divine life, which both Hellenism and
Hebraism, as we have said, fix as their crowning aim, Plato
expressly denies to the man of practical virtue merely, of
self-conquest with any other motive than that of perfect intellectual vision. He reserves it for the lover of pure knowledge, of
seeing things as they really are, – the φιλομαθής

Both Hellenism and Hebraism arise out of the wants of
human nature, and address themselves to satisfying those
wants. But their methods are so different, they lay stress on
such different points, and call into being by their respective
disciplines such different activities, that the face which human
nature presents when it passes from the hands of one of them
to those of the other, is no longer the same. To get rid of one's
ignorance, to see things as they are, and by seeing them as they
are to see them in their beauty, is the simple and attractive ideal
which Hellenism holds out before human nature; and from the
simplicity and charm of this ideal, Hellenism, and human life in
the hands of Hellenism, is invested with a kind of aërial ease,
clearness, and radiancy; they are full of what we call sweetness
and light. Difficulties are kept out of view, and the beauty and

rationalness of the ideal have all our thoughts. 'The best man is he who most tries to perfect himself, and the happiest man is he who most feels that he *is* perfecting himself,'[7] – this account of the matter by Socrates, the true Socrates of the *Memorabilia*, has something so simple, spontaneous, and unsophisticated about it, that it seems to fill us with clearness and hope when we hear it. But there is a saying which I have heard attributed to Mr Carlyle about Socrates, – a very happy saying, whether it is really Mr Carlyle's or not, – which excellently marks the essential point in which Hebraism differs from Hellenism. 'Socrates,' this saying goes, 'is terribly *at ease in Zion*.'[8] Hebraism, – and here is the source of its wonderful strength, – has always been severely preoccupied with an awful sense of the impossibility of being at ease in Zion; of the difficulties which oppose themselves to man's pursuit or attainment of that perfection of which Socrates talks so hopefully, and, as from this point of view one might almost say, so glibly. It is all very well to talk of getting rid of one's ignorance, of seeing things in their reality, seeing them in their beauty; but how is this to be done when there is something which thwarts and spoils all our efforts?

This something is *sin*; and the space which sin fills in Hebraism, as compared with Hellenism, is indeed prodigious. This obstacle to perfection fills the whole scene, and perfection appears remote and rising away from earth, in the background. Under the name of sin, the difficulties of knowing oneself and conquering oneself which impede man's passage to perfection, become, for Hebraism, a positive, active entity hostile to man, a mysterious power which I heard Dr Pusey[9] the other day, in one of his impressive sermons, compare to a hideous hunchback seated on our shoulders, and which it is the main business of our lives to hate and oppose. The discipline of the Old Testament may be summed up as a discipline teaching us to abhor and flee from sin; the discipline of the New Testament, as a discipline teaching us to die to it. As Hellenism speaks of thinking clearly, seeing things in their essence and beauty, as a grand and precious feat for man to achieve, so Hebraism speaks of becoming conscious of sin, of awakening to a sense of sin, as a feat of this kind. It is obvious to what wide divergence these differing tendencies, actively followed, must lead. As one passes and repasses from Hellenism to Hebraism, from Plato to St Paul, one feels inclined to rub one's eyes and ask oneself whether man is indeed a gentle and simple being, showing the traces of a noble and divine nature; or an unhappy chained creature, labouring with groanings that cannot be uttered to free himself from the body of this death.[10]

Apparently it was the Hellenic conception of human nature which was unsound, for the world could not live by it. Absolutely to call it unsound, however, is to fall into the common error of its Hebraizing enemies; but it was unsound at that particular moment of man's development, it was premature. The indispensable basis of conduct and self-control, the platform upon which alone the perfection aimed at by Greece can come into bloom, was not to be reached by our race so easily; centuries of probation and discipline were needed to bring us to it. Therefore, the bright promise of Hellenism faded, and Hebraism ruled the world. Then was seen that astonishing spectacle, so well marked by the often quoted words of the prophet Zechariah, when men of all languages and nations took hold of the skirt of him that was a Jew, saying: – '*We will go with you, for we have heard that God is with you.*'[11] And the Hebraism which thus received and ruled a world all gone out of the way and altogether become unprofitable, was, and could not but be, the later, the more spiritual, the more attractive development of Hebraism. It was Christianity; that is to say, Hebraism aiming at self-conquest and rescue from the thrall of vile affections, not by obedience to the letter of a law, but by conformity to the image of a self-sacrificing example. To a world stricken with moral enervation Christianity offered its spectacle of an inspired self-sacrifice; to men who refused themselves nothing, it showed one who refused himself everything; – '*my Saviour banished joy!*' says George Herbert.[12] When the *alma Venus*, the life-giving and joy-giving power of nature, so fondly cherished by the Pagan world, could not save her followers from self-dissatisfaction and ennui, the severe words of the apostle came bracingly and refreshingly: 'Let no man deceive you with vain words, for because of these things cometh the wrath of

God upon the children of disobedience.'[13] Through age after age and generation after generation, our race, or all that part of our race which was most living and progressive, was *baptized into a death*;[14] and endeavoured, by suffering in the flesh, to cease from sin. Of this endeavour, the animating labours and afflictions of early Christianity, the touching asceticism of mediæval Christianity, are the great historical manifestations. Literary monuments of it, each in its own way incomparable, remain in the Epistles of St Paul, in St Augustine's Confessions, and in the two original and simplest books of the Imitation.*

Of two disciplines laying their main stress, the one, on clear intelligence, the other, on firm obedience; the one, on comprehensively knowing the grounds of one's duty, the other, on diligently practising it; the one, on taking all possible care (to use Bishop Wilson's words again) that the light we have be not darkness, the other, that according to the best light we have we diligently walk, – the priority naturally belongs to that discipline which braces all man's moral powers, and founds for him an indispensable basis of character. And, therefore, it is justly said of the Jewish people, who were charged with setting powerfully forth that side of the divine order to which the words *conscience* and *self-conquest* point, that they were 'entrusted with the oracles of God;'[15] as it is justly said of Christianity, which followed Judaism and which set forth this side with a much deeper effectiveness and a much wider influence, that the wisdom of the old Pagan world was foolishness compared to it. No words of devotion and admiration can be too strong to render thanks to these beneficent forces which have so borne forward humanity in its appointed work of coming to the knowledge and possession of itself; above all, in those great moments when their action was the wholesomest and the most necessary.

But the evolution of these forces, separately and in themselves, is not the whole evolution of humanity, – their single history is not the whole history of man; whereas their admirers are always apt to make it stand for the whole history. Hebraism and Hellenism are, neither of them, the *law* of human

---

* The two first books.

development, as their admirers are prone to make them; they are, each of them, *contributions* to human development, – august contributions, invaluable contributions; and each showing itself to us more august, more invaluable, more preponderant over the other, according to the moment in which we take them, and the relation in which we stand to them. The nations of our modern world, children of that immense and salutary movement which broke up the Pagan world, inevitably stand to Hellenism in a relation which dwarfs it, and to Hebraism in a relation which magnifies it. They are inevitably prone to take Hebraism as the law of human development, and not as simply a contribution to it, however precious. And yet the lesson must perforce be learned, that the human spirit is wider than the most priceless of the forces which bear it onward, and that to the whole development of man Hebraism itself is, like Hellenism, but a contribution.

Perhaps we may help ourselves to see this clearer by an illustration drawn from the treatment of a single great idea which has profoundly engaged the human spirit, and has given it eminent opportunities for showing its nobleness and energy. It surely must be perceived that the idea of immortality, as this idea rises in its generality before the human spirit, is something grander, truer, and more satisfying, than it is in the particular forms by which St Paul, in the famous fifteenth chapter of the Epistle to the Corinthians, and Plato, in the *Phœdo*, endeavour to develop and establish it. Surely we cannot but feel, that the argumentation with which the Hebrew apostle goes about to expound this great idea is, after all, confused and inconclusive; and that the reasoning, drawn from analogies of likeness and equality, which is employed upon it by the Greek philosopher, is over-subtle and sterile. Above and beyond the inadequate solutions which Hebraism and Hellenism here attempt, extends the immense and august problem itself, and the human spirit which gave birth to it. And this single illustration may suggest to us how the same thing happens in other cases also.

But meanwhile, by alternations of Hebraism and Hellenism, of a man's intellectual and moral impulses, of the effort to see things as they really are, and the effort to win peace by self-conquest, the human spirit proceeds; and each of these two forces has its appointed hours of culmination and seasons of rule. As the great movement of Christianity was a triumph of Hebraism and man's moral impulses, so the great movement which goes by the name of the Renascence* was an uprising and re-instatement of man's intellectual impulses and of Hellenism. We in England, the devoted children of Protestantism, chiefly know the Renascence by its subordinate and secondary side of the Reformation. The Reformation has been often called a Hebraizing revival, a return to the ardour and sincereness of primitive Christianity. No one, however, can study the development of Protestantism and of Protestant Churches without feeling that into the Reformation too, – Hebraising child of the Renascence and offspring of its fervour, rather than its intelligence, as it undoubtedly was, – the subtle Hellenic leaven of the Renascence found its way, and that the exact respective parts, in the Reformation, of Hebraism and of Hellenism, are not easy to separate. But what we may with truth say is, that all which Protestantism was to itself clearly conscious of, all which it succeeded in clearly setting forth in words, had the characters of Hebraism rather than of Hellenism. The Reformation was strong, in that it was an earnest return to the Bible and to doing from the heart the will of God as there written. It was weak, in that it never consciously grasped or applied the central idea of the Renascence, – the Hellenic idea of pursuing, in all lines of activity, the law and science, to use Plato's words, of things as they really are. Whatever direct superiority, therefore, Protestantism had over Catholicism was a moral superiority, a superiority arising out of its greater sincerity and earnestness, – at the moment of its apparition at any rate, – in dealing with the heart and conscience. Its pretensions to an intellectual superiority are in general quite illusory. For Hellenism, for the thinking side in man as distinguished from the acting side, the attitude of mind of Protestantism towards the Bible in no

---

* I have ventured to give to the foreign word *Renaissance*, – destined to become of more common use among us as the movement which it denotes comes, as it will come, increasingly to interest us, – an English form.

respect differs from the attitude of mind of Catholicism towards the Church. The mental habit of him who imagines that Balaam's ass spoke, in no respect differs from the mental habit of him who imagines that a Madonna of wood or stone winked; and the one, who says that God's Church makes him believe what he believes, and the other, who says that God's Word makes him believe what he believes, are for the philosopher perfectly alike in not really and truly knowing, when they say *God's Church* and *God's Word*, what it is they say, or whereof they affirm.[16]

In the sixteenth century, therefore, Hellenism re-entered the world, and again stood in presence of Hebraism, – a Hebraism renewed and purged. Now, it has not been enough observed, how, in the seventeenth century, a fate befell Hellenism in some respects analogous to that which befell it at the commencement of our era. The Renascence, that great re-awakening of Hellenism, that irresistible return of humanity to nature and to seeing things as they are, which in art, in literature, and in physics, produced such splendid fruits, had, like the anterior Hellenism of the Pagan world, a side of moral weakness, and of relaxation or insensibility of the moral fibre, which in Italy showed itself with the most startling plainness, but which in France, England, and other countries was very apparent, too. Again this loss of spiritual balance, this exclusive preponderance given to man's perceiving and knowing side, this unnatural defect of his feeling and acting side, provoked a reaction. Let us trace that reaction where it most nearly concerns us.

Science has now made visible to everybody the great and pregnant elements of difference which lie in race, and in how signal a manner they make the genius and history of an Indo-European people vary from those of a Semitic people. Hellenism is of Indo-European growth, Hebraism is of Semitic growth; and we English, a nation of Indo-European stock, seem to belong naturally to the movement of Hellenism. But nothing more strongly marks the essential unity of man, than the affinities we can perceive, in this point or that, between members of one family of peoples and members of another. And no affinity of this kind is more strongly marked than that likeness in the strength and prominence of the moral fibre, which, notwithstanding immense elements of difference, knits in some special sort the genius and history of us English, and our American descendants across the Atlantic, to the genius and history of the Hebrew people. Puritanism, which has been so great a power in the English nation, and in the strongest part of the English nation, was originally the reaction in the seventeenth century of the conscience and moral sense of our race, against the moral indifference and lax rule of conduct which in the sixteenth century came in with the Renascence. It was a reaction of Hebraism against Hellenism; and it powerfully manifested itself, as was natural, in a people with much of what we call a Hebraizing turn, with a signal affinity for the bent which was the master-bent of Hebrew life. Eminently Indo-European by its *humour*, by the power it shows, through this gift, of imaginatively acknowledging the multiform aspects of the problem of life, and of thus getting itself unfixed from its own over-certainty, of smiling at its own over-tenacity, our race has yet (and a great part of its strength lies here), in matters of practical life and moral conduct, a strong share of the assuredness, the tenacity, the intensity of the Hebrews. This turn manifested itself in Puritanism, and has had a great part in shaping our history for the last two hunderd years. Undoubtedly it checked and changed among us that movement of the Renascence which we see producing in the reign of Elizabeth such wonderful fruits. Undoubtedly it stopped the prominent rule and direct development of that order of ideas which we call by the name of Hellenism, and gave the first rank to a different order of ideas. Apparently, too, as we said of the former defeat of Hellenism, if Hellenism was defeated, this shows that Hellenism was imperfect, and that its ascendency at that moment would not have been for the world's good.

Yet there is a very important difference between the defeat inflicted on Hellenism by Christianity eighteen hundred years ago, and the check given to the Renascence by Puritanism. The greatness of the difference is well measured by the difference in force, beauty, significance, and usefulness, between primitive Christianity and Protestantism. Eighteen hundred years ago it was altogether the hour of Hebraism. Primitive Christianity was legitimately and truly the ascendent force in the world at that time, and the way of mankind's progress lay through its full development. Another hour in man's development began in the fifteenth century, and the main road of his progress lay for a time through Hellenism. Puritanism was no longer the central current of the world's progress, it was a side stream crossing the central current and checking it. The cross and the check may have been necessary and salutary, but that does not do away with the essential difference between the main stream of man's advance and a cross or side stream. For more than two hundred years the main stream of man's advance has moved towards knowing himself and the world, seeing things as they are, spontaneity of consciousness; the main impulse of a great part, and that the strongest part, of our nation has been towards strictness of conscience. They have made the secondary the principal at the wrong moment, and the principal they have at the wrong moment treated as secondary. This contravention of the natural order has produced, as such contravention always must produce, a certain confusion and false movement, of which we are now beginning to feel, in almost every direction, the inconvenience. In all directions our habitual causes of action seem to be losing efficaciousness, credit, and control, both with others and even with ourselves. Everywhere we see the beginnings of confusion, and we want a clue to some sound order and authority. This we can only get by going back upon the actual instincts and forces which rule our life, seeing them as they really are, connecting them with other instincts and forces, and enlarging our whole view and rule of life.

From CHAPTER 5

Porro Unum Est Necessarium[1]

'Poor Mr Smith'

... The newspapers a short time ago contained an account of the suicide of a Mr Smith, secretary to some insurance company, who, it was said, 'laboured under the apprehension that he would come to poverty, and that he was eternally lost.' And when I read these words, it occurred to me that the poor man who came to such a mournful end was, in truth, a kind of type, – by the selection of his two grand objects of concern, by their isolation from everything else, and their juxtaposition to one another, – of all the strongest, most respectable, and most representative part of our nation. 'He laboured under the apprehension that he would come to poverty, and that he was eternally lost.' The whole middle class have a conception of things, – a conception which makes us call them Philistines, – just like that of this poor man; though we are seldom, of course, shocked by seeing it take the distressing, violently morbid, and fatal turn, which it took with him. But how generally, with how many of us, are the main concerns of life limited to these two: the concern for making money, and the concern for saving our souls! And how entirely does the narrow and mechanical conception of our secular business proceed from a narrow and mechanical conception of our religious business! What havoc do the united conceptions make of our lives! It is because the second-named of these two master-concerns presents to us the one thing needful in so fixed, narrow, and mechanical a way, that so ignoble a fellow master-concern to it as the first-named becomes possible; and, having been once admitted, takes the same rigid and absolute character as the other.

Poor Mr Smith had sincerely the nobler master-concern as well as the meaner, – the concern for saving his soul (according to the narrow and mechanical conception which Puritanism has of what the salvation of the soul is), as well as the concern for making money. But let us remark how many people there are, especially outside the limits of the serious and conscientious middle class to which Mr Smith belonged, who take up with a meaner master-concern, – whether it be pleasure, or field-sports, or bodily exercises, or business, or popular agitation, – who take up with one of these exclusively, and neglect Mr Smith's nobler master-concern, because of the mechanical form which Hebraism has given to this noble master-concern. Hebraism makes it stand, as we have said, as something talismanic, isolated, and all-sufficient, justifying our giving our ordinary selves free play in bodily exercises, or business, or popular agitation, if we have made our accounts square with this master-concern; and, if we have not, rendering other things indifferent, and our ordinary self all we have to follow, and to follow with all the energy that is in us, till we do. Whereas the idea of perfection at all points, the encouraging in ourselves spontaneity of consciousness, the letting a free play of thought live and flow around all our activity, the indisposition to allow one side of our activity to stand as so all-important and all-sufficing that it makes other sides indifferent, – this bent of mind in us may not only check us in following unreservedly a mean master-concern of any kind, but may even, also, bring new life and movement into that side of us with which alone Hebraism concerns itself, and awaken a healthier and less mechanical activity there. Hellenism may thus actually serve to further the designs of Hebraism.

Undoubtedly it thus served in the first days of Christianity. Christianity, as has been said, occupied itself, like Hebraism, with the moral side of man exclusively, with his moral affections and moral conduct; and so far it was but a continuation of Hebraism. But it transformed and renewed Hebraism by criticizing a fixed rule, which had become mechanical, and had thus lost its vital motive-power; by letting the thought play freely around this old rule, and perceive its inadequacy; by developing a new motive-power, which men's moral consciousness could take living hold of, and could move in sympathy with. What was this but an importation of Hellenism, as we have defined it, into Hebraism? St Paul used the contradiction between the Jew's profession and practice, his shortcomings on that very side of moral affection and moral conduct which the Jew and St Paul, both of them, regarded as all in all ('Thou that sayest a man should not steal, dost thou steal? thou that sayest a man should not commit adultery, dost thou commit adultery?'[2]), for a proof of the inadequacy of the old rule of life in the Jew's mechanical conception of it; and tried to rescue him by making his consciousness play freely around this rule, – that is, by a, so far, Hellenic treatment of it. Even so we, too, when we hear so much said of the growth of commercial immorality in our serious middle class, of the melting away of habits of strict probity before the temptation to get quickly rich and to cut a figure in the world; when we see, at any rate, so much confusion of thought and of practice in this great representative class of our nation, – may we not be disposed to say, that this confusion shows that his new motive-power of grace and imputed righteousness has become to the Puritan as mechanical, and with as ineffective a hold upon his practice, as the old motive-power of the law was to the Jew? and that the remedy is the same as that which St Paul employed, – an importation of what we have called Hellenism into his Hebraism, a making his consciousness flow freely round his petrified rule of life and renew it? Only with this difference: that whereas St Paul imported Hellenism within the limits of our moral part only, this part being still treated by him as all in all; and whereas he wellnigh exhausted, one may say, and used to the very uttermost, the possibilities of fruitfully importing it on that side exclusively; we ought to try and import it, – guiding ourselves by the ideal of a human nature harmoniously perfect in all points, – into all the lines of our activity. Only by so doing can we rightly quicken, refresh, and renew those very instincts, now so much baffled, to which Hebraism makes appeal . . .

From CHAPTER 6
Our Liberal Practitioners

But an unpretending writer, without a philosophy based on inter-dependent, subordinate, and coherent principles, must not presume to indulge himself too much in generalities. He must keep close to the level ground of common fact, the only safe ground for understandings without a scientific equipment. Therefore, since I have spoken so slightingly of the practical operations in which my friends and countrymen are at this moment engaged for the removal of certain definite evils, I am bound to take, before concluding, some of those operations, and to make them, if I can, show the truth of what I have advanced ...

'The Deceased Wife's Sister Bill'

... I was lucky enough to be present when Mr Chambers brought forward in the House of Commons his bill for ena- bling a man to marry his deceased wife's sister, and I heard the speech which Mr Chambers then made in support of his bill.[1] His first point was that God's law, – the name he always gave to the Book of Leviticus, – did not really forbid a man to marry his deceased wife's sister. God's law not forbidding it, the Lib- eral maxim, that a man's prime right and happiness is to do as he likes, ought at once to come into force, and to annul any such check upon the assertion of personal liberty as the prohib- ition to marry one's deceased wife's sister. A distinguished Liberal supporter of Mr Chambers, in the debate which fol- lowed the introduction of the bill, produced a formula of much beauty and neatness for conveying in brief the Liberal notions on this head: 'Liberty,' said he, 'is the law of human life.' And, therefore, the moment it is ascertained that God's law, the Book of Leviticus, does not stop the way, man's law, the law of lib- erty, asserts its right, and makes us free to marry our deceased wife's sister.

And this exactly falls in with what Mr Hepworth Dixon,[2] who may almost be called the Colenso of love and marriage,' – such a revolution does he make in our ideas on these matters, just as Dr Colenso does in our ideas on religion, – tells us of the notions and proceedings of our kinsmen in America. With that affinity of genius to the Hebrew genius which we have already noticed, and with the strong belief of our race that liberty is the law of human life, so far as that fixed, perfect, and paramount rule of conscience, the Bible, does not expressly control it, our American kinsmen go again, Mr Hepworth Dixon tells us, to their Bible, the Mormons to the patriarchs and the Old Testa- ment, Brother Noyes to St Paul and the New, and having never before read anything else but their Bible, they now read their Bible over again, and make all manner of great discoveries there. All these discoveries are favourable to liberty, and in this way is satisfied that double craving so characteristic of our Philistine, and so eminently exemplified in that crowned Philistine, Henry the Eighth, – the craving for forbidden fruit and the craving for legality.

Mr Hepworth Dixon's eloquent writings give currency, over here, to these important discoveries; so that now, as regards love and marriage, we seem to be entering, with all our sails spread, upon what Mr Hepworth Dixon, its apostle and evangelist, calls a Gothic Revival, but what one of the many newspapers that so greatly admire Mr Hepworth Dixon's lithe and sinewy style and form their own style upon it, calls, by a yet bolder and more striking figure, 'a great sexual insurrection of our Anglo-Teutonic race.'[3] For this end we have to avert our eyes from everything Hellenic and fanciful, and to keep them steadily fixed upon the two cardinal points of the Bible and liberty. And one of those practical operations in which the Liberal party engage, and in which we are summoned to join them, directs itself entirely, as we have seen, to these cardinal points, and may almost be regarded, perhaps, as a kind of first instalment, or public and parliamentary pledge, of the great sexual insurrection of our Anglo-Teutonic race.

But here, as elsewhere, what we seek is the Philistine's perfection, the development of his best self, not mere liberty for his ordinary self. And we no more allow absolute validity to his stock maxim, *Liberty is the law of human life*, than we allow it to the opposite maxim, which is just as true, *Renouncement is the law of human life*.[4] For we know that the only perfect freedom is, as our religion says, a service; not a service to any stock maxim, but an elevation of our best self, and a harmonizing in subordination to this, and to the idea of a perfected humanity, all the multitudinous, turbulent, and blind impulses of our ordinary selves. Now, the Philistine's great defect being a defect in delicacy of perception, to cultivate in him this delicacy, to render it independent of external and mechanical rule, and a law to itself, is what seems to make most for his perfection, his true humanity. And his true humanity, and, therefore, his happiness, appears to lie much more, so far as the relations of love and marriage are concerned, in becoming alive to the finer shades of feeling which arise within these relations, in being able to enter with tact and sympathy into the subtle instinctive propensions and repugnances of the person with whose life his own life is bound up, to make them his own, to direct and govern in harmony with them the arbitrary range of his personal action, and thus to enlarge his spiritual and intellectual life and liberty, than in remaining insensible to these finer shades of feeling and this delicate sympathy, in giving unchecked range, so far as he can, to his mere personal action, in allowing no limits or government to this except such as a mechanical external law imposes, and in thus really narrowing, for the satisfaction of his ordinary self, his spiritual and intellectual life and liberty.

Still more must this be so, when his fixed eternal rule, his God's law, is supplied to him from a source which is less fit, perhaps, to supply final and absolute instructions on this particular topic of love and marriage than on any other relation of human life. Bishop Wilson, who is full of examples of that fruitful Hellenizing within the limits of Hebraism itself, of that renewing of the stiff and stark notions of Hebraism by turning upon them a stream of fresh thought and consciousness, which we have already noticed in St Paul, – Bishop Wilson gives an admirable lesson to rigid Hebraizers, like Mr Chambers, asking themselves: Does God's law (that is, the Book of Leviticus) forbid us to marry our wife's sister? – Does God's law (that is, again, the Book of Leviticus) allow us to marry our wife's sister? – when he says: 'Christian duties are founded on reason, not on the sovereign authority of God commanding what He pleases; God cannot command us what is not fit to be believed or done, all his commands being founded in the necessities of our nature.' And, immense as is our debt to the Hebrew race and its genius, incomparable as is its authority on certain profoundly important sides of our human nature, worthy as it is to be described as having uttered, for those sides, the voice of the deepest necessities of our nature, the statutes of the divine and eternal order of things, the law of God, – who, that is not manacled and hoodwinked by his Hebraism, can believe that, as to love and marriage, our reason and the necessities of our humanity have their true, sufficient, and divine law expressed for them by the voice of any Oriental and polygamous nation like the Hebrews? Who, I say, will believe, when he really considers the matter, that where the feminine nature, the feminine ideal, and our relations to them, are brought into question, the delicate and apprehensive genius of the Indo-European race, the race which invented the Muses, and chivalry, and the Madonna, is to find its last word on this question in the institutions of a Semitic people, whose wisest king had seven hundred wives and three hundred concubines?[5] . . .

Conclusion

And so we bring to an end what we had to say in praise of culture, and in evidence of its special utility for the circumstances in which we find ourselves, and the confusion which environs us. Through culture seems to lie our way, not only to perfection, but even to safety. Resolutely refusing to lend a hand to the imperfect operations of our Liberal friends, disregarding their impatience, taunts, and reproaches, firmly bent on trying to find in the intelligible law of things a firmer and sounder basis for future practice than any which we have at present, and believing this search and discovery to be, for our generation and circumstances, of yet more vital and pressing importance than practice itself, we nevertheless may do more, perhaps, we poor disparaged followers of culture, to make the actual present, and the frame of society in which we live, solid and seaworthy, than all which our bustling politicians can do.

For we have seen how much of our disorders and perplexities is due to the disbelief, among the classes and combinations of men, Barbarian or Philistine, which have hitherto governed our society, in right reason, in a paramount best self; to the inevitable decay and break-up of the organizations by which, asserting and expressing in these organizations their ordinary self only, they have so longed ruled us; and to their irresolution, when the society, which their conscience tells them they have made and still manage not with right reason but with their ordinary self, is rudely shaken, in offering resistance to its subverters. But for us, – who believe in right reason, in the duty and possibility of extricating and elevating our best self, in the progress of humanity towards perfection, – for us the framework of society, that theatre on which this august drama has to unroll itself, is sacred; and whoever administers it, and however we may seek to remove them from their tenure of administration, yet, while they administer, we steadily and with undivided heart support them in repressing anarchy and disorder; because without order there can be no society, and without society there can be no human perfection.

And this opinion of the intolerableness of anarchy we can never forsake, however our Liberal friends may think a little rioting, and what they call popular demonstrations, useful sometimes to their own interests and to the interests of the valuable practical operations they had in hand, and however they may preach the right of an Englishman to be left to do as far as possible what he likes, and the duty of his government to indulge him and connive as much as possible and abstain from all harshness of repression. And even when they artfully show us operations which are undoubtedly precious, such as the abolition of the slave-trade, and ask us if, for their sake, foolish and obstinate governments may not wholesomely be frightened by a little disturbance, the good design in view and the difficulty of overcoming opposition to it being considered, – still we say no, and that monster-processions in the streets and forcible irruptions into the parks, even in professed support of this good design, ought to be unflinchingly forbidden and repressed; and that far more is lost than is gained by permitting them. Because a State in which law is authoritative and sovereign, a firm and settled course of public order, is requisite if man is to bring to maturity anything precious and lasting now, or to found anything precious and lasting for the future.

Thus, in our eyes, the very framework and exterior order of the State, whoever may administer the State, is sacred; and culture is the most resolute enemy of anarchy, because of the great hopes and designs for the State which culture teaches us to nourish. But as, believing in right reason, and having faith in the progress of humanity towards perfection, and ever labouring for this end, we grow to have clearer sight of the ideas of right reason, and of the elements and helps of perfection, and come gradually to fill the framework of the State with them, to fashion its internal composition and all its laws and institutions conformably to them, and to make the State more and more the expression, as we say, of our best self, which is not manifold, and vulgar, and unstable, and contentious, and ever-varying, but one, and noble, and secure, and peaceful, and the same for all mankind, – with what aversion shall we not *then* regard anarchy, with what firmness shall we not check it, when there is so much that is so precious which it will endanger!

So that, for the sake of the present, but far more for the sake of the future, the lovers of culture are unswervingly and with a good conscience the opposers of anarchy. And not as the Barbarians and Philistines, whose honesty and whose sense of humour make them shrink, as we have seen, from treating the State as too serious a thing, and from giving it too much power; – for indeed the only State they know of, and think they administer, is the expression of their ordinary self. And though the headstrong and violent extreme among them might gladly arm this with full authority, yet their virtuous mean is, as we have said, pricked in conscience at doing this; and so our Barbarian Secretaries of State let the park railings be broken down, and our Philistine Alderman-Colonels let the London roughs rob and beat the bystanders. But we, beholding in the State no expression of our ordinary self, but even already, as it were, the appointed frame and prepared vessel of our best self, and, for the future, our best self's powerful, beneficent, and sacred expression and organ, – we are willing and resolved, even now, to strengthen against anarchy the trembling hands of our Barbarian Home Secretaries, and the feeble knees of our Philistine Alderman-Colonels; and to tell them, that it is not really in behalf of their own ordinary self that they are called to protect the park railings, and to suppress the London roughs, but in behalf of the best self both of themselves and of all of us in the future.

Nevertheless, though for resisting anarchy the lovers of culture may prize and employ fire and strength, yet they must, at the same time, bear constantly in mind that it is not at this moment true, what the majority of people tell us, that the world wants fire and strength more than sweetness and light, and that things are for the most part to be settled first and understood afterwards. We have seen how much of our present perplexities and confusion this untrue notion of the majority of people among us has caused, and tends to perpetuate. Therefore, the true business of the friends of culture now is, to dissipate this false notion, to spread the belief in right reason and in a firm intelligible law of things, and to get men to try, in preference to staunchly acting with imperfect knowledge, to obtain some sounder basis of knowledge on which to act. This is what the friends and lovers of culture have to do, however the believers in action may grow impatient with us for saying so, and may insist on our lending a hand to their practical operations and showing a commendable interest in them.

To this insistence we must, indeed, turn a deaf ear. But neither, on the other hand, must the friends of culture expect to take the believers in action by storm, or to be visibly and speedily important, and to rule and cut a figure in the world. Aristotle says that those for whom alone ideas and the pursuit of the intelligible law of things can, in general, have much attraction, are principally the young, filled with generous spirit and with a passion for perfection; but the mass of mankind, he says, follow seeming goods for real, bestowing hardly a thought upon true sweetness and light; – 'and to *their* lives,' he adds mournfully, 'who can give another and a better rhythm?'[1] But, although those chiefly attracted by sweetness and light will probably always be the young and enthusiastic, and culture must not hope to take the mass of mankind by storm, yet we will not therefore, for our own day and for our own people, admit and rest in the desponding sentence of Aristotle. For is not this the right crown of the long discipline of Hebraism, and the due fruit of mankind's centuries of painful schooling in self-conquest, and the just reward, above all, of the strenuous energy of our own nation and kindred in dealing honestly with itself and walking steadfastly according to the best light it knows, – that when in the fulness of time it has reason and beauty offered to it, and the law of things as they really are, it should at last walk by this true light with the same staunchness and zeal with which it formerly walked by its imperfect light? And thus man's two great natural forces, Hebraism and Hellenism, will no longer be dissociated and rival, but will be a joint force of right thinking and strong doing to carry him on towards perfection. This is what the lovers of culture may perhaps dare to augur for such a nation as ours.

Therefore, however great the changes to be accomplished, and however dense the array of Barbarians, Philistines, and Populace, we will neither despair on the one hand, nor, on the other, threaten violent revolution and change. But we will look forward cheerfully and hopefully to 'a revolution,' as the Duke of Wellington said, 'by due course of law;' though not exactly such laws as our Liberal friends are now, with their actual lights, fond of offering to us.

But if despondency and violence are both of them forbidden to the believer in culture, yet neither, on the other hand, is public life and direct political action much permitted to him. For it is his business, as we have seen, to get the present believers in action, and lovers of political talking and doing, to make a return upon their own minds, scrutinize their stock notions and habits much more, value their present talking and doing much less; in order that, by learning to think more clearly, they may come at last to act less confusedly. But how shall we persuade our Barbarian to hold lightly to his feudal usages; how shall we persuade our Nonconformist that his time spent in agitating for the abolition of church-establishments would have been better spent in getting worthier ideas of God and the ordering of the world, or his time spent in battling for voluntaryism in education better spent in learning to value and found a public and national culture; how shall we persuade, finally, our Alderman-Colonel not to be content with sitting in the hall of judgment or marching at the head of his men of war, without some knowledge how to perform judgment and how to direct men of war, – how, I say, shall we persuade all these of this, if our Alderman-Colonel sees that we want to get his leading-staff

and his scales of justice for our own hands; or the Nonconformist, that we want for ourselves his platform; or the
Barbarian, that we want for ourselves his pre-eminence and
function? Certainly they will be less slow to believe, as we want
them to believe, that the intelligible law of things has in itself
something desirable and precious, and that all place, function,
and bustle are hollow goods without it, if they see that we ourselves can content ourselves with this law, and find in it our
satisfaction, without making it an instrument to give us for
ourselves place, function, and bustle.

And although Mr Sidgwick says that social usefulness really
means 'losing oneself in a mass of disagreeable, hard, mechanical details,'[2] and though all the believers in action are fond of
asserting the same thing, yet, as to lose ourselves is not what we
want, but to find ourselves through finding the intelligible law
of things, this assertion, too, we shall not blindly accept, but
shall sift and try it a little first. And if we see that because the
believers in action, forgetting Goethe's maxim, 'to act is easy,
to think is hard,' imagine there is some wonderful virtue in losing oneself in a mass of mechanical details, therefore they
excuse themselves from much thought about the clear ideas
which ought to govern these details, then we shall give our
chief care and pains to seeking out those ideas and to setting
them forth; being persuaded that if we have the ideas firm and
clear, the mechanical details for their execution will come a
great deal more simply and easily than we now suppose.

At this exciting juncture, then, while so many of the lovers
of new ideas, somewhat weary, as we too are, of the stock performances of our Liberal friends upon the political stage, are
disposed to rush valiantly upon this public stage themselves,
we cannot at all think that for a wise lover of new ideas this
stage is the right one. Plenty of people there will be without
us, – country gentlemen in search of a club, demagogues in
search of a tub, lawyers in search of a place, industrialists in
search of gentility, – who will come from the east and from the
west, and will sit down at that Thyestëan banquet of clap-trap[3]
which English public life for these many years past has been.
And, so long as those old organizations, of which we have seen

the insufficiency, – those expressions of our ordinary self, Barbarian or Philistine, – have force anywhere, they will have force in Parliament. There, the man whom the Barbarians send, cannot but be impelled to please the Barbarians' ordinary self, and their natural taste for the bathos: and the man whom the Philistines send, cannot but be impelled to please those of the Philistines. Parliamentary Conservatism will and must long mean this, that the Barbarians should keep their heritage; and Parliamentary Liberalism, that the Barbarians should pass away, as they will pass away, and that into their heritage the Philistines should enter. This seems, indeed, to be the true and authentic promise of which our Liberal friends and Mr Bright believe themselves the heirs, and the goal of that great man's labours. Presently, perhaps, Mr Odger and Mr Bradlaugh will be there with their mission to oust both Barbarians and Philistines, and to get the heritage for the Populace.

We, on the other hand, are for giving the heritage neither to the Barbarians nor to the Philistines, nor yet to the Populace; but we are for the transformation of each and all of these according to the law of perfection. Through the length and breadth of our nation a sense, – vague and obscure as yet, – of weariness with the old organizations, of desire for this transformation, works and grows. In the House of Commons the old organizations must inevitably be most enduring and strongest, the transformation must inevitably be longest in showing itself; and it may truly be averred, therefore, that at the present juncture the centre of movement is not in the House of Commons. It is in the fermenting mind of the nation; and his is for the next twenty years the real influence who can address himself to this.

Pericles was perhaps the most perfect public speaker who ever lived, for he was the man who most perfectly combined thought and wisdom with feeling and eloquence. Yet Plato brings in Alcibiades declaring, that men went away from the oratory of Pericles, saying it was very fine, it was very good, and afterwards thinking no more about it; but they went away from hearing Socrates talk, he says, with the point of what he had said sticking fast in their minds, and they could not get rid of it.[4] Socrates has drunk his hemlock and is dead; but in his own breast does not every man carry about with him a possible Socrates, in that power of a disinterested play of consciousness upon his stock notions and habits, of which this wise and admirable man gave all through his lifetime the great example, and which was the secret of his incomparable influence? And he who leads men to call forth and exercise in themselves this power, and who busily calls it forth and exercises it in himself, is at the present moment, perhaps, as Socrates was in his time, more in concert with the vital working of men's minds, and more effectually significant, than any House of Commons' orator, or practical operator in politics.

Everyone is now boasting of what he has done to educate men's minds and to give things the course they are taking. Mr Disraeli educates, Mr Bright educates, Mr Beales educates. We, indeed, pretend to educate no one, for we are still engaged in trying to clear and educate ourselves. But we are sure that the endeavour to reach, through culture, the firm intelligible law of things, we are sure that the detaching ourselves from our stock notions and habits, that a more free play of consciousness, an increased desire for sweetness and light, and all the bent which we call Hellenizing, is the master-impulse even now of the life of our nation and of humanity, – somewhat obscurely perhaps for this actual moment, but decisively and certainly for the immediate future; and that those who work for this are the sovereign educators.

Docile echoes of the eternal voice, pliant organs of the infinite will, such workers are going along with the essential movement of the world; and this is their strength, and their happy and divine fortune. For if the believers in action, who are so impatient with us and call us effeminate, had had the same good fortune, they would, no doubt, have surpassed us in this sphere of vital influence by all the superiority of their genius and energy over ours. But now we go the way the human race is going, while they abolish the Irish Church by the power of the Nonconformists' antipathy to establishments, or they enable a man to marry his deceased wife's sister.

FRIENDSHIP'S GARLAND

The acquaintance of the ever-to-be-lamented Arminius was made by the present Editor on the Continent in the year 1865. The early history of the noble family of Von-Thunder-ten-Tronckh, to which Arminius belonged, their establishment in Westphalia, the sack of their castle in the middle of the last century by the Bulgarians, the fate of their principal dependants (among whom was the famous optimist philosopher, Dr Pangloss), the adventures of Arminius's grandfather and his deportation to the Jesuits at Rome, are recorded in a well-known treatise of Voltaire.[1] Additional information is supplied in several of the following letters.

Arminius came to England in 1866, and the correspondence now given in a collected form to the public commenced in the summer of that year, at the outbreak of the war between Prussia and Austria.[2] Many will yet remember the thrill with which they originally received, through the unworthy ministry of the present Editor, the communication of the great doctrine of 'Geist.' What, then, must it have been to hear that doctrine in its first newness from the lips of Arminius himself! Yet it will, I hope, be admitted, that even in this position of exceptional privilege, the present Editor succeeded in preserving his coolness, his independent judgment, and his proper feelings as a Briton.) – ED.

LETTER I

I introduce Arminius and 'Geist' to the British Public

Sir, –   *Grub Street,*[1] *July 19, 1866*
   A Prussian acquaintance of mine, one of the party of foreigners who so offensively criticized my countrymen to me
when I was abroad last year, has been over here just now, and
for the last week or so he has been favouring me with his
remarks on all he hears us say about the present crisis in Germany. In confidence I will own to you that he makes himself
intensely disagreeable. He has the harsh, arrogant, Prussian
way of turning up his nose at things and laying down the law
about them; and though, as a lover of intellect, I admire him,
and, as a seeker of truth, I value his frankness, yet, as an Englishman, and a member of what the *Daily Telegraph* calls 'the
Imperial race,' I feel so uncomfortable under it, that I want,
through your kindness, to call to my aid the great British public, which never loses heart and has always a bold front and a
rough word ready for its assailants.
   My Prussian friend got a little mortification at the beginning
of his visit, and as it is my belief this mortification set him
wrong from the first, I shall relate what it was. I took him with
me down to Reigate by the railroad, and in the carriage was
one of our representative industrial men (something in the bottle way), a famous specimen of that great middle class whose
energy and self-reliance make England what it is, and who give
the tone to our Parliament and to our policy. News had just
come of the first bloodshed between the Austrians and Prussians now at war together in Germany. 'So they've begun fighting,'
cried my countryman; 'what fools they both are!' And he
handed us *Punch* with that masterly picture in it of 'Denmark
avenged;'[2] that scathing satire which represents the King of Denmark sitting with his glass of grog and his cigar, to gloat over
the terrible retribution falling upon his great enemy Prussia for
her misdeeds towards him. My Prussian glared at the striking
moral lesson thus brought to his notice, but rage and contempt

made him speechless. I hastened, with a few sentences taken from Mr Gladstone's recent advice to the Roumanians, to pay my homage to the great principles of peaceful, industrial development which were invoked by my countryman.[3] 'Yes; war,' I said, 'interrupts business, and brings intolerable inconvenience with it; whereas people have only to persist steadily in the manufacture of bottles, railways, banks, and finance companies, and all good things will come to them of their own accord.' Before I had finished we reached Reigate, and I got my still speechless Prussian quickly out of the train.

But never shall I forget the flood when speech came at last: 'The dolt! the dunderhead! His ignorance of the situation, his ignorance of Germany, his ignorance of what makes nations great, his ignorance of what makes life worth living, his ignorance of everything except bottles, – those infernal bottles!' I heard so much of all this that I am glad to forget it without going through it again with the British public. I only mention it to make the rudeness of expression in what follows less unaccountable.

The day before yesterday the *Daily News* published that powerful letter from Mr Goldwin Smith,[4] pronouncing in favour of the Prussian alliance. In great excitement I ran with it to my friend. 'At last I have got something,' I cried, 'which will please you; a declaration by one of our best writers, in one of our best newspapers, for a united Germany under Prussian headship. She and we are thereupon to combine to curb France. Wherever I go, I hear people admiring the letter and approving the idea.' A sardonic smile, such as Alexander von Humboldt[5] used to have when he contemplated the late King of Prussia's missionary deaconesses, came over my Berliner's harsh countenance. 'Good God!' said he, 'the miracles that needle-gun[6] is working! It is only a year ago you were threatening Prussia with France, and suggesting to that great and sagacious ruler, as you called him, the French Emperor, to take the Rhine Province from us; it is not six weeks since I saw him styled in this very newspaper, with the dignity usual in Englishmen at present, "the arbiter of Europe." He has done nothing in the meantime to injure you; he has done his best to keep well with you. How charmed he will be with his friends! But the declaration you are all so pleased at, who is it by?' 'Mr Goldwin Smith,' I answered. 'I know him,' he said; 'a good writer, but a fanatic.' 'Oh, no, no,' said I; 'a man of genius and virtue.'

Without answering, my Berliner took the newspaper and read the letter. 'He should have served with Nelson,' he said, as he finished it; 'he hates a Frenchman as he does the devil. However, it is true that a preponderance in the world such as the French, thanks to your stupidity, were fast getting, is enough to make any human being, let alone a Frenchman, unbearable; and it is a good thing to have a great Germany in the world as well as a great France. It would be a good thing to have a great England, too, if you would let us. But pray what is to unite Germany and England against France? What is to be the ground of sympathy between actual England and actual Germany?' 'You are a strong Liberal,' said I, 'so I can easily answer you. You are drawn towards England because of her liberalism, and away from the French Emperor because of his despotism.' 'Liberalism and despotism!' cried the Prussian; 'let us get beyond these forms and words. What unites and separates people now is "Geist".'[7]

I had not the slightest idea what he meant, and my looks told my bewilderment. 'I thought you had read Mr Grant Duff's chapters on Germany,' said he.[8] 'But Mr Grant Duff knows what he writes about, so I suppose you have not. Your great Lord Palmerston used to call Germany "that country of d—d professors;" and the English public, which supposes professors to be people who know something, and hates anybody who knows anything, has always kept its mind as clear of my unfortunate country as it could. But I advise you, for the sake of the events now passing, to read Mr Grant Duff's book. There you will find that in Berlin we oppose "Geist," – *intelligence*, as you or the French might say, – to "Ungeist." The victory of "Geist" over "Ungeist" we think the great matter in the world. The same idea is at the bottom of democracy; the victory of reason and intelligence over blind custom and prejudice. So we German Liberals who believe in "Geist" have a sympathy with France and its governors, so far as they are believers in democracy. We have no sympathy with English liberalism, whose centre is in the "Ungeist" of such people as your wiseacre in the Reigate train.'

'But then you play,' cried I, 'the game of the Tories; for listen to Mr Goldwin Smith: "The Tories in Europe, with the sure instinct of a party, recognize the great patron of reaction in the Emperor of the French." You and we are to unite, in order to defeat the Tories and the Emperor of the French.'

The Prussian answered: 'Mr Goldwin Smith blinds himself with the passions, as the Emperor of the French himself would say, of another age. The Tories of Europe have no real love for the Emperor of the French; they may admire and envy his absolutism and strength, but they hate his fundamental principles: they can have no real sympathy with the Sovereign who says boldly that he detests the actual public law of Europe, and who tells the people that it is among the people he finds the true genius of France, and breathes freely. Such a man works for "Geist" in his way;* not, perhaps, through a *Daily Telegraph*, or monster meetings in Trafalgar Square, or a Coles's Truss Manufactory standing where it ought not, a glorious monument of individualism and industrialism, to adorn the "finest site in Europe;"[9] but by making the common people feel they are alive and have a human spirit in them. We North-Germans have worked for "Geist" in our way, by loving knowledge, by having the best-educated middle and lower class in the world. You see what this has just done for us. France has "Geist" in her democracy, and Prussia in her education. Where have you got it? – got it as a force, I mean, and not only in a few scattered individuals. Your common people is barbarous; in your middle class "Ungeist" is rampant; and as for your aristocracy, you know "Geist" is forbidden by nature to flourish in an aristocracy.

'So do not,' he continued, 'suffer yourself to be deceived by parallels drawn from times before "Geist." What has won this Austrian battle for Prussia is "Geist;" "Geist" has used the

* The indulgence of Arminius for this execrable and unsuccessful tyrant was unworthy of a member of our great Teutonic family. Probably, after Sedan, he changed his opinion of him. – ED.

King, and Bismarck, and the Junkers, and "Ungeist in uniform," all for its own ends; and "Geist" will continue so to use them till it has triumphed.* It will ally itself with "Geist" where it finds it, because there it has a ground for mutual respect and understanding; and where there is no "Geist," it has none.

'And now,' this odious man went on, 'now, my dear friend, I shall soon be leaving you, so one word more. You have lately been writing about the Celts and the Germans, and in the course of your remarks on the Germans you have said, among many impertinences, one thing which is true. You have said that the strength of North Germany lay in this, that the idea of science governed every department of human activity there. You, my dear friend, live in a country where at present the idea of clap-trap governs every department of human activity. Great events are happening in the world, and Mr Goldwin Smith tells you that "England will be compelled to speak at last." It would be truly sad if, when she does speak, she should talk nonsense. To prevent such a disaster, I will give you this piece of advice, with which I take my leave: "*Get Geist.*"'

Thank God, this d—d professor (to speak as Lord Palmerston) is now gone back to his own *Intelligenz-Staat.*[10] I half hope there may next come a smashing defeat of the Prussians before Vienna, and make my ghostly friend laugh on the wrong side of his mouth. Meanwhile, I shall take care that he hears whatever answers he gets. I know that they will be conclusive, and I hope that they will be speedy, and in this hope,

I am, Sir,

Your obedient servant,

MATTHEW ARNOLD

To The EDITOR *of the* PALL MALL GAZETTE

---

* I am unwilling to triumph over Arminius in his grave; but I cannot help remarking that 'Ungeist in uniform,' as Mr Bottles observes to me, has just given a pretty good account of the 'Geist' in French democracy; and I have a shrewd suspicion it will give an equally good account of the 'Geist' of Arminius's educated and liberal friends in Prussia. Perhaps Arminius was taken away from the evil to come! – ED.

LETTER 2

Arminius Appears as his Own Interpreter

Sir, –   *Berlin, July 31, 1866*

An English friend of mine, Mr Matthew Arnold, seems to have rushed into print with an idea or two he picked up from me when I was in England, and to have made rather a mess of it; at least, he sends me some newspapers which have answered him, and writes me a helpless sort of a letter at the same time, asking me how he is to parry this, and what he is to say in reply to that. Now, I have a regard for this Mr Matthew Arnold, but I have taken his measure, and know him to be, as a disputant, rather a poor creature. Again and again I have seen him anxiously ruminating over what his adversary has happened to say against his ideas; and when I tell him (if the ideas were mine) that his adversary is a *dummkopf*, and that he must stand up to him firm and square, he begins to smile, and tells me that what is probably passing through his adversary's mind is so and so.*

I see your hideous truss manufactory in Trafalgar Square comes up in this controversy, and that very manufactory brings to my mind a ridiculous instance of my poor friend's weakness. I had been running over with him a few of the principal violations of æsthetic laws in London, illustrating the lesson by reference to the stucco palaces of my beautiful Berlin. After despatching the Duke of Wellington's statue and the black dome and grey pepper-boxes of your National Gallery, I came to Coles's manufactory. 'Can anything be more atrocious?' I asked. 'It is bad,' answered my poor friend; 'and yet,' he went on, 'and yet, Arminius, I have a tenderness for that manufactory. That manufactory, with other things in London like it, is one of my favourite arguments for the immortality of the soul.' 'What folly have you got in your head now?' said I. 'Remember,' said he, 'what is told us of the statue of the Olympian Zeus

---

* A very ill-natured and exaggerated description of my (I hope) not unamiable candour. – ED.

by Phidias. It was life enough to have seen it; felicity had then reached its consummation; the spirit could grasp no more, and the man might end. And what, therefore, I ask, must not be in store for the British ratepayer, who in his life has only seen the Duke of Wellington's statue and Coles's truss manufactory? His felicity must surely be yet to come. Somewhere, beyond the grave' . . . and for a good twenty minutes my simple friend went on with stuff like this, which I will not weary you with any more of.

I, Sir, as a true Prussian, have a passion for what is *wissen-schaftlich* (I do not say 'scientific,' because then you English will think I have an interest in the sea-bear, or in the blue lights and smells of a chemical lecture). I am, I say, *wissenschaftlich*;[1] I love to proceed with the stringency of a philosopher, and Mr Matthew Arnold with his shillyshallying spoils the ideas I confide to him. Therefore I write to you myself, to tell you (since I like your nation for the sake of the great men it has formerly produced, and of its brave-hearted, industrious people) where the pinch of the matter for you really lies.

It lies here – there is in you '*kein Ernst, der ins Ganze geht.*'[2] You peck at the mere outside of problems; you have not got your mind at work upon them; you fancy they will solve themselves without mind, if only you keep making bottles, and letting everyone do what is right in his own eyes, and congratulating yourselves at the top of your voices on your own success. 'Individualism and industrialism will in time replace Coles by a worthier edifice,' says one of your prophets. Not without an '*Ernst der ins Ganze geht,*' I answer. Not without 'Geist' and faith in 'Geist;' and this is just what your individualism and industrialism has not got. 'A self-administering community is surely an ideal.' – That depends entirely on what the self-administering community is like. If it has 'Geist,' and faith in 'Geist,' yes; if it has not, no. Then another of your prophets asks: 'Why should "Geist" care about democracy? Democracy is government by the masses, by the light of their own vulgar tastes.' – Your democracy perhaps, but this is just what makes your weakness; you have no *demos*, no people, but 'masses with vulgar tastes.' The top part of them are in training to be Philistines like your middle class; the lower part is a rabble.

Your democracy has not yet reached even the idea of country; the friends of your northern workmen tell us they read American newspapers, and care more for America than for England.[3] No wonder; they have never been quickened by an '*Ernst der ins Ganze geht*,' the only baptism that makes masses into a people; they have never been in contact with 'Geist,' only with clap-trap. To abate feudalism by providing that in one insignificant case out of one million land shall not follow the feudal law of descent; to abolish English church-rates because the English Dissenters are strong, and to spare the Irish Church Establishment because the Irish Catholics are weak;* to give a man leave to marry his deceased wife's sister; to give a man who lives in a particular kind of house a vote for members of Parliament – that is the pabulum by which the leaders of your people seek to develop 'Geist' in it, and to awaken an '*Ernst der ins Ganze geht*.' If this is not spiritual enough, as a final resource there is rioting in the parks, and a despotism of your penny newspapers tempered by the tears of your executive, to hasten the growth of English democracy in dignity and intelligence.

The French are not solid enough for my taste; but, *Gott in Himmel!* that people has had a fire baptism, and the democracy which is born of a fire baptism like theirs, 'Geist' cannot help caring about. They were unripe for the task they in '89 set themselves to do; and yet, by the strength of 'Geist' and their faith in 'Geist,' this 'mere viper brood of canting egotists' did so much that they left their trace in half the beneficial reforms through Europe; and if you ask how, at Naples, a convent became a school, or in Ticino an intolerable oligarchy ceased to govern, or in Prussia Stein was able to carry his land-reforms, you get one answer: *the French!*[4] Till modern society is finally formed, French democracy will still be a power in Europe, and it will manage to have effective leaders at the Tuileries, and not only in Cayenne.[5] It will live, though the classes above it may rot; because it has faith in 'Geist,' and does not think that

---

* No doubt this remark of Arminius had some share in producing that great measure which has since abolished the Irish Church by the power of the English Dissenters' enmity to Church establishments. – ED.

people can do without 'Geist' by dint of holding monster meetings, and having their *Star** and *Telegraph* every morning, and paying no church-rates, and marrying their deceased wife's sister.

We Prussians, Sir, have, as a people, no great love for the French, because we were blown into the air by the explosion of their 'Geist' some sixty years ago, and much quarrelling and ill-blood followed. But we saw then what a power the 'Geist' in their democracy gave them; and we set to work to make ourselves strong, not by a sort of wild fire-baptism of the mass, but in our steady German way, by culture, by *forming* our faculties of all kinds, by every man doing the very best he could with himself, by trusting, with an '*Ernst der ins Ganze geht*,' to mind and not to clap-trap. Your 'earnest Liberal' in England thinks culture all moonshine; he is for the spiritual development of your democracy by rioting in the parks, abolishing church-rates, and marrying a deceased wife's sister; and for leaving your narrow and vulgar middle class (of which I saw an incomparable specimen in a Reigate train when I was over in England) just as it is. On the other hand, Mr Matthew Arnold writes me word that a club has just been formed among you to do honour to the memory of that great man, Richard Cobden; that this club has taken for its motto, 'Peace, Retrenchment, and Reform;' and that these words, by a special command from Mr Cobden's ghost, are to bear the following interpretation: – 'Peace to our nonsense, retrenchment of our profligate expenditure of clap-trap, and reform of ourselves.' Whether this is true, or merely a stroke of my poor friend's so-called playfulness (Heaven save the mark!), I do not feel quite sure; I hope for your sakes it is true, as this is the very thing you want, and nothing else can save you from certain decline.

Do not be astonished at the aristocratic prefix to my name;

---

* The *Star*, like Arminius himself, has passed from among us; but may we not say that its work was done when it had once laid the bases of that admirable and fruitful alliance between Miallism and Millism, which the course of our politics is now every day consolidating? – ED.

I come of a family which has for three generations rubbed shoulders with philosophy.

Your humble servant,

VON THUNDER-TEN-TRONCKH

To The EDITOR *of the* PALL MALL GAZETTE

LETTER 3

*I expostulate with Arminius on his
Revolutionary Sentiments*

Sir, –   *Grub Street, August 6, 1866*

I thought it was very odd I got no answer from Arminius von Thunder-ten-Tronckh (he was christened Hermann, but I call him Arminius, because it is more in the grand style[1]), when I so particularly begged him to write soon, and save what rags he could of his tissue of nonsense about 'Geist,' after my countrymen had riddled it, as I knew they were sure to do. I supposed he had taken service, like the rest of the German Liberals, under Bismarck, and was too busy pillaging the poor Frankfurt people to think of intellectual matters,[2] but I now see he has been writing direct to you, and wants to leave me out in the cold altogether. I do not in the least care for his coarse Prussian sneers, but I must say it is rather good that he should not be above sponging on me week after week in Grub Street, swilling beer (none of your Bavarian wash, but sound English Bass) at my expense, filling my garret (for I don't smoke myself) with the smell of his execrable tobacco, getting the daily benefit of my *Star* and *Telegraph* (I take the *Star* for wisdom and charity, and the *Telegraph* for taste and style), and keeping me up yawning till two o'clock every morning to listen to his rubbishy transcendentalism, and yet be too fine a gentleman to make me the depositary of his ideas for transmission to the English public. But Arminius has the ridiculous pride of his grandfather, who, though the family estate had all gone to the dogs, and he was ruined and turned

priest, chose to set his stiff German face against Candide's marriage with his sister. He got shipped off to the Jesuits at Rome,
as everyone knows; but what is not so well known is,* that when
the French Revolution came, this precious priest, like Talleyrand,
married, and my Arminius is his grandson. Arminius came over
here to make acquaintance with Mr Lowe, who he has found out
is in some odd way descended from the philosopher Pangloss,†
a great friend of the Von Thunder-ten-Tronckh family; but
ever since the sack of their château by the Bulgarians, the Von
Thunder-ten-Tronckhs have not had a sixpence in the world
except what they could get by their 'Geist,' and what Arminius
gets by his is such beggar's allowance that he is hardly present-
able; well enough for Grub Street, but, as I told him, not at all
the sort of company Mr Lowe keeps.

I don't think Arminius has gained much by being his own
expounder, for more vague declamatory trash than his letter I
never read. The truth is, he cannot rise to an Englishman's conception of liberty, and understand, how liberty, like virtue, is its
own reward. 'We go for self-government,' I am always saying
to him. 'All right,' he says, 'if it is government by your better self.'³
'Fiddlesticks about our better self!' answer I. 'Who is to be the
judge? No, the self every man chooses.' 'And what is the self the
mass of mankind will choose,' cries he, 'when they are not told
there is a better and a worse self, and shown what the better is
like?' 'They will choose the worse, very likely,' say I, 'but that is
just liberty.' 'And what is to bring good out of such liberty as
that?' he asks. 'The glorious and sanative qualities of our match-
less Constitution,' I reply; and that is always a stopper for him.

But what I grieve most to observe in Arminius's letter, and
what will lead to my breaking with him in the long run, in spite

* It was necessarily unknown to Voltaire, who wrote the history of the Von T.
family. – ED.
† It is my firm belief that this relationship, which had become a fixed idea with
Arminius, never really existed. The optimism of Mr Lowe's estimate of the
British middle class and its House of Commons, in his celebrated speech on
Reform, had, in my opinion, struck Arminius's fancy, and made him imagine
a kinship in the flesh where there was in truth only a kinship in the
spirit. – ED.

of my love for intellect, is the bad revolutionary leaven which I
see works stronger and stronger in him, and which he no doubt
got from the worthless French company his grandfather kept.*
I noticed an instance of it while he was over here, and I have
had another instance, besides his letter to you, since he went
away. The instance while he was over here was this. I had taken
him down to Wimbledon to see the shooting; and there, walking
up and down before the grand tent, was Lord Elcho.⁴ Everybody knows Lord Elcho's appearance, and how admirably he
looks the part of our governing classes; to my mind, indeed, the
mere cock of his lordship's hat is one of the finest and most
aristocratic things we have. So of course I pointed Lord Elcho
out to Arminius. Arminius eyed him with a Jacobinical sort of
smile, and then: 'Cedar of Lebanon which God has not yet
broken!' sneered he. I was pleased at Arminius knowing his
St Augustine, for the Prussians are in general thought to be
much tainted with irreligion; but I felt at the time, and I feel
still, that this was not by any means the proper way of speaking
of a dashing nobleman like Lord Elcho.

The other instance is worse still. Besides writing Arminius
long letters, I keep him regularly supplied with the *Star*, sending
him my own copy after I have read it through twice. I particularly begged him to study the number for last Wednesday week,
in which there was that most beautiful account of 'An Aristocratic Reformer.' The other papers had not got it. It related how
the Honourable Charles Clifford, a gentleman of strikingly
handsome appearance, addressed the crowd in Hyde Park from
the foot-board of a Hansom. He told them he cared nothing for
the Walpoles or Pakingtons,⁵ who were for putting down the
voice of the people, for, said he, he was higher in social position
than they. He was the son of a peer, his son-in-law was a peer,
and all his family belonged to the aristocratic classes. This
announcement was received with enthusiastic applause by the
street-Hampdens present. 'May I ask you, right honourable sir,'

---

* This partially explains, no doubt, though it cannot altogether excuse, the
weak indulgence always cropping out in Arminius for France and its immoral
people. – ED.

cried one of them, 'why, as you are such a big man, you do not open the park gates to us poor people?' Mr C said he wished he had the keys of the park in his pocket. But he delivered himself of the great principle that it is the duty of the aristocratic classes to protect and promote the interests of the working men, and then he drove off in his Hansom amidst redoubled applause.

Now nothing, Sir, gives me such pride and pleasure as traits of this kind, which show that we have, as Lord Macaulay finely says, the most popular aristocracy and the most aristocratic people in the world.[6] I thought it would do Arminius good to study the incident, and I wrote him word to that effect. Would you believe it, Sir? Mr 'Geist' cannot condescend to write me a letter, but he sends me back my *Star* with a vile sketch, or rather caricature, of this touching incident; and opposite Mr C's gentlemanly figure he has written 'Esel,' and opposite the crowd 'Lumpenpack,' which a friend who knows German better than I do tells me are words of disrespect, and even contempt.[7] This is a spirit which I hate and abhor, and I tell Arminius plainly through your columns (since he chooses to adopt this way of corresponding) that unless he can break himself of it all is ended between him and me, and when next he comes to England he will find the garret-door in Grub Street bolted against him.

Your obedient servant,
MATTHEW ARNOLD

To The EDITOR *of the* PALL MALL GAZETTE

LETTER 4

Arminius assails the British Press for its Free and Independent Comments on Foreign Politics

Sir, –   *Berlin, August 11, 1866*

For Heaven's sake try and prevail upon your countrymen, who are so very anxious for peace for themselves, not to go on biting first the French Emperor's tail and then ours, merely for the fun of the thing apparently, and to have the pleasure of at least seeing a fight between other people, if they cannot have one of their own. You know that Michelet, the French historian, all through his history, familiarly talks of your people as *ce dogue*;[1] 'upon this *ce dogue mordit* such a one;' 'upon that *ce dogue déchira* such another.' According to him, you must always be *mordre*-ing or *déchirer*-ing[2] some one, at home or abroad, such is your instinct of savageness; and you have, – undoubtedly you have, – a strong share of pugnacity. When I was over in England the other day, my poor friend Mr Matthew Arnold insisted, with his usual blind adoration of everything English, on taking me down to admire one of your great public schools; precious institutions, where, as I tell him, for 250*l*. sterling a year your boys learn gentlemanly deportment and cricket. Well, down we went, and in the playing-fields (which with you are the school): 'I declare,' says Mr Matthew Arnold, 'if there isn't the son of that man you quarrelled with in the Reigate train! And there, close by him, is a son of one of our greatest families, a Plantagenet! It is only in England, Arminius, that this beautiful salutary intermixture of classes takes place. Look at the bottle-merchant's son and the Plantagenet being brought up side by side; none of your absurd separations and seventy-two quarterings here.[3] Very likely young Bottles will end by being a lord himself.' I was going to point out to Mr Matthew Arnold that what a middle class wants is ideas, and ideas an aristocracy has nothing to do with; so that that vulgar dog, Bottles the father, in sending his son to learn only cricket and a gentlemanly deportment, like the aristocracy, had done quite the wrong thing with him. But just at this moment our attention was attracted by what was passing between the boys themselves. First, a boy goes up to Bottles, and says: 'Bottles, Plantagenet says he could lick you with one hand; you are as big as he is, – you wouldn't take a licking from him, would you?' 'No!' answered poor Bottles, rather hesitatingly. Upon this another boy rushes to Plantagenet. 'Plantagenet,' cries he, 'that brute Bottles says he wouldn't take a licking from you.' 'Does he, the beast!' thunders Plantagenet, and, flying at Bottles, hits him full on the nose; and as Bottles's blood streamed out, and I turned away in disgust,

I heard the exulting cries of your young 'dogues' making the arrangements for a systematic encounter.

Now really, Sir, since I have been back in Germany your newspapers are perpetually bringing to my mind Michelet's 'dogue' and what I saw in your playing-fields. First you go to the French Emperor, and say: 'Ha, tyrant, we hope humble-pie agrees with you! We hope your tail between your legs is not productive of much inconvenience. Just as the intellectual Emperor was overmatched by an Italian statesman, he now finds himself outdone by a German statesman; a most agreeable thing for an intellectual Emperor – ha! ha! The intellectual Emperor distinctly intimated there must be no disturbing the European equilibrium, else he should interpose. Now the map has been altered enormously to the profit of Prussia, so what is the intellectual Emperor to do? Acknowledge himself outwitted by Count Bismarck, just as he was outwitted by Count Cavour? – ha, ha! Humble-pie! Humble pie!' – With the greatest alacrity the malcontents in France, the old Constitutional party,[4] take up your parable: 'France is eating humble-pie!' they scream out; 'that tyrant is making France eat humble-pie! France is humiliated! France is suffocating!' France is not difficult to stir up, and the French Emperor has already had to ask for the frontier of 1814. If you go on at this rate I expect he will have to ask for the Mark of Brandenburg next week.[5] Then you will come to Bismarck and say: 'Bismarck, the tyrant is stretching his greedy fist over German soil. Will you let him have it? Think of the prodigious strength you have just shown, of the glory you have just won. Think of French insolence, think of 1813, think of German honour, think of *sauer-kraut*, think of the moral support of England. Not an inch of German soil for the French tyrant!' And so, while you yourselves, – the new man in you, that is, – teach the nations, as Lord Stanley says, how to live, by peacefully developing your bottle-man in the Reigate train, your half-naked starvelings selling matches in St James's Park, your truss manufactories in Trafalgar Square, and your *Daily Telegraph* saying in spite of all powers human and divine what it likes, you at the same time want to throw a bone to the old 'dogue' in you, in the shape of a very pretty quarrel of your getting up between other people.

Do, Sir, let other people also have a chance of teaching the nations how to live, and emulate your bottle-man and your *Daily Telegraph*. For my part, I have the greatest aversion, and so have all the clearest-headed Germans of my acquaintance, to a quarrel with France. We, as genuine Liberals, know that French democracy is our natural ally. You will observe it is the Constitutionalists in France who are crying out so loudly for more territory to make their strength keep pace with ours. And then think of our poor delicate constitutionalism at home, and of the cruelty of leaving it with its work to do in the face of a war with France, and Bismarck made stronger than ever by such a war! I know our German constitutionalism pretty well. It comes up to the throne, 'With fullest heart-devotion we approach Prussia's King, reverently beseeching him to turn away his unconstitutional ministers.' Prussia's gracious King gives a grunt, and administers a sound kick to his petitioner's behind, who then departs, singing in fervent tones: '*Hoch* for King and fatherland!'

No, Sir; peace, the growth of a republican spirit all through Europe, and a mutual support between all those who share this spirit, are what I wish for. The French are vain; they have been spoilt; we have been going very fast; and you and the Orleanists[6] keep telling them they are humiliated if they do not get something. No doubt people have a right to go to war for the balance of power if they believe in it; you have gone to war for it often enough when it suited your turn. So the Emperor of the French, as you will not let him have a chance of being wise and of seeing that here is a new spiritual force he had not reckoned on, which yet he may perfectly make friends of and live happily with, thinks he must do something for the balance of power, must ask for some rectification or other of frontier. I only hope he will ask for something moderate, and that we shall be moderate when he asks for it. Pray, Sir, pray do not you play the 'dogue' and make moderation harder both for the Emperor and for us.

I assure you a war with France would be a curse to us which even the blessing of your moral support would hardly compensate. And supposing (for certainly you do hate the French pretty strongly) in a year or two you determined to give us your

active support,* and to send, with infinite crying out, an expedition of fifteen thousand men to the coast of Gothland or some
such place, I am afraid, Sir, with the vast armaments and rapid
operations of modern warfare, even this active support of yours
would not do us any great good.

Your humble servant,
VON THUNDER-TEN-TRONCKH

To The EDITOR *of the* PALL MALL GAZETTE

P.S. – By the way, I read poor Mr Matthew Arnold's letter to
you the other day. You see just what he is; the discursiveness,
the incapacity for arguing, the artlessness, the not very delicate
allusions to my private circumstances and his own. It is impossible to enter into any serious discussion with him. But on one
point of fact I will set him right. I saw Mr Lowe and found him
very affable; even more like his ancestor Pangloss than I should
have thought possible. 'The best of all possible worlds' was
always on his lips; 'a system of such tried and tested efficiency;'
'what can we want more?' 'the grumbler fails to suggest even
one grievance.' I told him of that bottle Barbarian in the Reigate train, and he said that on men of this kind rested 'the
mighty fabric of English prosperity.' I could not help saying
that in my opinion no country could longer stand being ruled
by the spirit (or rather matter) of men like that; that a discon-
tent with the present state of things was growing up, and that
tomorrow even, or next day, we might see a change. Upon this,
Mr Lowe threw himself into a theatrical attitude, and with the
most enthusiastic vehemence exclaimed: –

---

* This is puerile. War between France and Prussia has since happened. We
have not been able to give our undivided moral support to either combatant;
of our active support, therefore, there could be no question. But it may be fearlessly asserted, that the well-balanced alterations of our moral support, the
wise and steady advice given by our newspapers, and, in fact, our attitude
generally in regard to this war, have raised Great Britain to a height even more
conspicuous than she has ever yet occupied, in the esteem and admiration of
foreign countries. – ED.

> Tomorrow?
> Oh, spare it, spare it!
> It ought not so to die.*

In a man like poor Mr Matthew Arnold, this infatuation about everything English is conceivable enough, but in a man of Mr Lowe's parts I own I cannot quite make it out, notwithstanding his descent from Pangloss.

VON T.

LETTER 6

I become intrusted with the Views of Arminius on Compulsory Education

Sir, –   *Grub Street, April 20, 1867*

   It is a long while since you have heard anything of Arminius and me, though I do hope you have sometimes given a thought to us both. The truth is we have been in the country. You may imagine how horribly disagreeable Arminius made himself during the famous snow in London at the beginning of this year. About the state of the streets he was bad enough, but about the poor frozen-out working men who went singing without let or hindrance before our houses, he quite made my blood creep. 'The dirge of a society *qui s'en va*,' he used to call their pathetic songs. It is true I had always an answer for him – 'Thank God, we are not Haussmannized[1] yet!' and if that was not enough, and he wanted the philosophy of the thing, why I turned to a sort of constitutional common-place book, or true Englishman's *vade mecum*, which I have been these many years forming for my own use by potting extracts from the *Times* and which I hope one day

---

* As the sentiments here attributed to Mr Lowe, together with this very remarkable and splendid passage of poetry with which he concludes, are all taken from Mr Lowe's printed speeches, and may have been read by Arminius in the *Times*, I still retain my doubts whether his interview with Mr Lowe had ever any existence except in his own fertile imagination. – ED.

to give to the world, and I read him this golden aphorism: 'Administrative, military, and clerical tyranny are unknown in this country, because the educated class discharges all the corresponding functions through committees of its own body.' 'Well, then,' Arminius would answer, 'show me your administrative committee for ridding us of these cursed frozen-out impostors.' 'My dear Arminius,' was my quiet reply, 'voluntary organizations are not to be dealt with in this peremptory manner. The administrative committee you ask for will develop itself in good time; its future members are probably now at nurse. In England we like our improvements to *grow*, not to be manufactured.'

However, the mental strain, day after day, of this line of high constitutional argument was so wearing, that I gladly acceded to a proposal made by Arminius in one of his fits of grumbling to go with him for a little while into the country. So into the country we went, and there, under his able guidance, I have been assiduously pursuing the study of German philosophy. As a rule, I attend to nothing else just now; but when we were taking one of our walks abroad the other morning, an incident happened which led us to discuss the subject of compulsory education, and, as this subject is beginning to awaken deep interest in the public mind, I think you may be glad to have an account of the incident, and of the valuable remarks on compulsory education which were drawn from Arminius by it.

We were going out the other morning on one of our walks, as I said, when we saw a crowd before the inn of the country town where we have been staying. It was the magistrates' day for sitting, and I was glad of an opportunity to show off our local self-government to a bureaucracy-ridden Prussian like Arminius. So I stopped in the crowd, and there we saw an old fellow in a smock-frock, with a white head, a low forehead, a red nose, and a foxy expression of countenance, being taken along to the justice-room. Seeing among the bystanders a contributor to the *Daily Telegraph*,* whom I formerly knew well

---

* Do you recognize yourself, Leo? Is it presumptuous in me, upon giving this volume to the world, to bid you too, my friend, say with the poet: *Non omnis moriar*? – ED.

enough, – for he had the drawing-room floor underneath me in Grub Street, but the magnificent circulation of that journey has long since carried him, like the course of empire, westward, – I asked him if he could tell me what the prisoner was charged with. I found it was a hardened old poacher, called Diggs, – Zephaniah Diggs, – and that he was had up for snaring a hare, – probably his ten-thousandth. The worst of the story, to my mind, was that the old rogue had a heap of young children by a second wife whom he had married late in life, and that not one of these children would he send to school, but persisted in letting them all run wild, and grow up in utter barbarism.

I hastened to tell Arminius that it was a poaching case; and I added that it was not always, perhaps, in poaching cases that our local self-government appeared to the best advantage. 'In the present case, however, there is,' said I, 'no danger; for a representative of the *Daily Telegraph* is down here, to be on the lookout for justices' justice, and to prevent oppression.' Immediately afterwards I was sorry I had said this, for there are unfortunately several things which operate on Arminius like scarlet on a bull, making him vicious the moment he comes across them; and the *Daily Telegraph* is one of these things. He declares it foments our worst faults; and he is fond of applying to it Dryden's dictum on Elkanah Settle, that its style is boisterous and its prose incorrigibly lewd. Though I do certainly think its prose a little full-bodied, yet I cannot bear to hear Arminius apply such a term to it as 'incorrigibly lewd;' and I always remonstrate with him. 'No, Arminius,' I always say, 'I hope not *incorrigibly*; I should be sorry to think that of a publication which is forming the imagination and taste of millions of Englishmen.' 'Pleasant news,' was Arminius's answer, the last time I urged this to him, 'pleasant news; the next batch of you, then, will be even more charming than the present!'

I trouble you with all this, Sir, to account for the acerbity of tone in some of Arminius's subsequent conversation; an acerbity he too often manifests, and which tends, as I tell him, to detract from the influence which his talents and acquirements would otherwise give him. On the present occasion he took no direct notice of my mention of the *Daily Telegraph*, but seemed quite taken up with scrutinizing old Diggs. 'Such a peasant as that wretched old creature,' he said at last, 'is peculiar, my dear friend, to your country. Only look at that countenance! Centuries of feudalism have effaced in it every gleam of humane life'—'Centuries of fiddlesticks!' interrupted I (for I assure you, Sir, I can stand up to Arminius well enough on a proper occasion). 'My dear Arminius, how can you allow yourself to talk such rubbish? Gleam of humane life, indeed! do but look at the twinkle in the old rogue's eye. He has plenty of life and wits about him, has old Diggs, I can assure you; you just try and come round him about a pot of beer!' 'The mere cunning of an animal!' retorted Arminius. 'For my part,' pursued I, 'it is his children I think most about; I am told not one of them has ever seen the inside of a school. Do you know, Arminius, I begin to think, and many people in this country begin to think, that the time has almost come for taking a leaf out of your Prussian book, and applying, in the education of children of this class, what the great Kant calls the categorical imperative.[2] The gap between them and our educated and intelligent classes is really too frightful.' 'Your educated and intelligent classes!' sneered Arminius, in his very offensive manner; 'where are they? I should like to see them.'

I was not going to stand and hear our aristocracy and middle class set down in this way; so, treating Arminius's ebullition of spite as beneath my notice, I pushed my way through the crowd to the inn-door. I asked the policeman there what magistrates were on the bench today. 'Viscount Lumpington,' says the man, 'Reverend Esau Hittall, and Bottles Esquire.' 'Good heavens!' I exclaimed, turning round to Arminius, who had followed me, and forgetting, in my excitement, my just cause of offence with him, – 'Good heavens, Arminius, if Bottles hasn't got himself made a county magistrate! *Sic itur ad astra*.'[3] 'Yes,' says Arminius, with a smile, 'one of your educated and intelligent classes, I suppose. And I dare say the other two are to match. Your magistrates are a sort of judges, I know; just the people who are drawn from the educated and intelligent classes. Now, what's sauce for the goose is sauce for the gander; if you put a pressure on one class to make it train itself properly, you must put a pressure on others to the same end. That is what we do in Prussia, if you are going to take a leaf out of our book. I want to hear what steps you take to put this pressure on people above old Diggs there, and then I will talk to you about putting it on old Diggs. Take his judges who are going to try him today; how about them? What training have you made them give themselves, and what are their qualifications?'

I luckily happen to know Lord Lumpington and Hittall pretty well, having been at college with them in former days, when I little thought the Philistines would have brought grey hairs to a garret in Grub Street; and I have made the acquaint-ance of Mr Bottles since, and know all about him. So I was able to satisfy Arminius's curiosity, and I had great pleasure in mak-ing him remark, as I did so, the rich diversity of our English life, the healthy natural play of our free institutions, and the happy blending of classes and characters which this promotes. 'The three magistrates in that inn,' said I, 'are not three Govern-ment functionaries all cut out of one block; they embody our whole national life; – the land, religion, commerce, are all rep-resented by them. Lord Lumpington is a peer of old family and great estate; Esau Hittall is a clergyman; Mr Bottles is one of our self-made middle-class men. Their politics are not all of one colour, and that colour the Government's. Lumpington is a Constitutional Whig; Hittall is a benighted old Tory. As for Mr Bottles, he is a Radical of the purest water; quite one of the Manchester school. He was one of the earliest free-traders; he has always gone as straight as an arrow about Reform; he is an ardent voluntary in every possible line, opposed the Ten Hours' Bill, was one of the leaders of the Dissenting opposition out of Parliament which smashed up the education clauses of Sir James Graham's Factory Act;[4] and he paid the whole expenses of a most important church-rate contest out of his own pocket. And, finally, he looks forward to marrying his deceased wife's sister. Table, as my friend Mr Grant Duff says, the whole Lib-eral creed, and in not a single point of it will you find Bottles tripping!'

'That is all very well as to their politics,' said Arminius, 'but I want to hear about their education and intelligence.' 'There, too, I can satisfy you,' I answered. 'Lumpington was at Eton. Hittall was on the foundation[5] at Charterhouse, placed there by his uncle, a distinguished prelate, who was one of the trustees. You know we English have no notion of your bureaucratic tyranny of treating the appointments to these great foundations as public patronage, and vesting them in a responsible minister; we vest them in independent magnates, who relieve the State of all work and responsibility, and never take a shilling of salary for their trouble. Hittall was the last of six nephews nominated to the Charterhouse by his uncle, this good prelate, who had thoroughly learnt the divine lesson that charity begins at home.' 'But I want to know what his nephew learnt,' interrupted Arminius, 'and what Lord Lumpington learnt at Eton.' 'They followed,' said I, 'the grand, old, fortifying, classical curriculum.' 'Did they know anything when they left?' asked Arminius. 'I have seen some longs and shorts[6] of Hittall's,' said I, 'about the Calydonian Boar, which were not bad. But you surely don't need me to tell you, Arminius, that it is rather in training and bracing the mind for future acquisition, – a course of mental gymnastics we call it, – than in teaching any set thing, that the classical curriculum is so valuable.' 'Were the minds of Lord Lumpington and Mr Hittall much braced by their mental gymnastics?' inquired Arminius. 'Well,' I answered, 'during their three years at Oxford they were so much occupied with Bullingdon[7] and hunting that there was no great opportunity to judge. But for my part I have always thought that their both getting their degree at last with flying colours, after three weeks of a famous coach for fast men, four nights without going to bed, and an incredible consumption of wet towels, strong cigars, and brandy-and-water, was one of the most astonishing feats of mental gymnastics I ever heard of.'

'That will do for the land and the Church,' said Arminius. 'And now let us hear about commerce.' 'You mean how was Bottles educated?' answered I. 'Here we get into another line altogether, but a very good line in its way, too. Mr Bottles was brought up at the Lycurgus House Academy, Peckham. You are not to suppose from the name of Lycurgus that any Latin and

Greek was taught in the establishment; the name only indicates the moral discipline, and the strenuous earnest character, imparted there.[8] As to the instruction, the thoughtful educator who was principal of the Lycurgus House Academy, – Archimedes Silverpump, PhD, you must have heard of him in Germany? – had modern views. "We must be men of our age," he used to say. "Useful knowledge, living languages, and the forming of the mind through observation and experiment, these are the fundamental articles of my educational creed." Or, as I have heard his pupil Bottles put it in his expansive moments after dinner (Bottles used to ask me to dinner till that affair of yours with him in the Reigate train): "Original man, Silverpump! fine mind! fine system! None of your antiquated rubbish – all practical work – latest discoveries in science – mind constantly kept excited – lots of interesting experiments – lights of all colours – fizz! fizz! bang! bang! That's what I call forming a man."'

'And pray,' cried Arminius, impatiently, 'what sort of man do you suppose this infernal quack really formed in your precious friend Mr Bottles?' 'Well,' I replied, 'I hardly know how to answer that question. Bottles has certainly made an immense fortune; but as to Silverpump's effect on his mind, whether it was from any fault in the Lycurgus House system, whether it was that with a sturdy self-reliance thoroughly English, Bottles, ever since he quitted Silverpump, left his mind wholly to itself, his daily newspaper, and the Particular Baptist minister under whom he sate, or from whatever cause it was, certainly his mind, *quâ* mind—' 'You need not go on,' interrupted Arminius, with a magnificent wave of his hand, 'I know what that man's mind, *quâ* mind, is, well enough.'

But, Sir, the midnight oil is beginning to run very low; I hope, therefore, you will permit me to postpone the rest of Arminius's discourse till tomorrow. And meanwhile, Sir, I am, with all respect,

Your humble servant,
MATTHEW ARNOLD

To The EDITOR *of the* PALL MALL GAZETTE

LETTER 7

More about Compulsory Education

Sir, –   *Grub Street, April 21, 1867*

I take up the thread of the interesting and important discussion on compulsory education between Arminius and me where I left it last night.

'But,' continued Arminius, 'you were talking of compulsory education, and your common people's want of it. Now, my dear friend, I want you to understand what this principle of compulsory education really means. It means that to ensure, as far as you can, every man's being fit for his business in life, you put education as a bar, or condition, between him and what he aims at. The principle is just as good for one class as another, and it is only by applying it impartially that you save its application from being insolent and invidious. Our Prussian peasant stands our compelling him to instruct himself before he may go about his calling, because he sees we believe in instruction, and compel our own class, too, in a way to make it really feel the pressure, to instruct itself before it may go about its calling. Now, you propose to make old Diggs's boys instruct themselves before they may go bird-scaring or sheep-tending. I want to know what you do to make those three worthies in that justice-room instruct themselves before they may go acting as magistrates and judges.' 'Do?' said I; 'why, just look what they have done all of themselves. Lumpington and Hittall have had a public-school and university education; Bottles has had Dr Silverpump's, and the practical training of business. What on earth would you have us make them do more?' 'Qualify themselves for administrative or judicial functions, if they exercise them,' said Arminius. 'That is what really answers, in their case, to the compulsion, you propose to apply to Diggs's boys. Sending Lord Lumpington and Mr Hittall to school is nothing; the natural course of things takes them there. Don't suppose that, by doing this, you are applying the principle of compulsory education fairly, and as you apply it to Diggs's boys. You are not interposing, for the rich, education as a bar or condition between them and that which they aim at. But interpose it, as we do, between the rich and things they aim at, and I will say something to you. I should like to know what has made Lord Lumpington a magistrate?' 'Made Lord Lumpington a magistrate?' said I; 'why, the Lumpington estate, to be sure.' 'And the Reverend Esau Hittall?' continued Arminius. 'Why, the Lumpington living, of course,' said I. 'And that man Bottles?' he went on. 'His English energy and self-reliance,' I answered very stiffly, for Arminius's incessant carping began to put me in a huff; 'those same incomparable and truly British qualities which have just triumphed over every obstacle and given us the Atlantic telegraph![1] – and let me tell you, Von T., in my opinion it will be a long time before the "Geist" of any pedant of a Prussian professor gives us anything half so valuable as that.' 'Pshaw!' replied Arminius, contemptuously; 'that great rope, with a Philistine at each end of it talking inutilities!

'But in my country,' he went on, 'we should have begun to put a pressure on these future magistrates at school. Before we allowed Lord Lumpington and Mr Hittall to go to the university at all, we should have examined them, and we should not have trusted the keepers of that absurd cockpit you took me down to see, to examine them as they chose, and send them jogging comfortably off to the university on their lame longs and shorts. No; there would have been some Mr Grote[2] as School Board Commissary, pitching into them questions about history, and some Mr Lowe, as Crown Patronage Commissary, pitching into them questions about English literature; and these young men would have been kept from the university, as Diggs's boys are kept from their bird-scaring, till they had instructed themselves. Then, if, after three years of their university, they wanted to be magistrates, another pressure! – a great Civil Service examination before a board of experts, an examination in English law, Roman law, English history, history of jurisprudence—' 'A most abominable liberty to take with Lumpington and Hittall!' exclaimed I. 'Then your compulsory education is a most abominable liberty to take with Diggs's boys,' retorted Arminius. 'But good gracious! my dear Arminius,' expostulated I, 'do you really mean to maintain that a man can't put old Diggs in quod for snaring a hare without all this elaborate apparatus of Roman law and history of jurisprudence?' 'And do you really mean to maintain,' returned Arminius, 'that a man can't go bird-scaring or sheep-tending without all this elaborate apparatus of a compulsory school?' 'Oh, but,' I answered, 'to live at all, even at the lowest stage of human life, a man needs instruction.' 'Well,' returned Arminius, 'and to administer at all, even at the lowest stage of public administration, a man needs instruction.' 'We have never found it so,' said I.

Arminius shrugged his shoulders and was silent. By this time the proceedings in the justice-room were drawn to an end, the majesty of the law had been vindicated against old Diggs, and the magistrates were coming out. I never saw a finer spectacle than my friend Arminius presented, as he stood by to gaze on the august trio as they passed. His pilot-coat was tightly buttoned round his stout form, his light blue eyes shone, his sanguine cheeks were ruddier than ever with the cold morning and the excitement of discourse, his fell of tow was blown about by the March wind, and volumes of tobacco smoke issued from his lips. So in old days stood, I imagine, his great namesake by the banks of the Lippe, glaring on the Roman legions before their destruction.[3]

Lord Lumpington was the first who came out. His lordship good-naturedly recognized me with a nod, and then eyeing Arminius with surprise and curiosity: 'Whom on earth have you got there?' he whispered. 'A very distinguished young Prussian *savant*,' replied I; and then dropping my voice, in my most impressive undertones I added: 'And a young man of very good family, besides, my lord.' Lord Lumpington looked at Arminius again; smiled, shook his head, and then, turning away, and half aloud: 'Can't compliment you on your friend,' says he.

As for that centaur Hittall, who thinks of nothing on earth but field-sports, and in the performance of his sacred duties never warms up except when he lights on some passage about hunting or fowling, he always, whenever he meets me, remembers that in my unregenerate days, before Arminius inoculated me with a passion for intellect, I was rather fond of shooting, and not quite such a successful shot as Hittall himself. So, the moment he catches sight of me: 'How d'ye do, old fellow?' he blurts out; 'well, been shooting any straighter this year than you used to, eh?'[4]

I turned from him in pity, and then I noticed Arminius, who had unluckily heard Lord Lumpington's unfavourable comment on him, absolutely purple with rage and blowing like a turkey-cock. 'Never mind, Arminius,' said I soothingly; 'run after Lumpington, and ask him the square root of thirty-six.' But now it was my turn to be a little annoyed, for at the same instant Mr Bottles stepped into his brougham, which was waiting for him, and observing Arminius, his old enemy of the Reigate train, he took no notice whatever of me who stood there, with my hat in my hand, practising all the airs and graces I have learnt on the Continent; but, with that want of amenity I so often have to deplore in my countrymen, he pulled up the glass on our side with a grunt and a jerk, and drove off like the wind, leaving Arminius in a very bad temper indeed, and me, I confess, a good deal shocked and mortified.

However, both Arminius and I got over it, and have now returned to London, where I hope we shall before long have another good talk about educational matters. Whatever Arminius may say, I am still for going straight, with all our heart and soul, at compulsory education for the lower orders. Why, good heavens! Sir, with our present squeezable Ministry, we are evidently drifting fast to household suffrage, pure and simple; and I observe, moreover, a Jacobinical spirit growing up in some quarters which gives me more alarm than even household suffrage. My elevated position in Grub Street, Sir, where I sit commercing with the stars, commands a view of a certain spacious and secluded back yard; and in that back yard, Sir, I tell you confidentially that I saw the other day with my own eyes that powerful young publicist, Mr Frederic Harrison, in full evening costume, furbishing up a guillotine.[5] These things are very serious; and I say, if the masses are to have power, let them be instructed, and don't swamp with ignorance and unreason the education and intelligence which now bear rule among us. For my part, when I think of Lumpington's estate, family,

and connections, when I think of Hittall's shooting, and of the
energy and self-reliance of Bottles, and when I see the unexampled pitch of splendour and security to which these have
conducted us, I am bent, I own, on trying to make the new elements of our political system worthy of the old; and I say
kindly, but firmly, to the compound householder in the French
poet's beautiful words,* slightly altered: 'Be great, O working
class, for the middle and upper class are great!'

I am, Sir,

Your humble servant,

MATTHEW ARNOLD

To The EDITOR *of the* PALL MALL GAZETTE

(From the autumn of this year (1867) dates one of the most
painful memories of my life. I have mentioned in the last letter
but one how in the spring I was commencing the study of German philosophy with Arminius. In the autumn of that year the
celebrated young Comtist, Mr Frederic Harrison, resenting
some supposed irreverence of mine towards his master, permitted himself, in a squib, brilliant indeed, but unjustifiably severe,
to make game of my inaptitude for philosophical pursuits.[6] It
was on this occasion he launched the damning sentence: 'We
seek vainly in Mr A. a system of philosophy with principles
coherent, interdependent, subordinate, and derivative.' The blow
came at an unlucky moment for me. I was studying, as I have
said, German philosophy with Arminius; we were then engaged
on Hegel's 'Phenomenology of *Geist*,' and it was my habit to
develop to Arminius, at great length, my views of the meaning
of his great but difficult countryman. One morning I had,
perhaps, been a little fuller than usual over a very profound
chapter. Arminius was suffering from dyspepsia (brought on,
as I believe, by incessant smoking); his temper, always irritable,
seemed suddenly to burst from all control, – he flung the

---

* 'Et tâchez d'être grand, car le peuple grandit.'

Phänomenologie to the other end of the room, exclaiming: 'That smart young fellow is quite right! it is impossible to make a silk purse out of a sow's ear!' This led to a rupture, in which I think I may fairly say that the chief blame was not on my side. But two invaluable years were thus lost; Arminius abandoned me for Mr Frederic Harrison, who must certainly have many memoranda of his later conversations, but has never given them, as I always did mine of his earlier ones, to the world. A melancholy occasion brought Arminius and me together again in 1869; the sparkling pen of my friend Leo has luckily preserved the record of what then passed.) – Ed.

LETTER 8

Under a Playful Signature, my Friend Leo, of the 'Daily Telegraph,' advocates an Important Liberal Measure, and, in so doing, gives News of Arminius

Sir, –   *St James's Place, June 8, 1869*
For the sake of my health it is my custom at this full-blooded time of the year to submit myself to a lowering course of medical treatment, which causes me for a few days to be voted below par for Fleet Street; so I have bethought myself of utilizing my leisure, while universal humanity does not claim me, and while my style is reduced nearer the pitch of the *Pall Mall Gazette*, by writing to you on a subject in which I am strongly interested, and on which your ideas are, I am sorry to see, far from sound. I mean that great subject of which a fragment will be brought under discussion tonight, by the House of Commons going into Committee on Mr Chambers's admirable bill for enabling a woman to marry her sister's husband.[1]

My ideas on this subject have been stirred into lively activity by a visit I have just been making. I believe my name has been once or twice mentioned in your columns in connection with the Bottles family near Reigate, and with a group of friends gathered round them. Poor Mrs Bottles, I grieve to say, is not long for this world. She and her family showed an interest in me while I was rising to name and fame, and I trust I have never forgotten it. She sate, as Curran says, by my cradle, and I intend to follow her hearse. Meanwhile, with our Paris correspondent, who happens to be over here for a few days, I have been down to Reigate to inquire after her. The accounts were unhappily as bad as possible; but what I saw awakened a train of ideas and suggestions which I am going to communicate to you.

I found a good many people assembled, of whom several had come on the same errand as I. There was that broken-down acquaintance of my early youth, Mr Matthew Arnold, who has had many a dinner from Mrs Bottles (for she was kind to literature even in its humblest manifestations), snivelling and crying in a corner. There was that offensive young Prussian of his, who seems to have dropped him entirely, and to have taken up with a much younger man than my poor old acquaintance, and a much better-dressed man, with whom he is pursuing researches concerning labour and capital, which are hardly, as our Paris correspondent says, palpitating with actuality. There was a Baptist minister who had been the shepherd of the Bottles family in the old days when they were Dissenters, and who has never quite lost his hold upon Mrs Bottles. There was her sister Hannah, just about the same age as poor Sarah who married Bottles, and the very image of her. There was Job Bottles, Bottles's brother, who is on the Stock Exchange; a man with black hair at the sides of his head, a bald crown, dark eyes, and a fleshy nose, and a camellia in his button-hole. Finally, there was that handsome niece of Mr and Mrs Bottles, Mary Jane. *Mary Jane!*[2] I never pronounce the name without emotion; in season and out of season it keeps rising to my lips.* But the life we live in Fleet Street is devouring, and I have sacrificed to it all thought of marriage. Our Paris correspondent comforts me by saying that, even with the domestic affections suppressed, existence turns out to be a much more tolerable affair than humdrum people fancy.

---

* Leo here alludes, I imagine, to what the world has doubtless noticed, – the frequent introduction of *Mary Jane* into his articles for the *DT.* – ED.

Presently the members of the family left the room, and as the Baptist minister took the *Nonconformist* out of his pocket and began to read it, as the Prussian *savant* was quite absorbed with his new young man,[3] and as Mr Matthew Arnold counts for nothing, I was left to the conversation of our Paris correspondent, whom we call Nick because of the diabolical salt which sparkles in his deliverances. 'They say,' I began, 'that if Mr T. Chambers's excellent bill, which the Liberal party are carrying with such decisive majorities, becomes law, the place of poor Mrs Bottles will be taken by her sister Hannah, whom you have just seen. Nothing could be more proper; Mrs Bottles wishes it, Miss Hannah wishes it, this reverend friend of the family, who has himself made a marriage of the same kind, wishes it, everybody wishes it.' 'Everybody but old Bottles himself, I should think,' retorted my friend; 'don't envy him at all! – shouldn't so much mind if it were the younger one, though.'

These light words of my friend, Sir, seemed to touch a spring in me. Instantly I felt myself visited by a shower of ideas, full of import for the Liberal party and for the future, and which impel me to address to you the present letter. 'And why not the younger one, Nick?' said I, gently: 'why not? Either as a successor to Miss Hannah or in lieu of Miss Hannah, why not? Let us apply John Bright's crucial tests. Is she his first cousin? Could there be a more natural companion for Selina and the other Bottles girls? Or, – to take the moral ground so touchingly and irresistibly chosen by our great popular tribune, – if legislation on this subject were impeded by the party of bigotry, if they chose not to wait for it, if they got married without it, and if you were to meet them on the boulevard at Paris during their wedding tour, should you go up to Bottles and say: Mr Bottles, you are a profligate man?' 'Oh dear, no!' said Nick. 'I should never dream of it.' 'And if you met them a year later on the same spot,' I continued, 'with a Normandy nurse behind them carrying a baby, should you cry out to the poor little thing: Bastard?' 'Nothing of the kind,' he answered.

I noticed that my friend accompanied each of these assurances with a slight rapid droop of one eyelid. 'Let us have no flippancy, Nick,' I said. 'You mean that you hardly feel yourself

in a position to take high moral ground of this kind.' 'Well,' said
he, 'I suppose that even our great tribune, John Bright himself,
does not very often address people as bastards and profligates,
whatever he thinks of them. At least, I should imagine the
offender must almost be a bishop or some other high-placed
Anglican ecclesiastic to provoke him to do so.' 'A fig for your
fine distinctions,' cried I. 'Secretly or openly, will any one dare
call Bottles, if he contracts a marriage of this kind, a profligate
man?'

Poor Mr Matthew Arnold, upon this, emerged suddenly
from his corner, and asked hesitatingly: 'But will any one dare
call him a man of delicacy?' The question was so utterly unpractical that I took no notice of it whatever, and should not have
mentioned it if it had not led, by its extraordinary effect upon
our Paris correspondent, to the introduction and criticism of a
literary star of the first magnitude. My friend Nick, who has all
the sensitive temperament of genius, seemed inexplicably struck
by this word delicacy, which he kept repeating to himself. 'Delicacy,' said he, 'delicacy, – surely I have heard that word before!
Yes, in other days,' he went on dreamily, 'in my fresh, enthusiastic youth; before I knew Sala,[4] before I wrote for that infernal
paper, before I called Dixon's style lithe and sinewy—'

'Collect yourself, my friend,' said I, laying my hand on his
shoulder; 'you are unmanned. But in mentioning Dixon you
redouble my strength; for you bring to my mind the great sexual insurrection of the Anglo-Teutonic race,[5] and the master-spirit
which guides it. This illustrious man, who has invented a new
style—'

'He has, indeed,' said Mr Arminius the Prussian, turning
towards us for the first time; 'he has, indeed, and its right name
is middle-class Macaulayese.'

Now, I detest this German lecturer and his oracles, but as I
am, above everything, a man of letters myself, I never refuse to
listen to a remark upon style. 'Explain yourself,' said I; 'why do
you call Mr Hepworth Dixon's style middle-class Macaulayese?' 'I call it Macaulayese,' says the pedant, 'because it has
the same internal and external characteristics as Macaulay's style;

the external characteristic being a hard metallic movement with nothing of the soft play of life, and the internal characteristic being a perpetual semblance of hitting the right nail on the head without the reality. And I call it middle-class Macaulayese, because it has these faults without the compensation of great studies and of conversance with great affairs, by which Macaulay partly redeemed them.'

I turned away in pity. 'Let us leave the envious,' said I to Nick, 'to break their teeth on this magnificent file, the countlessness of whose editions has something analogous to the world-wide circulation of the *Daily Telegraph*. Let us pursue his fine regenerating idea of sexual insurrection. Let us deal with this question as a whole. Why, after Mr Chambers has succeeded at his one single point tonight, are we to have to begin afresh at other points tomorrow? We have established, I hope, that no man may presume to call Bottles profligate for marrying either his sister-in-law Hannah, or his niece Mary Jane. But this is not enough. A complication, like the complications of Greek tragedy, suggests itself to my mind. You noticed Mr Job Bottles. You must have seen his gaze resting on Mary Jane. But what with his cigars, his claret, his camellias, and the state of the money-market, Mr Job Bottles is not a marrying man just at this moment. His brother is; but his brother cannot last for ever. Job, on the other hand, is full of vigour and vitality. We have heard of the patience of Job; how natural, if his brother marries Mary Jane now, that Job, with his habits tempered, his view of life calmed, and the state of the money-market different, may wish, when she is a widow some five years hence, to marry her himself. And we have arrangements which make this illegal! At such arrangements I hurl, with scorn and disgust, the burning words of our great leader:[6] – Ecclesiastical rubbish!

I thank thee, Friend! for teaching me that word.[7]

Why, I ask, is Mr Job Bottles's liberty, his Christian liberty, as my reverend friend yonder would say, to be abridged in this manner? And why is Protestant Dissent to be diverted from its great task of abolishing State Churches for the purpose of removing obstacles to the sexual insurrection of our race? Why are its more devoted ministers to be driven to contract, in the interests of Christian liberty, illegal unions of this kind themselves, *pour encourager les autres*? Why is the earnest liberalism and nonconformity of Lancashire and Yorkshire to be agitated on this question by hope deferred? Why is it to be put incessantly to the inconvenience of going to be married in Germany or in the United States, that greater and better Britain

Which gives us manners, freedom, virtue, power.[8]

Why must ideas on this topic have to be incubated for years in that nest of spicery, as the divine Shakespeare says,[9] the mind of Mr T. Chambers, before they can rule the world? For my part, my resolve is formed. This great question shall henceforth be seriously taken up in Fleet Street. As a sop to those toothless old Cerberuses, the bishops, who impotently exhibit still the passions, as Nick's French friends say, of another age, we will accord the continuance of the prohibition which forbids a man to marry his grandmother. But in other directions there shall be freedom. Mr Chambers's admirable bill for enabling a woman to marry her sister's husband will doubtless pass triumphantly through Committee tonight, amidst the cheers of the ladies' gallery. The Liberal party must supplement that bill by two others: one enabling people to marry their brothers' and sisters' children, the other enabling a man to marry his brother's wife.'

But this glorious prospect fills me with an *afflatus* which can find its fit employment only in Fleet Street, and I am forced to subscribe myself,

Yours in haste,
A YOUNG LION

LETTER 12

'Life,' as Mr G. A. Sala says, 'a Dream!'

Mon Cher, –   *Versailles, November 26, 1870*[1]

An event has just happened which I confess frankly will afflict others more than it does me, but which you ought to be informed of.

Early this morning I was passing between Rueil and Bougival, opposite Mont Valérien. How came I in that place at that hour? *Mon cher,* forgive my folly! You have read *Romeo and Juliet,* you have seen me at Cremorne,[2] and though Mars has just now this *belle France* in his grip, yet you remember, I hope, enough of your classics to know that, where Mars is, Venus is never very far off. Early this morning, then, I was between Rueil and Bougival, with Mont Valérien in grim proximity. On a bank by a poplar-tree at the roadside I saw a knot of German soldiers, gathered evidently round a wounded man. I approached and frankly tendered my help, in the name of British humanity. What answer I may have got I do not know; for, petrified with astonishment, I recognized in the wounded man our familiar acquaintance, Arminius von Thunder-ten-Tronckh. A Prussian helmet was stuck on his head, but there was the old hassock of whity-brown hair, – there was the old square face, – there was the old blue pilot-coat! He was shot through the chest, and evidently near his end. He had been on outpost duty; – the night had been quiet, but a few random shots had been fired. One of these had struck Arminius in the breast, and gone right through his body. By this stray bullet, without glory, without a battle, without even a foe in sight, had fallen the last of the Von Thunder-ten-Tronckhs!

He knew me, and with a nod, 'Ah,' said he, 'the rowdy Philistine!' You know his turn, *outré* in my opinion, for flinging nicknames right and left. The present, however, was not a moment for resentment. The Germans saw that their comrade was in friendly hands, and gladly left him with me. He had evidently but a few minutes to live. I sate down on the bank by him, and asked him if I could do anything to relieve him. He shook his head. Any message to his friends in England? He nodded. I ran over the most prominent names which occurred to me of the old set. First, our Amphitryon,[3] Mr Bottles. 'Say to Bottles from me,' said Arminius coldly, 'that I hope he will be comfortable with his dead wife's sister.' Next, Mr Frederic Harrison. 'Tell him,' says Arminius, 'to do more in literature, – he has a talent for it; and to avoid Carlylese as he would the devil.' Then I mentioned a personage to whom Arminius had taken a great fancy last spring, and of whose witty writings some people had, absurdly enough, given Mr Matthew Arnold the credit, – Azamat-Batuk.[4] Both writers are simple; but Azamat's is the simplicity of shrewdness, the other's of helplessness. At hearing the clever Turk's name, 'Tell him only,' whispers Arminius, 'when he writes about the sex, not to show such a turn for sailing so very near the wind!' Lastly, I mentioned Mr Matthew Arnold. I hope I rate this poor soul's feeble and rambling performances at their proper value; but I am bound to say that at the mention of his name Arminius showed signs of tenderness. 'Poor fellow!' sighed he; 'he had a soft head, but I valued his heart. Tell him I leave him my ideas, – the easier ones; and advise him from me,' he added, with a faint smile, 'to let his Dissenters go to the devil their own way!'

At this instant there was a movement on the road at a little distance from where we were, – some of the Prussian Princes, I believe, passing; at any rate, we heard the honest German soldiers *Hoch-ing,* hurrahing, and God-blessing, in their true-hearted but somewhat *rococo* manner. A flush passed over Von Thunder-ten-Tronckh's face. 'God bless *Germany,*' he murmured, 'and confound all her kings and princelings!' These were his last coherent words. His eyes closed and he seemed to become unconscious. I stooped over him and inquired if he had any wishes about his interment. 'Pangloss – Mr Lowe – mausoleum – Caterham,'[5] was all that, in broken words, I could gather from him. His breath came with more and more difficulty, his fingers felt instinctively for his tobacco-pouch, his lips twitched; – he was gone.

So died, *mon cher,* an arrant Republican, and, to speak my

real mind, a most unpleasant companion. His great name and lineage imposed on the Bottles family, and authors who had never succeeded with the British public took pleasure in his disparaging criticisms on our free and noble country; but for my part I always thought him an over-rated man.

Meanwhile I was alone with his remains. His notion of their being transported to Caterham was, of course, impracticable. Still, I did not like to leave an old acquaintance to the crows, and I looked round in perplexity. Fortune in the most unexpected manner befriended me. The grounds of a handsome villa came down to the road close to where I was; at the end of the grounds and overhanging the road was a summer-house. Its shutters had been closed when I first discovered Arminius; but while I was occupied with him they had been opened, and a gay trio was visible within the summer-house at breakfast. I could scarcely believe my eyes for satisfaction. Three English members of Parliament, celebrated for their ardent charity and advanced Liberalism, were sitting before me adorned with a red cross and eating a Strasburg pie! I approached them and requested their aid to bury Arminius. My request seemed to occasion them painful embarrassment; they muttered something about 'a breach of the understanding,' and went on with their breakfast. I insisted, however; and at length, having stipulated that what they were about to do should on no account be drawn into a precedent, they left their breakfast, and together we buried Arminius under the poplar-tree. It was a hurried business, for my friends had an engagement to lunch at Versailles at noon. Poor Von Thunder-ten-Tronckh, the earth lies light on him, indeed! I could see, as I left him, the blue of his pilot-coat and the whity-brown of his hair through the mould we had scattered over him.

My benevolent helpers and I then made our way together to Versailles. As I parted from them at the Hôtel des Reservoirs I met Sala. Little as I liked Arminius, the melancholy scene I had just gone through had shaken me, and I needed sympathy. I told Sala what had happened. 'The old story,' says Sala; '*life a dream!* Take a glass of brandy.' He then inquired who my friends were. 'Three admirable members of Parliament,' I cried, 'who, donning the cross of charity—' 'I know,' interrupted Sala; 'the cleverest thing out!'

But the emotions of this agitating day were not yet over. While Sala was speaking, a group had formed before the hotel near us and our attention was drawn to its central figure. Dr Russell,[6] of the *Times,* was preparing to mount his war-horse. You know the sort of thing, – he has described it himself over and over again. Bismarck at his horse's head, the Crown Prince holding his stirrup, and the old King of Prussia hoisting Russell into the saddle. When he was there, the distinguished public servant waved his hand in acknowledgment, and rode slowly down the street, accompanied by the *gamins* of Versailles, who even in their present dejection could not forbear a few involuntary cries of '*Quel homme!*' Always unassuming, he alighted at the lodgings of the Grand Duke of Oldenburg, a potentate of the second or even the third order, who had beckoned to him from the window.

The agitation of this scene for me, however (may I not add, *mon cher,* for you also, and for the whole British press?), lay in a suggestion which it called forth from Sala. 'It is all very well,' said Sala, 'but old Russell's guns are getting a little honeycombed; anybody can perceive that. He will have to be pensioned off, and why should not you succeed him?' We passed the afternoon in talking the thing over, and I think I may assure you that a train has been laid of which you will see the effects shortly.

For my part, I can afford to wait till the pear is ripe; yet I cannot, without a thrill of excitement, think of inoculating the respectable but somewhat ponderous *Times* and its readers with the divine madness of our new style, – the style we have formed upon Sala. The world, *mon cher,* knows that man but imperfectly. I do not class him with the great masters of human thought and human literature, – Plato, Shakespeare, Confucius, Charles Dickens.[7] Sala, like us his disciples, has studied in the book of the world even more than in the world of books. But his career and genius have given him somehow the secret of a literary mixture novel and fascinating in the last degree: he blends the airy epicureanism of the *salons* of Augustus with the full-bodied gaiety of our English Cider-cellar.[8] With our people and country, *mon cher,* this mixture, you may rely upon it, is now the very thing to go down; there arises every day a larger public for it; and we, Sala's disciples, may be trusted not willingly to let it die. – *Tout à vous.*

A YOUNG LION*

To The EDITOR *of the* PALL MALL GAZETTE

---

* I am bound to say that in attempting to verify Leo's graphic description of Dr Russell's mounting on horseback, from the latter's own excellent correspondence, to which Leo refers us, I have been unsuccessful. Repeatedly I have seemed to be on the trace of what my friend meant, but the particular description he alludes to I have never been lucky enough to light upon.

I may add that, in spite of what Leo says of the train he and Mr Sala have said, of Dr Russell's approaching retirement, of Leo's prospect of succeeding him, of the charm of the leonine style, and of the disposition of the public mind to be fascinated by it, – I cannot myself believe that either the public, or the proprietors of the *Times,* are yet ripe for a change so revolutionary. But Leo was always sanguine. – ED.

ESSAYS IN CRITICISM:
SECOND SERIES

The Study of Poetry

'The future of poetry is immense, because in poetry, where it is worthy of its high destinies, our race, as time goes on, will find an ever surer and surer stay. There is not a creed which is not shaken, not an accredited dogma which is not shown to be questionable, not a received tradition which does not threaten to dissolve. Our religion has materialized itself in the fact, in the supposed fact; it has attached its emotion to the fact, and now the fact is failing it. But for poetry the idea is everything; the rest is a world of illusion, of divine illusion. Poetry attaches its emotion to the idea; the idea *is* the fact. The strongest part of our religion today is its unconscious poetry.'[1]

Let me be permitted to quote these words of my own, as uttering the thought which should, in my opinion, go with us and govern us in all our study of poetry. In the present work it is the course of one great contributory stream to the world-river of poetry that we are invited to follow. We are here invited to trace the stream of English poetry. But whether we set ourselves, as here, to follow only one of the several streams that make the mighty river of poetry, or whether we seek to know them all, our governing thought should be the same. We should conceive of poetry worthily, and more lightly than it has been the custom to conceive of it. We should conceive of it as capable of higher uses, and called to higher destinies, than those which in general men have assigned to it hitherto. More and more mankind will discover that we have to turn to poetry to interpret life for us, to console us, to sustain us. Without poetry, our science will appear incomplete; and most of what now passes with us for religion and philosophy will be replaced by poetry. Science, I say, will appear incomplete without it. For finely and truly does Wordsworth call poetry 'the impassioned expression which is in the countenance of all science';[2] and what is a countenance without its expression? Again, Wordsworth finely and truly calls poetry 'the breath and finer spirit of all knowledge':[3] our religion, parading evidences such as those on which the popular mind relies now; our philosophy, pluming itself on its reasonings about causation and finite and infinite being; what are they but the shadows and dreams and false shows of knowledge? The day will come when we shall wonder at ourselves for having trusted to them, for having taken them seriously; and the more we perceive their hollowness, the more we shall prize, 'the breath and finer spirit of knowledge' offered to us by poetry.

But if we conceive thus lightly of the destinies of poetry, we must also set our standard for poetry high, since poetry, to be capable of fulfilling such high destinies, must be poetry of a high order of excellence. We must accustom ourselves to a high standard and to a strict judgment. Sainte-Beuve relates that Napoleon one day said, when somebody was spoken of in his presence as a charlatan: 'Charlatan as much as you please; but where is there *not* charlatanism?' – 'Yes,' answers Sainte-Beuve, 'in politics, in the art of governing mankind, that is perhaps true. But in the order of thought, in art, the glory, the eternal honour is that charlatanism shall find no entrance; herein lies the inviolableness of that noble portion of man's being.' It is admirably said, and let us hold fast to it. In poetry, which is thought and art in one, it is the glory, the eternal honour, that charlatanism shall find no entrance; that this noble sphere be kept inviolate and inviolable. Charlatanism is for confusing or obliterating the distinctions between excellent and inferior, sound and unsound or only half-sound, true and untrue or only half-true. It is charlatanism, conscious or unconscious, whenever we confuse or obliterate these. And in poetry, more than anywhere else, it is unpermissible to confuse or obliterate them. For in poetry the distinction between excellent and inferior, sound and unsound or only half-sound, true and untrue or only half-true, is of paramount importance. It is of paramount importance because of the high destinies of poetry. In poetry, as a criticism of life[4] under the conditions fixed for such a criticism by the laws of poetic truth and poetic beauty, the spirit of our race will find, we have said, as time goes on and as other helps fail, its consolation and stay. But the consolation and stay will be of power in proportion to the power of the criticism of life. And the criticism of life will be of power in proportion as the poetry conveying it is excellent rather than inferior, sound rather than unsound or half-sound, true rather than untrue or half-true.

The best poetry is what we want; the best poetry will be found to have a power of forming, sustaining, and delighting us, as nothing else can. A clearer, deeper sense of the best in poetry, and of the strength and joy to be drawn from it, is the most precious benefit which we can gather from a poetical collection such as the present. And yet in the very nature and conduct of such a collection there is inevitably something which tends to obscure in us the consciousness of what our benefit should be, and to distract us from the pursuit of it. We should therefore steadily set it before our minds at the outset, and should compel ourselves to revert constantly to the thought of it as we proceed.

Yes; constantly in reading poetry, a sense for the best, the really excellent, and of the strength and joy to be drawn from it, should be present in our minds and should govern our estimate of what we read. But this real estimate, the only true one, is liable to be superseded, if we are not watchful, by two other kinds of estimate, the historic estimate and the personal estimate, both of which are fallacious. A poet or a poem may count to us historically, they may count to us on grounds personal to ourselves, and they may count to us really. They may count to us historically. The course of development of a nation's language, thought, and poetry, is profoundly interesting; and by regarding a poet's work as a stage in this course of development we may easily bring ourselves to make it of more importance as poetry than in itself it really is, we may come to use a language of quite exaggerated praise in criticising it; in short, to over-rate it. So arises in our poetic judgments the fallacy caused by the estimate which we may call historic. Then, again, a poet or a poem may count to us on grounds personal to ourselves. Our personal affinities, likings, and circumstances, have great power to sway our estimate of this or that poet's work, and to make us attach more importance to it as poetry than in itself it really possesses, because to us it is, or has been, of high importance. Here also we over-rate the object of our interest, and apply to it a language of praise which is quite exaggerated. And thus we get the source of a second fallacy in our poetic judgments – the fallacy caused by an estimate which we may call personal.

Both fallacies are natural. It is evident how naturally the study of the history and development of a poetry may incline a man to pause over reputations and works once conspicuous but now obscure, and to quarrel with a careless public for skipping, in obedience to mere tradition and habit, from one famous name or work in its national poetry to another, ignorant of what it misses, and of the reason for keeping what it keeps, and of the whole process of growth in its poetry. The French have become diligent students of their own early poetry, which they long neglected; the study makes many of them dissatisfied with their so-called classical poetry, the court-tragedy of the seventeenth century, a poetry which Pellisson[5] long ago reproached with its want of the true poetic stamp, with its *politesse stérile et rampante,* but which nevertheless has reigned in France as absolutely as if it had been the perfection of classical poetry indeed. The dissatisfaction is natural; yet a lively and accomplished critic, M. Charles d'Héricault,[6] the editor of Clément Marot, goes too far when he says that 'the cloud of glory playing round a classic is a mist as dangerous to the future of a literature as it is intolerable for the purposes of history.' 'It hinders,' he goes on, 'it hinders us from seeing more than one single point, the culminating and exceptional point; the summary, fictitious and arbitrary, of a thought and of a work. It substitutes a halo for a physiognomy, it puts a statue where there was once a man, and hiding from us all trace of the labour, the attempts, the weaknesses, the failures, it claims not

study but veneration; it does not show us how the thing is
done, it imposes upon us a model. Above all, for the historian
this creation of classic personages is inadmissible; for it withdraws the poet from his time, from his proper life, it breaks
historical relationships, it blinds criticism by conventional
admiration, and renders the investigation of literary origins
unacceptable. It gives us a human personage no longer, but a
God seated immovable amidst His perfect work, like Jupiter on
Olympus; and hardly will it be possible for the young student,
to whom such work is exhibited at such a distance from him,
to believe that it did not issue ready made from that divine head.'

All this is brilliantly and tellingly said, but we must plead for
a distinction. Everything depends on the reality of a poet's classic character. If he is a dubious classic, let us sift him; if he is a
false classic, let us explode him. But if he is a real classic, if his
work belongs to the class of the very best (for this is the true
and right meaning of the word *classic, classical*), then the great
thing for us is to feel and enjoy his work as deeply as ever we
can, and to appreciate the wide difference between it and all
work which has not the same high character. This is what is
salutary, this is what is formative; this is the great benefit to be
got from the study of poetry. Everything which interferes with
it, which hinders it, is injurious. True, we must read our classic
with open eyes, and not with eyes blinded with superstition; we
must perceive when his work comes short, when it drops out of
the class of the very best, and we must rate it, in such cases, at
its proper value. But the use of this negative criticism is not in
itself, it is entirely in its enabling us to have a clearer sense and
a deeper enjoyment of what is truly excellent. To trace the
labour, the attempts, the weaknesses, the failures of a genuine
classic, to acquaint oneself with his time and his life and his
historical relationships, is mere literary dilettantism unless it
has that clear sense and deeper enjoyment for its end. It may be
said that the more we know about a classic the better we shall
enjoy him; and, if we lived as long as Methuselah and had all
of us heads of perfect clearness and wills of perfect steadfast-
ness, this might be true in fact as it is plausible in theory. But
the case here is much the same as the case with the Greek and

Latin studies of our schoolboys. The elaborate philological groundwork which we require them to lay is in theory an admirable preparation for appreciating the Greek and Latin authors worthily. The more thoroughly we lay the groundwork, the better we shall be able, it may be said, to enjoy the authors. True, if time were not so short, and schoolboys' wits not so soon tired and their power of attention exhausted; only, as it is, the elaborate philological preparation goes on, but the authors are little known and less enjoyed. So with the investigator of 'historic origins' in poetry. He ought to enjoy the true classic all the better for his investigations; he often is distracted from the enjoyment of the best, and with the less good he over-busies himself, and is prone to over-rate it in proportion to the trouble which it has cost him.

The idea of tracing historic origins and historical relationships cannot be absent from a compilation like the present. And naturally the poets to be exhibited in it will be assigned to those persons for exhibition who are known to prize them highly, rather than to those who have no special inclination towards them. Moreover the very occupation with an author, and the business of exhibiting him, disposes us to affirm and amplify his importance. In the present work, therefore, we are sure of frequent temptation to adopt the historic estimate, or the personal estimate, and to forget the real estimate; which latter, nevertheless, we must employ if we are to make poetry yield us its full benefit. So high is that benefit, the benefit of clearly feeling and of deeply enjoying the really excellent, the truly classic in poetry, that we do well, I say, to set it fixedly before our minds as our object in studying poets and poetry, and to make the desire of attaining it the one principle to which, as the *Imitation* says, whatever we may read or come to know, we always return. *Cum multa legeris et cognoveris, ad unum semper oportet redire principium.*[7]

The historic estimate is likely in especial to affect our judgment and our language when we are dealing with ancient poets; the personal estimate when we are dealing with poets our contemporaries, or at any rate modern. The exaggerations due to the historic estimate are not in themselves, perhaps, of very much gravity. Their report hardly enters the general ear;

probably they do not always impose even on the literary men who adopt them. But they lead to a dangerous abuse of language. So we hear Cædmon, among our own poets, compared to Milton.[8] I have already noticed the enthusiasm of one accomplished French critic for 'historic origins.' Another eminent French critic, M. Vitet, comments upon that famous document of the early poetry of his nation, the *Chanson de Roland*.[9] It is, indeed, a most interesting document. The *joculator* or *jongleur*[10] Taillefer, who was with William the Conqueror's army at Hastings, marched before the Norman troops, so said the tradition, singing 'of Charlemagne and of Roland and of Oliver, and of the vassals who died at Roncevaux'; and it is suggested that in the *Chanson de Roland* by one Turoldus or Théroulde, a poem preserved in a manuscript of the twelfth century in the Bodleian Library at Oxford, we have certainly the matter, perhaps even some of the words, of the chant which Taillefer sang. The poem has vigour and freshness; it is not without pathos. But M. Vitet is not satisfied with seeing in it a document of some poetic value, and of very high historic and linguistic value; he sees in it a grand and beautiful work, a monument of epic genius. In its general design he finds the grandiose conception, in its details he finds the constant union of simplicity with greatness, which are the marks, he truly says, of the genuine epic, and distinguish it from the artificial epic of literary ages. One thinks of Homer; this is the sort of praise which is given to Homer, and justly given. Higher praise there cannot well be, and it is the praise due to epic poetry of the highest order only, and to no other. Let us try, then, the *Chanson de Roland* at its best. Roland, mortally wounded, lays himself down under a pine-tree, with his face turned towards Spain and the enemy –

> 'De plusurs choses à remembrer li prist,
> De tantes teres cume li bers cunquist,
> De dulce France, des humes de sun lign,
> De Carlemagne sun seignor ki l'nurrit.'*

---

* 'Then began he to call many things to remembrance, – all the land, which his valour conquered, and pleasant France, and the men of his lineage, and

That is primitive work, I repeat, with an undeniable poetic quality of its own. It deserves such praise, and such praise is sufficient for it. But now turn to Homer –

> "Ὣς φάτο τοὺς δ᾽ ἤδη κατέχεν φυσίζοος αἶα
> ἐν Λακεδαίμονι αὖθι, φίλῃ ἐν πατρίδι γαίῃ.*

We are here in another world, another order of poetry altogether; here is rightly due such supreme praise as that which M. Vitet gives to the *Chanson de Roland*. If our words are to have any meaning, if our judgments are to have any solidity, we must not heap that supreme praise upon poetry of an order immeasurably inferior.

Indeed, there can be no more useful help for discovering what poetry belongs to the class of the truly excellent, and can therefore do us most good, than to have always in one's mind lines and expressions of the great masters, and to apply them as a touchstone to other poetry. Of course, we are not to require this other poetry to resemble them; it may be very dissimilar. But if we have any tact we shall find them, when we have lodged them well in our minds, an infallible touchstone for detecting the presence or absence of high poetic quality, and also the degree of this quality, in all other poetry which we may place beside them. Short passages, even single lines, will serve our turn quite sufficiently. Take the two lines which I have just quoted from Homer, the poet's comment on Helen's mention of her brothers; – or take his

> Ἀ δειλώ, τί σφῶϊ δόμεν Πηλῆϊ ἄνακτι
> θνητᾷ ὑμεῖς δ᾽ ἐστὸν ἀγήρω Τ᾽ ἀθ̄ανάτω τε.
> ἦ ἵνα δυστήνοιαι μετ᾽ ἀνδράαιν ἄλγε᾽ ἔχητον,†

Charlemagne his liege lord who nourished him.' – *Chanson de Roland*, iii. 939–942.

* 'So said she; they long since in Earth's soft arms were reposing,
    There, in their own dear land, their fatherland, Lacedæmon,'
                    Iliad, iii. 243, 244 (translated by Dr Hawtrey).

† 'Ah, unhappy pair, why gave we you to King Peleus, to a mortal? but ye are without old age, and immortal. Was it that with men born to misery ye might have sorrow?' – *Iliad*, xvii. 443–445.

the address of Zeus to the horses of Peleus; – or take finally his

Καὶ σέ, γέρον, τὸ πρὶν μὲν ἀκούομεν ὄλβιον εἶναι.*

the words of Achilles to Priam, a suppliant before him. Take that incomparable line and a half of Dante, Ugolino's tremendous words –

> 'Io no piangeva; sì dentro impietrai.
> Piangevan elli . . .'†

take the lovely words of Beatrice to Virgil –

> 'Io son fatta da Dio, sua mercè, tale,
> Che la vostra miseria non mi tange,
> Nè fiamma d'esto incendio non m'assale . . .'‡

take the simple, but perfect single line –

> 'In la sua volontade è nostra pace.'§

Take of Shakespeare a line or two of Henry the Fourth's expostulation with sleep –

> 'Wilt thou upon the high and giddy mast
> Seal up the ship-boy's eyes, and rock his brains
> In cradle of the rude imperious surge . . .'[11]

and take, as well, Hamlet's dying request to Horatio –

---

* 'Nay, and thou too, old man, in former days wast, as we hear, happy.' – *Iliad*, xxiv. 543.
† 'I wailed not, so of stone grew I within; – *they* wailed.' – *Inferno*, xxxiii. 39, 40.
‡ 'Of such sort hath God, thanked be His mercy, made me, that your misery toucheth me not, neither doth the flame of this fire strike me.' – *Inferno*, ii. 91–93.
§ 'In His will is our peace.' – *Paradiso*, iii. 85.

'If thou didst ever hold me in thy heart,
Absent thee from felicity awhile,
And in this harsh world draw thy breath in pain
To tell my story . . .'[12]

Take of Milton that Miltonic passage –

'Darken'd so, yet shone
Above them all the archangel; but his face
Deep scars of thunder had intrench'd, and care
Sat on his faded cheek . . .'[13]

add two such lines as –

'And courage never to submit or yield
And what is else not to be overcome . . .'[14]

and finish with the exquisite close to the loss of Proserpine,
the loss

'. . . which cost Ceres all that pain
To seek her through the world.'[15]

These few lines, if we have tact and can use them, are enough
even of themselves to keep clear and sound our judgments
about poetry, to save us from fallacious estimates of it, to conduct us to a real estimate.

The specimens I have quoted differ widely from one another,
but they have in common this: the possession of the very highest poetical quality. If we are thoroughly penetrated by their
power, we shall find that we have acquired a sense enabling us,
whatever poetry may be laid before us, to feel the degree in
which a high poetical quality is present or wanting there. Critics give themselves great labour to draw out what in the abstract
constitutes the characters of a high quality of poetry. It is much
better simply to have recourse to concrete examples; – to take
specimens of poetry of the high, the very highest quality, and to
say: The characters of a high quality of poetry are what is

expressed *there*. They are far better recognized by being felt in the verse of the master, than by being perused in the prose of the critic. Nevertheless if we are urgently pressed to give some critical account of them, we may safely, perhaps, venture on laying down, not indeed how and why the characters arise, but where and in what they arise. They are in the matter and substance of the poetry, and they are in its manner and style. Both of these, the substance and matter on the one hand, the style and manner on the other, have a mark, an accent, of high beauty, worth, and power. But if we are asked to define this mark and accent in the abstract, our answer must be: No, for we should thereby be darkening the question, not clearing it. The mark and accent are as given by the substance and matter of that poetry, by the style and manner of that poetry, and of all other poetry which is akin to it in quality.

Only one thing we may add to the substance and matter of poetry, guiding ourselves by Aristotle's profound observation that the superiority of poetry over history consists in its possessing a higher truth and a higher seriousness (φιλοσοφώτερον καὶ σπουδαιότερον[16]). Let us add, therefore, to what we have said, this: that the substance and matter of the best poetry acquire their special character from possessing, in an eminent degree, truth and seriousness. We may add yet further, what is in itself evident, that to the style and manner of the best poetry their special character, their accent, is given by their diction, and, even yet more, by their movement. And though we distinguish between the two characters, the two accents, of superiority, yet they are nevertheless vitally connected one with the other. The superior character of truth and seriousness, in the matter and substance of the best poetry, is inseparable from the superiority of diction and movement marking its style and manner. The two superiorities are closely related, and are in steadfast proportion one to the other. So far as high poetic truth and seriousness are wanting to a poet's matter and substance, so far also, we may be sure, will a high poetic stamp of diction and movement be wanting to his style and manner. In proportion as this high stamp of diction and movement, again, is absent from a poet's style and manner, we shall find, also, that high poetic truth and seriousness are absent from his substance and matter.

So stated, these are but dry generalities; their whole force lies in their application. And I could wish every student of poetry to make the application of them for himself. Made by himself, the application would impress itself upon his mind far more deeply than made by me. Neither will my limits allow me to make any full application of the generalities above propounded; but in the hope of bringing out, at any rate, some significance in them, and of establishing an important principle more firmly by their means, I will, in the space which remains to me, follow rapidly from the commencement the course of our English poetry with them in my view.

Once more I return to the early poetry of France, with which our own poetry, in its origins, is indissolubly connected. In the twelfth and thirteenth centuries, that seed-time of all modern language and literature, the poetry of France had a clear predominance in Europe. Of the two divisions of that poetry, its productions in the *langue d'oil* and its productions in the *langue d'oc*,[17] the poetry of the *langue d'oc*, of southern France, of the troubadours, is of importance because of its effect on Italian literature; – the first literature of modern Europe to strike the true and grand note, and to bring forth, as in Dante and Petrarch it brought forth, classics. But the predominance of French poetry in Europe, during the twelfth and thirteenth centuries, is due to its poetry of the *langue d'oil*, the poetry of northern France and of the tongue which is now the French language. In the twelfth century the bloom of this romance-poetry was earlier and stronger in England, at the court of our Anglo-Norman kings, than in France itself. But it was a bloom of French poetry; and as our native poetry formed itself, it formed itself out of this. The romance-poems which took possession of the heart and imagination of Europe in the twelfth and thirteenth centuries are French; 'they are,' as Southey justly says, 'the pride of French literature, nor have we anything which can be placed in competition with them.' Themes were supplied from all quarters; but the romance-setting which was common to them all, and which gained the ear of Europe, was French. This constituted for the French poetry, literature, and languages, at the height of the Middle Age, an unchallenged predominance. The Italian Brunetto Latini, the master of Dante, wrote his *Treasure* in French because, he says, 'la parleure en est plus délitable et plus commune à toutes gens.'[18] In the same century, the thirteenth, the French romance-writer, Christian of Troyes, formulates the claims, in chivalry and letters, of France, his native country, as follows: –

'Or vous ert par ce livre apris,
Que Gresse ot de chevalerie
Le premier los et de clergie;
Puis vint chevalerie à Rome,
Et de la clergie la some,
Qui ore est en France venue.
Diex doinst qu'ele i soit retenue,
Et que li lius li abelisse
Tant que de France n'isse
L'onor qui s'i est arestée!'

'Now by this book you will learn that first Greece had the renown for chivalry and letters; then chivalry and the primacy in letters passed to Rome, and now it is come to France. God grant it may be kept there; and that the place may please it so well, that the honour which has come to make stay in France may never depart thence!'

Yet it is now all gone, this French romance-poetry, of which the weight of substance and the power of style are not unfairly represented by this extract from Christian of Troyes. Only by means of the historic estimate can we persuade ourselves now to think that any of it is of poetical importance.

But in the fourteenth century there comes an Englishman nourished on this poetry, taught his trade by this poetry, getting words, rhyme, metre from this poetry; for even of that stanza which the Italians used, and which Chaucer derived immediately from the Italians, the basis and suggestion was probably given in France. Chaucer (I have already named him) fascinated his contemporaries, but so too did Christian of Troyes and Wolfram of Eschenbach.[19] Chaucer's power of fascination, however, is enduring; his poetical importance does not need the assistance of the historic estimate; it is real. He is a genuine source of joy and strength, which is flowing still for us and will flow always. He will be read, as time goes on, far more generally than he is read now. His language is a cause of difficulty for us; but so also, and I think in quite as great a degree, is the language of Burns. In Chaucer's case, as in that of Burns, it is a difficulty to be unhesitatingly accepted and overcome.

If we ask ourselves wherein consists the immense superiority of Chaucer's poetry over the romance-poetry – why it is that in passing from this to Chaucer we suddenly feel ourselves to be in another world, we shall find that his superiority is both in the substance of his poetry and in the style of his poetry. His superiority in substance is given by his large, free, simple, clear yet kindly view of human life, – so unlike the total want, in the romance-poets, of all intelligent command of it. Chaucer has not their helplessness; he has gained the power to survey the world from a central, a truly human point of view. We have only to call to mind the Prologue to *The Canterbury Tales*. The right comment upon it is Dryden's: 'It is sufficient to say, according to the proverb, that *here is God's plenty*.' And again: 'He is a perpetual fountain of good sense.'[20] It is by a large, free, sound representation of things, that poetry, this high criticism of life, has truth of substance; and Chaucer's poetry has truth of substance.

Of his style and manner, if we think first of the romance-poetry and then of Chaucer's divine liquidness of diction, his divine fluidity of movement, it is difficult to speak temperately. They are irresistible, and justify all the rapture with which his successors speak of his 'gold dew-drops of speech.[21] Johnson misses the point entirely when he finds fault with Dryden for ascribing to Chaucer the first refinement of our numbers, and says that Gower also can show smooth numbers and easy rhymes.[22] The refinement of our numbers means something far more than this. A nation may have versifiers with smooth numbers and easy rhymes, and yet may have no real poetry at all. Chaucer is the father of our splendid English poetry; he is our 'well of English undefiled,[23] because by the lovely charm of his diction, the lovely charm of his movement, he makes an epoch and founds a tradition. In Spenser, Shakespeare, Milton, Keats, we can

follow the tradition of the liquid diction, the fluid movement, of
Chaucer; at one time it is his liquid diction of which in these
poets we feel the virtue, and at another time it is his fluid movement. And the virtue is irresistible.

Bounded as is my space, I must yet find room for an example
of Chaucer's virtue, as I have given examples to show the
virtue of the great classics. I feel disposed to say that a single
line is enough to show the charm of Chaucer's verse; that
merely one line like this –

'O martyr souded* in virginitee!'[24]

has a virtue of manner and movement such as we shall not find
in all the verse of romance-poetry; – but this is saying nothing.
The virtue is such as we shall not find, perhaps, in all English
poetry, outside the poets whom I have named as the special
inheritors of Chaucer's tradition. A single line, however, is too
little if we have not the strain of Chaucer's verse well in our
memory; let us take a stanza. It is from *The Prioress's Tale,* the
story of the Christian child murdered in a Jewry –

'My throte is cut unto my nekke-bone
Saidè this child, and as by way of kinde
I should have deyd, yea, longè time agone;
But Jesu Christ, as ye in bookès finde,
Will that his glory last and be in minde,
And for the worship of his mother dere
Yet may I sing O *Alma* loud and clere.'

Wordsworth has modernized this Tale, and to feel how delicate
and evanescent is the charm of verse, we have only to read
Wordsworth's first three lines of this stanza after Chaucer's –

'My throat is cut unto the bone, I trow,
Said this young child, and by the law of kind
I should have died, yea, many hours ago.'

* The French *soudé*; soldered, fixed fast.

The charm is departed. It is often said that the power of liquidness and fluidity in Chaucer's verse was dependent upon a free, a licentious dealing with language, such as is now impossible; upon a liberty, such as Burns too enjoyed, of making words like *neck, bird,* into a dissyllable by adding to them, and words like *cause, rhyme,* into a dissyllable by sounding the *e* mute. It is true that Chaucer's fluidity is conjoined with this liberty, and is admirably served by it; but we ought not to say that it was dependent upon it. It was dependent upon his talent. Other poets with a like liberty do not attain to the fluidity of Chaucer; Burns himself does not attain to it. Poets, again, who have a talent akin to Chaucer's, such as Shakespeare or Keats, have known how to attain to his fluidity without the like liberty.

And yet Chaucer is not one of the great classics. His poetry transcends and effaces, easily and without effort, all the romance-poetry of Catholic Christendom; it transcends and effaces all the English poetry contemporary with it, it transcends and effaces all the English poetry subsequent to it down to the age of Elizabeth. Of such avail is poetic truth of substance, in its natural and necessary union with poetic truth of style. And yet, I say, Chaucer is not one of the great classics. He has not their accent. What is wanting to him is suggested by the mere mention of the name of the first great classic of Christendom, the immortal poet who died eighty years before Chaucer, – Dante. The accent of such verse as

'In la sua volontade è nostra pace . . .'

is altogether beyond Chaucer's reach; we praise him, but we feel that this accent is out of the question for him. It may be said that it was necessarily out of the reach of any poet in the England of that stage of growth. Possibly; but we are to adopt a real, not a historic, estimate of poetry. However we may account for its absence, something is wanting, then, to the poetry of Chaucer, which poetry must have before it can be placed in the glorious class of the best. And there is no doubt what that something is. It is the σπουδαιότης, the high and excellent seriousness, which Aristotle assigns as one of the grand virtues of poetry. The substance of Chaucer's poetry, his view of things and his criticism of life, has largeness, freedom, shrewdness, benignity; but it has not this high seriousness. Homer's criticism of life has it, Dante's has it, Shakespeare's has it. It is this chiefly which gives to our spirits what they can rest upon; and with the increasing demands of our modern ages upon poetry, this virtue of giving us what we can rest upon will be more and more highly esteemed. A voice from the slums of Paris, fifty or sixty years after Chaucer, the voice of poor Villon out of his life of riot and crime, has at its happy moments (as, for instance, in the last stanza of *La Belle Heaulmière**) more of this important poetic virtue of seriousness than all the productions of Chaucer. But its apparition in Villon, and in men like Villon, is fitful; the greatness of the great poets, the power of their criticism of life, is that their virtue is sustained.

To our praise, therefore, of Chaucer as a poet there must be this limitation; he lacks the high seriousness of the great classics, and therewith an important part of their virtue. Still, the main fact for us to bear in mind about Chaucer is his sterling value according to that real estimate which we firmly adopt for all poets. He has poetic truth of substance, though he has not high

---

* The name *Heaulmière* is said to be derived from a headdress (helm) worn as a mark by courtesans. In Villon's ballad, a poor old creature of this class laments her days of youth and beauty. The last stanza of the ballad runs thus —

> 'Ainsi le bon temps regretons
> Entre nous, pauvres vieilles sottes,
> Assises bas, à croppetons,
> Tout en ung tas comme pelottes;
> A petit feu de chenevottes
> Tost allumées, tost estainctes.
> Et jadis fusmes si mignottes!
> Ainsi en prend à maintz et maintes.'

'Thus amongst ourselves we regret the good time, poor silly old things, low-seated on our heels, all in a heap like so many balls; by a little fire of hemp-stalks, soon lighted, soon spent. And once we were such darlings! So fares it with many and many a one.'

poetic seriousness, and corresponding to his truth of substance he has an exquisite virtue of style and manner. With him is born our real poetry.

For my present purpose I need not dwell on our Elizabethan poetry, or on the continuation and close of this poetry in Milton. We all of us profess to be agreed in the estimate of this poetry; we all of us recognize it as great poetry, our greatest, and Shakespeare and Milton as our poetical classics. The real estimate, here, has universal currency. With the next age of our poetry divergency and difficulty begin. An historic estimate of that poetry has established itself; and the question is, whether it will be found to coincide with the real estimate.

The age of Dryden, together with our whole eighteenth century which followed it, sincerely believed itself to have produced poetical classics of its own, and even to have made advance, in poetry, beyond all its predecessors. Dryden regards as not seriously disputable the opinion 'that the sweetness of English verse was never understood or practised by our fathers.'[25] Cowley could see nothing at all in Chaucer's poetry. Dryden heartily admired it, and, as we have seen, praised its matter admirably; but of its exquisite manner and movement all he can find to say is that 'there is the rude sweetness of a Scotch tune in it, which is natural and pleasing, though not perfect.'[26] Addison, wishing to praise Chaucer's numbers, compares them with Dryden's own. And all through the eighteenth century, and down even into our own times, the stereotyped phrase of approbation for good verse found in our early poetry has been, that it even approached the verse of Dryden, Addison, Pope, and Johnson.

Are Dryden and Pope poetical classics? Is the historic estimate, which represents them as such, and which has been so long established that it cannot easily give way, the real estimate? Wordsworth and Coleridge, as is well known, denied it; but the authority of Wordsworth and Coleridge does not weigh much with the young generation, and there are many signs to show that the eighteenth century and its judgments are coming into favour again. Are the favourite poets of the eighteenth-century classics?

It is impossible within my present limits to discuss the

question fully. And what man of letters would not shrink from seeming to dispose dictatorially of the claims of two men who are, at any rate, such masters in letters as Dryden and Pope; two men of such admirable talent, both of them, and one of them, Dryden, a man, on all sides, of such energetic and genial power? And yet, if we are to gain the full benefit from poetry, we must have the real estimate of it. I cast about for some mode of arriving, in the present case, at such an estimate without offence. And perhaps the best way is to begin, as it is easy to begin, with cordial praise.

When we find Chapman, the Elizabethan translator of Homer, expressing himself in his preface thus: 'Though truth in her very nakedness sits in so deep a pit, that from Gades to Aurora and Ganges few eyes can sound her, I hope yet those few here will so discover and confirm that, the date being out of her darkness in this morning of our poet, he shall now gird his temples with the sun,' – we pronounce that such a prose is intolerable. When we find Milton writing: 'And long it was not after, when I was confirmed in this opinion, that he, who would not be frustrate of his hope to write well hereafter in laudable things, ought himself to be a true poem,'[27] – we pronounce that such a prose has its own grandeur, but that it is obsolete and inconvenient. But when we find Dryden telling us: 'What Virgil wrote in the vigour of his age, in plenty and at ease, I have undertaken to translate in my declining years; struggling with wants, oppressed with sickness, curbed in my genius, liable to be misconstrued in all I write,'[28] – then we exclaim that here at last we have the true English prose, a prose such as we would all gladly use if we only knew how. Yet Dryden was Milton's contemporary.

But after the Restoration the time had come when our nation felt the imperious need of a fit prose. So, too, the time had likewise come when our nation felt the imperious need of freeing itself from the absorbing preoccupation which religion in the Puritan age had exercised. It was impossible that this freedom should be brought about without some negative excess, without some neglect and impairment of the religious life of the soul; and the spiritual history of the eighteenth century shows us that the freedom was not achieved without them. Still, the freedom was achieved; the preoccupation, an undoubtedly baneful and retarding one if it had continued, was got rid of. And as with religion among us at that period, so it was also with letters. A fit prose was a necessity; but it was impossible that a fit prose should establish itself among us without some touch of frost to the imaginative life of the soul. The needful qualities for a fit prose are regularity, uniformity, precision, balance. The men of letters, whose destiny it may be to bring their nation to the attainment of a fit prose, must of necessity, whether they work in prose or in verse, give a predominating, an almost exclusive attention to the qualities of regularity, uniformity, precision, balance. But an almost exclusive attention to these qualities involves some repression and silencing of poetry.

We are to regard Dryden as the puissant and glorious founder, Pope as the splendid high priest, of our age of prose and reason, of our excellent and indispensable eighteenth century. For the purposes of their mission and destiny their poetry, like their prose, is admirable. Do you ask me whether Dryden's verse, take it almost where you will, is not good?

> 'A milk-white Hind, immortal and unchanged,
> Fed on the lawns and in the forest ranged.'[29]

I answer: Admirable for the purposes of the inaugurator of an age of prose and reason. Do you ask me whether Pope's verse, take it almost where you will, is not good?

> 'To Hounslow Heath I point, and Banstead Down;
> Thence comes your mutton, and these chicks my own.'[30]

I answer: Admirable for the purposes of the high priest of an age of prose and reason. But do you ask me whether such verse proceeds from men with an adequate poetic criticism of life, from men whose criticism of life has a high seriousness, or even, without that high seriousness, has poetic largeness, freedom, insight, benignity? Do you ask me whether the application of ideas to life in the verse of these men, often a powerful application, no doubt, is a powerful *poetic* application? Do you ask me whether the poetry of these men has either the matter or the inseparable manner of such an adequate poetic criticism; whether it has the accent of

> 'Absent thee from felicity awhile . . .'

or of

> 'And what is else not to be overcome . . .'

or of

> 'O martyr souded in virginitee!'

I answer: It has not and cannot have them; it is the poetry of the builders of an age of prose and reason. Though they may write in verse, though they may in a certain sense be masters of the art of versification, Dryden and Pope are not classics of our poetry, they are classics of our prose.

Gray is our poetical classic of that literature and age; the position of Gray is singular, and demands a word of notice here. He has not the volume or the power of poets who, coming in times more favourable, have attained to an independent criticism of life. But he lived with the great poets, he lived, above all, with the Greeks, through perpetually studying and enjoying them; and he caught their poetic point of view for regarding life, caught their poetic manner. The point of view and the manner are not self-sprung in him, he caught them of others; and he had not the free and abundant use of them. But whereas Addison and Pope never had the use of them, Gray had the use of them at times. He is the scantiest and frailest of classics in our poetry, but he is a classic.

And now, after Gray, we are met, as we draw towards the end of the eighteenth century, we are met by the great name of Burns. We enter now on times where the personal estimate of poets begins to be rife, and where the real estimate of them is not reached without difficulty. But in spite of the disturbing pressures of personal partiality, of national partiality, let us try to reach a real estimate of the poetry of Burns.

By his English poetry Burns in general belongs to the eighteenth century, and has little importance for us.

> 'Mark ruffian Violence, distain'd with crimes,
> Rousing elate in these degenerate times;
> View unsuspecting Innocence a prey,
> As guileful Fraud points out the erring way;
> While subtle Litigation's pliant tongue
> The life-blood equal sucks of Right and Wrong!'[31]

Evidently this is not the real Burns, or his name and fame would have disappeared long ago. Nor is Clarinda's love-poet, Sylvander,[32] the real Burns either. But he tells us himself: 'These English songs gravel me to death. I have not the command of the language that I have of my native tongue. In fact, I think that my ideas are more barren in English than in Scotch. I have been at *Duncan Gray* to dress it in English, but all I can do is desperately stupid.'[33] We English turn naturally, in Burns, to the poems in our own language, because we can read them easily; but in those poems we have not the real Burns.

The real Burns is, of course, in his Scotch poems. Let us boldly say that of much of this poetry, a poetry dealing perpetually with Scotch drink, Scotch religion, and Scotch manners, a Scotchman's estimate is apt to be personal. A Scotchman is used to this world of Scotch drink, Scotch religion, and Scotch manners; he has a tenderness for it; he meets its poet half way. In this tender mood he reads pieces like the *Holy Fair* or *Halloween*. But this world of Scotch drink, Scotch religion, and Scotch manners is against a poet, not for him, when it is not a partial countryman who reads him; for in itself it is not a beautiful world, and no one can deny that it is of advantage to a poet to deal with a beautiful world. Burns's world of Scotch drink, Scotch religion, and Scotch manners, is often a harsh, a sordid, a repulsive world; even the world of his *Cotter's Saturday Night* is not a beautiful world. No doubt a poet's criticism of life may have such truth and power that it triumphs over its world and delights us. Burns may triumph over his world, often he does triumph over his world, but let us observe how and where. Burns is the first case we have had where the bias of the personal estimate tends to mislead; let us look at him closely, he can bear it.

Many of his admirers will tell us that we have Burns, convivial, genuine, delightful, here –

> 'Leeze me on drink! it gies us mair
>   Than either school or college;
> It kindles wit, it waukens lair,
>   It pangs us fou o' knowledge.
> Be 't whisky gill or penny wheep
>   Or ony stronger potion,
> It never fails, on drinking deep,
>   To kittle up our notion
>   By night or day.'[34]

There is a great deal of that sort of thing in Burns, and it is unsatisfactory, not because it is bacchanalian poetry, but because it has not that accent of sincerity which bacchanalian poetry, to do it justice, very often has. There is something in it of bravado, something which makes us feel that we have not the man speaking to us with his real voice; something, therefore, poetically unsound.

With still more confidence will his admirers tell us that we have the genuine Burns, the great poet, when his strain asserts the independence, equality, dignity, of men, as in the famous song For a' that and a' that –

> 'A prince can mak' a belted knight,
>   A marquis, duke, and a' that;
> But an honest man's aboon his might,
>   Guid faith he mauna fa' that!
> For a' that, and a' that,
>   Their dignities, and a' that,
> The pith o' sense, and pride o' worth
>   Are higher rank than a' that.'

Here they find his grand, genuine touches; and still more, when this puissant genius, who so often set morality at defiance, falls moralizing –

> 'The sacred lowe o' weel-placed love
>   Luxuriantly indulge it;
> But never tempt th' illicit rove,
>   Tho' naething should divulge it.
> I waive the quantum o' the sin,
>   The hazard o' concealing,
> But och! it hardens a' within,
>   And petrifies the feeling.'[35]

Or in a higher strain –

> 'Who made the heart, 'tis He alone
>   Decidedly can try us;
> He knows each chord, its various tone;
>   Each spring, its various bias.
> Then at the balance let's be mute,
>   We never can adjust it;
> What's *done* we partly may compute,
>   But know not what's resisted.'[36]

Or in a better strain yet, a strain, his admirers will say, unsurpassable –

> 'To make a happy fire-side clime
>   To weans and wife,
> That's the true pathos and sublime
>   Of human life.'[37]

There is criticism of life for you, the admirers of Burns will say to us; there is the application of ideas to life! There is, undoubtedly. The doctrine of the last-quoted lines coincides almost exactly with what was the aim and end, Xenophon tells us, of all the teaching of Socrates.[38] And the application is a powerful one; made by a man of vigorous understanding, and (need I say?) a master of language.

But for supreme poetical success more is required than the powerful application of ideas to life; it must be an application under the conditions fixed by the laws of poetic truth and poetic beauty. Those laws fix as an essential condition, in the poet's treatment of such matters as are here in question, high seriousness; – the high seriousness which comes from absolute sincerity. The accent of high seriousness, born of absolute sincerity, is what gives to such verse as

'In la sua volontade è nostra pace . . .'

to such criticism of life as Dante's, its power. Is this accent felt in the passages which I have been quoting from Burns? Surely not; surely, if our sense is quick, we must perceive that we have not in those passages a voice from the very inmost soul of the genuine Burns; he is not speaking to us from these depths, he is more or less preaching. And the compensation for admiring such passages less, from missing the perfect poetic accent in them, will be that we shall admire more the poetry where that accent is found.

No; Burns, like Chaucer, comes short of the high seriousness of the great classics, and the virtue of matter and manner which goes with that high seriousness is wanting to his work. At moments he touches it in a profound and passionate melancholy, as in those four immortal lines taken by Byron as a motto for *The Bride of Abydos,* but which have in them a depth of poetic quality such as resides in no verse of Byron's own –

> Had we never loved sae kindly,
> Had we never loved sae blindly,
> Never met, or never parted,
> We had ne'er been broken-hearted.'

But a whole poem of that quality Burns cannot make; the rest, in the *Farewell to Nancy,*[39] is verbiage.

We arrive best at the real estimate of Burns, I think, by conceiving his work as having truth of matter and truth of manner, but not the accent or the poetic virtue of the highest masters. His genuine criticism of life, when the sheer poet in him speaks, is ironic; it is not –

'Thou Power Supreme, whose mighty scheme
These woes of mine fulfil,
Here firm I rest, they must be best
Because they are Thy will!'[40]

It is far rather: *Whistle owre the lave o't!* Yet we may say of him as of Chaucer, that of life and the world, as they come before him, his view is large, free, shrewd, benignant, – truly poetic, therefore; and his manner of rendering what he sees is to match. But we must note, at the same time, his great difference from Chaucer. The freedom of Chaucer is heightened, in Burns, by a fiery, reckless energy; the benignity of Chaucer deepens, in Burns, into an overwhelming sense of the pathos of things; – of the pathos of human nature, the pathos, also, of non-human nature. Instead of the fluidity of Chaucer's manner, the manner of Burns has spring, bounding swiftness. Burns is by far the greater force, though he has perhaps less charm. The world of Chaucer is fairer, richer, more significant than that of Burns; but when the largeness and freedom of Burns get full sweep, as in *Tam o' Shanter,* or still more in that pleasant and splendid production, *The Jolly Beggars,* his world may be what it will, his poetic genius triumphs over it. In the world of *The Jolly Beggars* there is more than hideousness and squalor, there is bestiality; yet the piece is a superb poetic success. It has a breadth, truth, and power which make the famous scene in Auerbach's Cellar, of Goethe's *Faust,* seem artificial and tame beside it, and which are only matched by Shakespeare and Aristophanes.

Here, where his largeness and freedom serve him so admirably, and also in those poems and songs where to shrewdness he adds infinite archness and wit, and to benignity infinite pathos, where his manner is flawless, and a perfect poetic whole is the result, – in things like the address to the mouse whose home he had ruined, in things like *Duncan Gray, Tam Glen, Whistle and I'll come to you my Lad, Auld Lang Syne* (this list might be made much longer), – here we have the genuine Burns, of

whom the real estimate must be high indeed. Not a classic, nor
with the excellent σπουδαιότης of the great classics, nor with a
verse rising to a criticism of life and a virtue like theirs; but a
poet with thorough truth of substance and an answering truth
of style, giving us a poetry sound to the core. We all of us have
a leaning towards the pathetic, and may be inclined perhaps to
prize Burns most for his touches of piercing, sometimes almost
intolerable pathos; for verse like –

> 'We twa hae paidl't i' the burn
> From mornin' sun till dine;
> But seas between us braid hae roar'd
> Sin auld lang syne . . .'

where he is as lovely as he is sound. But perhaps it is by the
perfection of soundness of his lighter and archer masterpieces
that he is poetically most wholesome for us. For the votary
misled by a personal estimate of Shelley, as so many of us have
been, are, and will be, – of that beautiful spirit building his
many-coloured haze of words and images

> 'Pinnacled dim in the intense inane'[41] –

no contact can be wholesomer than the contact with Burns at
his archest and soundest. Side by side with the

> 'On the brink of the night and the morning
> My coursers are wont to respire,
> But the Earth has just whispered a warning
> That their flight must be swifter than fire . . .'[42]

of *Prometheus Unbound,* how salutary, how very salutary, to
place this from *Tam Glen* –

> 'My minnie does constantly deave me
> And bids me beware o' young men;
> They flatter, she says, to deceive me;
> But wha can think sae o' Tam Glen?'

But we enter on burning ground as we approach the poetry of times so near to us – poetry like that of Byron, Shelley, and Wordsworth – of which the estimates are so often not only personal, but personal with passion. For my purpose, it is enough to have taken the single case of Burns, the first poet we come to of whose work the estimate formed is evidently apt to be personal, and to have suggested how we may proceed, using the poetry of the great classics as a sort of touchstone, to correct this estimate, as we had previously corrected by the same means the historic estimate where we met with it. A collection like the present, with its succession of celebrated names and celebrated poems, offers a good opportunity to us for resolutely endeavouring to make our estimates of poetry real. I have sought to point out a method which will help us in making them so, and to exhibit it in use so far as to put any one who likes in a way of applying it for himself.

At any rate the end to which the method and the estimate are designed to lead, and from leading to which, if they do lead to it, they get their whole value, – the benefit of being able clearly to feel and deeply to enjoy the best, the truly classic, in poetry, – is an end, let me say it once more at parting, of supreme imporance. We are often told that an era is opening in which we are to see multitudes of a common sort of readers, and masses of a common sort of literature; that such readers do not want and could not relish anything better than such literature, and that to provide it is becoming a vast and profitable industry. Even if good literature entirely lost currency with the world, it would still be abundantly worth while to continue to enjoy it by oneself. But it never will lose currency with the world, in spite of momentary appearances; it never will lose supremacy. Currency and supremacy are insured to it, not indeed by the world's deliberate and conscious choice, but by something far deeper, – by the instinct of self-preservation in humanity.

Wordsworth

I remember hearing Lord Macaulay say, after Wordsworth's death, when subscriptions were being collected to found a memorial of him, that ten years earlier more money could have been raised in Cambridge alone, to do honour to Wordsworth, than was now raised all through the country. Lord Macaulay had, as we know, his own heightened and telling way of putting things, and we must always make allowance for it. But probably it is true that Wordsworth has never, either before or since, been so accepted and popular, so established in possession of the minds of all who profess to care for poetry, as he was between the years 1830 and 1840, and at Cambridge. From the very first, no doubt, he had his believers and witnesses. But I have myself heard him declare that, for he knew not how many years, his poetry had never brought him in enough to buy his shoe-strings. The poetry-reading public was very slow to recognize him, and was very easily drawn away from him. Scott effaced him with this public, Byron effaced him.

The death of Byron, seemed, however, to make an opening for Wordsworth. Scott, who had for some time ceased to produce poetry himself, and stood before the public as a great novelist; Scott, too genuine himself not to feel the profound genuineness of Wordsworth, and with an instinctive recognition of his firm hold on nature and of his local truth, always admired him sincerely, and praised him generously. The influence of Coleridge upon young men of ability was then powerful, and was still gathering strength; this influence told entirely in favour of Wordsworth's poetry. Cambridge was a place where Coleridge's influence had great action, and where Wordsworth's poetry, therefore, flourished especially. But even among the general public its sale grew large, the eminence of its author was widely recognized, and Rydal Mount became an object of pilgrimage. I remember Wordsworth relating how one of the pilgrims, a clergyman, asked him if he had ever written anything besides the *Guide to the Lakes*.[1] Yes, he answered modestly, he had written verses. Not every pilgrim was a reader, but the vogue was established, and the stream of pilgrims came.

Mr Tennyson's decisive appearance dates from 1842.[2] One cannot say that he effaced Wordsworth as Scott and Byron had effaced him. The poetry of Wordsworth had been so long before the public, the suffrage of good judges was so steady and so strong in its favour, that by 1842 the verdict of posterity, one may almost say, had been already pronounced, and Wordsworth's English fame was secure. But the vogue, the ear and applause of the great body of poetry-readers, never quite thoroughly perhaps his, he gradually lost more and more, and Mr Tennyson gained them. Mr Tennyson drew to himself, and away from Wordsworth, the poetry-reading public, and the new generations. Even in 1850, when Wordsworth died, this diminution of popularity was visible, and occasioned the remark of Lord Macaulay which I quoted at starting.

The diminution has continued. The influence of Coleridge has waned, and Wordsworth's poetry can no longer draw succour from this ally. The poetry has not, however, wanted eulogists; and it may be said to have brought its eulogists luck, for almost everyone who has praised Wordsworth's poetry has praised it well. But the public has remained cold, or, at least, undetermined. Even the abundance of Mr Palgrave's fine and skilfully chosen specimens of Wordsworth, in the *Golden Treasury*,[3] surprised many readers, and gave offence to not a few. To tenth-rate critics and compilers, for whom any violent shock to the public taste would be a temerity not to be risked, it is still quite permissible to speak of Wordsworth's poetry, not only with ignorance, but with impertinence. On the Continent he is almost unknown.

I cannot think, then, that Wordsworth has, up to this time, at all obtained his deserts. 'Glory,' said M. Renan[4] the other day, 'glory after all is the thing which has the best chance of not being altogether vanity.' Wordsworth was a homely man, and himself would certainly never have thought of talking of glory as that which, after all, has the best chance of not being altogether vanity. Yet we may well allow that few things are less vain than *real* glory. Let us conceive of the whole group of civilized nations as being, for intellectual and spiritual purposes, one great confederation, bound to a joint action and working towards a common result; a confederation whose members have a due knowledge both of the past, out of which they all proceed, and of one another. This was the ideal of Goethe,[5] and it is an ideal which will impose itself upon the thoughts of our modern societies more and more. Then to be recognized by the verdict of such a confederation as a master, or even as a seriously and eminently worthy workman, in one's own line of intellectual or spiritual activity, is indeed glory; a glory which it would be difficult to rate too highly. For what could be more beneficent, more salutary? The world is forwarded by having its attention fixed on the best things; and here is a tribunal, free from all suspicion of national and provincial partiality, putting a stamp on the best things, and recommending them for general honour and acceptance. A nation, again, is furthered by recognition of its real gifts and successes; it is encouraged to develop them further. And here is an honest verdict, telling us which of our supposed successes are really, in the judgment of the great impartial world, and not in our own private judgment only, successes, and which are not.

It is so easy to feel pride and satisfaction in one's own things, so hard to make sure that one is right in feeling it! We have a great empire. But so had Nebuchadnezzar. We extol the 'unrivalled happiness'[6] of our national civilization. But then comes a candid friend, and remarks that our upper class is materialized, our middle class vulgarized, and our lower class brutalized.[7] We are proud of our painting, our music. But we find that in the judgment of other people our painting is questionable, and our music non-existent. We are proud of our men of science. And here it turns out that the world is with us; we find that in the judgment of other people, too, Newton among the dead, and Mr Darwin among the living, hold as high a place as they hold in our national opinion.

Finally, we are proud of our poets and poetry. Now poetry is nothing less than the most perfect speech of man, that in which he comes nearest to being able to utter the truth. It is no small thing, therefore, to succeed eminently in poetry. And so much is required for duly estimating success here, that about poetry it is perhaps hardest to arrive at a sure general verdict, and takes longest. Meanwhile, our own conviction of the superiority of our national poets is not decisive, is almost certain to be mingled, as we see constantly in English eulogy of Shakespeare, with much of provincial infatuation. And we know what was the opinion current among our neighbours the French – people of taste, acuteness, and quick literary tact – not a hundred years ago, about our great poets. The old *Biographie Universelle*[8] notices the pretension of the English to a place for their poets among the chief poets of the world, and says that this is a pretension which to no one but an Englishman can ever seem admissible. And the scornful, disparaging things said by foreigners about Shakespeare and Milton, and about our national over-estimate of them, have been often quoted, and will be in everyone's remembrance.

A great change has taken place, and Shakespeare is now generally recognized, even in France, as one of the greatest of poets. Yes, some anti-Gallican cynic will say, the French rank him with Corneille and with Victor Hugo! But let me have the pleasure of quoting a sentence about Shakespeare, which I met with by accident not long ago in the *Correspondant*, a French review which not a dozen English people, I suppose, look at. The writer is praising Shakespeare's prose. With Shakespeare, he says, 'prose comes in whenever the subject, being more familiar, is unsuited to the majestic English iambic.' And he goes on: 'Shakespeare is the king of poetic rhythm and style, as well as the king of the realm of thought; along with his dazzling prose, Shakespeare has succeeded in giving us the most varied, the most harmonious verse which has ever sounded upon the human ear since the verse of the Greeks.' M. Henry Cochin, the writer of this sentence, deserves our gratitude for it; it would not be easy to praise Shakespeare, in a single sentence, more justly. And when a foreigner and a Frenchman writes thus of Shakespeare, and when Goethe says of Milton, in whom there was so much to repel Goethe rather than to attract him, that 'nothing has been ever done so entirely in the sense of the Greeks as *Samson Agonistes*,'[9] and that 'Milton is in very truth a poet whom we must treat with all reverence, then we under-stand what constitutes a European recognition of poets and poetry as contradistinguished from a merely national recogni-tion, and that in favour both of Milton and of Shakespeare the judgment of the high court of appeal has finally gone.

I come back to M. Renan's praise of glory, from which I started. Yes, real glory is a most serious thing, glory authenti-cated by the Amphictyonic Court[10] of final appeal, definitive glory. And even for poets and poetry, long and difficult as may be the process of arriving at the right award, the right award comes at last, the definitive glory rests where it is deserved. Every establishment of such a real glory is good and whole-some for mankind at large, good and wholesome for the nation which produced the poet crowned with it. To the poet himself it can seldom do harm; for he, poor man, is in his grave, prob-ably, long before his glory crowns him.

Wordsworth has been in his grave for some thirty years, and certainly his lovers and admirers cannot flatter themselves that this great and steady light of glory as yet shines over him. He is not fully recognized at home; he is not recognized at all abroad. Yet I firmly believe that the poetical performance of Words-worth is, after that of Shakespeare and Milton, of which all the world now recognizes the worth, undoubtedly the most consid-erable in our language from the Elizabethan age to the present time. Chaucer is anterior; and on other grounds, too, he cannot well be brought into the comparison. But taking the roll of our chief poetical names, besides Shakespeare and Milton, from the age of Elizabeth downwards, and going through it, – Spenser, Dryden, Pope, Gray, Goldsmith, Cowper, Burns, Coleridge, Scott, Campbell, Moore, Byron, Shelley, Keats (I mention those only who are dead), – I think it certain that Wordsworth's name deserves to stand, and will finally stand, above them all. Several of the poets named have gifts and excellences which Words-worth has not. But taking the performance of each as a whole, I say that Wordsworth seems to me to have left a body of poeti-cal work superior in power, in interest, in the qualities which give enduring freshness, to that which any one of the others has left.

But this is not enough to say. I think it certain, further, that if we take the chief poetical names of the Continent since the death of Molière, and, omitting Goethe, confront the remaining names with that of Wordsworth, the result is the same. Let us take Klopstock, Lessing, Schiller, Uhland, Rückert, and Heine for Germany; Filicaia, Alfieri, Manzoni, and Leopardi for Italy; Racine, Boileau, Voltaire, André Chenier, Béranger, Lamartine, Musset, M. Victor Hugo (he has been so long celebrated that although he still lives I may be permitted to name him) for France. Several of these, again, have evidently gifts and excellences to which Wordsworth can make no pretension. But in real poetical achievement it seems to me indubitable that to Wordsworth, here again, belongs the palm. It seems to me that Wordsworth has left behind him a body of poetical work which wears, and will wear, better on the whole than the performance of any one of these personages, so far more brilliant and celebrated, most of them, than the homely poet of Rydal. Wordsworth's performance in poetry is on the whole, in power, in interest, in the qualities which give enduring freshness, superior to theirs.

This is a high claim to make for Wordsworth. But if it is a just claim, if Wordsworth's place among the poets who have appeared in the last two or three centuries is after Shakespeare, Molière, Milton, Goethe, indeed, but before all the rest, then in time Wordsworth will have his due. We shall recognize him in his place, as we recognize Shakespeare and Milton; and not only we ourselves shall recognize him, but he will be recognized by Europe also. Meanwhile, those who recognize him already may do well, perhaps, to ask themselves whether there are not in the case of Wordsworth certain special obstacles which hinder or delay his due recognition by others, and whether these obstacles are not in some measure removable.

The *Excursion* and the *Prelude,* his poems of greatest bulk, are by no means Wordsworth's best work. His best work is in his shorter pieces, and many, indeed, are there of these which are of first-rate excellence. But in his seven volumes the pieces of high merit are mingled with a mass of pieces very inferior to them; so inferior to them that it seems wonderful how the same poet should have produced both. Shakespeare frequently has lines and passages in a strain quite false, and which are entirely unworthy of him. But one can imagine his smiling if one could meet him in the Elysian Fields and tell him so; smiling and replying that he knew it perfectly well himself, and what did it matter? But with Wordsworth the case is different. Work altogether inferior, work quite uninspired, flat and dull, is produced by him with evident unconsciousness of its defects, and he presents it to us with the same faith and seriousness as his best work. Now a drama or an epic fill the mind, and one does not look beyond them; but in a collection of short pieces the impression made by one piece requires to be continued and sustained by the piece following. In reading Wordsworth the impression made by one of his fine pieces is too often dulled and spoiled by a very inferior piece coming after it.

Wordsworth composed verses during a space of some sixty years; and it is no exaggeration to say that within one single decade of those years, between 1798 and 1808, almost all his really first-rate work was produced. A mass of inferior work remains, work done before and after this golden prime, imbedding the first-rate work and clogging it, obstructing our approach to it, chilling, not unfrequently, the high-wrought mood with which we leave it. To be recognized far and wide as a great poet, to be possible and receivable as a classic, Wordsworth needs to be relieved of a great deal of the poetical baggage which now encumbers him. To administer this relief is indispensable, unless he is to continue to be a poet for the few only, – a poet valued far below his real worth by the world.

There is another thing. Wordsworth classified his poems not according to any commonly received plan of arrangement, but according to a scheme of mental physiology. He has poems of the fancy, poems of the imagination, poems of sentiment and reflection, and so on. His categories are ingenious but far-fetched, and the result of his employment of them is unsatisfactory. Poems are separated one from another which possess a kinship of subject or of treatment far more vital and deep than the supposed unity of mental origin, which was Wordsworth's reason for joining them with others.

The tact of the Greeks in matters of this kind was infallible.

We may rely upon it that we shall not improve upon the classi-fication adopted by the Greeks for kinds of poetry; that their categories of epic, dramatic, lyric, and so forth, have a natural propriety, and should be adhered to. It may sometimes seem doubtful to which of two categories a poem belongs; whether this or that poem is to be called, for instance, narrative or lyric, lyric or elegiac. But there is to be found in every good poem a strain, a predominant note, which determines the poem as belonging to one of these kinds rather than the other; and here is the best proof of the value of the classification, and of the advantage of adhering to it. Wordsworth's poems will never produce their due effect until they are freed from their present artificial arrangement, and grouped more naturally.

Disengaged from the quantity of inferior work which now obscures them, the best poems of Wordsworth, I hear many people say, would indeed stand out in great beauty, but they would prove to be very few in number, scarcely more than half a dozen. I maintain, on the other hand, that what strikes me with admiration, what establishes in my opinion Wordsworth's superiority, is the great and ample body of powerful work which remains to him, even after all his inferior work has been cleared away. He gives us so much to rest upon, so much which communicates his spirit and engages ours!

This is of very great importance. If it were a comparison of single pieces, or of three or four pieces, by each poet, I do not say that Wordsworth would stand decisively above Gray, or Burns, or Coleridge, or Keats, or Manzoni, or Heine. It is in his ampler body of powerful work that I find his superiority. His good work itself, his work which counts, is not all of it, of course, of equal value. Some kinds of poetry are in themselves lower kinds than others. The ballad kind is a lower kind; the didactic kind, still more, is a lower kind. Poetry of this latter sort counts, too, sometimes, by its biographical interest partly, not by its poetical interest pure and simple; but then this can only be when the poet producing it has the power and importance of Wordsworth, a power and importance which he assuredly did not establish by such didactic poetry alone. Altogether, it is, I say, by the great body of powerful and significant work which remains to him, after every reduction and deduction has been made, that Wordsworth's superiority is proved.

To exhibit this body of Wordsworth's best work, to clear away obstructions from around it, and to let it speak for itself, is what every lover of Wordsworth should desire. Until this has been done, Wordsworth, whom we, to whom he is dear, all of us know and feel to be so great a poet, has not had a fair chance before the world. When once it has been done, he will make his way best, not by our advocacy of him, but by his own worth and power. We may safely leave him to make his way thus, we who believe that a superior worth and power in poetry finds in mankind a sense responsive to it and disposed at last to recognize it. Yet at the outset, before he has been duly known and recognized, we may do Wordsworth a service, perhaps, by indicating in what his superior power and worth will be found to consist, and in what it will not.

Long ago, in speaking of Homer, I said that the noble and profound application of ideas to life is the most essential part of poetic greatness. I said that a great poet receives his distinctive character of superiority from his application, under the conditions immutably fixed by the laws of poetic beauty and poetic truth, from his application, I say, to his subject, whatever it may be, of the ideas

'On man, on nature, and on human life,'[11]

which he has acquired for himself. The line quoted is Wordsworth's own; and his superiority arises from his powerful use, in his best pieces, his powerful application to his subject, of ideas 'on man, on nature, and on human life.'

Voltaire, with his signal acuteness, most truly remarked that 'no nation has treated in poetry moral ideas with more energy and depth than the English nation.' And he adds: 'There, it seems to me, is the great merit of the English poets.'[12] Voltaire does not mean, by 'treating in poetry moral ideas,' the composing moral and didactic poems; – that brings us but a very little way in poetry. He means just the same thing as was meant when I spoke above 'of the noble and profound application of ideas to life'; and he means the application of these ideas under the conditions fixed for us by the laws of poetic beauty and poetic truth. If it is said that to call these ideas *moral* ideas is to introduce a strong and injurious limitation, I answer that it is to do nothing of the kind, because moral ideas are really so main a part of human life. The question, *how to live,* is itself a moral idea; and it is the question which mosts interests every man, and with which, in some way or other, he is perpetually occupied. A large sense is, of course, to be given to the term *moral*. Whatever bears upon the question, 'how to live,' comes under it.

> 'Nor love thy life, nor hate; but, what thou liv'st,
> Live well; how long or short, permit to heaven.'[13]

In those fine lines Milton utters, as everyone at once perceives, a moral idea. Yes, but so, too, when Keats consoles the forward-bending lover on the Grecian Urn, the lover arrested and presented in immortal relief by the sculptor's hand before he can kiss, with the line,

> 'For ever wilt thou love, and she be fair' –

he utters a moral idea. When Shakespeare says, that

> 'We are such stuff
> As dreams are made of, and our little life
> Is rounded with a sleep,'[14]

he utters a moral idea.

Voltaire was right in thinking that the energetic and profound treatment of moral ideas, in this large sense, is what distinguishes the English poetry. He sincerely meant praise, not dispraise or hint of limitation; and they err who suppose that poetic limitation is a necessary consequence of the fact, the fact being granted as Voltaire states it. If what distinguishes the greatest poets is their powerful and profound application of

ideas to life, which surely no good critic will deny, then to prefix to the term ideas here the term moral makes hardly any
difference, because human life itself is in so preponderating a
degree moral.

It is important, therefore, to hold fast to this: that poetry is
at bottom a criticism of life; that the greatness of a poet lies in
his powerful and beautiful application of ideas to life, – to the
question: How to live. Morals are often treated in a narrow
and false fashion; they are bound up with systems of thought
and belief which have had their day; they are fallen into the
hands of pedants and professional dealers; they grow tiresome
to some of us. We find attraction, at times, even in a poetry of
revolt against them; in a poetry which might take for its motto
Omar Kheyam's words: 'Let us make up in the tavern for the
time which we have wasted in the mosque.'[15] Or we find attrac-
tions in a poetry indifferent to them; in a poetry where the
contents may be what they will, but where the form is studied
and exquisite. We delude ourselves in either case; and the best
cure for our delusion is to let our minds rest upon that great
and inexhaustible word *life,* until we learn to enter into its
meaning. A poetry of revolt against moral ideas is a poetry of
revolt against *life*; a poetry of indifference towards moral ideas
is a poetry of indifference towards *life*.

Epictetus had a happy figure for things like the play of the
sense, or literary form and finish, or argumentative ingenuity,
in comparison with 'the best and master thing' for us, as he
called it, the concern, how to live.[16] Some people were afraid of
them, he said, or they disliked and undervalued them. Such
people were wrong; they were unthankful or cowardly. But the
things might also be over-prized, and treated as final when they
are not. They bear to life the relation which inns bear to home.
'As if a man, journeying home, and finding a nice inn on the
road, and liking it, were to stay for ever at the inn! Man, thou
hast forgotten thine object; thy journey was not *to* this, but
through this. "But this inn is taking." And how many other
inns, too, are taking, and how many fields and meadows! but
as places of passage merely. You have an object, which is this:
to get home, to do your duty to your family, friends, and

fellow-countrymen, to attain inward freedom, serenity, happiness, contentment. Style takes your fancy, arguing takes your fancy, and you forget your home and want to make your abode with them and to stay with them, on the plea that they are taking. Who denies that they are taking? but as places of passage, as inns. And when I say this, you suppose me to be attacking the care for style, the care for argument. I am not; I attack the resting in them, the not looking to the end which is beyond them.'

Now, when we come across a poet like Théophile Gautier,[17] we have a poet who has taken up his abode at an inn, and never got farther. There may be inducements to this or that one of us, at this or that moment, to find delight in him, to cleave to him; but after all, we do not change the truth about him, – we only stay ourselves in his inn along with him. And when we come across a poet like Wordsworth, who sings

'Of truth, of grandeur, beauty, love and hope,
And melancholy fear subdued by faith,
Of blessed consolations in distress,
Of moral strength and intellectual power,
Of joy in widest commonalty spread'[18] –

then we have a poet intent on 'the best and master thing,' and who prosecutes his journey home. We say, for brevity's sake, that he deals with *life,* because he deals with that in which life really consists. This is what Voltaire means to praise in the English poets, – this dealing with what is really life. But always it is the mark of the greatest poets that they deal with it; and to say that the English poets are remarkable for dealing with it, is only another way of saying, what is true, that in poetry the English genius has especially shown its power.

Wordsworth deals with it, and his greatness lies in his dealing with it so powerfully. I have named a number of celebrated poets above all of whom he, in my opinion, deserves to be placed. He is to be placed above poets like Voltaire, Dryden, Pope, Lessing, Schiller, because these famous personages, with a thousand gifts and merits, never, or scarcely ever, attain the

distinctive accent and utterance of the high and genuine
poets –

'Quique pii vates et Phœbo digna locuti,'[19]

at all. Burns, Keats, Heine, not to speak of others in our list,
have this accent; – who can doubt it? And at the same time they
have treasures of humour, felicity, passion, for which in Wordsworth we shall look in vain. Where, then, is Wordsworth's
superiority? It is here; he deals with more of *life* than they do;
he deals with *life,* as a whole, more powerfully.

No Wordsworthian will doubt this. Nay, the fervent Wordsworthian will add, as Mr Leslie Stephen does, that Wordsworth's
poetry is precious because his philosophy is sound; that his
'ethical system is as distinctive and capable of expression as
Bishop Butler's'; that his poetry is informed by ideas which 'fall
spontaneously into a scientific system of thought.'[20] But we must
be on our guard against the Wordsworthians, if we want to
secure for Wordsworth his due rank as a poet. The Wordsworthians are apt to praise him for the wrong things, and to lay far
too much stress upon what they call his philosophy. His poetry
is the reality, his philosophy, – so far, at least, as it may put on
the form and habit of 'a scientific system of thought,' and the
more that it puts them on, – is the illusion. Perhaps we shall
one day learn to make this proposition general, and to say:
Poetry is the reality, philosophy the illusion. But in Wordsworth's case, at any rate, we cannot do him justice until we
dismiss his formal philosophy.

The *Excursion* abounds with philosophy, and, therefore, the
Excursion is to the Wordsworthian what it never can be to the
disinterested lover of poetry, – a satisfactory work. 'Duty
exists,' says Wordsworth, in the *Excursion*; and then he proceeds thus –

'. . . Immutably survive,
For our support, the measures and the forms,
Which an abstract Intelligence supplies,
Whose kingdom is, where time and space are not.'[21]

And the Wordsworthian is delighted, and thinks that here is a sweet union of philosophy and poetry. But the disinterested lover of poetry will feel that the lines carry us really not a step farther than the proposition which they would interpret; that they are a tissue of elevated but abstract verbiage, alien to the very nature of poetry.

Or let us come direct to the centre of Wordsworth's philosophy, as 'an ethical system, as distinctive and capable of systematical exposition as Bishop Butler's' –

> '. . . One adequate support
> For the calamities of mortal life
> Exists, one only; – an assured belief
> That the procession of our fate, howe'er
> Sad or disturbed, is ordered by a Being
> Of infinite benevolence and power;
> Whose everlasting purposes embrace
> All accidents, converting them to good.'[22]

That is doctrine such as we hear in church, too, religious and philosophic doctrine; and the attached Wordsworthian loves passages of such doctrine, and brings them forward in proof of his poet's excellence. But however true the doctrine may be, it has, as here presented, none of the characters of *poetic* truth, the kind of truth which we require from a poet, and in which Wordsworth is really strong.

Even the 'intimations' of the famous Ode, those corner-stones of the supposed philosophic system of Wordsworth, – the idea of the high instincts and affections coming out in childhood, testifying of a divine home recently left, and fading away as our life proceeds, – this idea, of undeniable beauty as a play of fancy, has itself not the character of poetic truth of the best kind; it has no real solidity. The instinct of delight in Nature and her beauty had no doubt extraordinary strength in Wordsworth himself as a child. But to say that universally this instinct is mighty in childhood, and tends to die away afterwards, is to say what is extremely doubtful. In many people, perhaps with the majority of educated persons, the love of nature is nearly imperceptible at ten years old, but strong and operative at thirty. In general we may say of these high instincts of early childhood, the base of the alleged systematic philosophy of Wordsworth, what Thucydides says of the early achievements of the Greek race: 'It is impossible to speak with certainty of what is so remote; but from all that we can really investigate, I should say that they were no very great things.'

Finally, the 'scientific system of thought' in Wordsworth gives us at last such poetry as this, which the devout Wordsworthian accepts –

> 'O for the coming of that glorious time
> When, prizing knowledge as her noblest wealth
> And best protection, this Imperial Realm,
> While she exacts allegiance, shall admit
> An obligation, on her part, to *teach*
> Them who are born to serve her and obey;
> Binding herself by statute to secure,
> For all the children whom her soil maintains,
> The rudiments of letters, and inform
> The mind with moral and religious truth.'[23]

Wordsworth calls Voltaire dull, and surely the production of these un-Voltairean lines must have been imposed on him as a judgment! One can hear them being quoted at a Social Science Congress; one can call up the whole scene.[24] A great room in one of our dismal provincial towns; dusty air and jaded afternoon daylight; benches full of men with bald heads and women in spectacles; an orator lifting up his face from a manuscript written within and without to declaim these lines of Wordsworth; and in the soul of any poor child of nature who may have wandered in thither, an unutterable sense of lamentation, and mourning, and woe!

'But turn we,' as Wordsworth says, 'from these bold, bad men,'[25] the haunters of Social Science Congresses. And let us be on our guard, too, against the exhibitors and extollers of a 'scientific system of thought' in Wordsworth's poetry. The poetry will never be seen aright while they thus exhibit it. The cause of its greatness is simple, and may be told quite simply. Words-worth's poetry is great because of the extraordinary power with which Wordsworth feels the joy offered to us in nature, the joy offered to us in the simple primary affections and duties; and because of the extraordinary power with which, in case after case, he shows us this joy, and renders it so as to make us share it.

The source of joy from which he thus draws is the truest and most unfailing source of joy accessible to man. It is also accessible universally. Wordsworth brings us word, therefore, according to his own strong and characteristic line, he brings us word

– 'Of joy in widest commonalty spread.'

Here is an immense advantage for a poet. Wordsworth tells of what all seek, and tells of it at its truest and best source, and yet a source where all may go and draw for it.

Nevertheless, we are not to suppose that everything is precious which Wordsworth, standing even at this perennial and beautiful source, may give us. Wordsworthians are apt to talk as if it must be. They will speak with the same reverence of *The Sailor's Mother*, for example, as of *Lucy Gray*. They do their master harm by such lack of discrimination. *Lucy Gray* is a beautiful success; *The Sailor's Mother* is a failure. To give aright what he wishes to give, to interpret and render successfully, is not always within Wordsworth's own command. It is within no poet's command; here is the part of the Muse, the inspiration, the God, the 'not ourselves.'[26] In Wordsworth's case, the accident, for so it may almost be called, of inspiration, is of peculiar importance. No poet, perhaps, is so evidently filled with a new and sacred energy when the inspiration is upon him; no poet, when it fails him, is so left 'weak as is a breaking wave.'[27] I remember hearing him say that 'Goethe's poetry was not inevitable enough.' The remark is striking and true; no line in Goethe, as Goethe said himself, but its maker knew well how it came there. Wordsworth is right, Goethe's poetry is not inevitable; not inevitable enough. But Wordsworth's poetry, when he is at his best, is inevitable, as inevitable as Nature herself. It might seem that Nature not only gave him the matter for his poem, but wrote his poem for him. He has no style. He was too conversant with Milton not to catch at times his master's manner, and he has fine Miltonic lines; but he has no assured poetic style of his own, like Milton. When he seeks to have a style he falls into ponderosity and pomposity. In the *Excursion* we have his style, as an artistic product of his own creation; and although Jeffrey completely failed to recognize Wordsworth's real greatness, he was yet not wrong in saying of the *Excursion*, as a work of poetic style: 'This will never do.'[28] And yet magical as is that power, which Wordsworth has not, of assured and possessed poetic style, he has something which is an equivalent of it.

Everyone who has any sense for these things feels the subtle turn, the heightening, which is given to a poet's verse by his genius for style. We can feel it in the

'After life's fitful fever, he sleeps well'[29] –

of Shakespeare; in the

'. . . though fall'n on evil days,
On evil days through fall'n, and evil tongues'[30] –

of Milton. It is the incomparable charm of Milton's power of poetic style which gives such worth to *Paradise Regained*, and makes a great poem of a work in which Milton's imagination does not soar high. Wordsworth has in constant possession, and at command, no style of this kind; but he had too poetic a nature, and had read the great poets too well, not to catch, as I have already remarked, something of it occasionally. We find it not only in his Miltonic lines; we find it in such a phrase as this, where the manner is his own, not Milton's –

'. . . the fierce confederate storm
Of sorrow barricadoed evermore
Within the walls of cities;'[31]

although even here, perhaps, the power of style, which is undeniable, is more properly that of eloquent prose than the subtle heightening and change wrought by genuine poetic style. It is style, again, and the elevation given by style, which chiefly makes the effectiveness of *Laodameia*. Still the right sort of verse to choose from Wordsworth, if we are to seize his true and most characteristic form of expression, is a line like this from *Michael* –

'And never lifted up a single stone.'

There is nothing subtle in it, no heightening, no study in poetic style, strictly so called, at all; yet it is expression of the highest and most truly expressive kind.

Wordsworth owed much to Burns, and a style of perfect plainness, relying for effect solely on the weight and force of that which with entire fidelity it utters, Burns could show him.

'The poor inhabitant below
Was quick to learn and wise to know,
And keenly felt the friendly glow
    And softer flame;
But thoughtless follies laid him low
    And stain'd his name.'[32]

Everyone will be conscious of a likeness here to Wordsworth; and if Wordsworth did great things with this nobly plain manner, we must remember, what indeed he himself would always have been forward to acknowledge, that Burns used it before him.

Still Wordsworth's use of it has something unique and unmatchable. Nature herself seems, I say, to take the pen out of his hand, and to write for him with her own bare, sheer, penetrating power. This arises from two causes; from the profound sincereness with which Wordsworth feels his subject, and also from the profoundly sincere and natural character of his subject itself. He can and will treat such a subject with nothing but the most plain, first-hand, almost austere naturalness. His expression may often be called bald, as, for instance, in the poem of *Resolution and Independence*; but it is bald as the bare mountain tops are bald, with a baldness which is full of grandeur.

Wherever we meet with the successful balance, in Wordsworth, of profound truth of subject with profound truth of execution, he is unique. His best poems are those which most perfectly exhibit this balance. I have a warm admiration for *Laodameia* and for the great *Ode*; but if I am to tell the very truth, I find *Laodameia* not wholly free from something artificial, and the great *Ode* not wholly free from something declamatory. If I had to pick out poems of a kind most perfectly to show Wordsworth's unique power, I should rather choose poems such as *Michael*, *The Fountain*, *The Highland Reaper*. And poems with the peculiar and unique beauty which distinguishes these, Wordsworth produced in considerable number; besides very many other poems of which the worth, although not so rare as the worth of these, is still exceedingly high.

On the whole, then, as I said at the beginning, not only is Wordsworth eminent by reason of the goodness of his best work, but he is eminent also by reason of the great body of good work which he has left to us. With the ancients I will not compare him. In many respects the ancients are far above us, and yet there is something that we demand which they can never give. Leaving the ancients, let us come to the poets and poetry of Christendom. Dante, Shakespeare, Molière, Milton, Goethe, are altogether larger and more splendid luminaries in the poetical heaven than Wordsworth. But I know not where else, among the moderns, we are to find his superiors.

To disengage the poems which show his power, and to present them to the English-speaking public and to the world, is the object of this volume. I by no means say that it contains all which in Wordsworth's poems is interesting. Except in the case of *Margaret*, a story composed separately from the rest of the *Excursion*, and which belongs to a different part of England, I have not ventured on detaching portions of poems, or on giving any piece otherwise than as Wordsworth himself gave it. But under the conditions imposed by this reserve, the volume contains, I think, everything, or nearly everything, which may best serve him with the majority of lovers of poetry, nothing which may disserve him.

I have spoken lightly of Wordsworthians; and if we are to get Wordsworth recognized by the public and by the world, we must recommend him not in the spirit of a clique, but in the spirit of disinterested lovers of poetry. But I am a Wordsworthian myself. I can read with pleasure and edification *Peter Bell*, and the whole series of *Ecclesiastical Sonnets*, and the addresses to Mr Wilkinson's spade,[33] and even the *Thanksgiving Ode;* – everything of Wordsworth, I think, except *Vaudracour and Julia*. It is not for nothing that one has been brought up in the veneration of a man so truly worthy of homage; that one has seen him and heard him, lived in his neighbourhood, and been familiar with his country. No Wordsworthian has a tenderer affection for this pure and sage master than I, or is less really offended by his defects. But Wordsworth is something more than the pure and sage master of a small band of devoted followers, and we ought not to rest satisfied until he is seen to be what he is. He is one of the very chief glories of English Poetry; and by nothing is England so glorious as by her poetry. Let us lay aside every weight which hinders our getting him recognized as this, and let our one study be to bring to pass, as widely as possible and as truly as possible, his own word concerning his poems: 'They will co-operate with the benign tendencies in human nature and society, and will, in their degree, be efficacious in making men wiser, better, and happier.'[34]

Byron

When at last I held in my hand the volume of poems which I had chosen from Wordsworth, and began to turn over its pages, there arose in me almost immediately the desire to see beside it, as a companion volume, a like collection of the best poetry of Byron. Alone among our poets of the earlier part of the century, Byron and Wordsworth not only furnish material enough for a volume of this kind, but also, as it seems to me, they both of them gain considerably by being thus exhibited. There are poems of Coleridge and of Keats equal, if not superior, to anything of Byron or Wordsworth; but a dozen pages or two will contain them, and the remaining poetry is of a quality much inferior. Scott never, I think, rises as a poet to the level of Byron and Wordsworth at all. On the other hand, he never falls below his own usual level very far; and by a volume of selections from him, therefore, his effectiveness is not increased. As to Shelley there will be more question; and indeed Mr Stopford Brooke, whose accomplishments, eloquence, and love of poetry we must all recognize and admire, has actually given us Shelley in such a volume.[1] But for my own part I cannot think that Shelley's poetry, except by snatches and fragments, has the value of the good work of Wordsworth and Byron; or that it is possible for even Mr Stopford Brooke to make up a volume of selections from him which, for real substance, power, and worth, can at all take rank with a like volume from Byron or Wordsworth.

Shelley knew quite well the difference between the achievement of such a poet as Byron and his own. He praises Byron too unreservedly, but he sincerely felt, and he was right in feeling, that Byron was a greater poetical power than himself. As a man, Shelley is at a number of points immeasurably Byron's superior; he is a beautiful and enchanting spirit, whose vision, when we call it up, has far more loveliness, more charm for our soul, than the vision of Byron. But all the personal charm of Shelley cannot hinder us from at last discovering in his poetry the incurable want, in general, of a sound subject-matter, and the incurable fault, in consequence, of unsubstantiality. Those who extol him as the poet of clouds, the poet of sunsets, are only saying that he did not, in fact, lay hold upon the poet's right subject-matter; and in honest truth, with all his charm of soul and spirit, and with all his gift of musical diction and movement, he never, or hardly ever, did. Except, as I have said, for a few short things and single stanzas, his original poetry is less satisfactory than his translations, for in these the subject-matter was found for him. Nay, I doubt whether his delightful Essays and Letters, which deserve to be far more read than they are now, will not resist the wear and tear of time better, and finally come to stand higher, than his poetry.

There remain to be considered Byron and Wordsworth. That Wordsworth affords good material for a volume of selections, and that he gains by having his poetry thus presented, is an old belief of mine which led me lately to make up a volume of poems chosen out of Wordsworth, and to bring it before the public. By its kind reception of the volume, the public seems to show itself a partaker in my belief. Now Byron also supplies plenty of material for a like volume, and he too gains, I think, by being so presented. Mr Swinburne urges, indeed, that 'Byron, who rarely wrote anything either worthless or faultless, can only be judged or appreciated in the mass; the greatest of his works was his whole work taken together.'[2] It is quite true that Byron rarely wrote anything either worthless or faultless; it is quite true also that in the appreciation of Byron's power a sense of the amount and variety of his work, defective though much of his work is, enters justly into our estimate. But although there may be little in Byron's poetry which can be pronounced either worthless or faultless, there are portions of it which are far higher in worth and far more free from fault than others. And although, again, the abundance and variety of his production is undoubtedly a proof of his power, yet I question whether by reading everything which he gives us we are so likely to acquire an admiring sense even of his variety and abundance, as by reading what he gives us at his happier moments. Varied and abundant he amply proves himself even by this taken alone. Receive him absolutely without omission or compression, follow his whole outpouring stanza by stanza and line by line from the very commencement to the very end, and he is capable of being tiresome.

Byron has told us himself that the *Giaour* 'is but a string of passages.' He has made full confession of his own negligence. 'No one,' says he, 'has done more through negligence to corrupt the language.' This accusation brought by himself against his poems is not just; but when he goes on to say of them, that 'their faults, whatever they may be, are those of negligence and not of labour,' he says what is perfectly true. '*Lara*,' he declares, 'I wrote while undressing after coming home from balls and masquerades, in the year of revelry, 1814. The *Bride* was written in four, the *Corsair* in ten days.' He calls this 'a humiliating confession, as it proves my own want of judgment in publishing, and the public's in reading, things which cannot have stamina for permanence.'[3] Again he does his poems injustice; the producer of such poems could not but publish them, the public could not but read them. Nor could Byron have produced his work in any other fashion; his poetic work could not have first grown and matured in his own mind, and then come forth as an organic whole; Byron had not enough of the artist in him for this, nor enough self-command. He wrote, as he truly tells us, to relieve himself, and he went on writing because he found the relief become indispensable. But it was inevitable that works so produced should be, in general, 'a string of passages,' poured out, as he describes them, with rapidity and excitement, and with new passages constantly suggesting themselves, and added while his work was going through the press. It is evident that we have here neither deliberate scientific construction, nor yet the instinctive artistic creation of poetic wholes; and that to take passages from work produced as Byron's was is a very different thing from taking passages out of the *Œdipus* or the *Tempest*, and deprives the poetry far less of its advantage.

Nay, it gives advantage to the poetry, instead of depriving it of any. Byron, I said, has not a great artist's profound and patient skill in combining an action or in developing a character, – a skill which we must watch and follow if we are to do justice to it. But he has a wonderful power of vividly conceiving a single incident, a single situation; of throwing himself upon it, grasping it as if it were real and he saw and felt it, and of making us see and feel it, too. The *Giaour* is, as he truly called it, 'a string of passages,' not a work moving by a deep internal law of development to a necessary end; and our total impression from it cannot but receive from this, its inherent defect, a certain dimness and indistinctness. But the incidents of the journey and death of Hassan, in that poem, are conceived and presented with a vividness not to be surpassed; and our impression from them is correspondingly clear and powerful. In *Lara*, again, there is no adequate development either of the character of the chief personage or of the action of the poem; our total impression from the work is a confused one. Yet such an incident as the disposal of the slain Ezzelin's body passes before our eyes as if we actually saw it. And in the same way as these bursts of incident, bursts of sentiment also, living and vigorous, often occur in the midst of poems which must be admitted to be but weakly-conceived and loosely-combined wholes. Byron cannot but be a gainer by having attention concentrated upon what is vivid, powerful, effective in his work, and withdrawn from what is not so.

Byron, I say, cannot but be a gainer by this, just as Wordsworth is a gainer by a like proceeding. I esteem Wordsworth's poetry so highly, and the world, in my opinion, has done it such scant justice, that I could not rest satisfied until I had fulfilled, on Wordsworth's behalf, a long-cherished desire; – had disengaged, to the best of my power, his good work from the inferior work joined with it, and had placed before the public the body of his good work by itself. To the poetry of Byron the world has ardently paid homage; full justice from his contemporaries, perhaps even more than justice, his torrent of poetry received. His poetry was admired, adored, 'with all its imperfections on its head,' – in spite of negligence, in spite of differences, in spite of repetitions, in spite of whatever faults it possessed. His name is still great and brilliant. Nevertheless the hour of irresistible vogue has passed away for him; even for Byron it could not but pass away. The time has come for him, as it comes for all poets, when he must take his real and permanent place, no longer depending upon the vogue of his own day and upon the enthusiasm of his contemporaries. Whatever we may think of him, we shall not be subjugated by him as they were; for, as he cannot be for us what he was for them, we cannot admire him so hotly and indiscriminately as they. His faults of negligence, of diffuseness, of repetition, his faults of whatever kind, we shall abundantly feel and unsparingly criticize; the mere interval of time between us and him makes disillusion of this kind inevitable. But how then will Byron stand, if we relieve him, too, so far as we can, of the encumbrance of his inferior and weakest work, and if we bring before us his best and strongest work in one body together? That is the question which I, who can even remember the latter years of Byron's vogue, and have myself felt the expiring wave of that mighty influence, but who certainly also regard him, and have long regarded him, without illusion, cannot but ask myself, cannot but seek to answer. The present volume is an attempt to provide adequate data for answering it.

Byron has been over-praised, no doubt. 'Byron is one of our French superstitions,' says M. Edmond Scherer;[4] but where has Byron not been a superstition? He pays now the penalty of this exaggerated worship. 'Alone among the English poets his contemporaries, Byron,' said M. Taine,[5] '*atteint à la cîme*, – gets to the top of the poetic mountain.' But the idol that M. Taine had thus adored, M. Scherer is almost for burning. 'In Byron,' he declares, 'there is a remarkable inability ever to lift himself into the region of real poetic art, – art impersonal and disinterested, – at all. He has fecundity, eloquence, wit, but even these qualities themselves are confined within somewhat narrow limits. He has treated hardly any subject but one, – himself; now the man, in Byron, is of a nature even less sincere than the poet. This beautiful and blighted being is at bottom a coxcomb. He posed all his life long.'

Our poet could not well meet with more severe and unsympathetic criticism. However, the praise often given to Byron has been so exaggerated as to provoke perhaps a reaction in which he is unduly disparaged. 'As various in composition as Shakespeare himself, Lord Byron has embraced,' says Sir Walter Scott, 'every topic of human life, and sounded every string on the divine harp, from its slightest to its most powerful and heart-astounding tones.' It is not surprising that some one with a cool head should retaliate, on such provocation as this, by saying: 'He has treated hardly any subject but one, *himself*.' 'In the very grand and tremendous drama of *Cain*,' says Scott, 'Lord Byron has certainly matched Milton on his own ground.'[6] And Lord Byron has done all this, Scott adds, 'while managing his pen with the careless and negligent ease of a man of quality.'

Alas, 'managing his pen with the careless and negligent ease of a man of quality,' Byron wrote in his *Cain* –

> 'Souls that dare look the Omnipotent tyrant in
> His everlasting face, and tell him that
> His evil is not good;'[7]

or he wrote –

> '. . . And *thou* would'st go on aspiring
> To the great double Mysteries! the *two Principles!*'[8]

One has only to repeat to oneself a line from *Paradise Lost* in order to feel the difference.

Sainte-Beuve, speaking of that exquisite master of language, the Italian poet Leopardi,[9] remarks how often we see the alliance, singular though it may at first sight appear, of the poetical genius with the genius for scholarship and philology. Dante and Milton are instances which will occur to everyone's mind. Byron is so negligent in his poetical style, he is often, to say the truth, so slovenly, slipshod, and infelicitous, he is so little haunted by the true artist's fine passion for the correct use and consummate management of words, that he may be described as having for this artistic gift the insensibility of the barbarian; – which is perhaps only another and a less flatering way of saying, with Scott, that he 'manages his pen with the careless and negligent ease of a man of quality.' Just of a piece with the rhythm of

> 'Dare you await the event of a few minutes'
> Deliberation?'

or of

> 'All shall be void –
> Destroy'd!'

is the diction of

> 'Which now is painful to these eyes,
> Which have not seen the sun to rise!'

or of

> '. . . there let him lay!'

or of the famous passage beginning

> 'He who hath bent him o'er the dead;'[10]

with those trailing relatives, that crying grammatical solecism,
that inextricable anacolouthon!'[11] To class the work of the author
of such things with the work of the authors of such verse as

> 'In the dark backward and abysm of time' –'[12]

or as

> 'Presenting Thebes, or Pelops' line,
> Or the tale of Troy divine"[13] –

is ridiculous. Shakespeare and Milton, with their secret of consummate felicity in diction and movement, are of another and
an altogether higher order from Byron, nay, for that matter,
from Wordsworth also; from the author of such verse as

> 'Sol hath dropt into his harbour"[14] –

or (if Mr Ruskin pleases) as

> 'Parching summer hath no warrant"[15] –

as from the author of

> 'All shall be void –
> Destroy'd!'

With a poetical gift and a poetical performance of the very highest order, the slovenliness and tunelessness of much of Byron's production, the pompousness and ponderousness of much of Wordsworth's are incompatible. Let us admit this to the full.

Moreover, while we are hearkening to M. Scherer, and going along with him in his fault-finding, let us admit, too, that the man in Byron is in many respects as unsatisfactory as the poet. And, putting aside all direct moral criticism of him, – with which we need not concern ourselves here, – we shall find that he is unsatisfactory in the same way. Some of Byron's most crying faults as a man, – his vulgarity, his affectation, – are really akin to the faults of commonness, of want of art, in his workmanship as a poet. The ideal nature for the poet and artist is that of the finely touched and finely gifted man, the εὐφυής of the Greeks; now, Byron's nature was in substance not that of the εὐφυής at all, but rather, as I have said, of the barbarian. The want of fine perception which made it possible for him to formulate either the comparison between himself and Rousseau,[16] or his reason for getting Lord Delawarr excused from a 'licking' at Harrow,[17] is exactly what made possible for him also his terrible dealings in, *An ye wool*; *I have redde thee*; *Sunburn me*; *Oons, and it is excellent well.*[18] It is exactly, again, what made possible for him his precious dictum that Pope is a Greek temple,[19] and a string of other criticisms of the like force; it is exactly, in fine, what deteriorated the quality of his poetic production. If we think of a good representative of that finely touched and exquisitely gifted nature which is the ideal nature for the poet and artist, – if we think of Raphael, for instance, who truly is εὐφυής just as Byron is not, – we shall bring into clearer light the connection in Byron between the faults of the man and the faults of the poet. With Raphael's character Byron's sins of vulgarity and false criticism would have been impossible, just as with Raphael's art Byron's sins of common and bad workmanship.

Yes, all this is true, but it is not the whole truth about Byron nevertheless; very far from it. The severe criticism of M. Scherer by no means gives us the whole truth about Byron, and we have not yet got it in what has been added to that criticism here. The negative part of the true criticism of him we perhaps have; the positive part, by far the more important, we have not. Byron's admirers appeal eagerly to foreign testimonies in his favour. Some of these testimonies do not much move me; but one testimony there is among them which will always carry, with me at any rate, very great weight, – the testimony of Goethe. Goethe's sayings about Byron were uttered, it must however be remembered, at the height of Byron's vogue, when that puissant and splendid personality was exercising its full power of attraction. In Goethe's own household there was an atmosphere of glowing Byron-worship; his daughter-in-law was a passionate admirer of Byron, nay, she enjoyed and prized his poetry, as did Tieck[20] and so many others in Germany at that time, much above the poetry of Goethe himself. Instead of being irritated and rendered jealous by this, a nature like Goethe's was inevitably led by it to heighten, not lower, the note of his praise. The Time-Spirit, or *Zeit-Geist*, he would himself have said, was working just then for Byron. This working of the *Zeit-Geist* in his favour was an advantage added to Byron's other advantages, an advantage of which he had a right to get the benefit. This is what Goethe would have thought and said to himself; and so he would have been led even to heighten somewhat his estimate of Byron, to accentuate the emphasis of praise. Goethe speaking of Byron at that moment was not and could not be quite the same cool critic as Goethe speaking of Dante, or Molière, or Milton. This, I say, we ought to remember in reading Goethe's judgments on Byron and his poetry. Still, if we are careful to bear this in mind, and if we quote Goethe's praise correctly, – which is not always done by those who in this country quote it, – and if we add to it that great and due qualification added to it by Goethe himself, – which so far as I have seen has never yet been done by his quoters in this country at all, – then we shall have a judgment on Byron, which comes, I think, very near to the truth, and which may well command our adherence.

In his judicious and interesting Life of Byron, Professor Nichol[21] quotes Goethe as saying that Byron 'is undoubtedly to be regarded as the greatest genius of our century.'[22] What Goethe did really say was 'the greatest *talent*,' not 'the greatest *genius*.' The difference is important, because, while talent gives the notion of power in a man's performance, genius gives rather the notion of felicity and perfection in it; and this divine gift of consummate felicity by no means, as we have seen, belongs to Byron and to his poetry. Goethe said that Byron 'must unquestionably be regarded as the greatest talent of the century.'* He said of him moreover: 'The English may think of Byron what they please, but it is certain that they can point to no poet who is his like. He is different from all the rest, and in the main greater.'[23] Here, again, Professor Nichol translates: 'They can show no (living) poet who is to be compared to him;' – inserting the word *living*, I suppose, to prevent its being thought that Goethe would have ranked Byron, as a poet, above Shakespeare and Milton. But Goethe did not use, or, I think, mean to imply, any limitation such as is added by Professor Nichol. Goethe said simply, and he meant to say, '*no* poet.' Only the words which follow† ought not, I think, to be rendered, 'who is to be compared to him,' that is to say, '*who is his equal as a poet*.' They mean rather, 'who may properly be compared with him,' '*who is his parallel*.' And when Goethe said that Byron was 'in the main greater' than all the rest of the English poets, he was not so much thinking of the strict rank, as poetry, of Byron's production; he was thinking of that wonderful personality of Byron which so enters into his poetry, and which Goethe called 'a personality such, for its eminence, as has never been yet, and such as is not likely to come again.' He was thinking of that 'daring, dash, and grandiosity,'‡ of Byron, which are indeed so splendid; and which were, so Goethe maintained, of a character to do good, because 'everything great is formative,' and what is thus formative does us good.

---

* 'Der ohne Frage als das grösste Talent des Jahrhunderts anzusehen ist.'
† 'Der ihm zu vergleichen wäre.'
‡ 'Byron's Kühnheit, Keckheit und Grandiositat, ist das nicht alles bildend? – Alles Grosse bildet, sobald wir es gewahr werden.'

The faults which went with this greatness, and which impaired Byron's poetical work, Goethe saw very well. He saw the constant state of warfare and combat, the 'negative and polemical working,' which makes Byron's poetry a poetry in which we can so little find rest; he saw the *Hang zum Unbegrenzten*, the straining after the unlimited,[24] which made it impossible for Byron to produce poetic wholes such as the *Tempest* or *Lear*; he saw the *zu viel Empirie*,[25] the promiscuous adoption of all the matter offered to the poet by life, just as it was offered, without thought or patience for the mysterious transmutation to be operated on this matter by poetic form. But in a sentence which I cannot, as I say, remember to have yet seen quoted in any English criticism of Byron, Goethe lays his finger on the cause of all these defects in Byron, and on his real source of weakness both as a man and as a poet. 'The moment he reflects, he is a child,' says Goethe; – '*sobald er reflectirt ist er ein Kind.*'[26]

Now if we take the two parts of Goethe's criticism of Byron, the favourable and the unfavourable, and put them together, we shall have, I think, the truth. On the one hand, a splendid and puissant personality – a personality 'in eminence such as has never been yet, and is not likely to come again'; of which the like, therefore, is not to be found among the poets of our nation, by which Byron 'is different from all the rest, and in the main greater.' Byron is, moreover, 'the greatest talent of our century.' On the other hand, this splendid personality and unmatched talent, this unique Byron, 'is quite too much in the dark about himself;'* nay, 'the moment he begins to reflect, he is a child.' There we have, I think, Byron complete; and in estimating him and ranking him we have to strike a balance between the gain which accrues to his poetry, as compared with the productions of other poets, from his superiority, and the loss which accrues to it from his defects.

A balance of this kind has to be struck in the case of all poets except the few supreme masters in whom a profound criticism of life exhibits itself in indissoluble connection with the laws of poetic truth and beauty. I have seen it said that I allege poetry

---

* 'Gar zu dunkel über sich selbst.'

to have for its characteristic this: that it is a criticism of life; and that I make it to be thereby distinguished from prose, which is something else. So far from it, that when I first used this expression, *a criticism of life*, now many years ago,[27] it was to literature in general that I applied it, and not to poetry in especial. 'The end and aim of all literature,' I said, 'is, if one considers it attentively, nothing but that: *a criticism of life*.' And so it surely is; the main end and aim of all our utterance, whether in prose or in verse, is surely a criticism of life. We are not brought much on our way, I admit, towards an adequate definition of poetry as distinguished from prose by that truth; still a truth it is, and poetry can never prosper if it is forgotten. In poetry, however, the criticism of life has to be made conformably to the laws of poetic truth and poetic beauty. Truth and seriousness of substance and matter, felicity and perfection of diction and manner, as these are exhibited in the best poets, are what constitute a criticism of life made in conformity with the laws of poetic truth and poetic beauty; and it is by knowing and feeling the work of those poets, that we learn to recognize the fulfilment and non-fulfilment of such conditions.

The moment, however, that we leave the small band of the very best poets, the true classics, and deal with poets of the next rank, we shall find that perfect truth and seriousness of matter, in close alliance with perfect truth and felicity of manner, is the rule no longer. We have now to take what we can get, to forgo something here, to admit compensation for it there; to strike a balance, and to see how our poets stand in respect to one another when that balance has been struck. Let us observe how this is so.

We will take three poets, among the most considerable of our century: Leopardi, Byron, Wordsworth. Giacomo Leopardi was ten years younger than Byron, and he died thirteen years after him; both of them, therefore, died young – Byron at the age of thirty-six, Leopardi at the age of thirty-nine. Both of them were of noble birth, both of them suffered from physical defect, both of them were in revolt against the established facts and beliefs of their age; but here the likeness between them ends. The stricken poet of Recanati[28] had no country, for an Italy in his day did not exist; he had no audience, no celebrity. The volume of his poems, published in the very year of Byron's death, hardly sold, I suppose, its tens, while the volumes of Byron's poetry were selling their tens of thousands. And yet Leopardi has the very qualities which we have found wanting to Byron; he has the sense for form and style, the passion for just expression, the sure and firm touch of the true artist. Nay, more, he has a grave fulness of knowledge, an insight into the real bearings of the questions which as a sceptical poet he raises, a power of seizing the real point, a lucidity, with which the author of *Cain* has nothing to compare. I can hardly imagine Leopardi reading the

> '. . . And *thou* would'st go on aspiring
> To the great double Mysteries! the *two Principles!*'

or following Byron in his theological controversy with Dr Kennedy,[29] without having his features overspread by a calm and fine smile, and remarking of his brilliant contemporary, as Goethe did, that 'the moment he begins to reflect, he is a child.' But indeed whoever wishes to feel the full superiority of Leopardi over Byron in philosophic thought, and in the expression of it, has only to read one paragraph of one poem, the paragraph of *La Ginestra*, beginning

> 'Sovente in queste piagge,'

and ending

> 'Non so se il riso ŏla pietà prevale.'[30]

In like manner, Leopardi is at many points the poetic superior of Wordsworth too. He has a far wider culture than Wordsworth, more mental lucidity, more freedom from illusions as to the real character of the established fact and of reigning conventions; above all, this Italian, with his pure and sure touch, with his fineness of perception, is far more of the artist. Such a piece of pompous dulness as

> 'O for the coming of that glorious time,'[31]

and all the rest of it, or such lumbering verse as Mr Ruskin's enemy,

'Parching summer hath no warrant' –

would have been as impossible to Leopardi as to Dante. Where, then, is Wordsworth's superiority? for the worth of what he has given us in poetry I hold to be greater, on the whole, than the worth of what Leopardi has given us. It is in Wordsworth's sound and profound sense

'Of joy in widest commonalty spread;'[32]

whereas Leopardi remains with his thoughts ever fixed upon the *essenza insanabile*, upon the *acerbo, indegno mistero delle cose*.[33] It is in the power with which Wordsworth feels the resources of joy offered to us in nature, offered to us in the primary human affection and duties, and in the power with which, in his moments of inspiration, he renders this joy, and makes us, too, feel it; a force greater than himself seeming to lift him and to prompt his tongue, so that he speaks in a style far above any style of which he has the constant command, and with a truth far beyond any philosophic truth of which he has the conscious and assured possession. Neither Leopardi nor Wordsworth are of the same order with the great poets who made such verse as

Τλητὸν γὰρ Μοῖραι θυμὸν θέασν ἀνθφώποισιν[34]

or as

'In la sua volontade è nostra pace;'[35]

or as

'. . . Men must endure
Their going hence, even as their coming hither;
Ripeness is all.'[36]

But as compared with Leopardi, Wordsworth, though at many points less lucid, though far less a master of style, far less of an artist, gains so much by his criticism of life being, in certain matters of profound importance, healthful and true, whereas Leopardi's pessimism is not, that the value of Wordsworth's poetry, on the whole, stands higher for us than that of Leopardi's, as it stands higher for us, I think, than that of any modern poetry except Goethe's.

Byron's poetic value is also greater, on the whole, than Leopardi's; and his superiority turns in the same way upon the surpassing worth of something which he had and was, after all deduction has been made for his shortcomings. We talk of Byron's *personality*, 'a personality in eminence such as has never been yet, and is not likely to come again;' and we say that by this personality Byron is 'different from all the rest of English poets, and in the main greater.' But can we not be a little more circumstantial, and name that in which the wonderful power of this personality consisted? We can; with the instinct of a poet Mr Swinburne has seized upon it and named it for us. The power of Byron's personality lies in 'the splendid and imperishable excellence which covers all his offences and out-weighs all his defects: *the excellence of sincerity and strength*.'

Byron found our nation, after its long and victorious strug-gle with revolutionary France, fixed in a system of established facts and dominant ideas which revolted him. The mental bondage of the most powerful part of our nation, of its strong middle class, to a narrow and false system of this kind, is what we call British Philistinism. That bondage is unbroken to this hour, but in Byron's time it was even far more deep and dark than it is now. Byron was an aristocrat, and it is not difficult for an aristocrat to look on the prejudices and habits of the British Philistine with scepticism and disdain. Plenty of young men of his own class Byron met at Almack's or at Lady Jersey's,[37] who regarded the established facts and reigning beliefs of the England of that day with as little reverence as he did. But these men, disbelievers in British Philistinism in private, entered English public life, the most conventional in the world, and at once they saluted with respect the habits and ideas of British

Philistinism as if they were a part of the order of creation, and as if in public no sane man would think of warring against them. With Byron it was different. What he called the *cant* of the great middle part of the English nation, what we call its Philistinism, revolted him; but the cant of his own class, deferring to this Philistinism and profiting by it, while they disbelieved in it, revolted him even more. 'Come what may,' are his own words, 'I will never flatter the million's canting in any shape.'[38] His class in general, on the other hand, shrugged their shoulders at this cant, laughed at it, pandered to it, and ruled by it. The falsehood, cynicism, insolence, misgovernment, oppression, with their consequent unfailing crop of human misery, which were produced by this state of things, roused Byron to irreconcilable revolt and battle. They made him indignant, they infuriated him; they were so strong, so defiant, so maleficent, – and yet he felt that they were doomed. 'You have seen every trampler down in turn,' he comforts himself with saying, 'from Buonaparte to the simplest individuals.' The old order, as after 1815 it stood victorious, with its ignorance and misery below, its cant, selfishness, and cynicism above, was at home and abroad equally hateful to him. 'I have simplified my politics,' he writes, 'into an utter detestation of all existing governments.' And again: 'Give me a republic. The king-times are fast finishing; there will be blood shed like water and tears like mist, but the peoples will conquer in the end. I shall not live to see it, but I foresee it.'[39]

Byron himself gave the preference, he tells us, to politicians and doers, far above writers and singers. But the politics of his own day and of his own class, – even of the Liberals of his own class, – were impossible for him. Nature had not formed him for a Liberal peer, proper to move the Address in the House of Lords, to pay compliments to the energy and self-reliance of British middle-class Liberalism, and to adapt his politics to suit it. Unfitted for such politics, he threw himself upon poetry as his organ; and in poetry his topics were not Queen Mab, and the Witch of Atlas, and the Sensitive Plant[40] – they were the upholders of the old order, George the Third and Lord Castlereagh and the Duke of Wellington and Southey, and they were the canters and tramplers of the great world, and they were his enemies and himself.

Such was Byron's personality, by which 'he is different from all the rest of English poets, and in the main greater.' But he posed all his life, says M. Scherer. Let us distinguish. There is the Byron who posed, there is the Byron with his affectations and silliness, the Byron whose weakness Lady Blessington, with a woman's acuteness, so admirably seized: 'His great defect is flippancy and a total want of self-possession.'[41] But when this theatrical and easily criticized personage betook himself to poetry, and when he had fairly warmed to his work, then he became another man; then the theatrical personage passed away; then a higher power took possession of him and filled him; then at last came forth into light that true and puissant personality, with its direct strokes, its ever-welling force, its satire, its energy, and its agony. This is the real Byron; whoever stops at the theatrical preludings does not know him. And this real Byron may well be superior to the stricken Leopardi, he may well be declared 'different from all the rest of English poets, and in the main greater,' in so far as it is true of him, as M. Taine well says, that 'all other souls, in comparison with his, seem inert'; in so far as it is true of him that with superb, exhaustless energy, he maintained, as Professor Nichol well says, 'the struggle that keeps alive, if it does not save, the soul;' in so far, finally, as he deserves (and he does deserve) the noble praise of him which I have already quoted from Mr Swinburne; the praise for 'the splendid and imperishable excellence which covers all his offences and outweighs all his defects: *the excellence of sincerity and strength*.'

True, as a man, Byron could not manage himself, could not guide his ways aright, but was all astray. True, he has no light, cannot lead us from the past to the future; 'the moment he reflects, he is a child.' The way out of the false state of things which enraged him he did not see, – the slow and laborious way upward; he had not the patience, knowledge, self-discipline, virtue, requisite for seeing it. True, also, as a poet, he has no fine and exact sense for word and structure and rhythm; he has not the artist's nature and gifts. Yet a personality of Byron's force counts for so much in life, and a rhetorician of Byron's force counts for so much in literature! But it would be most unjust to label Byron, as M. Scherer is disposed to label him, as a rhetorician only. Along with his astounding power and passion he had a strong and deep sense for what is beautiful in nature, and for what is beautiful in human action and suffering. When he warms to his work, when he is inspired, Nature herself seems to take the pen from him as she took it from Wordsworth, and to write for him as she wrote for Wordsworth, though in a different fashion, with her own penetrating simplicity. Goethe has well observed of Byron, that when he is at his happiest his representation of things is as easy and real as if he were improvising. It is so; and his verse then exhibits quite another and a higher quality from the rhetorical quality, – admirable as this also in its own kind of merit is, – of such verse as

'Minions of splendour shrinking from distress,'[42]

and of so much more verse of Byron's of that stamp. Nature, I say, takes the pen for him; and then, assured master of a true poetic style though he is not, any more than Wordsworth, yet as from Wordsworth at his best there will come such verse as

'Will no one tell me what she sings?'[43]

so from Byron, too, at his best, there will come such verse as

'He heard it, but he heeded not; his eyes
Were with his heart, and that was far away.'[44]

Of verse of this high quality, Byron has much; of verse of a quality lower than this, of a quality rather rhetorical than truly poetic, yet still of extraordinary power and merit, he has still more. To separate, from the mass of poetry which Byron poured forth, all this higher portion, so superior to the mass, and still so considerable in quantity, and to present it in one body by itself, is to do a service, I believe, to Byron's reputation, and to the poetic glory of our country.

Such a service I have in the present volume attempted to perform. To Byron, after all the tributes which have been paid to him, here is yet one tribute more –

'Among thy mightier offerings here are mine!'[45]

not a tribute of boundless homage certainly, but sincere; a tribute which consists not in covering the poet with eloquent eulogy of our own, but in letting him, at his best and greatest, speak for himself. Surely the critic who does most for his author is the critic who gains readers for his author himself, not for any lucubrations on his author; – gains more readers for him, and enables those readers to read him with more admiration.

And in spite of his prodigious vogue, Byron has never yet, perhaps, had the serious admiration which he deserves. Society read him and talked about him, as it reads and talks about *Endymion* today;[46] and with the same sort of result. It looked in Byron's glass as it looks in Lord Beaconsfield's, and sees, or fancies that it sees, its own face there; and then it goes its way, and straightway forgets what manner of man it saw. Even of his passionate admirers, how many never got beyond the theatrical Byron, from whom they caught the fashion of deranging their hair, or of knotting their neck-handkerchief, or of leaving their shirt-collar unbuttoned; how few profoundly felt his vital influence, the influence of his splendid and imperishable excellence of sincerity and strength!

His own aristocratic class, whose cynical make-believe drove him to fury; the great middle class, on whose impregnable Philistinism he shattered himself to pieces, – how little have either of these felt Byron's vital influence! As the inevitable break-up of the old order comes, as the English middle class slowly awakens from its intellectual sleep of two centuries, as our actual present world, to which this sleep has condemned us, shows itself more clearly, – our world of an aristocracy materialized and null, a middle class purblind and hideous, a lower class crude and brutal, – we shall turn our eyes again, and to more purpose, upon this passionate and dauntless soldier of a forlorn hope, who, ignorant of the future and unconsoled by its promises, nevertheless waged against the conservation of the old impossible world so fiery a battle; waged it till he fell, – waged it with such splendid and imperishable excellence of sincerity and strength.

Wordsworth's value is of another kind. Wordsworth has an insight into permanent sources of joy and consolation for mankind which Byron has not; his poetry gives us more which we may rest upon than Byron's, – more which we can rest upon now, and which men may rest upon always. I place Wordsworth's poetry, therefore, above Byron's on the whole, although in some points he was greatly Byron's inferior, and although Byron's poetry will always, probably, find more readers than Wordsworth's, and will give pleasure more easily. But these two, Wordsworth and Byron, stand, it seems to me, first and pre-eminent in actual performance, a glorious pair, among the English poets of this century. Keats had probably, indeed, a more consummate poetic gift than either of them; but he died having produced too little and being as yet too immature to rival them. I for my part can never even think of equalling with them any other of their contemporaries; – either Coleridge, poet and philosopher wrecked in a mist of opium; or Shelley, beautiful and ineffectual angel, beating in the void his luminous wings in vain. Wordsworth and Byron stand out by themselves. When the year 1900 is turned, and our nation comes to recount her poetic glories in the century which has then just ended, the first names with her will be these.

Letters

To A. H. Clough[1]

London. Tuesday.
[December 1847; or early part of 1848]

My dearest Clough

... One does not always remember that one of the signs of the Decadence of a literature, one of the factors of its decadent condition indeed, is this – that new authors attach themselves to the poetic expression the founders of a literature have flowered into, which may be *learnt* by a sensitive person, to the neglect of an inward poetic life. The strength of the German literature consists in this – that having no national models from whence to get an idea of *style* as half the work, they were thrown upon themselves, and driven to make the fulness of the content of a work atone for deficiencies of form. Even Goethe at the end of his life has not the inversions, the taking tourmenté style we admire in the Latins, in some of the Greeks, and in the great French and English authors. And had Shakespeare and Milton lived in the atmosphere of modern feeling, had they had the multitude of new thoughts and feelings to deal with a modern has, I think it likely the style of each would have been far less *curious* and exquisite. For in a *man* style is the saying in the best way *what you have to say*. The *what you have to say* depends on your age. In the seventeenth century it was *a smaller harvest than now*, and sooner to be reaped: and, therefore, to its reaper was left time to stow it more finely and curiously. Still more was this the case in the ancient world. The poet's matter being *the hitherto experience of the world, and his own*, increases with every century ...

To A. H. Clough

Lansdowne House Monday [March 6, 1848]

... It is this – this *wide and deepspread intelligence* that makes the French seem to themselves in the van of Europe. People compare a class here with a class there the best in each, and then wonder at Michelet's or Guizot's vanity. I don't think you have done them justice in this respect. Do you remember your pooh-poohing the revue des deux Mondes, and my expostulating that the final expression up to the present time of European opinion, without fantastic individual admixture, was *current* there; not emergent here and there in a great writer, – but the *atmosphere* of the commonplace man as well as of the Genius. This is the secret of their power: our weakness is that in an age where all tends to the triumph of the logical absolute reason we neither courageously have thrown ourselves into this movement like the French: nor yet have driven our feet into the solid ground of our individuality as spiritual, poetic, profound *persons*. Instead of this we have stood *up* hesitating: seeming to refuse the first line on the ground that the second is our *natural* one – yet not taking this. How long halt ye between two opinions: woe to the modern nation, which will neither be philosophe nor philosopher. Eh?

Yours with apologies for longness

M. Arnold

Yet is it something for a nation to feel that the only true line is its natural one?

To his Mother

Tuesday (March 7, 1848).

Dear Mamma – You need not return the *National;* I send you the *Examiner* with an article of Carlyle's.[2] How deeply restful it comes upon one, amidst the hot dizzy trash one reads about these changes everywhere. I send Price's letter. I think I thought much the same about the decisive point of ruin to the king's affairs.[3] As for his conscience, I incline to think he was only old and nervous. Certainly, taken individually, the French people, no more than one's own, are up to the measure of the ideal citizen they seem to propose to themselves; this thought constantly presses on me, but the question to be tried is whether the proclamation of this ideal city and public recognition of it may not bring a nation nearer to that measure than the professedly unbelieving Governments hitherto for some time in force everywhere. The source of repose in Carlyle's article is that he alone puts aside the din and whirl and brutality which envelop a movement of the masses, to fix his thoughts on its ideal invisible character. I was in the great mob in Trafalgar Square yesterday, whereof the papers will instruct you; but they did not seem dangerous, and the police are always, I think, needlessly rough in *manner*. English too often are. It will be *rioting* here, only; still the hour of the hereditary peerage and eldest sonship and immense properties has, I am convinced, as Lamartine would say, struck. You know I think papa would by this time have been a kind of Saint Martin – the writer, not the Saint proper. But I do not think England will be liveable-in just yet. I see a wave of more than American *vulgarity*, moral, intellectual, and social, preparing to break over us. In a few years people will understand better why the French are the most civilized of European peoples, when they see how fictitious our manners and civility have been, how little inbred in the race.   – Ever yours, M. Arnold

To his Eldest Sister, afterwards Mrs Forster

Lansdowne House, *Friday, March 10, 1848.*

My dearest K. – My excuse for not answering you, dear child, must be that not having been privately disposed lately, it mattered little, I thought, to whom my public general chronicles or remarks were addressed. Would that I were coming home. It is so hard to sequester oneself here from the rush of public changes and talk, and yet so unprofitable to attend to it. I was myself tempted to attempt some political writing the other day, but in the watches of the night I seemed to feel that in that direction I had some enthusiasm of the head perhaps, but no profound stirring. So I desisted, and have only poured forth a little to Clough, we two agreeing like two lambs in a world of wolves. I think you would have liked to see the correspondence.

What agitates me is this, if the new state of things succeeds in France, social changes are *inevitable* here and elsewhere, for no one looks on seeing his neighbour mending without asking himself if he cannot mend in the same way; but, without waiting for the result, the spectacle of France is likely to breed great agitation here, and such is the state of our masses that their movements now *can* only be brutal plundering and destroying. And if they wait, there is no one, as far as one sees, to train them to conquer, by their attitude and superior conviction; the deep ignorance of the middle and upper classes, and their feebleness of vision becoming, if possible, daily more apparent. You must by this time begin to see what people mean by placing France *politically* in the van of Europe; it is the *intelligence* of their *idea-moved masses* which makes them, politically, as far superior to the *insensible masses* of England as to the Russian serfs, and at the same time they do not threaten the educated world with the intolerable *laideur* of the well-fed American masses, so deeply anti-pathetic to continental Europe . . .

To his Mother

Wednesday (April 1848*).*

Dear Mamma – Don't trouble yourself to send me papers. I see all papers at clubs, and so forth. To say the truth, the responsibility of sending back a paper weighs on my mind. The *National* of yesterday reports that London was *en pleine insurrection*.[4] Do you wish for the *National* always, or only when I think it interesting? I saw Emerson the other day, and had a very pleasant interview. I did not think him just to Wordsworth. He had a very just appreciation of Miss Martineau, which indeed no man of a certain delicacy of intellectual organization can fail to have. He said Carlyle was much agitated by the course of things; he had known, he said, a European revolution was inevitable, but had expected the old state of things to last out his time. He gives our institutions, as they are called, aristocracy, Church, etc., five years, I heard last night; long enough, certainly, for patience, already at death's door, to have to die in. I was at the Chartist convention the other night, and was much struck with the ability of the speakers. However, I should be sorry to live under their government – nor do I intend to – though

Nemesis would rejoice at their triumph. The ridiculous terror of people here is beyond belief, and yet it is not likely, I fear, to lead to any good results. Tell Miss Martineau it is said here that Monckton Milnes[5] refused to be sworn in a special constable that he might be free to assume the post of President of the Republic at a moment's notice. – Ever yours,   M. Arnold

To his Eldest Sister

Wednesday (May 1848).

... How plain it is now, though an attention to the comparative literatures for the last fifty years might have instructed any one of it, that England is in a certain sense *far behind* the Continent. In conversation, in the newspapers, one is so struck with the fact of the utter insensibility, one may say, of people to the number of ideas and schemes now ventilated on the Continent – not because they have judged them or seen beyond them, but from sheer habitual want of wide reading and thinking: like a child's intellectual attitude *vis-à-vis* of the proposition that Saturn's apparent diameter subtends an angle of about 18°. Our practical virtues never certainly revealed more clearly their isolation. I am not sure but I agree in Lamartine's prophecy that 100 years hence the Continent will be a great united Federal Republic, and England, all her colonies gone, in a dull steady decay.   M. A.

To his Mother

London, *May* 7 (1848).

My dearest Mamma – Though I believe the balance of correspondence is in my favour at present, I will write to you a few lines instead of sitting idle till Lord L.[6] summons me. I have just finished a German book I brought with me here: a mixture of poems and travelling journal by Heinrich Heine, the most famous of the young German literary set. He has a good deal of power, though more trick; however, he has thoroughly disgusted me. The Byronism of a German, of a man trying to be gloomy, cynical, impassioned, *moqueur*, etc., all *à la fois*, with their honest bonhommistic language and total want of experience of the kind that

Lord Byron, an English peer with access everywhere, possessed, is the most ridiculous thing in the world. Goethe wisely said the Germans could not have a national comedy because they had no social life; he meant the social life of highly civilized corrupt communities like Athens, Paris, or London; and for the same reason they cannot have a Byronic poetry. I see the French call this Heine a 'Voltaire au clair de lune,' which is very happy.

I have been returning to Goethe's Life, and think higher of him than ever. His thorough sincerity – writing about nothing that he had not experienced – is in modern literature almost unrivalled. Wordsworth resembles him in this respect; but the difference between the range of their two experiences is immense, and not in the Englishman's favour. I have also been again reading Las Casas, and been penetrated with admiration for Napoleon, though his southern recklessness of assertion is sometimes staggering. But the astonishing clearness and width of his views on almost all subjects, and when he comes to practise his energy and precision in arranging details, never struck me so much as now. His contest with England is in the highest degree tragic. The inability of the English of that time in any way to comprehend him, and yet their triumph over him – and the sense of this contrast in his own mind – there lies the point of the tragedy. The number of ideas in his head which 'were not dreamed of in their philosophy,' on government and the *future of Europe*, and yet their crushing him, really *with the best intentions*, but a total ignorance of him – what a subject! But it is too near at hand to be treated, I am afraid. To one who knew the English, his fate must have seemed inevitable; and, therefore, his plans have seemed imperfect; but what foreigner could divine the union of invincibility and speculative dulness in England? – Ever yours,   M. A.

To A. H. Clough

London. Monday. [after September 1848–9]
My dearest Clough

What a brute you were to tell me to read Keats' Letters.[7] However it is over now: and reflection resumes her power over agitation.

What harm he has done in English Poetry. As Browning is a man with a moderate gift passionately desiring movement and fulness, and obtaining but a confused multitudinousness, so Keats with a very high gift, is yet also consumed by this desire: and cannot produce the truly living and moving, as his conscience keeps telling him. They will not be patient neither understand that they must begin with an Idea of the world in order not to be prevailed over by the world's multitudinousness: or if they cannot get that, at least with isolated ideas: and all other things shall (perhaps) be added unto them.

– I recommend you to follow up these letters with the Laocoön of Lessing: it is not quite satisfactory, and a little mare's nesty – but very searching.

– I have had that desire of fulness without respect of the means, which may become almost maniacal: but nature had placed a bar thereto not only in the conscience (as with all men) but in a great numbness in that direction. But what perplexity Keats Tennyson et id genus omne must occasion to young writers of the $\delta\pi\lambda\iota\tau\eta\varsigma$[8] sort: yes and those d—d Elizabethan poets generally. Those who cannot read Greek should read nothing but Milton and parts of Wordsworth: the state should see to it: for the failures of the $\sigma\tau\alpha\theta\mu o\iota$[9] may leave them good citizens enough, as Trench: but the others go to the dogs failing or succeeding.

So much for this inspired 'cheeper' as they are saying on the moon.

My own good man farewell.

M. A.

To A. H. Clough

Lansdowne House
Friday [early part of February 1849]

My dear Clough –

If I were to say the real truth as to your poems in general, as they impress me – it would be this – that they are not *natural*.

Many persons with far lower gifts than yours yet seem to find that natural mode of expression in poetry, and tho: the contents

may not be very valuable they appeal with justice from the judgment of the mere thinker to the world's general appreciation of
naturalness – i.e. – an absolute propriety – of form, as the sole
necessary of Poetry as such: whereas the greatest wealth and
depth of matter is merely a superfluity in the Poet *as such*.

– Form of Conception comes by nature certainly, but is generally developed late: but this lower form, of expression, is
found from the beginning among all born poets, even feeble
thinkers, and in an unpoetical age: as Collins, Green, and fifty
more, in England only.

The question is not of congruity between conception and
expression: which when both are poetical, is the poet's highest
result: – you say what you mean to say: but in such a way as to
leave it doubtful whether your mode of expression is not quite
arbitrarily adopted.

I often think that even a slight gift of poetical expression
which in a common person might have developed itself easily
and naturally, is overlaid and crushed in a profound thinker so
as to be of no use to him to help him to express himself. – The
trying to go into and to the bottom of an object instead of
grouping *objects* is as fatal to the sensuousness of poetry as the
mere painting, (for, *in Poetry*, this is not *grouping*) is to its airy
and rapidly moving life.

'Not deep the Poet sees, but wide':[10] – think of this as you gaze
from the Cumner Hill towards Cirencester and Cheltenham.

– You succeed best you see, in fact, in the hymn, where man,
his deepest personal feelings being in play, finds poetical expression as *man* only, not as artist: – but consider whether you
attain the *beautiful*, and whether your product gives PLEASURE,
not excites curiosity and reflection. Forgive me all this: but I am
always prepared myself to give up the attempt, on conviction:
and so, I know, are you: and I only urge you to reflect whether
you are advancing. Reflect, too, as I cannot but do here more and
more, in spite of all the nonsense some people talk, how deeply
unpoetical the age and all one's surroundings are. Not unpro-
found, not ungrand, not unmoving: – but *unpoetical*.

Ever yrs
M. A.

To A. H. Clough

[about March 1, 1849]

... It is true about form: something of the same sort is in my letter which crossed yours on the road. On the other hand, there are two offices of Poetry – one to add to one's store of thoughts and feelings – another to compose and elevate the mind by a sustained tone, numerous allusions, and a grand style. What other process is Milton's than this last, in Comus for instance. There is no fruitful analysis of character: but a great effect is produced. What is Keats? A style and form seeker, and this with an impetuosity that heightens the effect of his style almost painfully. Nay in Sophocles what is valuable is not so much his contributions to psychology and the anatomy of sentiment, as the grand moral effects produced by *style*. For the style is the expression of the nobility of the poet's character, as the matter is the expression of the richness of his mind: but on men character produces as great an effect as mind ...

To A. H. Clough

Thun. Sunday. Sept^ber 23 [1849]

My dear Clough

I wrote to you from this place last year. It is long since I have communicated with you and I often think of you among the untoward generation with whom I live and of whom all I read testifies. With me it is curious at present: I am getting to feel more independent and unaffectible as to all intellectual and poetical performance the impatience at being faussé in which drove me some time since so strongly into myself, and more snuffing after a moral atmosphere to respire in than ever before in my life. Marvel not that I say unto you, ye must be born again. While I will not much talk of these things, yet the considering of them has led me constantly to you the only living one almost that I know of of

> The children of the second birth
> Whom the world could not tame –[11]

for my dear Tom has not sufficient besonnenheit[12] for it to be any *rest* to think of him any more than it is a *rest* to think of mystics and such cattle – not that Tom is in any sense cattle or even a mystic but he has not a 'still, considerate mind'.

What I must tell you is that I have never yet succeeded in any one great occasion in consciously mastering myself: I can go thro: the imaginary process of mastering myself and see the whole affair as it would then stand, but at the critical point I am too apt to hoist up the mainsail to the wind and let her drive. However, as I get more awake to this it will I hope mend for I find that with me a clear almost palpable intuition (damn the logical senses of the word) is necessary before I get into prayer: unlike many people who set to work at their duty self-denial etc. like furies in the dark hoping to be gradually illuminated as they persist in this course. Who also perhaps may be sheep but not of my fold, whose one natural craving is not for profound thoughts, mighty spiritual workings etc. etc. but a distinct seeing of my way as far as my own nature is concerned: which I believe to be the reason why the mathematics were ever foolishness to me.

– I am here in a curious and not altogether comfortable state: however, tomorrow I carry my aching head to the mountains and to my cousin the Bhunlis Alp.

> Fast, fast by my window
> The rushing winds go
> Towards the ice-cumber'd gorges,
> The vast fields of snow.
> There the torrents drive upward
> Their rock strangled hum,
> And the avalanche thunders
> The hoarse torrent dumb.
> I come, O ye mountains –
> Ye torrents, I come,[13]

Yes, I come, but in three or four days I shall be back here, and then I must try how soon I can ferociously turn towards England.

My dearest Clough these are damned times – everything is

against one – the height to which knowledge is come, the spread of luxury, our physical enervation, the absence of great *natures*, the unavoidable contact with millions of small ones, newspapers, cities, light profligate friends, moral desperadoes like Carlyle, our own selves, and the sickening consciousness of our difficulties: but for God's sake let us neither be fantasies nor yet chaff blown by the wind but let us be *ὡς ὁ φρόνιμος διαρίσειεν* and not as any one else *διαρίσειεν*.[14] When I come to town I tell you beforehand I will have a real effort at managing myself as to newspapers and the talk of the day. Why the devil do I read about L^d. Grey's sending convicts to the Cape, and excite myself thereby, when I can thereby produce no possible good. But public opinion consists in a multitude of such excitements. Thou fool – that which is morally worthless remains so, and undesired by Heaven, whatever results flow from it. And which of the units which has felt the excitement caused by reading of Lord Grey's conduct has been made one iota a better man thereby, or can honestly call his excitement a *moral* feeling.

You will not I know forget me. You cannot answer this letter for I know not how I come home.

Yours faithfully,

M. A.

To his Wife

Oldham Road Lancasterian School,
Manchester, *October* 15, 1851.

I think I shall get interested in the schools after a little time; their effects on the children are so immense, and their future effects in civilizing the next generation of the lower classes, who, as things are going, will have most of the political power of the country in their hands, may be so important. It is really a fine sight in Manchester to see the anxiety felt about them, and the time and money the heads of their cotton-manufacturing population are willing to give to them. In arithmetic, geography, and history the excellence of the schools I have seen is quite wonderful, and almost all the children have an equal amount of information; it is not confined, as in schools of the richer classes, to the one or two cleverest boys. We shall certainly have a good deal of moving about; but we both like that well enough, and we can always look forward to retiring to Italy on £200 a year. I intend seriously to see what I can do in such a case in the literary way that might increase our income. But for the next three or four years I think we shall both like it well enough . . .

To A. H. Clough

6. Goldsmiths Building
Frances St. Edgbaston
June 7th 1852

. . . Au reste, a great career is hardly possible any longer – can hardly now be purchased even by the sacrifice of repose dignity and inward clearness – so I call no man unfortunate. I am more and more convinced that the world tends to become more comfortable for the mass, and more uncomfortable for those of any natural gift or distinction – and it is as well perhaps that it should be so – for hitherto the gifted have astonished and delighted the world, but not trained or inspired or in any real way changed it – and the world might do worse than to dismiss too high pretensions, and settle down on what it can see and handle and appreciate. I am sometimes in bad spirits, but generally in better than I used to be. I am sure however that in the air of the present times il nous manque d'aliment, and that we deteriorate in spite of our struggles – like a gifted Roman falling on the uninvigorating atmosphere of the decline of the Empire. Still nothing can absolve us from the duty of doing all we can to keep alive our courage and activity . . .

To A. H. Clough

Milford Boys School Oct[ber] 28 1852

. . . More and more I feel that the difference between a mature and a youthful age of the world compels the poetry of the former to use great plainness of speech as compared with that of the latter: and that Keats and Shelley were on a false track when they set themselves to reproduce the exuberance of expression, the charm, the richness of images, and the felicity, of the Elizabethan poets. Yet critics cannot get to learn this, because the Elizabethan poets are our greatest, and our canons of poetry are founded on their works. They still think that the object of poetry is to produce exquisite bits and images – such as Shelley's *clouds shepherded by the slow unwilling wind*, and Keats passim: whereas modern poetry can only subsist by its *contents*: by becoming a complete magister vitae as the poetry of the ancients did: by including, as theirs did, religion with poetry, instead of existing as poetry only, and leaving religious wants to be supplied by the Christian religion, as a power existing independent of the poetical power. But the language, style and general proceedings of a poetry which has such an immense task to perform, must be very plain direct and severe: and it must not lose itself in parts and episodes and ornamental work, but must press forwards to the whole ...

To A. H. Clough

Edgbaston. February 12th, 1853

My dear Clough

I received your letter ten days since – just as I was leaving London – but I have since that time had too much to do to attempt answering it, or indeed to attempt any thing else that needed any thing of 'recueillement'. I do not like to put off writing any longer, but to say the truth I do not feel in the vein to write even now, nor do I feel certain that I can write as I should wish. I am past thirty, and three parts iced over – and my pen, it seems to me, is even stiffer and more cramped than my feeling.

But I will write historically, as I can write naturally in no other way. I did not really think you had been hurt at anything I did or left undone while we were together in town: that is, I did not think any impression of hurt you might have had for a moment, had lasted. I remember your being annoyed once or twice, and that I was vexed with myself: but at that time I was absorbed in my speculations and plans and agitations respecting Fanny Lucy,[15] and was as egoistic and anti-social as possible. People in the condition in which I then was always are. I thought I had said this and explained one or two pieces of apparent carelessness in this way: and that you had quite understood it. So entirely indeed am I convinced that being in love generally unfits a man for the society of his friends, that I remember often smiling to myself at my own selfishness in half compelling you several times to meet me in the last few months before you left England, and thinking that it was only I who could make such unreasonable demands or find pleasure in meeting and being with a person, for the mere sake of meeting and being with them, without regarding whether they would be absent and preoccupied or not. I never, while we were both in London, had any feeling towards you but one of attachment and affection: if I did not enter into much explanation when you expressed annoyance, it was really because I thought the mention of my circumstances accounted for all and more than all that had annoyed you. I remember Walrond telling me you were vexed one day that on a return to town after a longish absence I let him stop in Gordon Square without me: I was then expecting to find a letter – or something of that sort – it all seems trivial now, but it was enough at the time to be the cause of heedlessness selfishness and heartlessness – in all directions but one – without number. It ought not to have been so perhaps – but it was so – and I quite thought you had understood that it was so.

There was one time indeed – shortly after you had published the Bothie – that I felt a strong disposition to intellectual seclusion, and to the barring out all influences that I felt troubled without advancing me: but I soon found that it was needless to secure myself against a danger from which my own weakness even more than my strength – my coldness and want of intellectual robustness – sufficiently exempted me – and besides your company and mode of being always had a charm and a salutary effect for me, and I could not have forgone these on a mere theory of intellectual dietetics.

In short, my dear Clough, I cannot say more than that I really have clung to you in spirit more than to any other man – and have never been seriously estranged from you at any time – for the estrangement I have just spoken of was merely a contemplated one and it never took place: I remember saying something about it to you at the time – and your answer, which

struck me for the genuineness and faith it exhibited as compared with my own – not want of faith exactly – but invincible
languor of spirit, and fickleness and insincerity even in the
gravest matters. All this is dreary work – and I cannot go on
with it now: but tomorrow night I will try again – for I have
one or two things more to say. Goodnight now. –

Sunday, 6 P.M.
I will not look at what I wrote last night – one endeavours to
write deliberately out what is in one's mind, without any veils
of flippancy levity metaphor or demi-mot, and one succeeds
only in putting upon the paper a string of dreary dead sentences that correspond to nothing in one's inmost heart or
mind, and only represent themselves. It was your own fault
partly for forcing me to it. I will not go on with it: only remember, *pray* remember that I am and always shall be, whatever I
do or say, powerfully attracted towards you, and vitally connected with you: this I am sure of: the period of my development
(God forgive me the d—d expression!) coincides with that of
my friendship with you so exactly that I am for ever linked
with you by intellectual bonds – the strongest of all: more than
you are with me: for your development was really over before
you knew me, and you had properly speaking come to your
assiette for life. You ask me in what I think or have thought you
going wrong: in this: that you would never take your assiette as
something determined final and unchangeable for you and proceed to work away on the basis of that: but were always poking
and patching and cobbling at the assiette itself – could never
finally, as it seemed – 'resolve to be thyself'[16] – but were looking
for this and that experience, and doubting whether you ought not
to adopt this or that mode of being of persons qui ne vous val-
aient pas because it might possibly be nearer the truth than your
own: you had no reason for thinking it *was*, but it *might* be – and
you would try to adapt yourself to it. You have I am convinced
lost infinite time in this way: it is what I call your morbid consci-
entiousness – you are the most conscientious man I ever knew:
but on some lines morbidly so, and it spoils your action.

There – but now we will have done with this: we are each

very near to each other – write and tell me that you feel this: as to my behaviour in London I have told you the simple truth: it is I fear too simple than that (excuse the idiom) you with your raffinements should believe and appreciate it.

There is a power of truth in your letter and in what you say about America and this country: yes – *congestion of the brain* is what we suffer from – I always feel it and say it – and cry for air like my own Empedocles. But this letter shall be what it is. I have a number of things I want to talk to you about – they shall wait till I have heard again from you. Pardon me, but we *will* exchange intellectual aperçus – we shall both be the better for it. Only let us pray all the time – God keep us both from aridity! *Arid* – that is what the times are. – Write soon and tell me you are well – I was sure you were not well. God bless you. Flu sends her kindest remembrances. ever yours.

M. A.

To A. H. Clough

Fox How. September 6ᵗʰ [1853]

. . . As to conformity I only recommend it in so far as it frees us from the unnatural and unhealthy attitude of contradiction and opposition – the *Qual der Negation* as Goethe calls it. Only positive convictions and feeling are worth anything – and the glow of these one can never feel so long as one is pugnacious and out of temper. This is my firm belief.

I do not believe that the Reformation caused the Elizabethan literature – but that both sprang out of the active animated condition of the human spirit in Europe at that time. After the fall of the Roman Empire the barbarians powerfully turned up the soil of Europe – and after a little time when the violent ploughing was over and things had settled a little, a vigorous crop of new ideas was the result. Italy bore the first crop – but the soil having been before much exhausted soon left bearing. The virgin soils of Germany and England went on longer – but they, too, are I think beginning to fail. I think there never yet has been a perfect literature or a perfect art because the energetic nations spoil them by their illusions and their want of taste – and the nations who lose their illusions lose also their energy and creative power. Certainly Goethe had all the *negative* recommendations for a perfect artist but he wanted the *positive* – Shakespeare had the positive and wanted the negative. The Iliad and what I know of Raphael's works seem to me to be in a juster measure and a happier vein than anything else.

If one loved what was beautiful and interesting in itself *passionately* enough, one would produce what was excellent without troubling oneself with religious dogmas at all. As it is, we are *warm* only when dealing with these last – and what is frigid is always bad. I would have others – most others stick to the old religious dogmas because I sincerely feel that this *warmth* is the great blessing, and this frigidity the great curse – and on the old religious road they have still the best chance of getting the one and avoiding the other.

ever yours

M. A.

To A. H. Clough

Derby, October 10th [1853]

... The Preface[17] is done – there is a certain *Geist* in it I think, but it is far less *precise* than I had intended. How difficult it is to write prose: and why? because of the *articulations of the discourse*: one leaps these over in Poetry – places one thought cheek by jowl with another without introducing them and leaves them – but in prose this will not do. It is, of course, not right in poetry either – but we all do it ...

To A. H. Clough

Coleby – November 30th [1853]

My dear Clough

I think 'if indeed this one desire rules all'[18] – *is* rather Tennysonian – at any rate it is not good.

The resemblance in the other passage I cannot for the life of me see.

I think the poem[19] has, if not the *rapidity*, at least the *fluidity* of Homer: and that it is in this respect that it is un-Tennysonian: and that it is a sense of this which makes Froude and Blackett say it is a step in advance of Tennyson in this strain.

A thousand things make one compose or not compose: composition seems to keep alive in me a *cheerfulness* – a sort of Tuchtigkeit, or natural soundness and valiancy, which I think the present age is fast losing – this is why I like it.

I am glad you like the Gipsy Scholar – but what does it *do* for you? Homer *animates* – Shakespeare *animates* – in its poor way I think Sohrab and Rustum *animates* – the Gipsy Scholar at best awakens a pleasing melancholy. But this is not what we want.

> The complaining millions of men
> Darken in labour and pain –[20]

what they want is something to *animate* and *ennoble* them – not merely to add zest to their melancholy or grace to their dreams. – I believe a feeling of this kind is the basis of my nature – and of my poetics.

You certainly do not seem to me sufficiently to desire and earnestly strive towards – assured knowledge – activity – happiness. You are too content to *fluctuate* – to be ever learning, never coming to the knowledge of the truth. This is why, with you, I feel it necessary to stiffen myself – and hold fast my rudder.

My poems, however, viewed *absolutely*, are certainly little or nothing . . .

To Mrs Forster

London, Saturday. 1853

. . . Fret not yourself to make my poems square in all their parts, but like what you can my darling. The true reason why parts suit you while others do not is that my poems are fragments – *i.e.* that I am fragments, while you are a whole; the whole effect of my poems is quite vague & indeterminate – this is their weakness; a person, therefore, who endeavoured to make them accord would only lose his labour; and a person who has any inward completeness can at best only like parts of them; in fact such a person stands firmly and knows what he is about while the poems stagger weakly & are at their wits end. I shall do better some day I hope – meanwhile change nothing, resign nothing that you have in deference to me or my oracles; & do not plague yourself to find a consistent meaning for these last, which in fact they do not possess through my weakness.

There – I would not be so frank as that with everyone ...

To W. D. Arnold[21]

Director of Public Instruction, Punjab, India.

Belgrave Street, London, March 31st, 1856.

My dearest Willy, –

... I too have felt the absurdity and disadvantage of our heredity connection in the minds of all people with education, and am always tempted to say to people, 'My good friends, this is a matter for which my father certainly had a specialité, but for which I have none whatever.' You, however, will throw yourself thoroughly into the work, and will do it well. You have more to do of an important kind than I have, certainly, but whatever you had to do, you would have thrown yourself heartily into and would have done it well – in this way you cease to feel the burden of the work. I on the contrary half cannot half will not throw myself into it, and feel the weight of it doubly in consequence. I am inclined to think it would have been the same with any active line of life on which I had found myself engaged – even with politics – so I am glad my sphere is a humble one and must try more and more to do something worth doing in my own way, since I cannot bring myself to do more than a halting sort of half-work in other people's way ...

To Mrs Forster

Martigny, September 6, 1858.

... Kingsley's remarks were very *handsome*, especially coming from a brother in the craft. I should like to send you a letter which I had from Froude about *Merope*, just at the same time that your record of Kingsley's criticisms reached me. If I can find it when I return to England I will send it to you. It was to beg me to discontinue the *Merope* line, but entered into very interesting developments, as the French say, in doing so. Indeed, if the opinion of the general public about my poems were the same as that of the leading literary men, I should make more money by them than I do. But, more than this, I should gain the stimulus necessary to enable me to produce my best – all that I have in me, whatever that may be, – to produce which is no light matter with an existence so hampered as mine is. People do not understand what a temptation there is, if you cannot bear anything not *very good*, to transfer your operations to a region where form is everything. Perfection of a certain kind may there be attained, or at least approached, without knocking yourself to pieces, but to attain or approach perfection in the region of thought and feeling, and to unite this with perfection of form, demands not merely an effort and a labour, but an actual tearing of oneself to pieces, which one does not readily consent to (although one is sometimes forced to it) unless one can devote one's whole life to poetry. Wordsworth could give his whole life to it, Shelley and Byron both could, and were besides driven by their demon to do so. Tennyson, a far inferior natural power to either of the three, can; but of the moderns Goethe is the only one, I think, of those who have had an *existence assujettie*, who has thrown himself with a great result into poetry. And even he felt what I say, for he could, no doubt, have done more, *poetically*, had he been freer; but it is not so light a matter, when you have other grave claims on your powers, to submit voluntarily to the exhaustion of the best poetical production in a time like this. Goethe speaks somewhere of the endless matters on which he had employed himself, and says that with the labour he had given to them he might have produced half a dozen more good tragedies; but to produce these, he says, I must have been *sehr zerrissen*.[22] It is only in the best poetical epochs (such as the Elizabethan) that you can descend into yourself and produce the best of your thought and feeling naturally, and without an overwhelming and in some degree morbid effort; for then all the people around you are more or less doing the same thing. It is natural, it is the bent of the time to do it; its being the bent of the time, indeed, is what makes the time a *poetical* one. But enough of this . . .

To Mrs Forster

London, *February* 16, 1859.
I thought of starting next Monday week, but I shall hardly be ready by that time, besides, I think of being presented at the *levée* on 2nd March, in order to be capable of going to Courts abroad, if necessary. I like the thoughts of the Mission more and more. You know that I have no special interest in the subject of public education, but a mission like this appeals even to the general interest which every educated man cannot help feeling in such a subject. I shall for five months get free from the routine work of it, of which I sometimes get very sick, and be dealing with its history and principles. Then foreign life is still to me perfectly delightful, and *liberating* in the highest degree, although I get more and more satisfied to live generally in England, and convinced that I shall work best in the long-run by living in the country which is my own. But when I think of the borders of the Lake of Geneva in May, and the narcissuses, and the lilies, I can hardly sit still . . .

To Mrs Forster

December 24, 1859.
. . . I thought the other day that I would tell you of a Frenchman whom I saw in Paris, Ernest Renan, between whose line of endeavour and my own I imagine there is considerable resemblance, that you might have a look at some of his books if you liked. The difference is, perhaps, that he tends to inculcate *morality*, in a high sense of the word, upon the French nation as what they most want, while I tend to inculcate *intelligence*, also in a high sense of the word, upon the English nation as what they most want; but with respect both to morality and intelligence, I think we are singularly at one in our ideas, and also with respect to the progress and the established religion of the present day. The best book of his for you to read, in all

ways, is his *Essais de Morale et de Critique*, lately published. I have read few things for a long time with more pleasure than a long essay with which the book concludes – 'Sur la poésie des races celtiques.' I have long felt that we owed far more, spiritually and artistically, to the Celtic races than the somewhat coarse Germanic intelligence readily perceived, and been increasingly satisfied at our own semi-Celtic origin, which, as I fancy, gives us the power, if we will use it, of comprehending the nature of both races. Renan pushes the glorification of the Celts too far; but there is a great deal of truth in what he says, and being on the same ground in my next lecture, in which I have to examine the origin of what is called the 'romantic' sentiment about women, which the Germans quite falsely are fond of giving themselves the credit of originating, I read him with the more interest . . .

To his Mother

2 Chester Square, *December* 31, 1859.

My dearest Mother – I have not much time, but must not fail to wish you many, many happy New Years. I keep planning and planning to pass Christmas and the New Year at Fox How, where I have passed them so often and so happily, now, alas! so long ago, but I do not see when it will be practicable. To make up, I think of you all more and oftener at this time of year than at any other. Poor little Tom[23] has been having, and has, one of his attacks, cough and fever, and yesterday was very ill, indeed; but he struggles on in the wonderful way that you know, and in every hour that he gets a little ease seems to recover his strength, which two or three hours of continuous cough try terribly. I hear his little voice now in the next room talking to his mamma about 'Brown, Jones, and Robinson.' It is one of his good hours, but this afternoon he has been very unwell. The others are very well indeed, and Lucy[24] making a great start in liveliness. Budge and Dick[25] went with us in the carriage this afternoon to make a call in the Regent's Park, and as the people were out, we took them on to the Zoological Gardens for an hour. It was Dick's first visit, and he shouted and danced for pleasure at the animals, above all the lion, who was in high excitement, and growling magnificently. I am very fond of the Gardens myself, and there are many new things this year. I must stop and go on looking over papers. Did you see a long article in the *Times* on Clough's *Plutarch*? It pleased me so much. Clough has just had the scarlatina, and is at Hastings to get well. Were you not agitated to hear of Macaulay's death? It has made a great sensation. But the *Times'* leading article on him is a splendid exhibition of what may be called the *intellectual vulgarity* of that newspaper. I had no notion Macaulay was so young a man. It is said he has left no more history ready, which is a national loss.

To his Mother

London, *October* 29, 1860.
My dearest Mother – I will not this time take a large sheet, I am so pressed for time; but I will not let more than a week pass without writing to you. I am in full work at my lecture on Homer, which you have seen advertised in the *Times*. I give it next Saturday. I shall try to lay down the true principles on which a translation of Homer should be founded, and I shall give a few passages translated by myself to add practice to theory. This is an off lecture, given partly because I have long had in my mind something to say about Homer, partly because of the complaints that I did not enough lecture on poetry. I shall still give the lecture, continuing my proper course, towards the end of the term. That, and preparing an introduction to my foreign Report, will keep me well employed up to January. But with the limited sphere of action in outward life which I have, what is life unless I occupy it in this manner, and keep myself from feeling starved and shrunk up? . . .

To Miss Arnold

2 Chester Square, *December* 17, 1860.
. . . I have not been in better case for a long time, and I attribute it entirely to making greater demands on myself. If you only half use the machine it goes badly, but its full play suits it; and if I live and do well from now to fifty (only twelve years!),

I will get something out of myself. I shall tomorrow finish my third lecture. It will not be given till the middle of January, but I want to get the subject done, and to have my mind free for other subjects. I have at last got the Commissioners' distinct leave to publish my Report, with additions, as a book. It will appear in February. By the time you come I hope to have finished the introduction to that and to have got it printed, and to be well plunged in the Middle Age. I have a strong sense of the irrationality of that period, and of the utter folly of those who take it seriously, and play at restoring it; still, it has poetically the greatest charm and refreshment possible for me. The fault I find with Tennyson in his *Idylls of the King* is that the peculiar charm and aroma of the Middle Age he does not give in them. There is something magical about it, and I will do something with it before I have done. The real truth is that Tennyson, with all his temperament and artistic skill, is deficient in intellectual power; and no modern poet can make very much of his business unless he is pre-eminently strong in this. Goethe owes his grandeur to his strength in this, although it even hurt his poetical operations by its immense predominance. However, it would not do for me to say this about Tennyson, though gradually I mean to say boldly the truth about a great many English celebrities, and begin with Ruskin in these lectures on Homer. I have been reading a great deal in the *Iliad* again lately, and though it is too much to say, as the writer in the *Biographie Universelle* says, that 'none but an Englishman would dream of matching Shakespeare with the Greeks,' yet it is true that Homer leaves him with all his unequalled gift – and certainly there never was any such naturally gifted poet – as far behind as perfection leaves imperfection.

To his Mother

2 Chester Square, *December 31*, 1860.
My dearest Mother – I ought long before this to have thanked all at Fox How, and you in particular, for all manner of affectionate letters and messages on my birthday; but along with my birthday arrived a frightful parcel from the Council Office of

grammar papers claiming to be returned, looked over, not later than today. Unluckily, at the same time I had entangled myself in the study of Greek accents, led thereto by some remarks on rhythm which I had to make in my lectures. Accent has a vital connection with the genius of a language, as any one can tell who has observed the effect of his own language spoken with a foreign accent, and anything in vital connection with the genius of such a language as the Greek must be interesting; still, the subject is one of those which lead you on and on, and I have been obliged to enter in my Diary a solemn resolution not to look again at a treatise on accents till I have sent in all my papers. Today, accordingly, I have sent in the great batch demanded of me, but with too great an effort, as in the early part of the week I had given too much time to my accents, and at the cost of nearly all duties of correspondence. I have still papers which will take me till the 24th of the month which begins tomorrow, but I have now got into the swing of them, and shall do my daily number with ease in two and a half hours in the evening, keeping my mornings for myself. In the next three or four mornings I must work at my Report for the past year, but then I hope to give my mornings steadily to preparing my French Report for the press.

The thaw has come, and I am glad of it, for the ice was spoiled for skating by the snow. I have had some pleasant days on the ice with Budge, Dick, and the nursemaid, but skating here reminds me too painfully of Westmorland. I begin now to count the weeks till you and Fan come. I must now go out and post this; it is past eleven o'clock, and I write after coming back from dinner in Eaton Place, and then before bed I must look over twenty papers. Little Tom is delightfully well; he and his brothers are to dine in Eaton Place at the late dinner on Twelfth Night. They are dear little boys, and as I work in a morning I hear Tom's voice in the dining-room reading aloud to his two brothers, who are seated one on each side of him. Lucy is getting a rogue of the first water. My love to all, not forgetting Rowland, and wishing you all a happy New Year, I am always, my dearest mother, your most affectionate son,

                                                                            M. A.

To his Mother

Norwich, July 30, 1861.

... I find the memory and mention of dear papa everywhere – far oftener than I tell you – among the variety of people I see. This variety is nowhere greater than on circuit. I find people are beginning to know something about *me* myself, but I am still far oftener an object of interest as his son than on my own account. You will have seen the attack on me in the *Saturday Review*, which I had heard a long time ago was coming. When first I read a thing of this kind I am annoyed; then I think how certainly in two or three days the effect of it upon me will have wholly passed off; then I begin to think of the openings it gives for observations in answer, and from that moment, when a free activity of the spirit is restored, my gaiety and good spirits return, and the article is simply an object of interest to me. To be able to feel thus, one must not have committed oneself on subjects for which one has no vocation, but must be on ground where one feels at home and secure – that is the great secret of good-humour ...

To Mrs Forster

Ipswich, July 31, 1861.

... You will have seen the amenities of the *Saturday Review*.[26] It seems affected to say one does not care for such things, but I do really think my spirits rebound after them sooner than most people's. The fault of the reviewer, as of English criticism in general, is that whereas criticism is the most delicate matter in the world, and wants the most exquisite lightness of touch, he goes to work in such a desperate heavy-handed manner, like a bear in a china-shop – if a bear can be supposed to have hands. I daresay I shall find an opportunity to set straight all that needs to be set straight in what both he and Newman[27] have brought forth. The disadvantage under which both of them labour is that the subject is not one for learning nor for violence, but rather for a certain *finesse* ...

To his Mother

February 19, 1862.
... I have just finished correcting the proofs of my article for *Fraser*,[28] and, what was harder, retouching and adding as was necessary. It will be very long, but I think not dull. Lowe's attack on the inspectors quite relieved me from all scruples in dealing with him, and I think my comments on his proceedings will be found vivacious. As to the article making a *sensation*, that I by no means expect. I never expect anything of mine to have exactly the popular quality necessary for making a sensation, and perhaps I hardly wish it. But I daresay it will be read by some influential people in connection with the debate which will soon come on. Froude's delay has certainly proved not unfortunate, as the present is a more critical moment for the article to appear than the beginning of the month, when Lowe's concessions were not answered, and could not be discussed.

Now I have to finish correcting my Homer lecture, which I am afraid will provoke some dispute. I sincerely say 'afraid,' for I had much rather avoid all the sphere of dispute. One begins by saying something, and if one believes it to be true one cannot well resist the pleasure of expanding and establishing it when it is controverted; but I had rather live in a purer air than that of controversy, and when I have done two more things I must do, – an article on Middle-Class Education and one on Academies (such as the French Academy), both of which will raise opposition and contradiction – I mean to leave this region altogether and to devote myself wholly to what is positive and happy, not negative and contentious, in literature ...

To Miss Arnold

The Athenæum (*November* 1865).
My dearest Fan – Thank dear mamma for her letter, but this week I will write to you, as I have two notes to thank you for. I have had a good deal from America, and was, therefore, the more interested in reading what you sent me. The *North American Review* for July had an article on me which I like as well as

anything I have seen.[29] There is an immense public there, and this alone makes them of importance; but besides that, I had been struck in what I saw of them on the Continent in the last few months, both with their intellectual liveliness and ardour, with which I had before been willing enough to credit them, as one of the good results of their democratic regime's emancipating them from the blinking and hushing-up system induced by our circumstances here – and also with the good effect their wonderful success had produced on them in giving them something really considerable to rest upon, and freeing them from the necessity of being always standing upon their toes, crowing. I quite think we shall see the good result of this in their policy, as well as in the behaviour of individuals. An English writer may produce plenty of effect there, and this would satisfy people like Bright who think successful America will do quite as well for all they want, or even better, than successful England; but it will never satisfy me. Whatever Mary may say, or the English may think, I have a conviction that there is a real, an almost imminent danger of England losing immeasurably in all ways, declining into a sort of greater Holland, for want of what I must still call ideas, for want of perceiving how the world is going and must go, and preparing herself accordingly. This conviction haunts me, and at times even overwhelms me with depression; I would rather not live to see the change come to pass, for we shall all deteriorate under it. While there is time I will do all I can, and in every way, to prevent its coming to pass. Sometimes, no doubt, turning oneself one way after another, one must make unsuccessful and unwise hits, and one may fail after all; but try I must, and I know that it is only by facing in every direction that one can win the day ...

To his Mother

The Athenæum, *February* 3, 1866.
My dearest Mother – It already seems a long, long time since I was with you, though you and dear Fan and the dear country often rise to my mind. I am now at work at my third lecture, to be delivered this day fortnight,[30] and from then till Easter I shall be incessantly at my Report. I mean to do hardly anything for the

Pall Mall Gazette, partly because it is not much use writing letters when I am immediately guessed, and so what I urge does not get the benefit of coming with the weight of impersonal newspaper authority – partly because the habit of newspaper writing would soon become too fascinating and exciting. I have the three next articles for the *Cornhill* as good as done. I think I told you that I cannot manage to send them to America, as Smith and Elder have an agreement with an American house which prevents me. But I shall publish in April my poem about Clough,[31] in *Macmillan*, and that I can send to America, and so fulfil my promise. There will be a good deal of talk about my *Cornhill* article.[32] I gather from Jane that you do not quite like it, but I am sure it was wanted, and will do good; and this, in spite of what the *Spectator* says, I really wish to do, and have my own ideas as to the best way of doing it. You see you belong to the *old* English time, of which the greatness and success was so immense and indisputable, that no one who flourished when it was at its height can ever lose the impression of it. Sir James Shuttleworth, who is a good judge, has just told me that without agreeing with every word, he entirely, on the whole, went along with the contents of the article, putting all questions of style and clever writing out of question, and that he thought the article timely and true. At the Stanleys' last night a good many people spoke to me about it, and with great amusement. I have received an indignant letter of expostulation from Lingen, however; but he thinks I want to exalt the actual aristocracy at the expense of the middle class, which is a total mistake, though I am obliged to proceed in a way which might lead a hasty and angry reader to think so. But there are certain things which it needs great dexterity to say in a receivable manner at all; and what I had to say I could only get said, to my thinking, in the manner I have said it. The *Spectator* you will see; the *Saturday* keeps silence; most of the other weekly newspapers mention it as the event of the *Cornhill*, very witty and suggestive, and so on.

Tonight we have a dinner party – the Forsters, the John Duke Coleridges, Lord and Lady Robert Montagu, Mallet of the Board of Trade, and Georgina. I think that will do very well. A kiss to Fan and my love to Rowland – Your ever most affectionate

                                                                M. A.

To his Mother

The Athenæum, *February* 23, 1866.
My dearest Mother – I have just finished my lecture, am not
satisfied with it, and feel bilious and good for nothing. Happily
it is often the case that what I am dissatisfied with at the time
of writing, turns out afterwards to be better than I expected;
and when one has to treat a subtle matter such as I have been
treating now, the marks of a Celtic leaven subsisting in the
English spirit and its productions, it is very difficult to satisfy
oneself. However, I shall see how it looks tomorrow; at any
rate, the lecture is finished, and now I can turn with uninter-
rupted constancy to my Report. We dine tonight at Lady
Wightman's; last night we dined with the Slades; the night
before dear K. dined with us, and that was the pleasantest dinner I have had for a long time; the night before that we dined
at Lady Westmorland's, and that was pleasant, though not so
pleasant as my dinner with Julian Fane at Vienna. I think I told
you of Carlyle's being so full of my article; I hear that Bright is
full of it also, but I have not yet heard any particulars of what
Bright says. Carlyle almost wholly approves, I hear; I am going
to see him. The country newspapers have had a great deal about
it; two leading articles in the *Edinburgh Courant*, not by any
means unfavourable, but trying to use it for their own Tory purposes. The Whig newspapers are almost all unfavourable, because
it tells disagreeable truths to the class which furnishes the great
body of what is called the Liberal interest. But I will really put my
hand on what I can collect and send it to you. I have been so
bothered with my lecture I have done nothing else I meant to do.
Thank dear Fan for sending me the *Westmorland Gazette*. Everyone is beginning to talk of a new religious book called *Ecce
Homo*.[33] Macmillan wanted to give me the book when it first
came out, but I said I should not read it till I must. I imagine it will
be infinitely more palatable to the English religious world than
Renan's book was; indeed, the review in the *Guardian* may be
taken, I suppose, as proof of this. Still the book is, by all accounts,
very far from what is called orthodoxy; it must be, when many
people attribute it to George Eliot, Miss Evans. However, James

Martineau told me today he was quite positive it was not by her.
My love to dear Fan. – Your ever most affectionate

M. A.

To his Mother

Athenæum, *November* 9, 1866.
... I slept at Copford the night before last, but now I have
done my country schools, and have nothing to take me out of
London till next April. I wrote in the train going down to Suf-
folk and posted from Melford, the place where I inspected, a
letter to the *Pall Mall Gazette* about Prussian tenant-right,[34]
based on what I got out of George Bunsen last Sunday in addition to what I had picked up at Berlin. I see the *Morning Star*
has reprinted the letter, and you would be amused to see
'Mr Matthew Arnold on the *Times*' placarded on the *Morning
Star* placards about London. The letter has been successful, and
Browning and John Duke Coleridge have both been telling me
that it is impossible to over-rate the effect these letters produce
and the change they promise to work. The fact is, it is the one
way in which in this country many things that have to be said
can be said so as to reach those who read them. I like to think
that the *Star*, in order to get the benefit of the irony on landlord-
ism, has to digest the irony on 'dissentism.' I daresay some of the
papers tomorrow will have something about it; at any rate I have
made the knowledge of Stein's land reforms *popular*, which was
no easy feat, any one would have said before yesterday ...

To his Mother

Stockwell Training School, *November* 8, 1867.
... I saw the *Spectator*, but indeed my name is getting familiar
in the newspapers. The *Saturday* had a reference to me which I
liked better than that in the *Spectator*. Lord Lytton's mention
of me was, as you may suppose, a pleasant surprise; I have not
time now to tell you about the whole affair, but in the morning
I had had no intention of going to dinner;[35] then I thought I
should like to hear the speeches, and with difficulty got a ticket

for a place at a crowded table at the bottom of the hall. As I was finishing my soup, arrive Edmund Yates, Levy the editor of the *Daily Telegraph*, and two of his young lions, and say they are charged to bring me up to the high table. I said I was very well where I was, but they insisted; then Dickens sent to say he hoped I would be one of the speakers, which I declined; finally Lord Lytton brought me in as you saw. It shows what comes, in the end, of quietly holding your own way, and bantering the world on the irrationality of its ways without losing temper with it . . .

. . . Thank you for the *Star* extract; but both the *Star* and *Telegraph* I shall contrive gently to touch up on occasion . . .

To his Mother

November 16, 1867.

. . . I am to meet Swinburne at dinner on Monday, at the Lockers'; Lady Charlotte Locker is Lady Augusta Stanley's sister. He expresses a great desire to meet me, and I should like to do him some good, but I am afraid he has taken some bent. His praise has, as was natural, inclined the religious world to look out in my writings for a crusade against religion, and the *Contemporary Review*, the *Christian World*, and other similar periodicals, fix on the speeches of Empedocles and Obermann, and calmly say, dropping all mention of the real speakers, 'Mr Arnold here professes his Pantheism,' or 'Mr Arnold here disowns Christianity.' However, the religious world is in so unsettled a state that this sort of thing does not do the harm it would have done two years ago. Meanwhile nearly 1,000 copies of my Poems are gone, which is very well. I have finished and corrected the preface to my Foreign Schools,[36] and am well pleased with it; part of it, where I touch on the Revised Code, needed very delicate handling. Now I have to do a sort of pendant to *Culture and its Enemies*, to be called *Anarchy and Authority*, and to appear in the Christmas *Cornhill*. It will amuse me to do it, as I have many things to say; and Harrison, Sedgwick, and others, who have replied to my first paper, have given me golden opportunities. – Your ever most affectionate

M. A.

To his Mother

Athenæum Club, Pall Mall, S.W.,
December 14, 1867.

... Everyone is full of the Clerkenwell blow-up;[37] I was dining at the Garrick Club last night, when one of the guests came in saying that his hansom had been nearly knocked down by a string of cabs with policemen filling them inside and out, hurrying to Clerkenwell Prison, which had been blown up by the Fenians. Later in the evening the newspaper came in and we learned what had really happened. You know I have never wavered in saying that the Hyde Park business eighteen months ago was fatal, and that a Government which dared not deal with a mob, of any nation or with any design, simply opened the flood-gates to anarchy. You cannot have one measure for Fenian rioting and another for English rioting, merely because the design of Fenian rioting is more subversive and desperate; what the State has to do is to put down *all* rioting with a strong hand, or it is sure to drift into troubles. Who can wonder at these Irish, who have cause to hate us, and who do not own their allegiance to us, making war on a State and society which has shown itself irresolute and feeble? But all these things are signs of the real hollowness and insufficiency of the whole system of our public life for these many years past, which could not but break down at last, just because it was hollow and insufficient. The great thing now is to try and build for the future, avoiding the faults which have done us so much mischief ...

To Mrs Forster

Athenæum Club, Pall Mall, S.W.,
December 20, 1867.

My dearest K. – The sight of my pile of grammar papers had already reminded me to write and ask you if I could bury myself, as in former years, in the solitude of Eccleston Square while I looked them over ...

We are in a strange uneasy state in London, and the profound sense I have long had of the hollowness and insufficiency of our whole system of administration does not inspire me with much confidence in this or any probable Government's plan of meeting it. To double the police on duty and to call out special constables seems a strange way of dealing with an enemy who is not likely to come in force into the streets, and who really needs a good secret police to track his operations – this, and nothing else. We shall get through this, and much besides we have in store, however, I hope and believe; but the amount of change and labour we have before us is immense, and few people, opening by degrees though their minds now are, can yet conceive it. It will be an amount of labour in proportion to the clap-trap we have tried to pass off on ourselves and others for truth; and one could hardly say more than that. Meanwhile, depend upon it that the great States of the Continent have two great elements of cohesion, in their administrative system and in their army, which we have not. Italy is like us in this respect, and her difficulties would be far less if she had a real administrative system and army, as France and Prussia have, and not, as she has, both the one and the other not really strong. The strength of the English character will have been never more tried than in having to go through, without army and administration, such a loosening of all old prejudices, respects, and habits as is beginning, and cannot be stopped, for it is the course of nature . . .

To his Mother

The Athenæum, *February* 22, 1868.
. . . Last night I dined with the Geological Society, at Huxley's invitation, who is President this year. My place was fixed between Lowe and Tyndall. Lowe's neighbourhood would have been amusing, but Lord de Grey failed to come. Lowe was moved into Lord de Grey's place, and I had another neighbour, Warrington Smyth, the ex-President. Tyndall was very pleasant. Lowe's speech not so good as people expected – rather a preachment about the Universities not giving enough of their prizes to reward natural science. Cardwell's speech was far better, and more amusing. Huxley is a capital speaker, and in one

of his speeches he brought in me and '*Arminius*' amusingly enough. But I had settled with him beforehand that I would not speak, and was not to be called upon. A clever, but raw and intemperate Scotch youth, Robert Buchanan, has been running rather a tilt against me and others. You will have seen his letters in the *Spectator*. Last night's *Pall Mall* had a tremendous onslaught upon him, which is very well, as showing that there are people ready to take up one's defence without having to do it oneself. Still, I had rather it was not done, as these bitter answers increase and perpetuate hatreds which I detest. Buchanan probably credits me with some of the severe reviews which have appeared of his verses, as doctrines of mine appear up and down in them. I am very sorry for this, and wish it could be known I never write anonymous criticisms. Then, too, the *Spectator* does me a very bad service by talking of my contempt for intellectual people. It is not at all true, and it sets people against one. You will laugh, but fiery hatred and malice are what I detest, and would always allay or avoid, if I could. Tonight I dine with Fitzjames Stephen, to talk over the Public Schools Bill. – Your ever most affectionate

M. A.

To *his Mother*

Harrow, *June* 5, 1869.

... My book[38] was out yesterday. This new edition is really a very pretty book, but you had better not buy it, because I am going to give it Fan, and shall bring it with me to Fox How, and the order of arrangement in this edition is not quite the final one I shall adopt. On this final order I could not decide till I saw this collected edition. The next edition will have the final order, and then the book will be stereotyped. That edition I shall have bound, and give you. I expect the present edition will be sold in about a year. Macmillan tells me the booksellers are subscribing very well for it. My poems represent, on the whole, the main movement of mind of the last quarter of a century, and thus they will probably have their day as people become conscious to themselves of what that movement of mind is, and interested in the literary productions which reflect it. It might be fairly urged that I have less poetical sentiment than Tennyson, and less intellectual vigour and abundance than Browning; yet, because I have perhaps more of a fusion of the two than either of them, and have more regularly applied that fusion to the main line of modern development, I am likely enough to have my turn, as they have had theirs . . .

To his Mother

Harrow, *June* 12, 1869.

. . . I heard the other day from Morier, the British Resident at Darmstadt, that Princess Alice is quite fascinated with my *Culture and Anarchy*, uses all its phrases, and knows long bits by heart. The Crown Princess is now reading the book. You will see that it will have a considerable effect in the end, and the chapters on Hellenism and Hebraism are in the main, I am convinced, so true that they will form a kind of centre for English thought and speculation on the matters treated in them . . .

To his Mother

Harrow, *November* 13, 1869.

My dearest Mother – I was much interested and touched by your letter, showing your willingness still, as always, to receive and comprehend what is new,[39] instead of shutting your mind against it. It was natural, too, that your thoughts should revert to your eldest brother. I had already thought of him. It is not man who determines what truths shall present themselves to this or that age, or under what aspect; and until the time is come for the new truth or the new aspect, they are presented unsatisfactorily or in vain. In papa's time the exploding of the old notions of literal inspiration in Scripture, and the introducing of a truer method of interpretation, were the changes for which, here in England, the moment had come. Stiff people could not receive this change, and my dear old Methodist friend, Mr Scott, used to say to the day of his death that papa and Coleridge might be excellent men, but that they had found and shown the rat-hole in the temple. The old notions about justification will undergo a like change, with a like opposition and cry of alarm from stiff people, with a like safety to true religion, as in the former case. It is not worth while to send you the lucubrations I receive, but the newspapers I forward (the organs of the Independents and Baptists) will show you how entirely I have reached the special Puritan class I meant to reach. Whether I have rendered St Paul's ideas with perfect correctness or not, there is no doubt that the confidence with which these people regarded their conventional rendering of them was quite baseless, made them narrow and intolerant, and prevented all progress. I shall have a last paper at Christmas, called 'Puritanism and the Church of England,' to show how the Church, though holding certain doctrines like justification in common with Puritanism, has gained by not pinning itself to those doctrines and nothing else, but by resting on Catholic antiquity, historic Christianity, development, and so on, which open to it an escape from all single doctrines as they are outgrown. Then I shall have done with the subject, and shall leave it . . . .

To his Mother

Harrow, *December* 4, 1870.

My dearest Mother – Tomorrow I dine with the Literary Society and sleep in Waterloo Place, as Mr George Smith kindly puts at my disposal his rooms over Smith and Elder's. The rooms are delightful, and the situation most convenient – at the bottom of Waterloo Place, and quite close to the Athenæum. My interview with the Income Tax Commissioners at Edgware the other day, who had assessed my profits at £1,000 a year, on the plea that I was a most distinguished literary man, my works were mentioned everywhere and must have a wide circulation, would have amused you. 'You see before you, gentlemen,' I said, 'what you have often heard of, *an unpopular author*.' It was great fun, though going to Edgware was a bore. The assessment was finally cut down to £200 a year, and I told them I should have to write more articles to prevent my being a loser by submitting to even that assessment, upon which the Chairman politely said, 'Then the public will have reason to be much obliged to us.' . . .

To Cardinal Newman

THE ATHENÆUM, *May 28, 1872.*

My dear Sir, –

You will have felt, I am sure, that your letter would give me very great pleasure. There are four people, in especial, from whom I am conscious of having learnt – a very different thing from merely receiving a strong impression – learnt habits, methods, ruling ideas, which are constantly with me; and the four are – Goethe, Wordsworth, Sainte-Beuve, and yourself. You will smile and say I have made an odd mixture and that the result must be a jumble: however that may be as to the whole, I am sure in details you must recognize your own influence often, and perhaps this inclines you to indulgence. What you say about the reception of the prophetical Scriptures by the young has great weight; if I were to say the very truth I should say that I thought the typical side alone would perhaps be best and safest for them, if it were given to them rightly; but that it is so wrongly, for the most part, conceived and given to them that it is better to give them the historical side plainly. But I did not mean to write of this; only to thank you, and to beg you, if any criticisms on the corrections adopted in the revision occur to you, to let me know them. They would be of the greatest possible weight with me, I need hardly say . . .

To his Sister, Mrs Cropper

October 26, 1878.

My dear Susy – I have sent you *Light* with a rather rhapsodical review of my poetry, because it praises and quotes a poem[40] which I remember repeating to you just after it was composed, and I can see your dear face now as you listened to it, and were touched by it. My poems have had no better friends in their early and needy days than my own sisters. It is curious how the public is beginning to take them to its bosom after long years of comparative neglect. The wave of thought and chance has rolled on until people begin to find a significance and an attraction in what had none for them formerly. Send *Light* to Fan when you have read it, she will like to see it. I believe the article is by Robert Buchanan. The writers of poetry have been better friends to me than the mass of readers of poetry. – Your affectionate

M. A.

To Miss Arnold

Cobham, *Sunday, May* 15 (1880).

... On Thursday I got a card from the Duchess of Norfolk for a party that evening, to meet Newman. I went, because I wanted to have spoken once in my life to Newman, and because I wanted to see the house. The house was not so fine as I expected. Newman was in costume – not full Cardinal's costume, but a sort of vest with gold about it and the red cap; he was in state at one end of the room, with the Duke of Norfolk on one side of him and a chaplain on the other, and people filed before him as before the Queen, dropping on their knees when they were presented and kissing his hand. It was the faithful who knelt in general, but then it was in general only the faithful who were presented. That old mountebank Lord — dropped on his knees, however, and mumbled the Cardinal's hand like a piece of cake. I only made a deferential bow, and Newman took my hand in both of his and was charming. He said, 'I ventured to tell the Duchess I should like to see you.' One had to move on directly, for there was a crowd of devotees waiting, and he retires at eleven. But I am very glad to have seen him ...

To Miss Arnold

(*November* 1880.)

... I have been reading Chaucer a great deal, the early French poets a great deal, and Burns a great deal. Burns is a beast, with splendid gleams, and the medium in which he lived, Scotch peasants, Scotch Presbyterians, and Scotch drink, is repulsive. Chaucer, on the other hand, pleases me more and more, and his medium is infinitely superior. But I shall finish with Shakespeare's *King Lear* before I finally write my Introduction,[41] in order to have a proper taste in my mind while I am at work.

To Miss Arnold

Athenæum Club, *February* 21 (1881).

. . . On Friday night I had a long talk with Lord Beaconsfield at Lady Airlie's. He was in a good humour, and had evidently resolved to be civil. He got up, took me to a settee at the end of the room, and said, pointing to it – The poet's sofa! I told him of my having mentioned to Gladstone some of the epigrammatic things in *Endymion*, and he said – 'But I don't want to talk about my things, I want to talk about *you*.' He went on to say that he read me with delight, that I was doing very great good, and ended by declaring that I was the only living Englishman who had become a classic in his own lifetime. The fact is that what I have done in establishing a number of current phrases – such as Philistinism, sweetness and light, and all that – is just the sort of thing to strike him. He had told Lady Airlie before I came that he thought it a great thing to do, and when she answered that she thought it was rather a disadvantage, for people got hold of my phrases and then thought they knew all about my work, he answered – Never mind, it's a great achievement! . . .

To Miss Arnold

Cobham, *New Year's Day*, 1882.

My dearest Fan – A happy New Year to you! I think the beginning of a New Year very animating, it is so visible an occasion for breaking off bad habits and carrying into effect good resolutions. I am glad to find that in the past year I have at least accomplished more than usual in the way of reading the books which at the beginning of the year I had put down to be read. I always do this, and I do not expect to read all I put down, but sometimes I fall much too short of what I proposed, and this year things have been a good deal better. The importance of reading, not slight stuff to get through the time, but the best that has been written, forces itself upon me more and more every year I live; it is living in good company, the best company, and people are generally quite keen enough, or too keen, about doing that, yet they will not do it in the simplest and most innocent manner by reading. However, if I live to be eighty I shall probably be the only person left in England who reads anything but newspapers and scientific publications. We have Nelly at home again; she enjoyed herself greatly at the Goschens', and they were very kind to her. Mr Goschen danced the polka with her, she being the only young lady on whom he bestowed this mark of favour. They wanted her to stay over the New Year with them, but she said she must go home ... She certainly is both gay herself and makes other young people so. We have had a pleasant week, not one single rainy day; but today it has begun to rain – thermometer 47. The primroses are coming out in all directions, and so is the pyrus japonica. We have also our first camellia out. Now I must stop. – Ever your most affectionate

                                                                    M. A.

NOTES

PREFACE TO FIRST EDITION OF *POEMS* (1853)

Arnold had published two earlier volumes of poetry: *The Strayed Reveller and Other Poems* (1849) and *Empedocles on Etna and Other Poems* (1852), with only his initial 'A' appearing on the title pages. *Poems* (1853) consisted mainly of reprints from the two earlier volumes together with some new poems (including 'Sohrab and Rustum' and 'The Scholar Gypsy') and the Preface. Arnold's full name was printed on the title page for the first time. For the second edition (1854) he added a further brief preface slightly modifying his original critical position. Both prefaces were reprinted in the third edition (1857). Neither appeared in subsequent volumes of Arnold's poetry, but were included in *Irish Essays and Others* (1882) from which the present text is taken.

1. (p. 3) 'Empedocles on Etna'. Arnold reprinted it, at Robert Browning's request, in *New Poems* (1867).
2. (p. 4) Aristotle, *Poetics*, IV: 'Imitation is natural to man from childhood, one of his advantages over the lower animals being this, that he is the most imitative creature in the world, and learns at first by imitation. And it is also natural for all to delight in works of imitation.' Tr. Ingram Bywater, *Aristotle on the Art of Poetry* (1920).
3. (p. 5) Throughout the Preface Arnold is taking issue with his fellow poets and with the reviewers; the first examples of a technique he later developed with enormous skill. For a detailed study of this particular controversy, see Sidney M. B. Coulling, 'Matthew Arnold's 1853 Preface: Its Origin and Aftermath', *Victorian Studies* VII, March 1964.

    It was a common complaint in the 1830s and 40s that poetry was becoming irrelevant to life because it dealt with an ideal

rather than a real world. Sandy Mackaye's advice to the young
Alton Locke typifies the kind of attitude Arnold has in mind:
'What do ye ken anent the Pacific? Which is maist to your business? – thae bare-backed hizzies that play the harlot o' the other
side o' the warld, or these – these thousands o' bare-backed hizzies that play the harlot o' your ain side – made out o' your ain
flesh and blude? You a poet! True poetry, like true charity, my
laddie, begins at hame.' Charles Kingsley, *Alton Locke* (1850),
Chapter 8.

4.   (p. 6) Achilles, the *Iliad*; Prometheus, Aeschylus's *Prometheus
     Bound*; Clytemnestra, Aeschylus's *Agamemnon*; Dido, Virgil,
     Aeneid.

5.   (p. 6) The authors are: Goethe, Byron, Lamartine and Words-
     worth.

6.   (p. 7) *the grand style*: see *On Translating Homer: Last Words*
     (pp. 58–62).

7.   (p. 15) 'It's hard to be good.'

8.   (p. 16) Johann Wolfgang von Goethe (1749–1832), German
     poet, novelist, dramatist and scientist. One of the four men from
     whom, as Arnold later claimed, he was 'conscious of having
     learnt'. See his letter to Newman, 28 May 1872 (p. 432). Bar-
     thold Georg Niebuhr (1776–1831), German historian, author of
     The History of Rome (1827–8). He was the first historian to
     view historical change in terms of social conflict, and was vener-
     ated by Arnold's father.

9.   (p. 16) Virgil, *Aeneid*, XII, 894–5: 'It is not your fiery words that
     daunt me . . . it is the Gods and the enmity of Jupiter.'

ON THE MODERN ELEMENT IN LITERATURE

Originally delivered as Arnold's inaugural lecture as Professor of
Poetry at Oxford on 14 November 1857, 'On the Modern Element in
Literature' was not published until February 1869 when it appeared
in *Macmillan's Magazine* with a brief apologetic note. Arnold never
included it in any of his collections of essays.

1.   (p. 20) *Hellenism and Hebraism*: see *Culture and Anarchy*,
     Chapter 4 (pp. 253–65).

2.   (p. 21) There are many references in Arnold's early writing to his
     enthusiastic study of Indian philosophy, especially the *Bhagavad
     Gita*. This influenced his important concept of disinterestedness.

In 'The Function of Criticism' it is described as 'the Indian virtue of detachment' (p. 122).

3. (p. 24) Johnson, 'Pope', *Lives of the Poets*. Arnold's dislike of eighteenth-century English literature is so notorious that it is worth noting the many favourable references to writers of this period scattered throughout his work, especially Johnson, Swift, Defoe and Fielding.

4. (p. 32) *A distinguished person:* Mr Gladstone.

5. (p. 33) *Lucretius:* Arnold had long planned to write a tragedy on Lucretius, and refers to it as late as 1886. Only a few fragments of the projected work have survived.

6. (p. 35) Niebuhr and Gladstone.

ON TRANSLATING HOMER 1861

Arnold's three lectures 'On Translating Homer' were delivered at Oxford on 3 November and 8 December 1860 and 26 January 1861. One reason for choosing this subject was the large number of translations of, and writings about, Homer published in the 1850s; another, more significant reason was, as Arnold explained in a letter to his mother, 'because of the complaints that I did not enough lecture on poetry'. The lectures were published as a book in 1861. The present text is that of the first edition.

1. (p. 42) *The Iliad of Homer, faithfully translated into unrhymed English metre* by F. W. Newman (1856). Francis Newman (1805–97), who bears the brunt of Arnold's attack in the Homer lectures, was the brother of Cardinal Newman and Professor of Latin at University College, London.

2. (p. 43) Edward Craven Hawtrey, Provost of Eton, had published some translations from Homer in 1847.

3. (p. 44) William Hepworth Thompson was Regius Professor of Greek, University of Cambridge; Benjamin Jowett, Regius Professor of Greek, University of Oxford. In his first lecture Arnold had described Hawtrey, Thompson and Jowett as men 'who both know Greek and can appreciate poetry'.

4. (p. 44) *Troilus and Cressida*, Prologue.

5. (p. 44) ibid.

6. (p. 46) *Thersites and Irus:* both are low characters. Thersites, a scurrilous Greek soldier in the *Iliad*; Irus, a beggar in the *Odyssey*.

ON TRANSLATING HOMER: LAST WORDS 1862

Arnold's 'Last Words' on translating Homer were delivered at Oxford on 30 November 1861 and published in book form the following year. His principal reason for returning to the subject was Francis Newman's *Homeric Translation in Theory and Practice. A Reply to Matthew Arnold* (1861), but Arnold also took the opportunity to answer criticisms that he had used his privileged position to indulge in personal attacks. The present text is that of the first edition.

1. (p. 53) Arnold's allusion is both appropriate and ironic. When Achilles sulkily withdrew from the Trojan War his close friend Patroclus returned to the battle and was killed by Hector. Hector foolishly taunted Achilles and was killed by him. In the battle over translating Homer, Arnold, the modern Achilles, stands poised to slay Newman, the modern Hector.

2. (p. 54) The offending passage, a striking early example of Arnold's ability to coin telling phrases, comes in his third lecture: ' "To grunt and sweat under a weary load;" – that does perfectly well where it comes in Shakespeare; but if the translator of Homer, who will hardly have wound up our minds to the pitch at which these words of Hamlet find them, were to employ when he has to speak of one of Homer's heroes under the load of calamity, this figure of "grunting" and "sweating," we should say, *He Newmanizes*, and his diction would offend us.'

3. (p. 54) Arnold is referring to an article in the *Saturday Review*, 27 July 1861, 'Homeric Translators and Critics', which pointed out that Newman's academic record at Balliol was better than Arnold's. Newman obtained a double first; Arnold, a second-class degree.

4. (p. 57) *digamma*: the sixth letter of the original Greek alphabet, representing a sound approximately that of the English *w*, which early fell into disuse.

5. (p. 57) Newman was renowned for his knowledge of obscure languages: 'Besides Hebrew, Greek, Latin, Sanscrit, French, Spanish, Italian and Danish, he learned Berber, Libyan, Arabic, Abyssinian, Gothic, Chaldean, Syriac and Numidian; he translated Horace into English, *Hiawatha* into Latin and *Robinson Crusoe* into Latin and Arabic.' Lionel Trilling, *Matthew Arnold* (1939), Chapter 6.

6. (p. 58) Montaigne, 'Des Livres', *Essais*: 'Plutarque est plus uniforme et constant; Seneque, plus ondoyant et divers.'

7.   (p. 59) Milton, *Paradise Lost*, VII, 23–6.
8.   (p. 62) John Spedding, 'Arnold on Translating Homer', *Fraser's Magazine*, June 1861.
9.   (p. 64) Tennyson, *The Princess*, VII, 182; 'Merlin and Vivien', 633–4, *Idylls of the King*; ibid., 638–9; *The Princess*, V, 20–21; 'Marriage of Geraint', 74–8, *Idylls*.
10. (p. 64) Tennyson, *Ulysses*, 16–17.
11. (p. 66) *Moschus:* a Greek pastoral poet.
12. (p. 66) Arthur Hugh Clough (1819–61), close friend of Arnold's and the subject of 'Thyrsis'. Some of Clough's most successful poems were written in English hexameters, and during the last years of his life he was translating Homer into this metre.
13. (p. 67) From *The Bothie of Tober-Na-Vuolich* (1848).

DEMOCRACY

In 1859 Arnold was appointed Foreign Assistant Commissioner to the Royal Commission on Education which had been set up in the previous year under the chairmanship of the Duke of Newcastle. His task was to examine and report upon the methods of popular education in France, the French cantons of Switzerland and Holland. He spent nearly five months (March–August 1859) on the Continent and submitted his report in 1860. The importance Arnold attached to his findings can be seen by his wish to publish the report. It appeared as *The Popular Education of France* in 1861, with 'Democracy' acting as an introduction. Arnold described the essay as 'one of the things I have taken most pains with', and reprinted it in *Mixed Essays* (1879), from which the present text is taken.

1.   (p. 73) *the grand style*: see *On Translating Homer: Last Words* (pp. 58–62).
2.   (p. 80) In 1856 Sir James Parke was raised to a life peerage, but the Lords determined that the Crown had lost by disuse the power of creating life peers, and he was given a hereditary peerage. R. H. Super (editor), *The Complete Prose Works of Matthew Arnold*, II (1962), 332.
3.   (p. 82) Virgil, *Aeneid*, V, 231: 'They have the capacity because they think they have it.'
4.   (p. 84) Arnold's fear that with the advent of democracy England would become Americanized stayed with him all his life. His American lecture tours in 1883 and 1886 did little to dispel the

fear: 'Whatever one may think of the general danger to the world from the Anglo-Saxon contagion, it appears to me difficult to deny that the growing greatness and influence of the United States does bring with it some danger to the ideal of a high and rare excellence. The *average man* is too much a religion there; his performance is unduly magnified, his shortcomings are not duly seen and admitted.' 'Milton', *Essays in Criticism: Second Series* (1888).

5.   (p. 85) The *Constitutionnel*, founded in 1815, was strongly Bonapartist in sympathy.

6.   (p. 85) *Morning Star:* a radical newspaper founded in 1856 to express the views of the Manchester School. It was edited by Samuel Lucas, John Bright's brother-in-law.

7.   (p. 85) S. Butler, *Hudibras*, I, i, 215–16.

8.   (p. 87) The belief that the industrial society of the nineteenth century was inferior to the non-industrial society of the Middle Ages was expressed in a variety of ways throughout the Victorian period. Here Arnold is probably referring to Carlyle, *Past and Present* (1843), and Ruskin, *The Stones of Venice* (1853).

9.   (p. 88) Acts passed by the first Restoration Parliament (1661–5) to restrict the activity of the Nonconformists.

10. (p. 89) Matthew 9.12: 'They that are whole have no need of a physician, but they that are sick.'

11. (p. 90) *Classical and Commercial Academy:* Arnold uses the phrase to describe the various kinds of private schools (patronized mainly by the middle classes) set up in competition with the public and grammar schools.

12. (p. 94) Super, quoting R. C. Tobias, notes that this favourite quotation of Arnold's is wrong: 'Although Burke uses both the words *collective* and *corporate* in describing the State, he nowhere uses the exact phrase that Arnold credits him with here.' *Complete Prose Works*, II, 377.

13. (p. 97) Matthew 5.48; Philippians 3.13.

ESSAYS IN CRITICISM

The first edition of *Essays in Criticism* contained, apart from the essays printed here, 'The Literary Influence of Academies', 'Eugénie de Guérin', 'Pagan and Mediaeval Religious Sentiment', 'Spinoza', and 'Marcus Aurelius'. For the second edition (1869) Arnold shortened the Preface, reorganized the 'Spinoza' essay and renamed it 'Spinoza and the Bible'. A new essay, 'A Persian Passion Play', was added to the third edition (1875). The present text is that of the third edition. Arnold's Preface to the first edition is a superb example of his polemic at its most savage. It is available, fully annotated, in Fraser Neiman (editor), *Essays, Letters and Reviews by Matthew Arnold* (1960).

Preface

1. (p. 101) The first volume of Ichabod Wright's translation of the *Iliad* (1859) had been attacked by Arnold in his lectures on Homer. Wright replied with *A Letter to the Dean of Canterbury, on the Homeric Lectures of Matthew Arnold* (1864).

2. (p. 103) Professors Pepper, Anderson and Frickel were theatrical performers, renowned for their ghost effects and conjuring tricks.

3. (p. 103) Arnold is paraphrasing points made by James Fitzjames Stephen in 'Mr Matthew Arnold and his Countrymen', *Saturday Review*, 3 December 1864, a reply to 'The Function of Criticism at the Present Time', which was first published in the *National Review*, November 1864. This was the first exchange in a debate that leads directly to 'My Countrymen', *Culture and Anarchy* and *Friendship's Garland*.

4. (p. 103) Franz Müller, a German tailor, murdered Thomas Briggs on the North London Railway on 9 July 1864. He escaped to New York, was extradited and hanged.

5. (p. 104) *Exeter Hall:* a building in the Strand used for evangelical meetings.

6. (p. 104) *Marylebone Vestry:* the governing body of the parish of St Marylebone, popularly elected and solidly bourgeois.

7. (p. 104) Jeremy Bentham bequeathed his body to University College, London, where it is still preserved. Arnold's grim parody of the Benthamite utilitarian is his revenge for the parody of himself as a 'transcendentalist'.

8. (p. 105) Byron, *Childe Harold*, IV, cxli, 5 ('There *were* . . .' in the original).

9. (p. 105) *Tübingen:* a German school of theology associated with the scientific explanation of the Scriptures.

10. (p. 105) Goethe, 'Epilog zu Schillers Glocke', 32: 'the material world which ties us down'. *Das gemeine* is not capitalized in the original.

The Function of Criticism at the Present Time

1. (p. 112) On Sunday, 23 July 1637, Jenny Geddes threw a stool at the Bishop of Edinburgh in St Giles's Church as a protest at the use of Laud's service-book.

2. (p. 112) A bill for the decimalization of weights and measures was introduced in the House of Commons in 1863 but withdrawn after the second reading.

3. (p. 114) Richard Price (1723–91) was a Unitarian minister whose sermon praising the French Revolution provoked Burke to write *Reflections on the Revolution in France* (1790).

4. (p. 114) Goldsmith, 'Retaliation', 32.

5. (p. 115) Numbers 22.38.

6. (p. 116) Aesop: the fable of the wind and the sun.

7. (p. 119) *Sir Charles Adderley:* Conservative M.P. for North Staffordshire.

8. (p. 119) John Arthur Roebuck (1801–79), M.P. for Sheffield, was more radical and independent than Arnold makes him sound. In 1855 he had played a central part in the setting up of a select committee to investigate the condition of the army in the Crimean War, and he was an advocate of further parliamentary reform. But his radicalism was tempered by a vociferous nationalism and it is this that Arnold seizes on.

9. (p. 123) *Lord Somers* (1651–1716): lawyer and statesman, who presided over the drafting of the Declaration of Rights on the accession of William and Mary in 1689.

10. (p. 123) William Cobbett (1763–1835), radical journalist, author of *Rural Rides* (1830). He became M.P. for Oldham in 1832.

11. (p. 123) The hysterical tone of *Latter-day Pamphlets* (1850) repelled Arnold, together with many other admirers of Carlyle's earlier social criticism.

12. (p. 123) Ruskin, *Unto This Last* (1862), the work in which Ruskin finally committed himself to a detailed programme of economic and social reform. It was severely criticized on publication.

13. (p. 123) *terræ filii:* a colloquial expression describing a person of low birth or obscurity. Super points out that Arnold is replying to criticisms of the sentence in 'The Bishop and the Philosopher': 'the highly instructed few, and not the scantily instructed many, will ever be the organ to the human race of knowledge and truth.' *Complete Prose Works*, III (1962), 479.

14. (p. 124) *Obermann* (1804) by Étienne Pivert de Senancour

(1770–1846), a romantic, melancholy novel in the tradition of Goethe's *Werther*; it was greatly admired by Arnold, who wrote two poems on the subject, 'Obermann' and 'Obermann Once More'.

15. (p. 124) John William Colenso (1814–83), Bishop of Natal. The first volume of his *The Pentateuch and the Book of Joshua Critically Examined* (1862–79) caused a considerable stir and was regarded as a daring, even heretical, book. Arnold savaged Colenso and the 'uncritical spirit of our race' in 'The Bishop and the Philosopher', *Macmillan's Magazine*, January 1863. Some passages from 'The Bishop and the Philosopher' were later incorporated into the Spinoza article which appeared in *Essays in Criticism* (second edition, 1869) as 'Spinoza and the Bible'.

16. (p. 125) Arnold had favourably reviewed A. P. Stanley's *Lectures on the History of the Jewish Church* in the same periodical, the month following his Colenso article. Arnold may be replying to personal criticisms here; Stanley was a close friend and his father's official biographer.

17. (p. 125) *the eighty and odd pigeons:* Arnold is mocking Colenso's technique of criticism by 'arithmetical demonstration'.

18. (p. 126) David Friedrich Strauss (1808–74), *Leben Jesu* (1835), translated into English by George Eliot (1846).

19. (p. 126) Ernest Renan (1823–92), French critic and orientalist, author of *La Vie de Jésus* (1863). Arnold had met Renan in France. See letter to Mrs Forster, 24 December 1859 (pp. 415–6).

20. (p. 127) The British College of Health was founded in 1828 by James Morrison for the dispensing of his vegetable pills. Carlyle had used the phrase 'Morrison's Pill' in *Past and Present* (1843) to describe any vain remedy for the ills of society.

21. (p. 128) *English Divorce Court:* established by the Divorce Law, 1857.

22. (p. 129) Virgil, *Eclogues*, IV, 5: 'The cycle of the ages is born afresh.'

Maurice de Guérin

1. (p. 133) Linnaeus (1707–78), botanist and zoologist; Cavendish (1731–1801), chemist and physicist; Cuvier(1769–1832), naturalist.

2. (p. 133) *The Winter's Tale*, IV, iii, 118–20.

3. (p. 133) Wordsworth, 'The Solitary Reaper'.

4. (p. 134) Keats, 'Bright Star' (*'pure* ablution' in the original).

5.   (p. 134) Chateaubriand, 'Les Chasseurs'.

6.   (p. 134) *Senancour:* see note 14 on 'The Function of Criticism'.

Heinrich Heine

1.   (p. 137) *Soli:* a town in Asia Minor whose inhabitants were reputed to speak bad Greek; hence the word 'solecism'.

2.   (p. 137) Goliath was the champion of the Philistines. The English are like Goliath; they have great strength but this alone is not enough.

3.   (p. 137) Carlyle, 'Count Cagliostro', *Critical and Miscellaneous Essays.*

4.   (p. 139) Jeremiah 8.22: 'Is there no balm in Gilead? Is there no physician there?'

5.   (p. 139) Bismarck became Prime Minister of Prussia in 1862.

6.   (p. 140) Wordsworth, 'Resolution and Independence', 77.

7.   (p. 140) Job 12.23.

8.   (p. 141) Lucan, *Pharsalia*, i, 135: 'He stands, the shadow of a mighty name.'

Joubert

1.   (p. 143) Arnold particularly admired Coleridge's influence on religious thought: 'my dear old Methodist friend, Mr Scott, used to say to the day of his death that papa and Coleridge might be excellent men, but that they had found and shown the rat-hole in the temple.' Letter to his mother, 13 November 1869 (p. 00).

2.   (p. 147) Eugène Scribe (1791–1861), French dramatist, author of an enormous number of light comedies.

3.   (p. 148) *Lord Jeffrey* (1773–1850): editor of the *Edinburgh Review* 1802–29, renowned for the partisan severity of his criticism.

4.   (p. 148) *Lord Macaulay* (1800–1859): essayist, historian, poet and politician. His essays for the *Edinburgh Review* (1825–44) and his *Lays of Ancient Rome* (1842) and *History of England* (1849–61) were immensely popular. Criticisms of him appear throughout Arnold's work. See especially: letter to his mother, 31 December 1859 (p. 416); *Friendship's Garland*, 8 (pp. 284–319); and 'A French Critic on Milton', *Mixed Essays.*

5.   (p. 149) Jean François de La Harpe (1739–1803), French critic and dramatist.

6.   (p. 149) *Dagon:* the god of the Philistines. See Judges 16.23.

MY COUNTRYMEN

'My Countrymen' was first published in the *Cornhill*, February 1866, a belated, though long-contemplated, reply to James Fitzjames Stephen's article 'Mr Matthew Arnold and his Countrymen', *Saturday Review*, 3 December 1864, which was in turn a criticism of Arnold's 'The Function of Criticism'. It should be seen as part of a running debate Arnold conducted with his critics throughout the 1860s. Arnold's contributions to the debate are collected, in chronological order, in Super (editor), *Complete Prose Works*, V (1965). When the Arminius letters were published as *Friendship's Garland* in 1871, Arnold closed the volume with 'My Countrymen', placing it after Letter 12, adding the footnotes and introducing it with the following note:

(I have thought that the memorial raised to Arminius would not be complete without the following essay, in which, though his name is not actually mentioned, he will be at once recognized as the leading spirit of the foreigners whose conversation is quoted.

Much as I owe to his intellect, I cannot help sometimes regretting that the spirit of youthful paradox which led me originally to question the perfections of my countrymen, should have been, as it were, prevented from dying out by my meeting, six years ago, with Arminius. The *Saturday Review*, in an article called 'Mr Matthew Arnold and his Countrymen,' had taken my correction in hand, and I was in a fair way of amendment, when the intervention of Arminius stopped the cure, and turned me, as has been often said, into a mere mouthpiece of this dogmatic young Prussian. It was not that I did not often dislike his spirit and boldly stand up to him; but, on the whole, my intellect was (there is no use denying it) overmatched by his. The following essay, which appeared at the beginning of 1866, was the first proof of this fatal predominance, which has in many ways cost me so dear.) – ED.

1. (p. 150) For 'the return of Burke upon himself', see 'The Function of Criticism'.
2. (p. 151) Sir Thomas Bazley (1797–1885), wealthy cotton manufacturer, M.P. for Manchester. The speech from which Arnold quotes was concerned with the setting up of the Schools Inquiry Commission (1865).
3. (p. 151) *Mr Miall . . . the Nonconformist:* Edward Miall (1809–81), editor of the *Nonconformist*, a weekly Congregational

paper established in 1841, and one of the leaders of the Voluntaryist Society, which opposed state intervention in education.

4.   (p. 153) In, respectively, *A French Eton* (1864) and 'The Literary Influence of Academies', *Essays in Criticism*.

5.   (p. 153) From April to October 1865 Arnold toured the Continent as Foreign Assistant Commissioner to the Schools Inquiry Commission. Part of his report was published as *Schools and Universities on the Continent* (1868).

6.   (p. 153) Robert Burns, 'To a Louse', stanza 8.

7.   (p. 154) Arnold is referring to a leading article in *The Times* on the death of Palmerston: 'It must awake a sort of envy' in France that England can be guided by 'a perfect representative of the country, a thoroughly popular chief, a mean between all classes, without the surrender of our liberties or the formality of several revolutions.' Super (editor), *Complete Prose Works*, V, 365.

8.   (p. 155) In 1860 England signed a 'most favoured nation' treaty with France. It was hailed as a great triumph for Cobden, who negotiated the treaty, and for the Manchester School's free-trade policies.

9.   (p. 155) In 'The Literary Influence of Academies' Arnold had quoted an extract from the *Saturday Review* describing foreign criticism of English precautions against invasion as 'eminently worthy of a great fool'.

10.   (p. 155) Palmerston died on 18 October 1865.

11.   (p. 156) *Heu incredibiles humanarum rerum mutationes!* 'Alas, the unbelievable changes in human affairs.'

12.   (p. 156) Robert Lowe (1811–92), M.P. for Kidderminster (1852–9) and for the pocket borough of Calne (1859–67). When Calne was swept away by the 1867 Reform Bill, he was returned for the University of London. As vice-president of the committee of council on education (1859–64), he introduced a bill to Parliament whereby government grants for education would be allotted to schools in proportion to the number of pupils who had passed examinations set by the school Inspectors: the method of 'payment by results', as it was popularly known. In spite of Lowe being his superior in the department of education, Arnold wrote a series of anonymous articles and letters attacking 'payment by results', and his action helped bring about an eventual compromise. Lowe was also prominent in the 1860s as a vociferous opponent of working-class enfranchisement, while at the same time constantly eulogizing the middle-class society that had developed out of the 1832 Reform Bill.

13. (p. 157) In 1864 Prussia and Austria invaded Denmark and annexed the duchies of Schleswig-Holstein.

14. (p. 157) English middle-class radicals were sharply divided over the American civil war. Many opposed the Northern blockade because it interfered with trade but as the war progressed they came to support the Federal cause.

15. (p. 158) John Parry was an entertainer who specialized in one-man comedy sketches. The specific relevance of the sketch Arnold describes is uncertain.

16. (p. 160) Judges 5.20.

17. (p. 162) Lowe's speech was on the Borough Franchise Extension Bill, 3 May 1865.

18. (p. 163) John Bright (1811–89), Liberal politician and reformer, M.P. for Manchester (1847–57) and for Birmingham (1857–89). A leader of the Manchester School, Bright campaigned for the repeal of the Corn Laws, and for free trade, reduced taxation and parliamentary reform. Primarily a representative of the new industrial middle class, he also supported the extension of the franchise to the working classes in 1867, thus having, as Arnold says in *Culture and Anarchy*, a foot in both camps. He was also a great admirer of American democracy.

19. (p. 163) In the speech to which Arnold refers, Bright had claimed that if the Tories had been in power for the previous forty years England would have collapsed into a state of anarchy and the members of the House of Lords would have been emptied into the Thames. Super (editor), *Complete Prose Works*, V, 368.

20. (p. 166) *Hamlet*, IV, v, 84.

21. (p. 167) Arnold pursued this comparison in *Friendship's Garland*, 5, and in a letter to the *Pall Mall Gazette*, 'Stein Plus Hadenberg'.

22. (p. 170) Count Pococurante, in Voltaire's *Candide*, epitomizes aristocratic *ennui*.

23. (p. 171) *Areopagus:* the supreme tribunal of Athens.

24. (p. 171) *Sardinia's course:* i.e. in the unification of Italy. Francis II, King of Naples, was defeated by Garibaldi in 1860. Arnold does not make it clear here that his narrative has jumped forward a year. Hitherto he has been discussing the reaction of *The Times* to *Napoleon the Third and Italy* (1859) by Arthur, vicomte de La Guéronnière.

25. (p. 172) Arnold is being doubly ironic. The views being put to him are, of course, his own; views which the *Saturday Review* had already frequently criticized.

26. (p. 173) *Othello*, V, ii, 242.
27. (p. 174) 'A Roland for an Oliver': tit for tat.
28. (p. 175) *penny gaff*: a low-class theatre.
29. (p. 175) *Strathmore . . . the one-pound-eleven-and-sixpenny gaff*: *Strathmore* was a romantic three-volume novel by Ouida. Each volume cost 10s. 6d.
30. (p. 176) *Buncombe*: bunkum.
31. (p. 177) Virgil, *Aeneid*, II, 287: 'He answers nothing, nor does he heed my idle questions.'
32. (p. 177) Arnold, 'Heine's Grave'. The poem was unpublished at this time.

CULTURE AND ANARCHY

Arnold's final lecture as Professor of Poetry, 'Culture and Its Enemies', was delivered at Oxford on 7 June 1867 and published in the *Cornhill* the following month. He had planned to write a sequel to 'Culture and Its Enemies' but the criticism of his original lecture was so widespread that by August 1868 his reply had expanded to a further five articles which were published in the *Cornhill* under the general title 'Anarchy and Authority'. These articles, together with the original lecture and a preface, were slightly rearranged and published as *Culture and Anarchy* (1869). For the second edition (1875) Arnold deleted many of the topical and personal allusions, and added the chapter headings. The present text is that of the third edition (1882).

Introduction

1. (p. 181) *Mr Bright*: see note 18 on 'My Countrymen'.
2. (p. 181) *Frederic Harrison* (1831–1923): barrister and critic, a leading English disciple of Auguste Comte's positivist philosophy and a supporter of working-class reforms. In 'Our Venetian Constitution', *Fortnightly Review*, March 1867, the article from which Arnold is quoting here, Harrison had argued that the 'best part' of the working class was perfectly capable of exercising political power. A second article by Harrison, referred to by Arnold throughout *Culture and Anarchy* and *Friendship's Garland*, 'Culture, A Dialogue', *Fortnightly Review*, November 1867, was a reply to 'My Countrymen' and the early Arminius letters. Arnold said of this article that it made him laugh till he cried. *Letters*, I, 372.

3. (p. 182) *Daily Telegraph:* established in 1855, the first penny paper in London, it claimed to have the largest circulation in the world, and had replied to Arnold's earlier gibes at 'the young lions of the *Daily Telegraph*' by describing him as 'an elegant Jeremiah'.

Chapter 1. Sweetness and Light

1. (p. 183) In 'The Function of Criticism' (p. 141).
2. (p. 183) Charles Augustin Sainte-Beuve (1804–69), French critic, greatly admired by Arnold and a major influence on his literary essays. For Arnold's obituary article on Sainte-Beuve, see Super (editor), *Collected Prose Works*, V.
3. (p. 185) Thomas Wilson (1663–1755), Bishop of Sodor and Man. Arnold discovered a copy of the *Maxims* in his father's library in 1866 and was delighted with it. Bishop Wilson was so little known that Arnold was accused of having invented him.
4. (p. 187) Luke 17.21.
5. (p. 187) In *A French Eton* (1864).
6. (p. 188) cf. Carlyle: 'Were we required to characterise this age of ours by any single epithet, we should be tempted to call it . . . the Mechanical Age. It is the Age of Machinery, in every outward and inward sense of that word.' 'Signs of the Times' (1829).
7. (p. 189) *Mr Roebuck's:* see note 8 on 'The Function of Criticism', *Essays in Criticism*.
8. (p. 192) In *The Battle of the Books* Aesop acts as arbiter in a quarrel between the Spider (representing the moderns) and the Bee (representing the ancients). He decides in favour of the latter: 'The difference is, that, instead of dirt and poison, we have rather chosen to fill our hives with honey and wax; thus furnishing mankind with the two noblest of things, which are sweetness and light.'
9. (p. 194) *The Nonconformist:* see note 3 on 'My Countrymen'.
10. (p. 194) 1 Peter 3.8.
11. (p. 196) T. H. Huxley (1825–95), scientist, educationist and agnostic. He frequently championed Darwin's theory of evolution against attacks from religious leaders.
12. (p. 196) Sallust, *Catilina*, LII, 22: 'in public life penury, in private, luxury.'
13. (p. 197) *muscular Christianity:* the form of religion associated with Charles Kingsley: hearty and non-intellectual.
14. (p. 198) Edmond Beales (1803–81), president of the Reform

League founded in 1865 to campaign for the extension of the franchise to the working classes; Charles Bradlaugh (1833–91), a member of the League and at this time best known as a fiery orator, atheist and republican.

15. (p. 199) The Oxford or Tractarian Movement began in 1833 with the attempts by Keble, Pusey and Newman to re-examine the doctrinal and historical validity of the Anglican Church; the first phase ended with Newman joining the Church of Rome in 1845. Arnold was not associated with the Oxford Movement, but see his letter to Cardinal Newman, 28 May 1872 (p. 432); also his description of Newman at Oxford in 'Emerson', *Discourses in America* (1885).

16. (p. 199) 'My battle was with liberalism; by liberalism I mean the anti-dogmatic principle and its developments. This was the first point on which I was certain.' Newman, *Apologia Pro Vita Sua*, Chapter 2.

17. (p. 199) Virgil, *Aeneid*, I, 460: 'What quarter of the globe is not full of our toils?'

18. (p. 200) *Lowe*: see note 12 on 'My Countrymen'.

19. (p. 202) *the Journeyman Engineer*: pseudonym of Thomas Wright, author of *Some Habits and Customs of the Working Classes* (1867).

20. (p. 204) *men of a system . . .*: Auguste Comte (positivism), H. T. Buckle (the scientific interpretation of history), John Stuart Mill (utilitarianism).

21. (p. 204) Matthew 23.8: 'But be not ye called Rabbi: for one is your teacher, and all ye are brethren.'

22. (p. 205) See especially 'On the Modern Element in Literature' (pp. 20–38).

23. (p. 206) Peter Abelard (1079–1142), French scholar, best known for his tragic love affair with Heloisa, but also a popular and influential teacher.

24. (p. 206) Gotthold Ephraim Lessing (1729–81), dramatist and critic; a central figure in the development of German naturalism. Johann Gottfried Herder (1744–1803), critic and historian. His relativist approach to literature and history influenced Goethe, and would have appealed strongly to Arnold.

Chapter 2. Doing as One Likes

1. (p. 207) *Alcibiades*: a brilliant but irresponsible leader of the Athenians in the Peloponnesian War. *Morning Star*: see note 6 on 'Democracy'.

2. (p. 208) Frederic Harrison, 'Culture, A Dialogue'. For Harrison's relations with Arminius, see *Friendship's Garland*, 7 (pp. 289–323).

3. (p. 209) *the British Constitution . . . a system of checks:* the theory that the British Constitution protects the liberty of the individual and makes dictatorship impossible by a tripartite division of power (Crown, Lords and Commons), each of which acts as a check upon the others. Arnold may be referring specifically to Walter Bagehot, *The English Constitution* (1867), VII.

4. (p. 209) See note 12 on 'Democracy'.

5. (p. 210) In *The Popular Education of France*.

6. (p. 211) *breaks down the park railings:* on 23 July 1866 the Reform League organized a monster meeting in Hyde Park. The leaders were Edmond Beales, Charles Bradlaugh, Colonel Dickson and C. J. Holyoake. When admission to the park was refused, some of the demonstrators broke down the railings. The skirmishes that followed, though hardly serious, caused a public outcry, and became known as the 'Hyde Park riots'.

7. (p. 211) *invades a Secretary of State's office:* on 18 September 1867 the Fenians (an Irish-American revolutionary organization) killed a police sergeant while attempting to rescue two of their members from arrest, and were sentenced to death. On 18 November a mob of English sympathizers broke into the Home Secretary's office and demanded that the condemned men be given a pardon. On 13 December an attempt by the Fenians to dynamite the walls of Clerkenwell prison killed twelve people living in the locality.

8. (p. 211) *Mr Murphy . . .:* on 16 June 1867 William Murphy began a series of anti-Catholic lectures in Birmingham which led to riots in the Midlands. Murphy defended his actions by invoking the right of free speech.

9. (p. 213) *Fenianism:* see note 7 above.

10. (p. 213) Coles's Truss Manufactory was situated on the corner of Trafalgar Square, which had been described by Sir Robert Peel as 'the finest site in Europe'.

11. (p. 214) *Sir Daniel Gooch* (1816–89): engineer and inventor, Chairman of the Great Western Railway.

12. (p. 215) Carlyle, *Shooting Niagara* (1867).

13. (p. 216) John 12.31.

14. (p. 217) See especially 'Democracy' (pp. 71–97).

15. (p. 217) Dives and Lazarus, Luke 16.19–31.

16. (p. 218) *Oxford in the bad old times:* before the Oxford University Act of 1854.

17. (p. 218) In a speech on 'Primary and Classical Education' at Edinburgh, 1 November 1867, Lowe argued that English education should place more stress on modern, and less on ancient, languages. Arnold ignores the more serious side of Lowe's speech and seizes upon his remark that a knowledge of modern languages would enable an Englishman to order a meal in Paris without making himself a laughingstock. Super (editor), *Complete Prose Works*, V, 429.

18. (p. 218) Aristotle defined virtue as a mean 'lying between two forms of badness, one being excess and the other deficiency'. *Ethics*, II, vi.

19. (p. 218) In the first edition Arnold named his 'well-known lord and well-known baronet' as Lord Elcho (who reappears in *Friendship's Garland*, 3) and Sir Thomas Bateson.

20. (p. 220) *Mr Miall:* see note 3 on 'My Countrymen'.

21. (p. 221) Arnold's 'representative man' is Sir Thomas Bazley (see note 2 on 'My Countrymen'). This whole passage was rewritten for the second edition. In the first edition, after excluding John Bright as a representative member of the middle class because of his genius, Arnold instanced Bright's brother, Jacob, as a perfect example; Bazley was then classified with Jacob Bright.

22. (p. 222) *Dissenting minister from Walsall:* the Reverend William Cattle, who was chairman at Mr Murphy's lectures. See note 8 above.

23. (p. 223) *Melanchhon:* Philip Melanchthon (1497–1560), German humanist and reformer who helped Luther in his German translation of the New Testament, and played a leading role in the Reformation.

24. (p. 223) On 3 June 1867, the City of London Militia, led by Alderman Samuel Wilson, the Colonel of the Regiment, marched through London and were followed by gangs of roughs who assaulted and robbed spectators. Colonel Wilson refused to let his soldiers intervene and justified his action in the words Arnold quotes.

25. (p. 225) George Odger (1820–77), secretary of the London Trades Council (1862–72), and a leading working-class advocate of parliamentary reform, though also a moderate with regard to trade-union militancy.

26. (p. 227) In the debate on the Reform Bill of 1832.

Chapter 3. Barbarians, Philistines, Populace

1.   (p. 230) 'The Friend of Humanity and the Knife-Grinder', a skit on Robert Southey by George Canning, published in the *Anti-Jacobin*, 27 November 1797.

2.   (p. 230) *Zephaniah Diggs*: see *Friendship's Garland*, 6 (pp. 301-7).

3.   (p. 230) See especially 'Heine', *Essays in Criticism*.

4.   (p. 231) *Barbarians*: Arnold had used the word earlier (quoting from Byron) in the Preface to *Essays in Criticism* (pp. 101-5).

5.   (p. 235) 'From the son of his father and the pupil of his teacher [Wordsworth] none would have looked for such an efficient assault and battery of the Philistine outworks ... A profane alien in my hearing once defined him as "David, the son of Goliath."' A. C. Swinburne, 'Mr Arnold's New Poems', *Fortnightly Review*, October 1867.

6.   (p. 235) Arnold was notoriously fond of shooting and fishing: 'The shooting here is superb, and I am shooting if possible worse than I did at Hampden; but this last year I shall go on blazing away, and then abandon for ever the vain attempt to mingle in the sports of the Barbarians.' *Letters*, II, 107.

7.   (p. 236) *rattening*: 'abstracting tools, destroying machinery or appliances, etc., as a means of enforcing compliance with the rules of a trade-union'.

8.   (p. 238) *The Memoirs of Martinus Scriblerus* (1741), a satire on 'all the false tastes in learning' by John Arbuthnot.

9.   (p. 238) The *Saturday Review*, founded in 1855, was one of the liveliest of Victorian periodicals and renowned for its sharp social criticism. In spite of his disagreements with the *Saturday Review*, Arnold always treats it with respect.

10. (p. 239) The *British Banner* (1847-58), a weekly Nonconformist paper.

11. (p. 239) *Dixon's ... The Mormons ...*: William Hepworth Dixon (1821-79), historian and travel-writer, editor of the *Athenaeum* (1853-68), author of *New America* (1867), from which Arnold is quoting here, and *Spiritual Wives* (1868).

12. (p. 239) Joe Smith was the founder of the Mormons; his successor was Brigham Young, referred to in the next sentence.

13. (p. 240) *Shakerism*: the Shakers were a millenarian sect founded in 1747 in England, but with a considerable following in America.

14. (p. 241) Proverbs 28.26.

15. (p. 241) Tennyson, *The Princess*, conclusion.
16. (p. 242) In the debate on the Reform Bill, 13 March 1866: 'If you want venality, if you want ignorance, if you want drunkenness, and facility for being intimidated; or if, on the other hand, you want impulsive, unreflecting, and violent people, where do you look for them in the constituencies? Do you go to the top or the bottom?'
17. (p. 244) *Sir James Graham's useful Education Clauses in 1843*: clauses in the Factory Act which allowed for children working in factories to receive religious instruction according to the tenets of the Church of England; they were opposed by the Nonconformists and withdrawn.
18. (p. 245) Wilhelm von Humboldt (1767–1835), the first Prussian Minister of Education, founder of the State University of Berlin, in which he was helped by his friend Friedrich Schleiermacher (1768–1834), theologian and educationist.
19. (p. 248) *Daily News*: founded in 1846 by Charles Dickens, it represented moderate Liberalism.
20. (p. 252) *Renan*: see note 19 on 'The Function of Criticism', *Essays in Criticism*.

Chapter 4. Hebraism and Hellenism

1. (p. 254) 2 Peter 1.4.
2. (p. 254) *Frederick Robertson* (1816–53): popular preacher of Trinity Chapel, Brighton.
3. (p. 254) It was from Heine that Arnold took the terms 'Hebraism', 'Hellenism' and 'Philistine'.
4. (p. 255) Proverbs 29.18; Psalms 112.1.
5. (p. 256) Romans 3.31.
6. (p. 257) Aristotle, *Ethics*, II, iv.
7. (p. 258) Socrates, *Memorabilia*, IV, viii.
8. (p. 258) Carlyle to John Llewelyn Davies, 27 April 1852. Super (editor), *Complete Prose Works*, V, 437.
9. (p. 258) Edward Bouverie Pusey (1800–1882), Regius Professor of Hebrew at Oxford, and one of the founders of the Oxford Movement. See note 15 on Chapter 1 above.
10. (p. 259) Romans 8.26, 7.24.
11. (p. 259) Zechariah 8.23.
12. (p. 259) George Herbert (1593–1633), 'The Size'. The original reads: 'Thy Saviour sentenc'd joy.'

13. (p. 260) Ephesians 5.6.
14. (p. 260) Romans 6.3.
15. (p. 260) Romans 3.2.
16. (p. 263) 1 Timothy 1.7.

From Chapter 5. Porro Unum Est Necessarium

1. (p. 265) 'One thing is needful'. Luke 10.42.
2. (p. 267) Romans 2.22.

From Chapter 6. Our Liberal Practitioners

1. (p. 269) On 2 May 1866, Thomas Chambers moved the second reading of his bill to repeal the Act of 1835 by which it was made illegal for a man to marry his deceased wife's sister. The bill was defeated and was not passed until 1907. For Arnold's most biting treatment of the subject, see *Friendship's Garland*, 8 (pp. 313–18).
2. (p. 269) *Hepworth Dixon:* see note 11 on Chapter 3 above. *Colenso:* see note 15 on 'The Function of Criticism', *Essays in Criticism*.
3. (p. 270) The final chapter of Dixon's *Spiritual Wives* (1868) is called 'The Gothic Revival' and contains the following sentence: 'All the Teutonic seers and scribes have more or less this mystic sense of a higher sexual affinity than that of ordinary wedlock.' Super (editor), *Complete Prose Works*, V, 442.
4. (p. 270) cf. Carlyle: 'Well did the Wisest of our time write: "It is only with Renunciation (Entsagen) that Life, properly speaking, can be said to begin."' *Sartor Resartus*, II, ix. The 'Wisest of our time' is Goethe.
5. (p. 272) 1 Kings 11.3.

Conclusion

1. (p. 275) Aristotle, *Ethics*, X, ix. In this chapter Aristotle is arguing that education in virtue is best undertaken by the State.
2. (p. 277) Henry Sidgwick, 'The Prophet of Culture', *Macmillan's Magazine*, August 1867.
3. (p. 277) *Thyesteän banquet of clap-trap*: i.e. Parliament. Atreus revenged himself upon his brother Thyestes by inviting him to a banquet and serving him the flesh of his children to eat. Arnold's

grotesque image expresses even more disillusionment with the parliamentary system than Carlyle's 'The Collective Wisdom of the Nation' and Dickens's 'The Great Dust-Heap'.

4. (p. 279) Plato, *Symposium*.

FRIENDSHIP'S GARLAND

The twelve letters that make up the central text of *Friendship's Garland* were published originally in the *Pall Mall Gazette*. Letters 1–7 appeared between July 1866 and April 1867; Letters 8–12 between June 1869 and November 1870. When Arnold gathered the letters together to publish them as a book (February 1871), he added a 'Dedicatory Letter', 'My Countrymen' (in which Arminius, though unnamed, first appeared), 'A Courteous Explanation' (a letter he had published in the *Pall Mall Gazette* in reply to a French critic of 'My Countrymen') and a few paragraphs of commentary linking the letters. He greatly enjoyed himself in the role of editor and wrote to his publisher: 'I think it is more self-important and *bête* if I put Ed. after every note. It is rather fun making the notes.' *Friendship's Garland* should be read, as Arnold intended, in conjunction with *Culture and Anarchy*. The present text is that of the first edition.

Introductory paragraphs

1. (p. 283) Voltaire, *Candide* (1759). Dr Pangloss is Candide's teacher. His optimistic philosophy is founded on the assumption that 'things cannot be other than they are, for since everything was made for a purpose, it follows that everything is made for the best purpose.' Tr. John Butt (Penguin Books, 1947), Chapter 1.

2. (p. 283) The war between Austria and Prussia lasted for seven weeks, June–July 1866.

Letter 1

1. (p. 284) *Grub Street*: the traditional abode of hack-writers.

2. (p. 284) *'Denmark avenged'*: by Charles Keene, *Punch*, 7 July 1866.

3. (p. 285) It was a fundamental belief of the 'Manchester School' that the expansion of international trade would eventually make

war obsolete. Gladstone, who was Chancellor of the Exchequer in 1866, subscribed to this belief and offered it to the Rumanians as the reason why they should peacefully settle their constitutional crisis.

4. (p. 285) *Goldwin Smith* (1823–1910): Regius Professor of Modern History at Oxford (1858–66), an ardent Liberal, a regular contributor to the periodicals, and a personal friend of Arnold's.

5. (p. 285) *Humboldt:* Alexander von Humboldt (1769–1859), German statesman. He used the phrase 'missionary deaconesses' to describe the religious courtiers who surrounded King Frederick William IV of Prussia during the early years of his reign.

6. (p. 285) *needle-gun:* a rapid-firing breech-loading rifle used by the Prussian army.

7. (p. 286) *Geist:* intelligence, light, reason. Although Arnold claims here to be introducing the word to the British public, it had long been a favourite with him. See his letter to Clough, 10 October 1853 (p. 411). Arnold also named his pet dachshund Geist and wrote a poem to his memory, 'Geist's Grave'.

8. (p. 286) Grant Duff, *Studies in European Politics* (1866).

9. (p. 287) *Coles's Truss Manufactory . . . finest site in Europe:* see note 10 on Chapter 2, *Culture and Anarchy*.

10. (p. 288) *Intelligenz-Staat:* probably Arnold's own coinage. It refers to Prussia, a state governed by, and permeated with, 'light'.

Letter 2

1. (p. 290) *wissenschaftlich:* learned, scholarly, embracing both the arts and sciences. Arminius is pointing out that the word has a sense of scientific application unknown to the English.

2. (p. 290) *kein Ernst, der ins Ganze geht:* 'no earnest attempt to grasp the whole.' Eckermann, *Conversations with Goethe*, 20 April 1825.

3. (p. 291) A reference to John Bright who, quoting a Northern manufacturer, made the remark used by Arminius. Super (editor), *Complete Prose Works*, V, 383.

4. (p. 291) The point Arnold is making is that reforms in nineteenth-century Europe owed everything to the inspiration of the French. (1) In Naples convents were suppressed and turned into schools. (2) Ticino, a Swiss canton, rebelled against the Swiss League in 1798 and came under Napoleon's protection in 1803. (3) Karl Stein was the architect of Prussian tenant-right land reforms (1807–11). In Letter 5 of *Friendship's Garland*

Arnold argued that England should follow Stein's example with regard to the settlement of the Irish question.

5. (p. 291) *Cayenne:* in French Guiana, the site of a prison for political exiles.

Letter 3

1. (p. 293) Hermann was a German national hero known to the Romans as Arminius. For 'the grand style' see *On Translating Homer: Last Words* (pp. 58–62).

2. (p. 293) Frankfurt fell to the Prussians on 16 July 1866. Bismarck was said to have dealt severely with the city because of attacks made upon him by the Frankfurt press. Super (editor), *Complete Prose Works*, V, 389.

3. (p. 294) *better self:* see *Culture and Anarchy*, Chapter 2 (pp. 207–28).

4. (p. 295) *Lord Elcho:* the 'well-known lord' of *Culture and Anarchy*, Chapter 2, who exemplified the happy mean of aristocracy. He was a Conservative M.P. and an opponent of parliamentary reform.

5. (p. 295) *Walpoles or Pakingtons:* Spencer Walpole, Home Secretary during the Hyde Park riots (1866). See note 6 on Chapter 2, *Culture and Anarchy*. Sir James Pakington was First Lord of the Admiralty at the same time.

6. (p. 296) Macaulay, *History of England* (1849–61), I, i.

7. (p. 296) *Esel:* ass. *Lumpenpack:* rabble.

Letter 4

1. (p. 297) *dogue:* mastiff.

2. (p. 297) *mordre-ing or déchirer-ing: mordre,* to bite; *déchirer,* to tear. Arminius is obviously aware that this curious way of anglicizing French verbs was common usage in popular literature and songs of the Victorian period. It expresses the cheerful English contempt for foreigners that Arnold so detested. The most famous example is Mr Meagles in *Little Dorrit*, Chapter 2: 'I mean the French people. They're always at it ... allonging and marshonging to something or other.'

3. (p. 297) *seventy-two quarterings:* Candide's request to marry Cunégonde is indignantly rejected by the Baron: 'You have the impudence to think of marrying my sister, who has seventy-two quarterings in her coat of arms.' *Candide*, Chapter 15.

4. (p. 298) *Constitutional party:* the supporters of the Republican Constitution of 1848, overthrown by Napoleon III.

5. (p. 298) *Mark of Brandenburg:* one of the largest provinces of Prussia.

6. (p. 299) *Orleanists:* the French Royalists.

Letter 6

1. (p. 301) *Haussmanniszed:* Georges-Eugène Haussmann (1809-91), prefect of the Seine (1853-70), encouraged by Napoleon III, ruthlessly demolished large areas of Paris and replanned the entire city. He was criticized for the hardship caused to the poor by his demolitions.

2. (p. 304) *Kant . . . the categorical imperative:* 'I ought never to act except in such a way that I can also will that my maxim should become a universal law.'

3. (p. 304) Virgil, *Aeneid,* IX, 641: 'This is the way to the stars.'

4. (p. 305) *Sir James Graham's Factory Act:* see note 17 on Chapter 3, *Culture and Anarchy.*

5. (p. 306) *on the foundation:* educated at the expense of the endowment of the school.

6. (p. 306) *longs and shorts:* Latin verses.

7. (p. 306) *Bullingdon:* a social club at Oxford University.

8. (p. 307) *Lycurgus:* the legendary architect of Sparta's constitution.

Letter 7

1. (p. 309) The laying of the Atlantic cable was completed on 27 July 1866. *The Times* proclaimed: 'The two most active and energetic nations of the globe are placed in hourly communication.' Super (editor), *Complete Prose Works,* V, 403.

2. (p. 309) George Grote (1823-1910), historian, classical scholar and Benthamite, vice-chancellor of the University of London.

3. (p. 310) Arminius's namesake Hermann defeated the Romans in a battle on the banks of the Lippe, in the Teutoburg Forest, in A.D. 9.

4. (p. 311) See note 6 on Chapter 3, *Culture and Anarchy.*

5. (p. 311) As a Comtist, Frederic Harrison hailed the coming of a bloodless revolution brought about not by class conflict but by the scientific examination and understanding of society. Hence Arnold's ironic description of him as a Jacobin.

6. (p. 312) Frederic Harrison's article 'Culture, A Dialogue' took the form of a conversation between Harrison and Arminius. Hitherto

Arnold has merely been answering Harrison's criticisms; he now claims that Arminius has deserted him in favour of Harrison's more scientific philosophy. This fiction is employed to explain the two-year gap in the letters; it also enables Arnold to introduce Harrison as a character.

Letter 8

1. (p. 313) The Deceased Wife's Sister Bill: see note 1 on Chapter 6, *Culture and Anarchy*.
2. (p. 314) *Mary Jane*: a generic name for female domestics, used by the *Daily Telegraph* in articles on the servant question.
3. (p. 315) *his new young man*: Frederic Harrison.
4. (p. 316) George Augustus Sala (1828–96) joined the *Daily Telegraph* in 1857 and became its special foreign correspondent. He was often credited with establishing the florid literary style of the *Daily Telegraph*, a style of which the paper was extremely proud. Arnold is also responding to a personal attack: in *Rome and Venice* (1869) Sala had described him as a 'shallow and conceited sciolist'. Super (editor), *Complete Prose Works*, V, 469.
5. (p. 316) *sexual insurrection of the Anglo-Teutonic race*: see note 3 on Chapter 6, *Culture and Anarchy*.
6. (p. 317) *our great leader*: John Bright.
7. (p. 317) *The Merchant of Venice*, IV, i, 341. As Bright was a Quaker, Arnold substitutes 'Friend' for 'Jew'.
8. (p. 318) Wordsworth, 'London, 1802'. The original line reads: 'And give us manners, virtue, freedom, power.'
9. (p. 318) *Richard III*, IV, iv, 424.

Letter 12

1. (p. 319) Versailles was the headquarters of the Prussian army besieging Paris. War had been declared by Napoleon III on 14 July 1870. In Letter 9, dated 9 August, Arminius announced his intention of leaving England to join the Prussian army: 'I am a republican, I desire a republic for every country in Europe … But the present war, though we are led by the old drill-sergeant and his wire puller [the King of Prussia and Bismarck] is a war of Germany against France. I must go and take part in it.'
2. (p. 319) *Cremorne*: a pleasure garden in Chelsea.
3. (p. 320) In Plautus's play, Amphitryon married his niece Alcmene.

4.   (p. 320) *Azamat-Batuk:* the pseudonymous author of a series of letters about England published in the *Pall Mall Gazette* in 1869.

5.   (p. 320) Arminius is hoping that as he and Lowe are both descended from Pangloss, he will be laid to rest in Lowe's family mausoleum at Caterham.

6.   (p. 322) *Dr Russell:* William Howard Russell (1820–1907), the famous war correspondent of *The Times*. In his dispatches from the Franco-German War Russell frequently stressed his intimacy with the Prussian leaders.

7.   (p. 322) *Dickens:* Arnold is probably referring to the fact that Sala was a friend of Dickens and an early contributor to *Household Words*. He is certainly not being serious in placing Dickens in such distinguished literary company. In the first edition of the Preface to *Essays in Criticism* (1865), Arnold included *Little Dorrit* in a gruesome list of books to be found in the typical Philistine's library.

8.   (p. 322) *Cider-cellar:* a tavern which featured musical entertainment; a forerunner of the music halls.

ESSAYS IN CRITICISM: SECOND SERIES

The second series of *Essays in Criticism* was published in November 1888, seven months after Arnold's death. In addition to the essays reprinted here it contained: 'Milton', 'Thomas Gray', 'John Keats', 'Shelley', 'Count Leo Tolstoi' and 'Amiel'. 'The Study of Poetry' had been published originally as the introduction to *The English Poets* (4 vols., 1880), edited by T. H. Ward. 'Wordsworth' had appeared in *Macmillan's Magazine*, July 1879, and as the Preface to *Poems of Wordsworth* (1879); 'Byron' in *Macmillan's Magazine*, March 1881, and as the Preface to *Poetry of Byron* (1881). The present text is that of the first edition.

The Study of Poetry

1.   (p. 327) Arnold, Introduction to the first volume of *The Hundred Greatest Men* (8 vols., 1880). Arnold slightly altered the original wording of this paragraph, and omitted the sentence: 'Compare the stability of Shakespeare with the stability of the Thirty-Nine Articles!'

2.   (p. 328) Wordsworth, Preface to the second edition of *Lyrical Ballads* (1802).

3.   (p. 328) ibid.

4.   (p. 329) *poetry, as a criticism of life:* for Arnold's earlier use of this famous phrase, see 'Joubert', *Essays in Criticism* (pp. 142–9).

5.   (p. 330) Paul Pellisson (1624–93), French historian and poet; the first historian of the French Academy (1652).

6.   (p. 330) *Charles d'Héricault* (1823–99): French novelist and historian; his edition of the French poet Clément Marot (1496–1544) was published in 1867.

7.   (p. 332) Thomas à Kempis, *Imitatio Christi*, III, xliii: 'Read much, learn much, yet you must always come to one beginning –'

8.   (p. 333) *Cædmon:* an Anglo-Saxon poet of the seventh century, to whom at this time was wrongly attributed the old English *Genesis* which, like *Paradise Lost*, describes the fall of the Angels.

9.   (p. 333) *Chanson de Roland:* a French epic which tells of Charlemagne's expedition against the Moors in 778. The earliest extant version was composed in the eleventh century.

10.   (p. 333) *joculator or jongleur:* court jester or minstrel.

11.   (p. 335) *Henry IV, Part 2*, III, i, 18–20.

12.   (p. 336) *Hamlet*, V, ii, 360–63.

13.   (p. 336) *Paradise Lost*, I, 599–602.

14.   (p. 336) *Paradise Lost*, I, 108–9.

15.   (p. 336) *Paradise Lost*, IV, 271–2.

16.   (p. 337) Aristotle, *Poetics*, IX: 'Poetry is something more philosophic and of graver import than history since its statements are of the nature rather of universals, whereas those of history are singulars.'

17.   (p. 338) *langue d'oil ... langue d'oc:* the languages spoken respectively in the North and South of France; the phrases are derived from the different pronunciation of the word 'oui'.

18.   (p. 339) *Brunetto Latini* (1220–94): Florentine philosopher and politician who did most of his writing during six years' exile in France. His *Trésor* was an encyclopedic survey of knowledge. *La parleure ... gens:* 'The language is more pleasing and universal.'

19.   (p. 339) *Wolfram of Eschenbach:* a medieval German poet, author of the epic *Parzival*.

20.   (p. 340) Dryden, Preface to *Fables Ancient and Modern* (1700), which included adaptations from Chaucer.

21.   (p. 340) *gold dew-drops of speech:* John Lydgate, *The Life of Our Lady* (c. 1411).

22.   (p. 340) Johnson, 'Dryden', *Lives of the Poets*.

23. (p. 340) *well of English undefiled:* Spenser, *Faerie Queene*, IV, ii, stanza 32.
24. (p. 341) Chaucer, *The Prioress's Tale*, stanza 14 ('*to* virginitee' in the original).
25. (p. 344) Dryden, *An Essay of Dramatic Poesy.*
26. (p. 344) Dryden, Preface to *Fables.*
27. (p. 345) Milton, *An Apology against a Pamphlet . . . against Smectymnuus* (1642).
28. (p. 345) Dryden, Postscript to his translation of the *Aeneid* (1697).
29. (p. 346) Dryden, *The Hind and the Panther* (1687), I, 1–2.
30. (p. 346) Pope, *Imitations of Horace*, II, 143–4.
31. (p. 348) Burns, 'On the Death of Lord President Dundas'.
32. (p. 348) *Clarinda's love-poet, Sylvander:* Clarinda was the name given by Burns to Mrs Maclehose, with whom he corresponded under the name of Sylvander.
33. (p. 348) Burns in a letter to George Thomson (1794). *The Letters of Robert Burns*, ed. J. DeLancey Ferguson (1931), II, 268.
34. (p. 349) Burns, 'The Holy Fair'.
35. (p. 350) Burns, 'Epistle to a Young Friend'.
36. (p. 350) Burns, 'Address to the Unco Guid'.
37. (p. 350) Burns, 'Epistle to Dr Blacklock'.
38. (p. 350) Xenophon, *Memorabilia*, II, ii.
39. (p. 351) *Farewell to Nancy:* Burns's title is 'Ae Fond Kiss'.
40. (p. 352) Burns, 'Winter'.
41. (p. 353) Shelley, *Prometheus Unbound*, III, iv, 204.
42. (p. 353) *Prometheus Unbound*, II, v, 1–4.

Wordsworth

1. (p. 355) *Guide to the Lakes:* Wordsworth's *Guide Through the District of the Lakes in the North of England* was first published in 1810 as an introduction to a series of drawings by Joseph Wilkinson.
2. (p. 356) *Tennyson . . . 1842:* the publication of *Poems* (1842) established Tennyson as the leading poet of the Victorian period. He succeeded Wordsworth as Poet Laureate in 1850.
3. (p. 356) *The Golden Treasury of Songs and Lyrics*, edited by F. T. Palgrave, was first published in 1861.
4. (p. 356) *Renan:* see note 19 on 'The Function of Criticism', *Essays in Criticism.*
5. (p. 357) *the ideal of Goethe:* 'National literature is now rather an unmeaning term. The epoch of world-literature is at hand, and

everyone must strive to hasten its approach.' Eckermann, *Conversations with Goethe*, 31 January 1827.

6. (p. 357) *unrivalled happiness:* Roebuck's phrase mocked by Arnold in 'The Function of Criticism' (pp. 119–22).

7. (p. 357) The 'candid friend' is Arnold himself. He had used these terms to describe the three classes in 'Ecce Convertimur Ad Gentes', *Fortnightly Review*, February 1879, reprinted in *Irish Essays* (1882).

8. (p. 358) *The old Biographie Universelle:* a French biographical dictionary (1810–28), edited by Joseph François Michaud and Louis Gabriel Michaud.

9. (p. 358) Eckermann, *Conversations with Goethe*, 31 January 1830.

10. (p. 359) *Amphictyonic Court:* a council, supposedly founded by Amphictyon, at which most of the states of ancient Greece were represented.

11. (p. 363) Wordsworth, from a fragment of 'The Recluse' printed in the Preface to *The Excursion* (1814).

12. (p. 363) Voltaire, *Histoire du siècle de Louis XIV*, Chapter 24.

13. (p. 364) *Paradise Lost*, XI, 553–4.

14. (p. 364) *The Tempest*, IV, i, 156–8.

15. (p. 365) In spite of the popularity at this time of Fitzgerald's *Rubaiyat*, Arnold uses a prose translation, and his own spelling of 'Khayyam'.

16. (p. 365) Epictetus, *Moral Discourses*, III, vii.

17. (p. 366) *Théophile Gautier* (1811–72): French poet and novelist. The Preface to his novel *Mademoiselle de Maupin* (1835) was a manifesto of the *L'art pour l'art* doctrine, an anti-utilitarian approach to poetry completely contrary to everything that Arnold represents.

18. (p. 366) Wordsworth, Preface to *The Excursion*, 14–18.

19. (p. 367) Virgil, *Aeneid*, VI, 662: 'And they who were pious bards and spoke things meet for the ear of Phoebus.'

20. (p. 367) Leslie Stephen, 'Wordsworth's Ethics', *Hours in a Library*, II.

21. (p. 367) *The Excursion*, IV, 73–6.

22. (p. 368) *The Excursion*, IV, 10–17.

23. (p. 369) *The Excursion*, IX, 293–302.

24. (p. 369) The National Association for the Promotion of Social Science was founded in 1857. Annual congresses were held in provincial cities throughout England at which leading intellectuals and reformers read and discussed papers on social problems,

published each year in a volume of *Transactions*. It was by no
means the ridiculous institution Arnold makes it sound.

25. (p. 369) *bold, bad men:* Wordsworth, 'To the Lady Fleming', 81.
26. (p. 370) *not ourselves:* the phrase is Arnold's own: 'Something
    not ourselves which makes for righteousness'. *Literature and
    Dogma*, Chapter 8.
27. (p. 370) *weak as is a breaking wave:* Wordsworth, 'A Poet's Epi-
    taph', 58.
28. (p. 371) *This will never do:* the opening words of Lord Jeffrey's
    review of *The Excursion* in the *Edinburgh Review*, November
    1814.
29. (p. 371) *Macbeth*, III, ii, 23.
30. (p. 371) *Paradise Lost*, VII, 25–6.
31. (p. 371) Wordsworth, Preface to *The Excursion*, 78–80.
32. (p. 372) Burns, 'A Bard's Epitaph', stanza 4.
33. (p. 374) *Mr Wilkinson's spade:* Wordsworth's title is 'To the Spade
    of a Friend'.
34. (p. 374) Wordsworth, letter to Lady Beaumont, 21 May 1807.

Byron

1. (p. 375) Stopford Brooke (editor), *Poems from Shelley* (1880).
2. (p. 376) A. C. Swinburne, Preface to *A Selection from the Works
   of Lord Byron* (1866).
3. (p. 377) The Byron quotations are from letters to John Murray,
   29 November 1813, and Thomas Moore, 8 June 1822 and
   3 March 1814.
4. (p. 379) *Edmond Scherer* (1815–89): French journalist, editor of
   Le Temps, and the French critic of Arnold's essay 'A French
   Critic on Milton', *Mixed Essays*.
5. (p. 379) Hippolyte Taine (1828–93), French critic and literary historian, author of the influential *Histoire de la littérature anglaise*
   (1865).
6. (p. 379) Sir Walter Scott, 'Lord Byron', *Miscellaneous Prose Works*.
7. (p. 380) Byron, *Cain*, I, i, 138–40.
8. (p. 380) *Cain*, II, ii, 403–4.
9. (p. 380) Giacomo Leopardi (1798–1837), Italian poet and scholar.
   His profoundly melancholy poetry appealed strongly to Arnold.
10. (p. 381) The five Byron quotations come from: *Werner*, V, i, 383–
    4; *Heaven and Earth*, I, iii, 94–5; *The Prisoner of Chillon*, 42–3;
    Childe Harold's Pilgrimage, IV, stanza 180; *The Giaour*, 68.
11. (p. 381) *anacolouthon:* lack of grammatical sequence.

12. (p. 381) *The Tempest*, I, ii, 50.

13. (p. 381) Milton, *Il Penseroso*, 99–100.

14. (p. 381) *Sol hath dropt into his harbour*: 'The Longest Day', 3. In choosing this particular line to criticize, Arnold was being either exceptionally careless (his quotations are often incorrect) or deliberately unfair to Wordsworth. Up to *Poetical Works* 1836, the line reads 'Sol has dropped into his harbour'; but for *Poetical Works* 1843 it was changed to 'For the sun is in his harbour'. In this case, at least, Wordsworth was obviously aware of the weakness picked on by Arnold.

15. (p. 381) *if Mr Ruskin pleases . . . 'Parching summer hath no warrant'*: This line, from Wordsworth's 'Inscriptions supposed to be found in and near a Hermit's Cell', was ridiculed by Ruskin in an article 'Fiction – Fair and Foul', *Nineteenth Century*, September 1880.

16. (p. 382) *the comparison between himself and Rousseau*: made by Byron's mother but rejected by Byron himself.

17. (p. 382) *Lord Delawarr . . .*: a school friend. He was excused a beating on Byron's plea that he was a 'brother-peer'.

18. (p. 382) *An ye wool . . . well*: Arnold is mocking Byron's taste for archaisms.

19. (p. 382) *Pope is a Greek temple*: letter to Thomas Moore, 3 May 1821.

20. (p. 383) Ludwig Tieck (1773–1853), German poet, novelist, critic and dramatist; editor of A. W. and Dorothea Schlegel's translation of Shakespeare (1797–1810).

21. (p. 383) John Nichol (1833–94), Professor of English at Glasgow University. His study of Byron (1880) was published in the English Men of Letters series.

22. (p. 384) *greatest genius of our century*: Eckermann, *Conversations with Goethe*, 5 July 1827.

23. (p. 384) ibid., 26 March 1826.

24. (p. 385) *'negative and polemical working' . . . straining after the unlimited*: ibid., 24 February 1825.

25. (p. 385) *zu viel Empirie*: too much experience, i.e. too worldly. ibid., 8 November 1826.

26. (p. 385) ibid., 18 January 1825.

27. (p. 386) *a criticism of life*: first used by Arnold in 'Joubert', *Essays in Criticism* (pp. 142–9).

28. (p. 386) *Recanati*: Leopardi's birthplace.

29. (p. 387) *Dr Kennedy*: a Scottish physician who, in a series of long conversations with the poet, tried to convert Byron during his

last days in Greece. The conversations were published in James Kennedy, *Conversations on Religion with Lord Byron and Others* (1830).

30. (p. 387) *La Ginestra:* the broom plant. *Sovente . . . piagge (rive* not *piagge* in the original): 'Often on these hillsides (banks)'. *Non . . . prevale:* 'I do not know if laughter or pity prevails.'

31. (p. 387) Wordsworth, *The Excursion,* IX, 293.

32. (p. 388) Wordsworth, Preface to *The Excursion,* 18.

33. (p. 388) *essenza insanabile:* incurable essence. *Acerbo, indegno mistero delle cose:* the bitter, unworthy mystery of things.

34. (p. 388) *Iliad,* XXIV, 45: 'For the Fates have set an enduring spirit in men.'

35. (p. 388) *In la sua . . . pace:* one of Arnold's 'touchstones' in 'The Study of Poetry' (pp. 335–6).

36. (p. 388) *King Lear,* V, ii, 9–11.

37. (p. 389) *Almack's . . . Lady Jersey's:* Almack's Assembly Rooms in King Street, St James's, where famous society balls were held: they were organized by a committee of aristocratic women. Lady Jersey was a leading member of the Almack's committee and a close friend of Byron's.

38. (p. 390) Letter to John Murray, 1 August 1819.

39. (p. 390) *Journal, 1813–14: Diary,* 13 January 1821.

40. (p. 390) *Queen Mab . . . the Witch of Atlas . . . the Sensitive Plant:* all poems by Shelley. Arnold is contrasting the more visionary aspect of Shelley's work with Byron's harsh satire.

41. (p. 391) Lady Blessington, *Conversations of Lord Byron* (1834).

42. (p. 392) Byron, *Childe Harold's Pilgrimage,* II, xxvi.

43. (p. 392) Wordsworth, 'The Solitary Reaper', 17.

44. (p. 392) Byron, *Childe Harold,* IV, cxli.

45. (p. 393) *Childe Harold,* IV, cxxxi.

46. (p. 393) *Endymion:* a society novel by Disraeli, published in 1880.

LETTERS

There is no collected edition of Arnold's letters, though one is projected and a descriptive checklist of the material available has been compiled by Arthur Kyle Davis, Jr. It is published by the Bibliographical Society of the University of Virginia (1969). The letters reprinted here are taken from the following: G. W. E. Russell (editor), *Letters of Matthew Arnold 1848–1888* (2 vols., 1895); A. Whitridge (editor), *Unpublished Letters of Matthew Arnold* (New Haven, 1923);

and H. F. Lowry (editor), *The Letters of Matthew Arnold to Arthur Hugh Clough* (1932).

1.   (p. 395) *A. H. Clough:* see note 12 on *On Translating Homer: Last Words.*
2.   (p. 396) Carlyle, 'Louis Philippe', *The Examiner,* 4 March 1848.
3.   (p. 396) *king's affairs:* Louis Philippe was deposed in the French Revolution of 1848.
4.   (p. 398) *London was en pleine insurrection:* on 10 April 1848 the Chartists held a mass demonstration on Kennington Common before delivering a petition to Parliament. Extreme measures were taken to prevent violence breaking out but the event passed peacefully.
5.   (p. 399) Richard Monckton Milnes, later Lord Houghton (1809–85), M.P. for Pontefract. His yearning for political and social position was notorious. Arnold's joke about Milnes interestingly anticipates the kind of humour he was later to use in his portrait of Frederic Harrison as a Jacobin. See note 5 on Letter 7, *Friendship's Garland.*
6.   (p. 399) *Lord L.:* Arnold was private secretary to Lord Lansdowne, a leading Liberal peer, from 1847 to 1851.
7.   (p. 400) *Life, Letters and Literary Remains of John Keats,* edited by R. M. Milnes (2 vols., 1848). Like many Victorian critics Arnold despised Keats's letters for their 'unmanly' qualities, an attitude later felt to be confirmed by the publication of Keats's letters to Fanny Brawne (1878). Arnold pursues this subject at length in 'John Keats', *Essays in Criticism: Second Series* (1888), and makes an important qualification: 'But the thing to be seized is, that Keats had flint and iron in him, that he had character.'
8.   (p. 401) 'heavy-armed foot soldier'.
9.   (p. 401) 'stages along the royal road'.
10.   (p. 402) Arnold, 'Resignation'.
11.   (p. 403) Arnold, 'Stanzas in Memory of the author of Obermann'.
12.   (p. 404) *besonnenheit:* prudence.
13.   (p. 404) Arnold, 'Parting'.
14.   (p. 405) Arnold means: 'But let us be "as the prudent man would define", and not as anyone else would "define".' H. F. Lowry (editor), *Letters to A. H. Clough* (1932), 112.
15.   (p. 407) *Fanny Lucy:* Arnold's wife, elsewhere in the letters usually called Flu. They were married on 10 June 1851.
16.   (p. 409) Arnold, 'Self-Dependence'.

17. (p. 411) *The Preface:* to *Poems* (1833) (pp. 00–00).

18. (p. 411) Arnold, 'Sohrab and Rustum'. The line (74) was later slightly changed.

19. (p. 411) *the poem:* 'Sohrab and Rustum'.

20. (p. 412) Arnold, 'The Youth of Nature'.

21. (p. 413) William Delafield Arnold (1828–59), Matthew Arnold's younger brother. He held the post of Director of Public Instruction in the Punjab, and was the author of a novel about Anglo-Indian life: *Oakfield* (1853).

22. (p. 414) *sehr zerrissen:* a German equivalent of Arnold's earlier phrase in the same paragraph, a 'tearing of oneself to pieces'.

23. (p. 416) *Tom:* Arnold's eldest son, who died, aged sixteen, in 1868.

24. (p. 416) *Lucy:* Arnold's eldest daughter.

25. (p. 416) *Budge:* the family nickname of his second son, William Trevenen, who died, aged eighteen, in 1872. *Dick:* Arnold's third son.

26. (p. 420) 'Homeric Translators and Critics', *Saturday Review,* 27 July 1861.

27. (p. 420) Francis W. Newman, *Homeric Translation in Theory and Practice: A Reply to Matthew Arnold* (1861).

28. (p. 421) *my article for Fraser:* 'The Twice-Revised Code', *Fraser's Magazine,* March 1862.

29. (p. 422) The article was a review of *Essays in Criticism.*

30. (p. 422) *my third lecture:* 'The Study of Celtic Literature', delivered at Oxford on 24 February 1866.

31. (p. 423) *my poem about Clough:* 'Thyrsis', *Macmillan's Magazine,* April 1866.

32. (p. 423) *my Cornhill article:* 'My Countrymen', *Cornhill,* February 1866.

33. (p. 424) *Ecce Homo:* by Sir John Seeley, published anonymously in 1865.

34. (p. 425) *letter . . . about Prussian tenant-right:* Letter 5 of *Friendship's Garland,* first published in the *Pall Mall Gazette,* 8 November 1866.

35. (p. 425) A farewell dinner for Charles Dickens before his departure on a tour of America, held on 2 November 1867.

36. (p. 426) *preface to my Foreign Schools: Schools and Universities on the Continent* (1868).

37. (p. 427) *Clerkenwell blow-up:* see note 7 on Chapter 2, *Culture and Anarchy.*

38. (p. 429) *My book*: *Poems* (2 vols., 1869).
39. (p. 430) *what is new*: a reference to Arnold's articles 'St Paul and Protestantism', *Cornhill*, October and November 1869.
40. (p. 432) *quotes a poem*: 'Switzerland'.
41. (p. 434) *my Introduction*: 'The Study of Poetry', first published as an introduction to *The English Poets* (1880).

PENGUIN CLASSICS

DIALOGUES CONCERNING NATURAL RELIGION
DAVID HUME

'Were this world ever so perfect a production, it must still remain uncertain,
whether all the excellences of the work can justly be ascribed to the workman'

In the posthumously published *Dialogues Concerning Natural Religion*, the
Enlightenment philosopher David Hume attacked many of the traditional
arguments for the existence of God, expressing the belief that religion is founded
on ignorance and irrational fears. Though calm and courteous in tone – at times
even tactfully ambiguous – the conversations between Hume's vividly realized
fictional figures form perhaps the most searching case ever mounted against
orthodox Christian theological thinking and the 'deism' of the time, which pointed
to the wonders of creation as conclusive evidence of God's Design. Hume's
characters debate these issues with extraordinary passion, lucidity and humour, in
one of the most compelling philosophical works ever written.

Based on Hume's own manuscript, Martin Bell provides an accessible modern
edition, while his fascinating introduction sets Hume's religious scepticism in the
philosophical and scientific context of its time.

Edited with an introduction by Martin Bell

PENGUIN CLASSICS

A VINDICATION OF THE RIGHTS OF WOMAN
MARY WOLLESTONECRAFT

Writing in an age when the call for the rights of man had brought revolution to America and France, Mary Wollstonecraft produced her own declaration of female independence in 1792. Passionate and forthright, *A Vindication of the Rights of Woman* attacked the prevailing view of docile, decorative femininity, and instead laid out the principles of emancipation: an equal education for girls and boys, an end to prejudice and a plea for women to become defined by their profession, not their partner. Wollstonecraft's work was received with a mixture of admiration and outrage – Walpole called her 'a hyena in petticoats' – and it established her as the mother of modern feminism.

This revised edition contains a new chronology, updated further reading, greatly expanded notes and an updated introduction. The text of the second edition of 1792, including original punctuation, is printed with emendations listed.

'Her pioneering demand for equality' Sheila Rowbotham

'She is alive and active ... we hear her voice and trace her influence even now' Virginia Woolf

Edited with an introduction and notes by Miriam Brody

PENGUIN CLASSICS

COMMON SENSE
THOMAS PAINE

> 'When my country ... was set on fire about my ears, it was time to stir.
> It was time for every man to stir'

Published anonymously in 1776, six months before the Declaration of
Independence, Paine's *Common Sense* was a radical and impassioned call for
America to free itself from British rule and set up an independent republican
government. Savagely attacking hereditary kingship and aristocratic institutions,
Paine urged a new beginning for his adopted country in which personal freedom
and social equality would be upheld and economic and cultural progress
encouraged. His pamphlet was the first to speak directly to a mass audience – it
went through fifty-six editions within a year of publication – and its assertive
and often caustic style both embodied the democratic spirit he advocated, and
converted thousands of citizens to the cause of American independence.

Isaac Kramnick's introduction examines Paine's life and work within the context
of the political and social changes taking place in Europe and America in the late
eighteenth century.

Edited with an introduction by Isaac Kramnick

PENGUIN CLASSICS

REFLECTIONS ON THE REVOLUTION IN FRANCE
EDMUND BURKE

'To make a revolution is to subvert the ancient state of our country;
and no common reasons are called for to justify so violent a proceeding'

Burke's seminal work was written during the early months of the French
Revolution, and it predicted with uncanny accuracy many of its worst excesses,
including the Reign of Terror. A scathing attack on the revolution's attitudes to
existing institutions, property and religion, it makes a cogent case for upholding
inherited rights and established customs, argues for piecemeal reform rather than
revolutionary change – and deplores the influence Burke feared the revolution
might have in Britain. *Reflections on the Revolution in France* is now widely
regarded as a classic statement of conservative political thought, and is one of the
eighteenth century's great works of political rhetoric.

Conor Cruise O'Brien's introduction examines the contemporary political situation
in England and Ireland and its influence on Burke's point of view. He highlights
Burke's brilliant grasp of social and political forces and discusses why the book
has remained so significant for over two centuries.

Edited with an introduction by Conor Cruise O'Brien

PENGUIN CLASSICS

DEMOCRACY IN AMERICA *AND*
TWO WEEKS IN THE WILDERNESS
ALEXIS DE TOCQUEVILLE

'A new political science is needed for a totally new world'

In 1831 Alexis de Tocqueville, a young French aristocrat and ambitious civil servant, made a nine-month journey throughout America. The result was *Democracy in America,* a monumental study of the strengths and weaknesses of the nation's evolving politics and institutions. Tocqueville looked to the flourishing democratic system in America as a possible model for post-revolutionary France, believing that the egalitarian ideals it enshrined reflected the spirit of the age and even that they were the will of God. His insightful work has become one of the most influential political texts ever written on America and an indispensable authority for anyone interested in the future of democracy. This volume includes the rarely translated *Two Weeks in the Wilderness*, an evocative account of Tocqueville's travels in Michigan among the Iroquois and Chippeway, and *The Excursion to Lake Onéida.*

This is the only edition that contains all Tocqueville's writings on America. Gerald Bevan's translation is accompanied by an introduction by Isaac Kramnick, which discusses Tocqueville's life and times, and the enduring significance of *Democracy in America.*

Translated by Gerald Bevan with an introduction by Isaac Kramnick

---

PENGUIN CLASSICS

THE DESCENT OF MAN
CHARLES DARWIN

'With all these exalted powers – Man still bears in his bodily frame the indelible
stamp of his lowly origin'

In *The Origin of Species*, 1859, Charles Darwin refused to discuss human
evolution, believing the subject too 'surrounded with prejudices'. He had been
reworking his notes since the 1830s, but only with much trepidation did he finally
publish *The Descent of Man* in 1871. The book notoriously put apes in our family
tree and made the races one family, diversified by 'sexual selection': Darwin's
provocative theory that female choice among competing males leads to diverging
racial characteristics. Named by Sigmund Freud as 'one of the ten most significant
books' ever written, Darwin's *Descent of Man* continues to shape the way we think
about what it is that makes us uniquely human.

In their introduction, James Moore and Adrian Desmond, acclaimed biographers of
Charles Darwin, call for a radical re-assessment of the book, arguing that its core
ideas on race were fired by Darwin's hatred of slavery. This reprint of the second
and definitive edition also contains suggestions for further reading, a chronology
and biographical sketches of prominent individuals.

Edited with an introduction by James Moore and Adrian Desmond

PENGUIN CLASSICS

ON LIBERTY
JOHN STUART MILL

> 'The only freedom which deserves the name
> is that of pursuing our own good in our own way'

On Liberty is dedicated to one simple principle: that men and women should be free to do as they please, without interference from society or the State, unless their actions might cause harm to others. While many of his immediate predecessors and contemporaries, from Adam Smith to William Godwin and Thoreau, had celebrated liberty, it was Mill who transformed the concept into a philosophy, claiming for it a central role in social policy and government and arguing for a redrawing of the line between the authority wielded by the State and the independence of the individual – a view that continues to inform debates about personal liberty to this day.

This edition contains an introduction, which puts the work in its biographical and political context, and explores the unresolved contradictions in liberal philosophy.

Edited with an introduction by Gertrude Himmelfarb

PENGUIN CLASSICS

CONFESSIONS OF AN ENGLISH OPIUM EATER
THOMAS DE QUINCEY

'Thou hast the keys of Paradise, oh just, subtle, and mighty opium!'

Confessions is a remarkable account of the pleasures and pains of worshipping at the 'Church of Opium'. Thomas De Quincey consumed large daily quantities of laudanum (at the time a legal painkiller), and this autobiography of addiction hauntingly describes his surreal visions and hallucinatory nocturnal wanderings though London, along with the nightmares, despair and paranoia to which he became prey. The result is a work in which the effects of drugs and the nature of dreams, memory and imagination are seamlessly interwoven. *Confessions* forged a link between artistic self-expression and addiction, paving the way for later generations of literary drug-users from Baudelaire to Burroughs, and anticipating psychoanalysis with its insights into the subconscious.

This edition is based on the original serial version of 1821, and reproduces the two 'sequels', 'Suspiria De Profundis' (1845) and 'The English Mail-Coach' (1849). It also includes a critical introduction discussing the romantic figure of the addict and the tradition of confessional literature, and an appendix on opium in the nineteenth century.

Edited with an introduction by Barry Milligan

PENGUIN CLASSICS

SELECTED ESSAYS, POEMS AND OTHER WRITINGS
GEORGE ELIOT

'We can often detect a man's deficiencies in what he admires more clearly than in what he condemns'

The works collected in this volume provide an illuminating introduction to George Eliot's incisive views on religion, art and science, and the nature and purpose of fiction. Essays such as 'Evangelical Teaching' show her rejecting her earlier religious beliefs, while 'Woman in France' questions conventional ideas about female virtues and marriage, and 'Notes on Form in Art' sets out theories of idealism and realism that she developed further in *Middlemarch* and *Daniel Deronda*. It also includes selections from Eliot's translations of works by Strauss and Feuerbach that challenged many ideas about Christianity; excerpts from her poems; and reviews of writers such as Wollstonecraft, Goethe and Browning. Wonderfully rich in imagery and observations, these pieces reveal the intellectual development of this most challenging and rewarding of writers.

This volume, the first paperback collection of George Eliot's non-fiction, makes available many works never before published in book form. In her introduction, A. S. Byatt discusses Eliot's place in the literary world of Victorian London and the views expounded in these works.

Edited by A. S. Byatt and Nicholas Warren

With an introduction by A. S. Byatt

PENGUIN CLASSICS

THE LIFE OF CHARLOTTE BRONTË
ELIZABETH GASKELL

> 'Wild, strong hearts, and powerful minds,
> were hidden under an enforced propriety and regularity of demeanour'

Elizabeth Gaskell's biography of her close friend Charlotte Brontë was published in 1857 to immediate popular acclaim, and remains the most significant study of the enigmatic author who gave *Jane Eyre* the subtitle 'An Autobiography'. It recounts Charlotte Brontë's life from her isolated childhood, through her years as a writer who had 'foreseen the single life' for herself, to her marriage at thirty-eight and death less than a year later. The resulting work – the first full-length biography of a woman novelist by a woman novelist – explores the nature of Charlotte's genius and almost single-handedly created the Brontë myth.

Elisabeth Jay's introduction discusses Gaskell's artistic construction of The Life and its lasting influence. The text follows the controversial first edition of 1857 throughout, and all the variations of the revised third edition are contained in an appendix.

'It will stand in the first rank, of Biographies, till the end of time' Patrick Brontë

'A classic in its own right, still read today as one of the great works of Victorian literature' Lucasta Miller

Edited with an introduction and notes by Elisabeth Jay

PENGUIN CLASSICS

MARY BARTON
ELIZABETH GASKELL

'O Jem, her father won't listen to me, and it's you must save Mary!
You're like a brother to her'

Mary Barton, the daughter of disillusioned trade unionist, rejects her working-class
lover Jem Wilson in the hope of marrying Henry Carson, the mill owner's son,
and making a better life for herself and her father. But when Henry is shot down
in the street and Jem becomes the main suspect, Mary finds herself painfully torn
between the two men. Through Mary's dilemma, and the moving portrayal of her
father, the embittered and courageous activist John Barton, *Mary Barton* (1848)
powerfully dramatizes the class divides of the 'hungry forties' as personal tragedy.
In its social and political setting, it looks towards Elizabeth Gaskell's great novels
of the industrial revolution, in particular *North and South*.

In his introduction Macdonald Daly discusses Elizabeth Gaskell's first novel as
a pioneering book that made public the great division between rich and poor – a
theme that inspired much of her finest work.

Edited with an introduction and notes by Macdonald Daly

THE STORY OF PENGUIN CLASSICS

Before 1946 ...'Classics' are mainly the domain of academics and students, without readable editions for everyone else. This all changes when a little-known classicist, E. V. Rieu, presents Penguin founder Allen Lane with the translation of Homer's *Odyssey* that he has been working on and reading to his wife Nelly in his spare time.

1946 *The Odyssey* becomes the first Penguin Classic published, and promptly sells three million copies. Suddenly, classic books are no longer for the privileged few.

1950s Rieu, now series editor, turns to professional writers for the best modern, readable translations, including Dorothy L. Sayers's *Inferno* and Robert Graves's *The Twelve Caesars*, which revives the salacious original.

1960s The Classics are given the distinctive black jackets that have remained a constant throughout the series's various looks. Rieu retires in 1964, hailing the Penguin Classics list as 'the greatest educative force of the 20th century'.

1970s A new generation of translators arrives to swell the Penguin Classics ranks, and the list grows to encompass more philosophy, religion, science, history and politics.

1980s The Penguin American Library joins the Classics stable, with titles such as *The Last of the Mohicans* safeguarded. Penguin Classics now offers the most comprehensive library of world literature available.

1990s The launch of Penguin Audiobooks brings the classics to a listening audience for the first time, and in 1999 the launch of the Penguin Classics website takes them online to a larger global readership than ever before.

The 21st Century Penguin Classics are rejacketed for the first time in nearly twenty years. This world famous series now consists of more than 1300 titles, making the widest range of the best books ever written available to millions – and constantly redefining the meaning of what makes a 'classic'.

The Odyssey continues ...

The best books ever written

PENGUIN CLASSICS

SINCE 1946